FILM SCRIPTWRITING

■ ■ ■ ■ ■

FILM SCRIPTWRITING

■ ■ ■ ■ ■ ■ ■

A Practical Manual

by

DWIGHT V. SWAIN

COMMUNICATION ARTS BOOKS

HASTINGS HOUSE, PUBLISHERS

New York 10016

O Joye!

Copyright ©1976 by Dwight V. Swain
Reprinted, June, 1977

Library of Congress Cataloging in Publication Data

Swain, Dwight V
    Film scriptwriting.
    (Communication arts books)
    Bibliography: p. 352
    Includes index.
    1. Moving-picture authorship. I. Title.
PN1996.S9   808.2'3   76-17315
ISBN 0-8038-2318-5
ISBN 0-8038-2319-3 pbk.

Published simultaneously in Canada by
Saunders of Toronto, Ltd., Don Mills, Ontario

Printed in the United States of America

CONTENTS

FOREWORD:

Before We Start

Just what should you expect from a book on film scriptwriting? Answer: Tools.

Let me elaborate. Too many years ago, I took a job as scriptwriter for a producer of informational films despite the fact I'd never seen a film script.

What followed was a groping, nerve-gnawing nightmare. Endlessly, it seemed, I ran pictures back and forth through a battered Bell & Howell projector, trying to figure out what made them tick. On the side, I carried lights, dressed sets, played cable boy, and on occasion swept the editing room floor.When I came upon Vladimir Nilsen's *The Cinema as a Graphic Art* and V. I. Pudovkin's *Film Technique and Film Acting* in the local library, it rated as a major breakthrough. The Calvin Company's annual production workshop in Kansas City had me shaking with excitement, even while I begged scripts from any and all in order to get some idea of proper format.

This is a process called learning the hard way. I don't recommend it.

Eventually, I discovered that writing a successful film script is not one thing, but many; for writing is a process made up of an infinity of sub-processes. "Learning to write" means learning how to go through the steps involved in such sub-processes with facility, and how to relate these various sub-processes to each other and to incorporate them into an integrated whole.

Three elements are involved in such learning: work, luck, and talent.

Why do I give work first place? Because it stands as far and away the most important of the trio. As the old line has it, the way to learn to write is by writing. Given enough time, enough patience, enough practice, even the most inept novice will improve. No amount of talk or theory or study can substitute for it.

Though its role is secondary, luck too plays a major role in writing. Call it serendipity, if you will: the faculty for stumbling onto the things you need even when you aren't hunting for them; the blind, unmotivated impulse that leads you to read the right book, talk to the right man, juxtapose the right words or ideas, capture the right insight. And let no one laugh at such a notion who hasn't awakened in the middle of the night with the perfect solution to a problem, then drifted off to sleep again—only to find when he got up that the thought had vanished.

What about talent?

Well, what about it? Obviously, some of us have greater aptitude than others, whether the area involved be auto mechanics or violin playing or bread baking.

Or writing.

Why this should be so remains open to question, and really doesn't matter anyhow. After all, and regardless of who wins the arguments about heredity versus conditioning, you have to start where you are; work with what you've got. Certainly it's nice to have some sort of built-in facility and/or insight at your fingertips. But I can assure you from a fair amount of experience at both writing and teaching that minimal talent plus work will carry you infinitely farther than maximum aptitude lackadaisically applied.

So where does that leave you—you, beginning scriptwriter?

Not too badly off, really. Mostly, what you need is a willingness to acknowledge that you *are* a beginner: a man or woman essaying a creative task that calls for skills you've never mastered.

That being the case, what you need is less theory and generalization than specific, concrete, step-by-step procedures. Whether the approaches and devices you acquire are the ultimate "best" for their purpose is unimportant, for "best" is a tricky concept—that mode of handling which constitutes perfection for one man may prove awkward to the point of uselessness to another. What counts is discovering some way—any way—of coping with your problems effectively. —The simpler, the better. Later on, as you gain experience, you'll dig out methods optimally suited to your own taste and temperament. Now, what you need is much more basic: down-to-earth tools to help you get your job done.

So. That's what this book is all about: tools, scriptwriting tools and how to use them. And it matters not at all that some old hand takes umbrage and cries, "But that's not the way *I* do it!" or that ten years from now you'll smile wryly at the idea that these procedures once were your standbys, for by then you'll know yourself and your craft a full ten years better.

Meanwhile, day by day and step by step, these techniques will help you turn out solid scripts.

Good luck, friends! It's from the heart.

*   *   *

It goes without saying that no one puts together a book such as this one by himself. Ever and always, a writer must fall back on the experience of others: those who have gone before; those with whom he's worked; those who out of the kindness of their hearts are willing to lend a hand.

Especially is this true of *Film Scriptwriting*. I owe a real debt of gratitude to the many writers, directors, producers, studio officials, teachers, and friends who have contributed so generously of their time and talent: John Bennett, producer; Robert Bethard, president, Visual Presentations, Inc.; Harold Black, director, Allende Productions; Irwin R. Blacker, scriptwriter and professor of cinema, University of Southern California; Robert Bloch, scriptwriter; Howard Browne, scriptwriter; Oliver Crawford, scriptwriter and Writers Guild of America, west, board member; Frank Davis, studio manager, Metro-Goldwyn-Mayer, Inc.; Gerald Di Pego, scriptwriter; Bob and Wanda Duncan, scriptwriters; Herbert Farmer, professor of cinema, University of Southern California; Edward Fischer, professor, Department of Communication Arts, University of Notre Dame; Julian Fowles, law department, Universal Pictures, Inc.; David Gerrold, scriptwriter; Don A. Hart, assistant secretary and patent counsel, Sunkist Growers, Inc.; Charles N. Hockman, associate professor of journalism and director of motion picture production, University of Oklahoma; Gerald Isenberg, president, The Jozak Company; Don Jardine, editor, *The Palmer Writer*; Frances Kimbrough, story editor, New World Pictures, Inc.; Robert Knudson, special collections librarian, University of Southern California; G. E. ("Skip") Landen, supervisor, motion picture production, Ithaca College and former general manager, Landon & Landen Productions; Caryl Ledner, scriptwriter; Robert S. Levy, producer, Pebble Productions, Inc.; Raymond Friday Locke, scriptwriter; Layton Mabrey, former producer, TLM Productions; William P. and Maureen McGivern, scriptwriters; Gordon Molson, Molson-Stanton Associates Agency, Inc.; Lewis Morton, former executive story editor, Metro-Goldwyn-Mayer, Inc.; Charles A. Palmer, executive producer, Parthenon Pictures; Vaughn Paul, producer, Cascade Pictures of California, Inc.; Lee Preston, senior vice president, Bureau of Engraving, Inc.; William E. Pryor, producer-director, William E. Pryor & Associates; Allen Rivkin, public relations director, Writers Guild of America, west; Howard Rodman, scriptwriter, and Writers Guild of America, west, board member; Carl Steward, director; Larry Sugar, Twentieth Century-Fox Film Corporation; James A. Stabile, vice president, Metromedia Producers Corporation; Jack Turley, scriptwriter; plus the many crews and clients with whom I've worked on films through lo these 25 happy if horrendous years.

I probably should add that not all of these people are going to agree with everything I've said. And, obviously, none of them is responsible for errors or opinions expressed herein.

Organizations which have granted much-appreciated permission to use script excerpts include Allende Productions (*Riding Holiday in Mexico*), The Jozak Company (*Winner Take All*), Metro-Goldwyn-Mayer, Inc. (*Night World*), Palo Alto Productions, Inc. and Twentieth Century-Fox Film Corporation (*Capone*), Parthenon Pictures (the proposal and "Bait and Switch" episode of *The Gullies*), and Sunkist Growers, Inc. and Cascade Pictures of California, Inc. (*The Real Talking Singing Action Movie About Nutrition*).

Appreciation also is due *The Palmer Writer* for permission to use my articles, "A Premise Is Basic" and "Look Who's Talking!" in somewhat altered form.

Finally, a very special thank you goes to Russell F. Neale, executive vice president, Hastings House, for more patience than anyone should be called upon to exercise, and to my wife, Joye Raechel Swain, not only for her aid in typing and copyreading my manuscript, but also for her fortitude in surviving the year-long trauma that went into its writing.

D.V.S.

San Miguel de Allende,
Gto.
Mexico

CHAPTER 1:

Film and You

One of the nicest things about film scriptwriting is that it offers not just a living, but a way of life which allows you to make full use of your potential.

In addition, if you're cut out for it, it can prove a tremendous lot of fun.

Next question: What do you need to become a film scriptwriter? Seven things:

1. The kind of rhinoceros hide and iron backbone that won't take "no" for an answer.
2. The ability to become excited about any subject on ten minutes' notice—or no notice at all.
3. Resilience on a level that enables you to take the worst punch in the teeth or knife in the back where your ego is concerned and still come up affable and smiling.
4. Conscience of a brand that keeps you dedicated to making the best of a bad job, even when your every atom churns with resentment/ disappointment.
5. An understanding of how to make the most of your creative talent.
6. A decision as to the area in which you wish to work.
7. A knowledge of the scriptwriter's ground rules and technical devices.

Does this mean that if you have these attributes, success is automatically assured you?

1

Oh, come, now! Becoming a film scriptwriter is one thing; becoming a *successful* film scriptwriter, a rather different matter.

You see, in this life there's an element known as competition. Certain things loom as desirable—things like high pay, congenial work, ego satisfaction. In consequence, more people want them than can get them.

Result: survival of the fittest . . . an unhappy state, for many, in view of the fact that "fittest" may, upon occasion, mean anything from pure genius to possession of an uncle with an inside track. But that's the way of the world, as they say, and the ability to face it and fight it is part of the stubbornness and resilience on which we focused in points 1 and 3 above.

On the other hand, breaks alone can carry you only so far, especially where scriptwriting is concerned. How much success you achieve in the long haul will depend pretty much on your own ability as a writer . . . your ability, plus the seven points listed above, that is.

So, what about those points? Let's consider them one at a time.

1. *The kind of rhinoceros hide and iron backbone that won't take "no" for an answer.*

If your father is a major movie star, a top director, a seven-figure investor in a film company or a company that buys films, it's quite possible your desire to become a scriptwriter will win a reasonably warm reception. Agents will agree to read your efforts. Producers will chat with you over drinks. A director may even go so far as to take you under his wing; hire you for some minor job so you can observe the process and problems of film making at first hand.

You understand, they still won't buy your scripts or hire you as a writer; not unless said scripts are in and of themselves of top quality, fully up to the level of the competition. Film production is far too expensive a proposition for it to be otherwise. But, you *will* have a built-in "in"—a breach of sorts in the towering walls which otherwise seem to surround the motion picture market.

Most of us, for better or worse, have no such entrée. In consequence, we have no choice but to storm the barricades on our own.

There are easier tasks, believe me. For one thing, scripts submitted by mail ordinarily come back unopened. (I'll explain why in Chapter 16.)

So, you have to shoot angles, start on a different level. Maybe that means doing films on your own, in Super 8 or whatever, in hopes someone will recognize your talent. Or taking film courses in schools that bring in people from the industry to lecture. Or scraping acquaintances with studio personnel, on the theory that sooner or later you'll meet someone with the authority to buy scripts. Or taking jobs as page boy or typist or sweeper, in order to scrape up such acquaintances.

I wish I could pretend that any or all of these approaches held your answer. Unfortunately, they don't. Scriptwriting is a rough field to crack, and as one Writers Guild official commented to me recently, "Three hundred of our members have more work than they can handle. The other 3,000 are working part time in filling stations."

What it comes down to is that *if* you learn the ropes, and *if* you persevere, and *if* you have the writing skill, then maybe—just "maybe," mind you—you'll eventually make the grade.

This doesn't discourage you? Good! Because if you *can* be discouraged, you're better off not to start. Only if the writing of film scripts enthralls you to the point that you can't be stopped do you have any business in this field.

2. *The ability to become excited about any subject on ten minutes' notice— or no notice at all.*

A friend of mine, half of a husband/wife team long prominent in the ranks of TV and film writers, once told me, "One thing I know. In this business, can you do it in a hurry counts for a lot more than can you do it good." Then he added, "You can't imagine how many jobs we've cinched because we could leave a conference, bounce ideas off each other for five minutes in the reception room, and then walk back in with a fresh angle."

My own experience in the fact-film field echoes that in spades. I have, on numerous occasions, discovered on entering a meeting that someone had billed me as being wild to do a script on quail-hunting, or the acidizing of oil wells, or promotion of a backwoods women's college. Once, even, my phone rang and when I answered I found I was talking to a psychiatrist who wanted a film scripted from a citation in a medical text. On another occasion, a feature producer thrust an abstract painting at me and was shocked when my interpretation of it as springboard to a film didn't match his.

The point? You'd better be fast on your feet, Jack, and this is no field for negative thinkers.

3. *Resilience on a level that enables you to take the worst punch in the teeth or knife in the back where your ego is concerned and still come up affable and smiling.*

This is the morning after a week in which you've worked your heart out to build a really spectacular angle for the bright new producer of a science fiction film. He listens while you try to sell it . . . then informs you he isn't interested in "hack work" or "linear thinking" and exercises his right to cut you off the job.

The technical consultant on an industrial relations film accuses you of being a "racist bastard" because you've differentiated two characters in your script by labeling one a Serbian, the other an Italian.

The star of a feature finds your very presence so distasteful that she demands the director bar you from the set. Her stand-in tips you off that the real issue is that Star thinks you've given a bit player better lines than hers in a 30-second exchange.

Yes, you do need resilience!

4. Conscience of a brand that keeps you dedicated to making the best of a bad job, even while your every atom churns with resentment/ disappointment.

The film is on deer hunting. A conservation man insists that you include a shot of a knife ripping open a doe shot out of season . . . hands lifting out a dead fawn's blood-dripping fetus. You point out it's going to make half the viewers sick, but you get nowhere.

A film on mental retardation for a national agency. A petty bureaucrat, afraid of repercussions, wants to carve the guts out of it for fear of offending one state's medical association.

A feature with a hideously weak director. The male lead continually bollixes plot lines. When you protest, the actor retorts, "George S. Kaufman never made me memorize my sides. Why should you?"

In each of these instances, you have a decision to make. Since you're not in charge, you can't control the situation. So, will you slack off and say, "The hell with it," or will you go on sweating, trying to make the film as good as you can, within the limits of your predicament?

If your answer is, "The hell with it"—please quit before you start. This business has enough eight-balls already. Which is not to say you may not withdraw or demand that your name be taken from the credits, upon occasion. The man I'm objecting to is the one who stays on the job but quits trying.

5. An understanding of how to make the most of your creative powers.

It goes without saying that a film scriptwriter must above all be creative. Creativity is one of the major—if not *the* major—tools in his craft-kit.

Some people, obviously, are more creative than others.

It's also a fact, however, that most of us can become infinitely more creative than we are, if we learn how to make the most of our abilities.

The creative person, you see, is one somehow conditioned to make multiple responses to single stimuli. That is, he tends to have a variety of reactions to whatever he perceives. Most often, he's not even conscious that he does this. But—spontaneously, habitually—it's become an integral part of his overall pattern of behavior to operate in this manner.

Thus, consider a candlestick. The non-creative among us see it for what it is and nothing more—as some sort of holder with a socket for a candle.

The creative person, on the other hand, looks beyond this obvious function to see the candlestick's further potentials, based on its size, shape, material, components, relationship to the room and its furnishings, and so on. So if I ask him to devise ten ways to murder someone with a candlestick, odds are that sooner or later he'll come up with something fresh and original, simply because he's formed the habit of envisioning more than one possibility per situation.

You, in turn, can through practice train yourself to apply this same principle to every phase of your writing. If a character seems trite and obvious, *make a list* of half a dozen ways you might increase his individuality via unique goals, background, attitudes, appearance, mannerisms, speech, or what have you. Look what Terry Southern did with *Candy* by reversing Sweet Innocence's normally anticipated reactions. Or the characterization of *Ironside* as a wheelchair invalid . . . Puzo's *Godfather* portrayal of the Mafia as a benevolent society . . . *Easy Rider,* with its happy dopers biking cross-country to their doom. Does a dialogue passage sound dull? Try different lines—a dozen of them! Let the little old lady carry a switchblade in her reticule, or the preacher's wife sleep around. How about a monster of a man who faints at the sight of blood? The bathing beauty who's scared of water? The tycoon who can't read? (Pardon me—better skip that last one; Somerset Maugham built a classic short story around it!)

Similarly, your film's key statement may be dull or it may be spritely (or provocative, or profound, or what have you). Your own taste and judgment will be the deciding factor. Given "What about Susie Schnickelfritz's party?" as a central question, you may come up with answers ranging from "Seven close friends attended" to "Any birthday can be a disaster, if Susie bakes the cake!"

But remember, it takes practice to change habit patterns. Get in the swing of creative thinking *before* crucial need for it arises. To that end, look for faces in clouds. Compare people with animals as to manners or appearance. Devise outrageously appropriate replies to propriety's questions—even if you don't have the nerve to voice them. Leave a movie two-thirds through the picture, set up five possible endings of your own, and then go back for the next performance and see if the scriptwriter resolved the situation as cleverly.

Do keep the fitness of things in mind, however. That is, be sure your characters—whether people, products, or principles—stay in character. Don't throw your picture out of kilter with shock for shock's sake. You'll still have plenty of room to move around, once you learn to devise a variety of fresh handlings—via lists—for every mundane circumstance.

6. A decision as to the area in which you wish to work.

Film production today is a fantastically big field—and all of it needs competent scriptwriters. But you're the one who has to decide which road you want to take.

Thus, there are art films, business films, documentary films, educational films, entertainment films, experimental films, government films, industrial films, medical films, promotional films, religious films, sales films, scientific films, slide films, travel films, and a host of others. Each area offers strengths and weaknesses, advantages and opportunities and headaches.

You need to find out about these various specialities: the demands they make, the rewards they offer. Here, we can strike little more than a glancing blow at an issue that warrants all sorts of study.

Where you're concerned, the important thing is not to fall prey to snap judgments, slap-dash decisions. Above all, recognize that Hollywood represents only the tip of the film world's iceberg. Other types of scriptwriting may, for you, prove far more congenial.

7. A knowledge of the scriptwriter's ground rules and technical devices.

By and large, all films fall into one of two categories: fact films, designed primarily to inform; and feature films, whose main purpose is to entertain. And while the degree of overlap between these two fields is great, the differences between them are sufficiently marked as to warrant giving each separate treatment.

Such being the case, I've divided this book into three major segments.

Part 1 concerns how to script fact films.

Part 2 deals with the writing of feature film scripts.

Part 3 is devoted to what I hope are practical suggestions on how to survive and prosper as a writer—especially during that crucial period when you're trying to break in; examples of film script form and technique, drawn from the scripts of produced films and here presented in their typescript versions, complete with detailed comments.

I recommend that you begin your study by scanning the book in its entirety, in order to get an idea of each chapter's contents. Particularly, do *not* slight the fact film chapters because your main interest lies in features, or vice versa. Otherwise, you'll miss many things you'll need to know.

Bear in mind too that I, like any writer, have my own notions as to how my subject matter should be presented. Thus, the traditional approach to scriptwriting tends to act as if all scripts follow a rigid, neatly-ordered pattern of development: outline, treatment, screenplay, shooting script. While in general I agree, I also see the picture as a good deal more flexible—even fluid—and so treat it in these pages.

And that's enough and too much of preliminaries. Now, let's get going . . . with a step-by-step look at how to organize a fact film.

PART ONE

THE FACT FILM

■ ■ ■ ■ ■ ■ ■

CHAPTER 2:

The Proposal Outline

Just what is a fact film, anyhow?

In contrast to the theatrical release feature film, the traditional entertainment "movie," the fact film is one designed primarily to inform and/or influence and/or inspire. A "message" picture, it sells ideas in virtually every field of human knowledge. Thousands of such films are made each year, by hundreds of producing units, at a cost that runs high into the millions.

(This is where you come in, of course. Someone has to write a script for each and every one of those thousands of pictures. In consequence, opportunities for the writer are far greater than in the entertainment film field. But more of that later.)

The feature film in most cases is based on a story, fiction. It's produced in the expectation of making money directly, from paid theatre admissions.

The fact film, on the other hand, ordinarily is rooted in life, reality, nonfiction. Most often shown in classrooms, union halls, churches, club meetingrooms, and the like, it's paid for by a client/sponsor whose main object is to communicate knowledge, arouse interest, or induce belief, on topics ranging from how to increase production of telephone components to discouraging suicide to demonstrating improved methods of garbage collection. Titles from one distributor's brochure on my desk include *The Mighty Western Forest, Wall to Wall Decorating, The Charolais Report, How Much Is A Miracle, The Fine Art of Sterling Design,* and *Modern Mosquito Control.*

9

All of which is not to say that some fact films may not entertain to a greater degree than some features. Or that some features may not inform or influence more than some fact films. Or that fact films may not be designed to cash in at the box office or on TV, or that features may not stand first and foremost as propaganda.

Overall, nonetheless, the fact film zeroes in on information/influence/inspiration. To function effectively in this role, it must be properly organized.

Next question: How do you organize a fact film?

You prepare a proposal outline, a film treatment, a sequence outline, and a shooting script.

That is, sometimes you do. But sometimes you don't, for each and every producer—indeed, each and every film—tends to be a law unto himself/itself. Procedures differ from shop to shop, and if there's one thing you need in your survival kit, it's flexibility.

The general principles set forth here are sound, however. Adapt them to each specific situation as it arises and you'll have no trouble.

Back to the fact film and how to organize it:

Step 1: the proposal outline.

The idea for a film may originate with a producer, a writer, an advertising agency, within the potential client's operation, or wherever. Eventually, however, Idea has to be cast into some kind of comprehensible form.

That form in most instances is what is termed a *film proposal.*

Heart of the proposal is the *proposal outline.* Often, it's where the writer makes his first appearance, for he's likely to be the man (or woman) called upon to get the key facts down on paper.

The proposal is exactly what it sounds like—a bid to make a film. Ordinarily, it lays out the specifications for the project, and sets forth the basic concept the picture is supposed to communicate. In so doing, it establishes a foundation of agreement between client and producer . . . tells the potential sponsor what he may expect for his money, and lets the filmmaker know what he'll be called on to deliver. The document involved—that is, the proposal—may be short or long, simple or elaborate. (The trend is to the short and simple.) All points are subject to negotiation.

For you, the writer, all this probably will first come into focus at a preliminary conference, to which you've been invited by producer/agency/client. (How you get that invitation is something we'll take up in a later chapter. Same for financial arrangements and how you get your money.)

On to the conference!

Hopefully, it will be small—six or eight people at most. Big conferences tend to spell trouble. It's just too hard to work things out or get agreement when 20 or 30 participants are involved.

So: Here you are, sitting down with Client and an aide or two . . . producer and partner . . . ad agency account executive . . . maybe a couple of other intermediaries or abettors of uncertain status.

The business of conference strategy is another item we'll take up later. Right now, for you, the issue is one of digging out certain critical information. Simply put, you need to learn three things: the topic of the proposed picture, its purpose, and who will comprise its audience. But like most things that are simply put, that tends to end up just a bit *too* simple. So let's go a step further and focus your probings into ten specific questions:

1. What's Client's purpose in making the proposed film?
2. What's the film's topic, and what does Client want to say about it?
3. Who does he want to say it to?
4. How much does that audience already know about the topic?
5. What does Client want Audience to do when the lights come on?
6. What are the film's technical specifications, including conditions of use?
7. What's the budget?
8. Are there any particular cost factors on which Client has his heart set?
9. Who's to be your technical advisor?
10. Who has the power, the muscle, the final say?

At first glance, it would appear that some of these matters are primarily problems of the producer, rather than the writer; and first glance would be right. But experience also says Writer too had better bear them firmly in mind, lest later his neglect of matters apparently outside his bailiwick should box him into unanticipated—and uncomfortable—corners.

Now, what is there to say about each question?

1. What's Client's purpose in making the proposed film?

Shall we be blunt? There is only one reason why anyone makes a fact film, and that reason is dissatisfaction. That is to say, client wouldn't be spending his money on a picture if he were happy with the way things are, the *status quo*. Always, he seeks change . . . change in somebody's state of affairs and/or state of mind, even if the issue is only to bring new awareness of the nesting habits of the rosy-breasted pushover. To that end, he proposes to produce a picture.

This is a matter of vital concern to you, because it poses one of your major tasks: to discover what it is your client is dissatisfied with in his present situation and how he'd like to see it changed.

Unfortunately, this isn't always easy. A good place to start, however, is with the question of purpose.

Said question is one you should raise early in the meeting, pinning down what the film is supposed to achieve in the most practical terms possible: "Who do you want to do what?" "Why is this film being made?" "What are you trying to prove?" Then, listen with all three ears—and not just to Client's words.

Your answer, you see, if you're properly perceptive, will come through on at least two levels. The first will be the film's *ostensible* purpose; the other, its *true* purpose.

Ostensible purposes will be obvious indeed, and frankly stated: "We want to improve our company image." "We want to sell more widgets." "We want to help kids understand ionization." "We want to reduce crime in the streets." "We want to teach doctors how to cope with staph infections."

True purposes may prove more difficult to zero in on: "We want to make the competition look like small potatoes." "We want to do a little empire-building—corner a bigger share of next year's appropriation." "We want to take the edge off those things that damn' Congressional committee said about us." "I want to register as a comer—improve my chances for that promotion." "I want to make time with that cute doll in Department 7 by getting her a part in this picture."

Obviously, you won't always be able to pin down the true issues behind production of a film. Indeed, upon occasion you'll find situations where everything is out in the open, sans guile. But it's still important that you have your antennae up and quivering for any clues Client or his colleagues may drop as to their motives. After all, making the competition look like small potatoes may involve trying to buy $100,000 worth of cinematic flash and glamor for $30,000. Empire building or over-ambition may rouse antagonism in people in a position to sabotage the project. That cute doll in Department 7, on film, may prove an utter disaster.

Being aware of such, it's possible you can walk wide around the traps these gambits represent . . . not to mention improving your chances of preparing a script that satisfies *both* Client goals.

2. What's the film's topic, and what does Client want to say about it?

Every film's pattern of organization is built on the same two underpinnings: a topic, and a point of view.

The topic element is simple enough. It's the answer you get when you ask, "What's this film to be about?"

Back comes the answer: "Ulcers." "Wire rope." "Executive aircraft." "Cockroaches." And there's your topic.

Point of view is something else again. Assuming there's a client/sponsor, it's his *subjective attitude* towards the topic. You uncover it by asking, "But what *about* ulcers/wire rope/executive aircraft/cockroaches?"

Now quite obviously there are a number of possible answers to these questions. Take cockroaches, for example. Is Client for them or against them? Does he look on them as pests, or playmates, or the firm foundation on which he's built his extermination business, or potential laboratory livestock for cancer research?

Your goal as writer is to sift through all such possibilities until, ultimately, you come up with a *core assertion:* a clear, concise statement of precisely what point the film is to sell to the audience.

Again, this will not necessarily be an easy task. Client and colleagues may themselves disagree, for instance—I once ached through a college chemistry faculty's eight-hour debate as to precisely how to define the pH system for measurement of acidity and basicity of aqueous solutions. Or, no one may have thought the matter through beyond the "Let's make a movie about our new framistan" level. It's entirely possible two or three sessions may pass before you arrive at the right answer.

But then, who said writing film scripts would be easy? The big thing is that if you know what you're after and you keep plugging, sooner or later you'll come up with the right core assertion, the key point your client really wants to make: "Modern farm equipment gives you extra hours—and time is money." "Those happy, happy college days. I grew up here. I found the real me." "Get more fencerows for bobwhite. Help our quail to find an Oklahoma home."

I can't overemphasize the importance of this phase of your work. Pinning down the right core assertion takes you a giant step along the road to building a solid script, an effective film. Failing to do so is a virtual guarantee of later headaches.

Two hints: It will be to your advantage if you research your film's topic thoroughly at your earliest opportunity, both on your own and in company with your technical advisor. Only as you know your subject can you hope to capture its essence in a razor-sharp core assertion.

Also, often, it will help if you throw out hypotheses as to what Client seeks vainly to put into words: "You mean, then, that when an Indian wears one of these ceremonial masks, he feels that he and the god are one?" "So the big edge Angus have over other cattle is that they're natural polls?" "In other words, it's the man and not the gun that does the killing?"

You'll miss the target more often than not, of course. But the very fact that you've injected a fresh viewpoint has a tendency to jar Client loose from dead center. That helps him—and you—to come up with an intelligent statement that captures the heart of what your picture's all about.

3. Who does he want to say it to?

Implicitly or explicitly, every film has a target audience—a particular group Client seeks to inform or influence or inspire, whether it be eighth grade science students, suburban Parent-Teacher Associations, potential polar bear hunters, or oil field drilling contractors.

Quite possibly you'll have trouble finding just what group this is, because Client, lost in ego inflation, will claim that "everyone" or "the general public" or "the whole Yew-nited States" is his bull's-eye.

This just won't do. You *must* narrow the field. Why? Because you'll need one mode of attack for salesmen, another for engineers, yet a third for consumers.

Further, what fascinates a network TV audience may very well drive surgeons (or artists, or numismatists, or pro football players) to snorts of disgust.

In general, the broader the audience, the harder it will be to hit it with anything meaningful. A mass audience is infinitely more interested in dramatic action than it is in content.

The narrower your audience, in turn, the greater your chances of really striking home. Tailoring your presentation to viewer interests, attitudes, and feelings, you can maximize appeal and impact.

One final point: Be sure the audience your client says he's seeking is actually the one to shoot for. Why? Because Client won't accept blame for steering you wrong if you miss the target. He'll just say the film's a failure.

Thus, once upon a time, I took on the scripting of a film for an expensive summer resort. The audience? Young swingers, the way the owner told it.

Prowling the grounds, however, I soon discovered that the clientele was middle-aged at least.

Had Client been lying to me, then?

Not really. It was just that, aging himself, he zeroed in on the younger patrons to the point that, in his mind's eye, the older majority faded to minor significance.

4. How much does the target audience already know about the topic?

The greater the prior interest of an audience in your subject, the less your need to fancy up the presentation.

Embellishing a film that's intended for an audience of experts frequently will alienate that audience. If you're writing for surgeons about a new operative technique, dragging in Dr. Kildare will outrage them.

If viewers know and/or care nothing about your topic, on the other hand, you'd better scratch around till you find a way to hook their interest. Then, *Symptomatology of Undetected Diabetes* becomes *Diabetes and You Too,* complete with a high-school girl who tires too easily to make the swimming team and a fat widowed mother looking for a husband.

Don't take it for granted that your client is correct in his assumptions about audience knowledge. He may assume too much or too little.

How does a scriptwriter learn whether his potential viewers are interested in a subject, or know about it?

He puts on his hat and goes out and asks questions of said viewers. He does *not* take it for granted that their tastes and level of information are the same as his—or his client's.

Neither does he kid himself that giving heed to audience consists merely of eliminating polysyllables from narration about how to operate a new-type manure spreader.

5. *What does Client want Audience to do when the lights come on?*

Action—*audience* action—is ever and always your ultimate goal when you script a fact film. So it makes good sense to try to decide just *what* action will best relieve your client's dissatisfaction with the World That Is.

Perhaps client's dream of paradise is to see Audience head en masse for a mobile chest x-ray clinic. Or to watch brain surgeons step into the operating theatre tomorrow morning with total confidence in their mastery of a new technique. Or a sales staff move to the attack selling boxer shorts. Or customers clutch pens in frantic haste to sign insurance policy applications.

Isn't this all the same as film purpose? No, not quite. Purpose tends to drift up into generality and abstraction on occasion. "What do you want the audience to do when the lights come on?" yanks goals back down to earth.

6. *What are the film's technical specifications, including conditions of use?*

Is this picture to be sound or silent? Narrated or lip sync? Color or b&w? Live action or animation? 8mm, Super 8, 16mm, 35mm 70mm? What length? Under what conditions will the film be shown? Do facilities exist to bring it to the target audience?

Yes, you do need to know these things. They'll have an influence on the kind of script you write.

Thus, shooting lip-synchronized sound involves an infinity of problems absent in the narrated film. For one, you the writer have to come up with acceptable dialogue! A five-minute picture can be highly effective for some topics; impossible for others. Color can make some pictures—yet spoil a mood piece. Sound seldom is the best when a 16mm print is shown in theatre-size facilities. The list goes on and on.

7. *What's the budget?*

Here the main part of your function will be to keep quiet while Client and Producer wrestle this weighty question. But you do need to pay attention, because the size of the budget will play a large role indeed in determining what you can or can't include in your script for the forthcoming epic. Awareness now will help you to avoid shocks later. But more of that elsewhere.

8. Are there any particular cost factors on which Client has his heart set?

In general, this too is a matter which you can leave to the producer. But you do need to keep your ears open.

Consider, for example, the client who stands fast in his determination to have key scenes shot at his cabin in the woods, where the sun and a Coleman lantern are the only sources of light. But that's all right, because Client wants this to be a historical sequence, featuring Abe Lincoln's boyhood and starring Bob Hope as the friendly neighbor—you know how name talent adds audience interest! And then, of course, Client really wouldn't mind if you included *him* in a few brief bridging scenes; after all, his stutter isn't *that* bad. . . .

Well, you get the idea.

9. Who's to be your technical advisor?

Now hear this: *There's no such thing as a film on which you don't need a technical advisor.*

That is to say, some people have more expertise in a given area than do others.

Expertise is a thing you need, even if the film you're scripting is a saga of a freshman's college year, *A Trip to the Zoo with Jen and Jerry,* or the doings of a housewife in her native habitat. So insist that your client assign you an appropriate technical advisor—a man or woman who knows the film's topic intimately and has the ability and willingness to talk about it freely.

How can a good technical advisor help you?

Well, he can save you endless hours of research, for one thing. He can catch slips which otherwise would make you look like a fool and maybe cost you future assignments. He can clue you in on company/ organization/agency personalities, policies, problem areas. He can brief you on specialized terms, help you brighten narration or dialogue with "insider" touches. Oh, there are so many things he can do!

To manage all these chores, however, he's going to have to be the right person—one who's interested enough in your project to want to help.

Your client, in turn, must be willing to make this paragon available to you, so that you can reach him when you need him. An international authority is worthless if it takes you three days to get an appointment, or if he never seems able to spare you more than five minutes.

Public relations types may prove splendid technical aides, or they may be a total waste of time. It all depends on whether they really know the operation. My own all-time favorite tech advisor was a metallurgical engineer who'd transferred to Sales.

Have your technical advisor assigned before you leave Meeting No. 1. It can make all the difference between a good, pleasant, profitable job of which you can be proud, and a financial disaster on which you want to slash your wrists.

10. Who has the power, the muscle, the final say?

Whether your client be a business, an industry, a governmental unit, an association, or what have you, know in advance that a pecking order exists within it.

It's important to you to determine precisely who speaks with the voice of authority where your script is concerned. Failure to do so can have horrifying results, in terms of your doing your work under the impression that one man is in command, when actually another has the final say. As a case in point, I once worked up an entire treatment for a group I falsely assumed represented an organization, only to have the treasurer, who viewed them as dissidents, refuse to pay a nickel for it.

Along this line, it should be mentioned that at all stages of any script work, it is highly desirable—indeed essential—to get approval signatures from the client; and to make it clear in your contract or letter of agreement that later deviations from such approved handling will result in increased charges.

*   *   *

At last the preliminary conference is over. You go away and do some thinking; some checking with your technical advisor.

Part of your cogitations should be devoted to a question too often slighted: Is this material best presented on film?

It would be nice, you see, if film were the answer to everybody's problems. Regrettably, sometimes it doesn't work that way. If you, the writer, are to keep out of hot water and impossible assignments, you need to know the factors to consider.

Thus, film has these advantages:

a. Film shows motion.

A horse running, a machine operating, a fight in progress—all come through vividly on the screen.

b. Film reveals what the eye can't see.

With time-lapse photography, you can watch a year of plant growth in a minute. Slow motion reveals how the magician performs his sleight. Animation lets you see the moving parts within an engine.

c. Film transcends time and space.

It enables you to stretch a minute to ten or reduce it to nothing . . . to jump from the North Pole to the South, from New York to London to Moscow to Peking.

d. Film enables you to pinpoint the exact audience you want.

If you prefer that only psychiatrists or coffee shop managers or demolitions experts view a picture, you can so stipulate. Many films have been made whose sole audience was to be a seven-man board of directors or the president of a company.

e. Film is reusable.

Which same is why live TV drama went down the drain. Once a play's filmed, you can run it over and over, not to mention selling or renting prints to each new station as it opens. Similarly, fact films can be shown to generation after generation of school children, to each new group of employees, and so on.

f. Film repeats accurately.

This obviously is a tremendous advantage. Memory is fallible, and no speaker does precisely the same job every time. So, if you're a college football coach, you don't need to rely on your recollections of last week's game. Good and bad plays, filmed and shown in slow motion, can help you pinpoint errors and devise more effective strategy.

g. Film is visual.

The importance of this comes into focus when you realize that assorted studies indicate human beings learn at least 75 per cent by sight.

h. Film may have color or sound.

Color isn't always an unmixed blessing, but there certainly are some things you can't show properly without it—the look of growing grain, for instance; or diseased tissue vs. normal; or paintings, fashions, hair colors, etc.

Sound, in turn, may change the whole world film reveals, as well as our reactions to it—witness the horrors perpetrated via TV laugh tracks.

i. Film emphasizes, emotionalizes.

By filling the screen with the right details, you can create virtually any feeling you want in an audience. Consider the World War 2 German newsreels used to soften up countries soon to be invaded: Their graphic portrayal of the destruction wrought by Panzer divisions and Stuka dive-bombers so terrified viewers that they fled at the first rumor of attack.

j. Film may offer extra attention value.

A good case in point is film's use in suitcase units that include both projector and screen. "I want to show you a film," says the salesman who brings it. "The time involved will be precisely ten minutes. If you're not interested in my proposition after you see the picture, I'll leave without a word." An incredibly high proportion of the time, the prospect will agree . . . which clears the way for a 10-minute presentation put together by master sales psychologists and seen sans interruptions by secretaries or phone calls.

So much for film's advantages. Now, what about the disadvantages?

These break down into three categories: subject factors, production factors, and use factors.

a. Subject factors.

(1) STATICITY. . . . which is just a fancy way of saying the subject doesn't move. Consequently, film's wasted on it, even though *camera* movement may lend it some air of vitality. An example? Consider the film which shows a painting. True, you can zoom in on specific details or pan across it while a narrator comments, voice over. But the subject is still static, still poorly adapted to filmic treatment.

(2) COMPLEXITY. Your topic is *The Causes of Poverty.* Granted, you can make a film about it. But the problem itself is so complex, so subject to controversy, that you can deal with it only by resorting to a simplistic treatment that does it less than justice or even distorts the facts. There's just too much ground to cover in one picture. So, either break it down into smaller bites or leave it alone.

(3) SIMULTANEITY. Remember *The Thomas Crown Affair,* or the *Mannix* titles? Using split screen techniques, several pictures are shown to the viewer at the same time. While gimmicky and often fascinating for the moment, such tends to confuse more than to enlighten in many cases. If you can break the simultaneous element down into a series of *sequential* developments ("This happens . . . and, meanwhile, this is happening . . . and this . . . and this . . ."), fine. But if you have to show 17 things happening at once and there's no way of separating or categorizing them, forget it.

(4) LENGTH. Much as in the case of complex subjects, you sometimes are confronted with topics which demand such a length of film (and running time) as to make them impractical—and this in spite of the fact that, upon occasion, the entire history of the United States has been compressed into a three-minute montage.

Consider, for example, various psychological/psychiatric case studies. Months—perhaps years—of psychotherapy are involved, with little clear-cut progress at any given moment. Any film you make of such will either have to oversimplify, or to deteriorate into an Andy Warhol sleeping-the-happy-hours-away movie.

(5) ABSTRACTION. Art has a concept called "negative space." But I'd hate to have to film it. Same for the philosophy of Zen, statistical analysis, or "vaginal politics."

Understand, films can—and probably have—been made in defiance of virtually every one of these factors. But they do complicate the writer's life by forcing him to oversimplify or to make use of strained parallels or false analogies.

b. Production factors.

(1) COST. No doubt about it, movie-making costs money. But more important than cost itself, by far, is the ratio of expense to return. In other words, it doesn't matter if a neo-*Cleopatra* costs $50 million, if the box office returns total $250 million. On the other hand, a $7,500 industrial film may prove a disaster for a small company's public relations man if the firm's president secretly views the whole project as a needless frill and is anticipating a bill for $1,500

(2) TECHNICAL DIFFICULTIES. Closely related to cost is the fact that virtually anything in this world can be filmed if you're willing to spend enough money. But entirely apart from expense, if a crane shot is essential in a factory sequence and you haven't got a crane, you're in trouble. Even a baby elephant that refuses to behave can throw your budget—and story line—out of kilter, as I once witnessed during the filming of an episode of Ziv's old *Science Fiction Theatre.*

(3) TIME PROBLEMS. A friend of mine was forced out of the film business because he hadn't given proper weight to the fact that the writer of a picture he'd contracted to produce had set sequences in each of the four seasons—which meant production was going to have to extend over an entire year.

Similarly, it may prove impractical to schedule filming of a particular rock festival, to obtain the services of a particular actor for a particular time, or to push through the editing or processing of a film to meet a deadline.

Any number of producers have bucked these odds, you understand. But you do need to consider them before you sign on to do a script.

c. Use factors.

(1) LACK OF VIEWING FACILITIES. Most of us take screens and projectors for granted. It's a mistake. The sheepherder or pipeline walker your film is designed to influence may never get to see it, simply because there's no place to show it. In the same way, many educational films win few viewings because teachers don't want to bother with requisitioning, setting up, learning to operate, and operating projectors.

Or how about the picture shown in a packed union hall, with the air conditioning turned off because it interferes with the sound? And that's not even mentioning lack of competent projectionists, erratic power sources, broken film stuck together with cellulose tape, and a dozen other potential disaster areas.

(2) LACK OF PRINTS. You know about a good film on some phase of chemistry, or algebra, or history. You'd like to show it to your pupils. But can you get a print when you need it, or will you have to wait till the class is seven weeks past the topic? For my own part, when I was teaching scriptwriting at the University of Oklahoma, at least half the pictures I wanted to show students as classic examples of particular techniques had been withdrawn from circulation.

(3) PROBLEM AUDIENCES. How do you show a film—effectively, that is—to an audience that doesn't speak the narrator's language? How do you show it to primitives in New Guinea who haven't yet learned to see in two dimensions and so view the images on the screen as mere flickering shadows? How do you show it to Kurd tribesmen who've never seen or heard of a refrigerator and so don't know what the one in the film is for? How do you show it to guerrilla-indoctrinated *campesinos* who think the film is part of an imperialist plot against them?

Summing up, then, film is a great thing—but not at all times nor in all situations. Sometimes the smartest thing you can do when someone comes to you with a great idea—and yes, he *does* have money and *is* prepared to pay you—is to forget film in favor of still pix, slides, a brochure, or even just a simple sheet of printed instructions.

Now, three frequently-raised questions:

1. Is it really necessary to organize a film completely before the shooting starts?

Or, to put it more bluntly, why bother to write a script at all? Why not just go out and shoot whatever footage comes handy and worry about organization later?

No, this is not a rhetorical issue. The world is full of would-be filmmakers eager to plunge into production with no time wasted on pre-planning.

Trouble is, any writer could retire on the money spent by befuddled clients on "shot-off-the-cuff" films that never reached the screen. For there's more—much more—to making any film than simply shooting pictures. Both time and money enter, and the question that always arises is what shots to shoot, how to shoot them, and in what order to arrange them *in order to end up with an effective film.*

There, of course, is the issue. It's easy enough to make a fact film. But to make an *effective* one—in terms of audience, purpose, and client satisfaction—is something else again.

The shot-off-the-cuff film begins by being wasteful. Instead of tying up the time of one man—the writer—it ties up the time of an entire crew. Then, lacking a carefully laid-out script—which is to say, lacking adequate pre-planning—it racks up fantastic bills for raw stock and processing.

Later, when editing time comes, this waste grows even greater because, lacking a clear-cut concept and chain of logic, it's hard to put the thing together. In addition, many vital shots are bound to turn up missing, simply because no one realized that this closeup would prove essential, or that jump cut would require a covering cutaway.

Finally, like a joke told by an inept comic, all too often the whole thing somehow ends up both looking like amateur night and missing the point the client wanted to make.

Yes, it *is* important to organize a film as completely as possible before the shooting starts!

2. *Doesn't this kind of pre-planning limit the director's creativity—his opportunities for improvisation, capturing the insights and inspirations of the moment?*

Alfred Hitchcock speaking: "When I hear of a man shooting a film off the cuff, making it up as he goes along, I think it's like a composer composing a symphony before a full orchestra. I like to improvise in an office, not on a stage in front of a hundred technicians." (page 98, *The Celluloid Muse: Hollywood Directors Speak,* by Charles Higham and Joel Greenberg. New York: New American Library, 1969.)

Actually, of course, having a well-planned script is a help rather than a hindrance to a competent director. In the first place, in all likelihood he'll have worked with the writer and/or studied the script in detail, incorporating his own pet notions in the process. In the second, he'll still be able to improvise within the framework of the script, should something that develops on the set or location give him a fresh idea.

The only thing he's really barred from doing is based on the ethics of his relationship to the client. That is, he shouldn't abandon the script's plan of action, its line of development. That plan, that line, has been worked out with painstaking care so that it makes the client's point. To throw it out the window during filming is to betray the trust the client has placed in him.

3. *What do you as a scriptwriter do when you find yourself stuck with a pre-shot film?*

A film shot without a script, that is; and yes, it *does* happen, and writers *are* called in to help cope with the problem. In fact, often it's an entirely legitimate situation: The circumstances were such that it simply wasn't possible to plan things in advance, as in the case of some friends of mine who spent six weeks with the Lacandon Indians of Chiapas, four days on foot from the nearest road. They had no real idea of what they'd find when they arrived, so they flew by the seat of their pants, as it were—shot footage of everything that looked interesting and hoped it could be cut into some kind of meaningful pattern later.

Similarly, you some day may find yourself confronted with 9,000 feet—four hours plus—of 16mm film taken by Joe Bigbux on his

African safari, or a mile or two of catch-as-catch-can shots of Guatemalan guerrillas in action, or reel after reel of coverage of the various steps in the construction of a new housing development.

You meet such challenges in much the same way you'd attack any other picture topic. That is to say, you hunt for a point of view, an angle: some kind of core assertion that makes sense and captures the idea. *But you do it within the limitations of the footage at hand.*

Thus, in the Lacandon Indian epic cited above, I ended up with the core assertion, "The Lacandones are a people trapped between two worlds." The unifying concept behind endless footage of kindergarten children was finally sifted down to "Play is children's work, a tool for growth." A mass of ill-assorted campus shots gave birth to "A school's spirit is what shapes its students' futures."

What—? You lack essential footage? Well, I agree that can be a problem. But sometimes there are ways around it. We'll take them up in a later chapter.

*   *   *

And so, at long last, this first phase of your thinking's done; your questions answered, your concepts organized. It's time to put your proposal down on paper.

How to go about it? A system that's worked well for me is simply to ask the producer for a copy of his favorite presentation. Then, I follow that pattern.

Make it a rule to keep your writing style as clear and simple as possible. Also, incorporate your core assertion, if you've developed one that satisfies you. (If you haven't, it's no sin to hold off on it till you write your film treatment.)

At this point, just in case you haven't found another model, a format may prove useful—not the only possible format, you understand, nor even necessarily the best. Indeed, many presentations will be much more elaborate. But a handling such as this one is acceptable in most situations.

Among items often (but not always) included are:

Heading: designation of your presentation as a proposal . . . working title, so labeled.

Content outline: purpose of film, audience, summary of key data to be included.

Specifications: length, color, sound, animation or major special effects (if any).

Shooting schedule: where and when the picture will be shot.

Production schedule: any and all deadlines, up to and including delivery date for the finished film.

Budget: details as required.

Approvals: producer, client, dates.

What does an actual proposal look like? Here's an example:

Film Proposal

WHAT THE TEACHER SEES

(Working Title)

This 16mm film is intended for teachers in the elementary schools --primarily those teachers with relatively limited experience. Its purpose is to give them an approach to the problem of pupil health appraisal, and to provide them with key data needed in order to make such appraisals intelligently.

The film will be approximately 20 minutes in length, and will be shot in sound and color. Both voice-over narration and lip-synchronized dialogue will be used.

On the assumption that client will provide technical advisor and all players without cost to producer, budget is estimated at $12,500. This estimate is subject to revision upwards if animation is required. Additional charges for travel will also be made if filming outside the Oklahoma City area becomes necessary.

Revised version prepared for

OKLAHOMA STATE DEPARTMENT OF HEALTH

Approved:

For the Producer_____Date_____

For Department of Health_____Date_____

So there's your proposal, signed and sealed. What comes next? Why, obviously, you proceed to your film treatment.

CHAPTER 3:

The Film Treatment

The film treatment (or "treatment outline") is a succinct, third-person, present tense summary of your proposed film. Its purpose is to flesh out your proposal outline into a more detailed presentation of material and approach, so dramatized—that is, made vividly expressive—as to excite your client in regard to the picture-to-be, as well as to inform him. It also serves as a preliminary check on weaknesses and/or disagreements before you proceed to the even more comprehensive development known as the sequence outline.

To these ends, the treatment should block in approach and handling, specify (at least in broad outline) the information to be included, and otherwise capture the essence of your thinking. It may be of almost any length, from two or three to 40 or 50 pages—the briefer, the better, in most cases.

I like to divide the building of an effective film treatment into two phases: a *thinking through* phase and a *writing* phase.

THINKING THROUGH YOUR TREATMENT

I hope no one who reads this book thinks writing a filmscript is just a matter of putting words on paper, for such a belief could hardly be farther from the truth.

Actually, most "writing" is essentially complete before a typewriter key is struck. It takes place in the writer's head as he figures out how to attack his topic.

25

I can't overemphasize how important this is. Please, please, if you have any desire at all to succeed in this field, do think things through! Or, as the old gag has it, don't put typewriter in motion until brain is in gear.

My own approach to this thinking-through process tends to involve three elements: an *information line*, an *interest line*, and a *presentation structure*.

This is not to say that these constitutents are treated in that particular order. Rather, the trick is to catch any passing thought in notes as it flashes by, weaving it into an integrated pattern later. But just knowing you do have an information line and interest line and presentation structure helps keep you from forgetting or leaving out some vital factor. Also, it gives you solid answers when Client or Producer asks why you're handling this or that in some particular way.

So. Let's take a look at

1. The information line

The purpose of the information line is to insure inclusion and effective arrangement of your film's key data. To this end,

1. You research your film's topic and point of view.
b. You frame a core assertion for your film to make.
c. You back up this core assertion with subassertions, proof points.
d. You prove each of these points visually.
Shall we consider these issues one by one?

a. You research your film's topic and point of view.

As pointed out in the preceding chapter, the primary goal of the fact film is to inform and/or influence and/or inspire a specified target audience; to sell its viewers a particular attitude on a given topic.

It's an axiom of successful salesmanship that you first must know your product. Similarly, in scripting successful fact films, you first must know as much as possible about your topic/attitude package.

Sound research attacks this issue on three fronts, digging up information via print, interview, and field investigation. Slight any one of these and you're tempting disaster.

Print research means reading books, brochures, catalogues, trade journals, company reports—anything whatever about your topic on which you can lay your hands. Not too much at first, however, and not in too great depth. There's a mass of data available on almost every subject. Much of it is bound to be outdated, or unrelated, or inapplicable. What you need at the beginning is less true expertise than a sort of scanning knowledge, designed to fill in on the big picture, the broad panorama, *to a point where you can ask at least semi-intelligent questions.*

Now, enter *interview research*: specifically, talk with your technical advisor.

This is where your preliminary print research will pay off. Experts often tend to be short of patience. If they feel they're dealing with a total idiot, they give said idiot short shrift.

If, on the other hand, you've already briefed yourself in private to a point where you know the difference between a walking beam and a Christmas tree, an id and an ego, a Doppler shift and a *doppelganger*, Advisor may conclude it's worth his while to fill in your blind spots, bring you up to date, and explain confusing details.

The value of this just can't be overstated. Ever so much rule-of-thumb procedure in any field simply never gets into print. Slang, trade jargon, specialized terminology can leave you staring slack-jawed. New developments render whole textbooks obsolete. But with the right technical advisor on call, you'll weather such perils with minimal damage.

Too, a good t.a. often can and will refer you to other, associated experts. Before you know it, you'll find the impossibly complex come clear; the inscrutable unscrewed.

Somewhere along the line, hopefully, you'll also find yourself involved in *field research*, a term which means simply that you go forth and examine your topic in its natural habitat, alive and breathing. This may involve anything from running an obstacle course to observing a swimming class; invading a steel plant to peering through a microscope. The important thing is: If at all possible, *do it*. Realistic writing demands experience, not just talk and reading. Good copy is built on feelings, sensory perceptions—sights, sounds, smells, tastes, touches; how hot, how cold, how frightening, how overwhelming, how pitiful, how stirring. The counterculture will mean more to you if you've been moved off Venice Beach by the Los Angeles Police Department's Tactical Squads, along with 20,000 other rock fans. You'll understand mental illness better if you, too, have heard the clang of iron doors closing.

It also should be mentioned that research is seldom a thing once done, then over. Throughout your work on any given script, you'll find yourself stumbling or hung up for lack of some fragment of information. When that time comes, don't stall and don't fake. Just plunge back into further research, digging until you find your answers.

Remember, too, that things are not always what they seem. Thus, in preparing the script for a film designed to sell executive aircraft, I kept running into endless nit-picking hassles that at first glance seemed totally without meaning. Only after hours of digging did it finally come out that certain key personnel felt their product's strongest selling point was its potential for use by buyers to transport young ladies other than their wives to resort areas with minimal risk of discovery.

Resolution of the problem consisted of including footage that showed mountains, beaches, luxury hotels, and the like, plus an assortment of alleged secretaries boarding the featured plane for duty at conferences. If anyone wanted to draw conclusions from same, that was his business.

As pointed out earlier, research *can* help!

b. You frame a core assertion for your film to make.

This is an issue we've already dealt with in some detail, in the preceding chapter. I mention it here only to reemphasize (1) its importance and (2) the fact that it's not always easily managed. You definitely should have it worked out to everyone's satisfaction by the time you write your treatment, however, Otherwise, your film's line of development will almost certainly prove weak and wandering.

c. You back up this core assertion with subassertions, proof points.

Every core assertion of necessity rests on an undergirding of subassertions—sound reasons why the core assertion is true.

Thus, a core assertion that "Colorado is a wonderful place to vacation" may rest on such subassertions as "The Rockies are spectacular in their beauty," "Swimming in Colorado lakes is fun," "Is fishing your thing? You'll catch the big ones here," "Ghost towns are fascinating to explore," "Comfortable tourist facilities are available throughout the state on every budget level," and so on.

Apply this pattern to your own script jobs.

First, list all the reasons your core assertion is true.

Second, arrange these reasons in some sort of order that is (1) logical, and (2) of increasing interest, with the most impressive reasons at the climax. Your goal should be to make it as clear as possible how, individually and/or in sequence, the subassertions lead to the conclusion that is your core assertion.

It may help if you simply type out everything you can recall which seems at all pertinent to your topic/assertion, paying no attention whatever to arrangement beyond placing each thought, each idea, each unit of information in a separate paragraph.

Finally, you'll run out of things to say. When that happens, snip apart the paragraphs and group like with like, until the key points stand out sharp and clear.

Arranging these key points logically will vary from script to script. A historical subject, for example, might best be presented *chronologically*, in the order in which the events took place. If a number of locations are involved, it may seem preferable to attack *spatially*, moving from one setting to another. Other common approaches are *simple to complex*, *specific to general*, *familiar to unfamiliar*, *problem to solution*, *cause to effect*, or what have you. Or, you may choose to combine various of these patterns—*chronological* with *spatial* with *problem to solution*, for example, in the case of how a company with plants in seven states dealt with a pollution hazard first discovered in 1969.

Often, too, logic will prove to be something you invent; and the same for the matter of increasing interest. That is, no one line of attack is necessarily right, let alone the only one possible.

Thus, what is the reasoning behind my attack on the Colorado vacation issue? Let's reduce it to the sketchiest of outlines.

First, I wanted something to catch the eye—and what's more eye-catching than the Rockies?

But mountains are remote and lack the human factor, so I visualized turning next to crowds of happy swimmers . . . then closing in to the isolated individual, fishing.

Finally, what's most important to most people in planning a vacation? Answer: Money. So, we conclude with a brief montage of footage emphasizing the attractive facilities and comfort available "on every budget level."

Is this the only way to approach the issue? Of course not. The elements available may be arranged in almost any pattern, *provided you develop some sort of order of presentation and emphasis that makes sense*—first to you; then, through you, to your film's ultimate viewers.

Working out this kind of thing won't necessarily be quick or easy, of course. Count on it, you'll find yourself repeatedly bogged down by false starts, holes in your thinking, inadequate information. Don't let such discourage you. The difference between the amateur and the professional, often, is that the amateur gives up. The old pro, in contrast, knows that if he keeps banging his square Dutch head against the apparently insurmountable stone wall of his current stumblingblock, sooner or later that wall will fall down. The issue is merely to pinpoint the problem and then work out a solution—with additional research, with rethinking, with rearrangement of ideas.

d. You prove each of these points visually.

Back to the statements that back our Colorado core assertion: "The Rockies are spectacular," "Swimming is fun," "You'll catch the big ones," and so on. Note that each of these subassertions (that is, proof points) is subject to cinematic demonstration. A camera crew can take appropriate footage to make every point visual.

These filmed fragments, in turn, convince your audience, because *seeing is believing*. It forces automatic agreement.

A point *without* such visual backup, on the other hand, offers no conclusive end to the argument; in the last analysis, it rests on opinion. "This is a film" is instantly and demonstrably true. "This is a *good* film" introduces an element subject to endless debate.

It's also wise to remember that the true basis for any "proof" or "reason" always comes down to the individual case, the illustrative instance. That's why the "case study" approach is so common: By following one person as he experiences a situation, the writer acquires a built-in story line. Indeed, there are worse rules of thumb to follow than that of thinking first in terms of translating your data into terms of people doing things.

Whatever road you take, the trick always is to figure out specific action/incidents which will *show* your assertion is true. *Telling* just isn't good enough.

Thus, if I *tell* you I have the power to levitate myself, to float through the air without support, you may or may not believe me—with the odds strongly on the "not" side.

If, on the other hand, I simply say, "Look, I want to show you something," and then, before your very eyes, still in a sitting position, rise slowly from my chair into the air, drifting here and there about the room above your head, you may be tempted to refuse to believe me. Yet you dare not, for how can you deny the evidence of your own senses? I shall have proved my point in spite of you.

Where you the writer are concerned, this means you must train yourself to translate glib generalities into photographable specifics ("spiritual forces" become churches and religious rites of every faith), and to draw generalities *from* specifics (ghetto shacks and ragged children become "the blight of poverty"). You must devise ways to put abstractions like *fun* and *love* and *culture* on the screen . . . figure out how to *show* a girl as sloppy, a man conniving, a child evil-minded. Only as you learn to combine clips of film to establish a firm's reliability, a city's corruption, a party's dedication to the people's welfare can you say you've mastered your craft.

The road to such mastery lies in practice, endless practice; plus the nerve and experimental turn of mind that sees you eager to try something new.

Nor will it hurt you any to study others' films, just in case they in their turn have come up with something new and different.

So much for your factual content, your information line; an organized, unified, effective pattern for presenting the ideas and data necessary to bring alive your client's core assertion, the things he wants the film to say.

Your next step is to devise a plan of action to hold your viewers' attention—what I choose to call

2. The interest line.

The purpose of the interest line is to capture and hold your viewers' attention.

Obviously, there are a host of ways to do this. Self-interest, spectacle, shock, contrast, the impossible, the unattainable, the forbidden, the disastrous, the incongruous, the logical yet unanticipated—all have their devotees, their demonstrated values.

The most consistently useful device, in my own experience, is injection of a conflict element, a struggle between two opposing forces. Why? Because conflict, on whatever level, automatically raises a question as to which side will win. In so doing, it also creates tension in an audience.

Tension is the basis of *attention*. It's what keeps your viewers awake—maybe on the edge of their seats.

If they're awake and excited, they may even catch the message your client is trying to put across. Which same will prove a star in your crown, not to mention getting you new assignments.

Next question: How do you put this principle to practical use in your film script?

    a. You develope a character (or characters) with whom viewers can empathize.

    b. You face this character with danger.

    c. You draw a conclusion, make a point from the conflict.

Again, we'll take the process a step at a time.

a. You develop a character (or characters) with whom viewers can empathize.

In any filmed conflict, it helps if you can involve your audience in the struggle. How? By means of what the psychologists call *empathy*—the tendency of people to share the feelings and experiences of others. "To see with the eyes of another, to hear with the ears of another, to feel with the heart of another," as someone has said. It's the thing that makes you yawn when the man beside you yawns; flush or clench your fists at the humiliation of another; cringe back when a passing car splashes water on someone else.

To achieve empathy with an audience, you introduce some character who, in effect, is on the audience's side. That is, he shares your viewers' desires and attitudes and feelings. Thus, *Love That Car*, a hilarious yet effective five-minute short from Parthenon Pictures, featured vignettes of eight motorists whose carelessness regarding car care got them into trouble. Viewers laughed and empathized—because they too were motirists and had had car trouble brought on by such neglect.

In planning conflict situations, bear in mind that your audience can empathize with anything, animate or inanimate. So characters may be individuals, groups, objects, phenomena: witness Pare Lorentz's famed *The River*, with the Mississippi as star. A germ or an elephant or a tractor, skillfully handled, can play hero or villain just as well as a man.

In each case, however, you must be able to impute a goal, a desire, to the "character." Why? Because that which can desire and strive has in it the potential for success or failure and, therefore, for an implied "story question": "Will this striver succeed or fail in its strivings?" Viewers then become involved as they do with one or the other of the opposing teams at a football game.

Without desire, on the other hand, there can be no conflict—and no conflict, no interest.

Which is not to say that goals necessarily have to be spelled out. The fact that a given character is driving to work or cooking dinner or running a milling machine *implies* a goal and/or direction, even if it isn't stated.

Handling, in turn, can be on any level, from cool understatement to slapstick, so long as it fulfills your client's needs effectively.

Once you've built your empathetic character or characters (Chapter 8 will give you additional help), you're ready to add interest line component number two:

b. You face your character with danger.

Conflict is a man trying to walk through a locked door. It's attempting to attain goals in the face of opposition, obstacles.

This being the case, you not only give your empathetic character something to strive for. You also confront him with something to *struggle against*. Whether he's a man or a carburetor or a theory, you make it hard for him. You emphasize the obstacle, the irritation, the pain in the neck.

This opposing element, this factor which threatens your character's chances to attain his goal, I label *danger*. It comes in three categories.

First, there's that old reliable of melodrama, the *threat to life itself*. In film, you see it on levels ranging from the mad killer with the axe to the Anopheles mosquito; from the car roaring out of control to the improperly packed parachute or the crumbling cement at the dam base.

Second, there's drama's standby the *threat to happiness*: the boy whose girl says no, the aging executive whose company folds, the family whose home is to be sacrificed for a freeway.

Third, comedy chuckles at the *threat to dignity*. Here stands the lonely bachelor whose brags about a non-existent sweetheart are about to be unmasked; the male chauvinist pig whose new boss turns out to be a female; the woman who discovers that her husband has invited in his Dirty Old Men's Club for the same night she's entertaining the Temperance Circle.

Why do I belabor this breakdown of danger in such detail? I do so because too many writers—and not just beginners, either—see danger only in terms of blood-and-thunder, threat to life . . . when, actually, for most of us, threat to happiness or to dignity are infinitely more useful working tools.

At any rate, and one way or another, it helps to hold viewer interest if your script incorporates struggles between desire and danger.

This conflict element may run through an entire picture, or it may be limited to bits or a sequence or two, depending on your needs. Thus, a typical college recruitment film invariably includes a tour of the campus. Equally invariably, said tour proves a drag and a bore where the audience is concerned.

Suppose, however, that we incorporate a pretty blonde freshman taking such a tour. Then, give Blonde a pair of brand new, too-tight shoes so that her feet are killing her.

Result: humorous conflict, girl versus shoes. The curse is taken off the tour sequence, and there's even a payoff when another girl loans Blonde more comfortable footgear, thus demonstrating what a friendly campus this really is.

Conflict to run throughout a film? My *Retire to Life* dealt with retirement problems . . . the conflict, with a man versus old age.

Non-human conflict? How about a grain of sand versus a pump valve? Acid battling oil-bearing rock strata? Wind and water against topsoil? In each case, danger battles desire—and viewers pay attention.

c. You draw a conclusion, make a point from the conflict.

This is what's known as stitching your interest line and your information line together. It's based on the rule-of-thumb that any conflicts you introduce into a script should be indigenous to your topic, born of it, rather than grafted on outside.

Thus, a tour of the campus is pretty much indigenous to college recruitment, and so are new freshmen. Q.E.D.: A blonde heroine with aching feet fits in. And the payoff, the friendly campus bit, makes a point that helps to prove the core assertion—that this is a good place to go to school.

Similarly, there's nothing alien about sand and pump valves. Reality sees them fight it out with devastating regularity. Their conflict is part and parcel of the topic. Same for erosion and conservation, man and old age, careless motorists and car problems.

In contrast, the phoniness of talking clocks, "investigations" of the facilities of luxury resorts by private detectives, ghosts who fight or try to force change, and the like, can prove disastrous, simply because they're so obviously hokey as to turn audiences off.

A final question: How much of an interest line do you need?

If any.

This is no idle matter. There's a tendency in the fact film business, too often, to assume that some kind of story line, some sort of interest hook, is ever and always an essential.

Such isn't necessarily true. For as mentioned in the proceding chapter, too great a preoccupation with noninformational elements may irritate or distract rather than enhance.

It's wise, therefore, to consider three points before you plunge headlong into development of an all-out interest line:

(1) *What is this film's job?* Specifically, what does Client seek to

accomplish? Is his goal to inform, to influence, or to inspire? Does he want to show workers how to tie a bowline knot, persuade citizens to pledge to the United Fund, or convince unbelievers that God is love?

(2) *Why are the viewers watching this film?* Are they already interested in the topic? Is knowledge of the picture's contents important to them? Are they killing time, seeking entertainment, fighting boredom?

(3) *Under what conditions are they viewing it?* Is viewing a voluntary act, or do we have a captive audience? Of individuals, small groups, large groups? Are they at home, at work, among friends, in a social or business situation?

There is no "right" answer to these questions. All they give you are raw materials of varying weight on which to base a private judgment—and yes, you *can* guess wrong.

In general, though, straight-out instruction—the bowline knot bit, for example—requires no "interest" dressing. Neither does the documentary of events at the top of the news, or the film whose contents have a built-in importance to Audience.

(I still remember the outburst of a technical consultant on *Microscopic Studies of Fluids in Porous Matrices*: "I don't give a damn if the audience *doesn't* understand this film the first time round. These men are engineers. They'll keep on running it till it *does* make sense; their jobs depend on it!"

On the other hand, dramatized "most needy" incidents within a fact film framework may go miles in coaxing charity contributions; and there's a sound reason the popular *Insight* TV program uses fully dramatized, professionally written and acted stories, rather than pulpiteering, to get across its ideological messages.

It's also important to consider the competition. If your public service film on psychological factors in home accidents is to run in the time slot in which another TV channel has a John Wayne western on deck, you'd better come out swinging with a strong, clever interest line. And double that in spades for the training film scheduled for showing after lunch to troops already worn down by a morning's hard-at-it physical activity.

3. The presentation structure.

The purpose of setting up a presentation structure is to insure that the materials incorporated in interest and information lines reach the audience in the most effective order.

The simplest fact film organization formula I know to achieve this goal is the old familiar "Hey!—You—See?—So . . ." I like it because it's so loose it accommodates almost anything you can think of, rather than restricting your creativity; yet applied with a little imagination, it gets the job done.

The formula works this way:

Hey! = some element of your film's topic that strikes you as holding potential for capturing your audience's attention—an intriguing situation, a change in that situation, a bit of action, an interesting character, you name it.

You = something to involve the viewer subjectively . . . draw him into the topic on a personal level. A starting place? Try striking for known target audience attitudes. Or ringing changes on sociologist W.I. Thomas's famed "four wishes": adventure, security, response, recognition. Or the Gypsy fortune teller's love, health, wealth, trouble.

See? = the evidence you introduce to develop your subject, prove your point.

So . . . = the conclusion you draw, the point you make, the residual impression you leave.

Beyond this, and like any other "linear" literary form, a well-constructed film treatment is laid out in terms of beginning, middle, and end.

a. The beginning.

The good beginning does two things:

(1) It sets forth an audiovisual "hook" with which to catch the viewer's interest.
(2) It establishes the core assertion, the point the client wants to make and around which the film is to be built.

There are, at a conservative estimate, an infinity of ways to accomplish these worthy ends. You learn them by viewing films without number—viewing them critically, with an eye to their strengths and weaknesses—and then experimenting with your own film topic plus imagination.

Thus, by way of yelling "Hey!" a good beginning may fade in on an ambulance racing down the street, siren screaming; or on the house at which said ambulance eventually will stop; or on the patient within the house; or on the operating room to which he will be taken. But it can equally well open on bacteria on a slide viewed through a microscope, or on a clinician on his way to work, or on Patient-to-be eating a picnic dinner, or on his wife calling the hospital, or any number of other ways.

You see, the good opening's "Hey!" isn't necessarily shouted in a loud voice. Bomb-bursts or rifle shots are seldom vital.

What, then, does it take to make a good beginning?

Three elements: *curiosity, change,* and *consequences.*

The curiosity factor is more or less self-explanatory. Open with the ambulance, and Viewer wonders where it's going and why. Show him the house, and he puzzles over what's happening there, that we should focus on it. Zero in on the patient, and people ponder the poor man's fate: What's wrong with him? Will he live or die? Why?

But curiosity will carry a film only so far. In an appallingly short time, Audience will begin to grunt, "Get on with it!"

In other words, "Why did you show us that first shot? What's its purpose? Where's it leading?"

And believe me, it had better be leading somewhere, if you hope to hold your viewers!

The best place for it to lead—directly or indirectly, swiftly or slowly, subtly or without ceremony—is to a *change* of some sort, or at least the promise of change.

What's change? Let's define it as some aspect of reality becoming different in some way.

Change is, of course, the source of every news story: something has happened, is happening, will happen. Or here's something we want to happen.

Change is also an aspect of life that intrigues us immeasurably. For the best of reasons, too. Change almost invariably has *consequences* . . . consequences which very well may warp our lives or shape our destinies on any and all levels.

Let a film rouse our curiosity with its opening shots, then springboard from them into some change that has consequences which, via empathy, hold our interest, and that film is off to a good start.

Thus, the folksy, familiar pleasure of Patient-to-be eating a picnic dinner builds from mild curiosity to a deeper involvement as we cut to his home that night and watch him writhing in pain, then see him—in consequence of this anguish—rushed to the hospital for diagnosis and treatment.

Especially if his ailment is such that *you* might very well be in his place!

This principle is equally valid for the most pedestrian of intructional films, if it's handled rightly. Topic: the life of the spider. The opening shot centers on the mass of eggs, rousing curiosity by the very fact that only the experienced eye can identify them for what they are. Then—change—the eggs begin to hatch and—consequence—tiny spiders in motion fill the frame.

Is this curiosity-change-consequence the only way to start a picture? Of course not. But I like it because it does have the advantage of forcing you to think of your topic as a dynamic, developing entity rather than a static thing.

On to *core assertion*.

Though in and of itself a statement about your topic, often the core assertion is best presented in question form: "Is there really hope for Man, then? Is there really a chance to build a better world?" "Just what *can* a public health nurse do for the mentally retarded child?" ". . . so now, let's take a closer look at scientific occupations. Is there really room for your kind of gal or guy within the field?"

The important thing is to get that point you want to make in early. For until it—your core assertion—is established, your picture hasn't really started.

In turn, where your interest line's concerned, the beginning's the place to introduce your empathetic element—your central character, animate or otherwise—and plunge said element into the conflict with the opposition.

b. The middle.

A film's middle sequences constitute the "See?" element of our formula. The "See?" in turn is made up of the subassertions on which your core assertion is based, linking them into a chain of logic designed to prove the assertion.

The main thing to bear in mind when doing this is that it's of more than passing importance to set up your major points in ascending order of importance/intensity/interest. For as it has been noted since Aristotle, anything which follows a climax must be either a greater climax or an anti-climax, and tension—and attention—diminishes if you allow anti-climax to take over.

This being the case, the middle sees the clash between the interest line's "character(s)" and opposition build to a peak.

c. The end.

The "So . . ." of our formula is the conclusion our film draws . . . a reiteration of the core assertion. It comes at the film's end, and preferably should hammer home the assertion in a summarizing "key phrase" which nails down the residual impression with which you hope to leave the audience.

Here, too, you resolve any remaining conflicts your interest line has developed. If you can do so in appropriately clever and pertinent fashion, so much the better. In *Love That Car*, the twist was the garage's tow truck running out of gas—a neat reversal that brought yet another laugh even while it wiped out any chance viewers might feel they were being lectured to by some authority figure who was never himself careless or neglectful.

d. Special tools.

So far, I've tried to avoid mention of anything too specifically cinematic. But now, the time has come.

Why? Because occasionally, in preparing a treatment, you're going to encounter a situation where nothing you can think of seems to solve the problems. When that moment arrives you may find your answer in *special effects* or *animation*.

Special effects—that is, footage unobtainable by ordinary routine shooting techniques—makes it possible for the filmmaker to freeze action, slow it down, allow time to pass between frames, modify or obstruct light, put foreground action against different backgrounds, superimpose one shot upon another, split frames, and perform a host of other visual miracles.

Animation is a cinematic procedure for giving apparent life and movement to inanimate objects. By means of photographed drawings, it enables you to minimize, maximize, go inside the human body, or capture both the history and spirit of science in a 15-minute film.

The problem with both animation and special effects is that all too often they prove fantastically expensive. But they're such valuable tools you can't afford not to be aware of their potential.

Because they're too complex to discuss in detail here, I suggest you investigate them by means of the various books on the subject listed in Appendix C, "For Further Reading."

WRITING YOUR TREATMENT

Planning's one thing, writing another. The initial thinking through of how best to handle your topic is vital, to say the least. But once that's out of the way, the less attention you pay to mechanics when you sit down at the typewriter to hammer out your first draft treatment, the better. Write from the moment's impulse, rather, getting down everything in the wildest rush of enthusiasm you can muster. Hunt for the aspects that intrigue you, excite you, turn you on.

Rules? Patterning? Structure? Use them as checklists later, not as guidelines to creation. That is, get the picture you visualize down on paper and *then* go back and see if you've left out anything essential.

Where your information line and interest line are concerned, neither *as such* goes into the treatment. What you describe is an integration of them, a presentation drawn from them. Or, to put it in another way, they exist only as part of your planning. Writing, you incorporate their essence, not their form.

The cardinal sin in the treatment is to reduce it to a dry-as-dust outline. You *must* dramatize to some degree, in all but the most technical of cases, if you hope to prove effective. To that end, present your ideas in descriptions that enable producer and client to *experience* with the audience . . . *understand and empathize* with the characters. Tell your man the conclusions you want him to draw, the way you seek to have him react. If that takes occasional brief passages of dialogue, or dramatic descriptions of action, or inclusion of emotionally pertinent detail—fine! The important thing is to get your concepts across, with pictorial nouns and action verbs and short, simple declarative sentences.

What about format? Actually, there's no such thing as *a* treatment format. There are only the formats for specific treatments.

Herewith, a sample of one I like, one that also shows how a preliminary outline or proposal expands as it reaches the treatment stage. Accept it as that and nothing more, and then go on to develop the private pattern *you* prefer.

Proposed

Film Treatment Outline

WHAT THE TEACHER SEES

(Working Title)

Opening titles will be (1) sponsoring organization's name, (2) main titles, and (3) production credit titles. These titles will appear over shots of children (ages 5 to 12) at play on school playground.

The titles fade as school bell rings and the children enter the school. Our central character, an attractive young teacher, monitors them as they push through the doorway. Narrator raises the central question which the film proposes to answer: Miss Jackson wants to be a good teacher. She knows that to be taught effectively, children must be in good health. But inexperienced as she is, what standard should she use to judge her pupils? Are there danger signals she should watch for? Above all, how can she recognize the signs of health?

The main body of the film demonstrates that careful, continuing observation is the key to success. Or, as a friendly older teacher (portrayed as a model well worthy of emulation) explains it to Miss Jackson: "Just remember one thing, my dear. A good teacher doesn't teach just subjects; she teaches children."

Under this teacher's tutelage, Miss Jackson considers a variety of typical children...learns how to use the youngsters themselves as the basis for a norm by which to judge health. Included are children who show (1) good body development, (2)

good nurture, (3) good posture, (4) good motor coordination,
(5) good respiration, (6) good skin, (7) good vision, (8) good
hearing, (9) good speech, (10) good emotional health, (11)
freedom from disease, and (12) freedom from injury. Children
who deviate from this norm also are shown, by way of contrast,
but the dominant emphasis remains strongly on the side of
normality. As Miss Jackson observes the signs of health or
deviation, she makes written notes of her observations of
significant health and behavioral problems, consults with the
school nurse, talks with parents, etc. However, it is stressed
throughout that the teacher's role is not and should not be
that of diagnostician. Her function is only to observe the
norm and deviations from the norm.

Concluding scenes show children leaving Miss Jackson's
class for recess. Miss Jackson joins Mrs. Carter, the older
teacher. "How best can you make sure you're doing right by
your class?" narrator asks the audience, recapitulating. "It's
simple, really. Just use your eyes and ears, your senses.
Watch for the signs of health. Get to know each and every
pupil as an individual. As Mrs. Carter says--a really good
teacher doesn't just teach subjects; she teaches children!"

Laughing and talking (and with Miss Jackson's
admiration for Mrs. Carter plainly showing) the two teachers
cross to a window and look out. They see the children at
play on the playground, in a shot which roughly matches the
one on which the film opened. Concluding narration emphasizes
Miss Jackson's growth and development, and the emotional
satisfaction it gives her.

End titles come on over.

The End

Revised version prepared for

OKLAHOMA STATE DEPARTMENT OF HEALTH

Approved:

For the Producer_____Date_____

For Department of Health_____Date_____

So much for the film treatment. With practice, you too can learn to write it.

But you can't stop there. Not when you still have to learn about the sequence outline.

CHAPTER 4:

The Sequence Outline

Seq. 7: In his lab, Dr. Smith
works on his immunology
project. Narrator
emphasizes that entirely
apart from the project's
importance, Smith gains
tremendous satisfaction
from the work itself.
But work's only one part
of his life. Outside the
lab lie a host of other
interests.
                    DISSOLVE TO:

Seq. 8: Dr. Smith and family at
symphony concert.
Narrator's comments
enlarge on the normal life
angle.

DISSOLVE TO:

Seq. 9: The Smith kids romp with their parents in bed on Saturday morning. Appropriate comments.

DISSOLVE TO:

Seq. 10: Dr. Smith and friends play golf. Appropriate comments.

DISSOLVE TO:

Seq. 11: Dr. Smith and family watch Sunday night TV. Appropriate comments.

DISSOLVE TO:

What you see above is an excerpt from what's known as a *sequence outline,* the phase in script preparation that ordinarily follows writing of the treatment.

Next question: Just what is a sequence?

A motion picture is made up of a series of still pictures (each termed a *frame*) taken at the rate of 24 pictures per second.* The illusion of movement is the result of a physiological phenomenon known as *persistence of vision*—the fact that the image of Picture 1 lingers long enough in the eye to overlap Picture 2, thus making it seem to the viewer that he is observing continuous action rather than a series of separate photographs.

The piece of film resulting from a single camera run—that is, the series of still pictures taken between the moment a motion picture camera starts and the moment it stops—is called a *shot.*

A *sequence* is a related series of shots—a group of individual film cuts tied together by some element they hold in common. A *sequence outline* is a succinct list/description of the sequences to be included in a film.

Just as the film treatment fleshes out the proposal outline, so the sequence outline elaborates on the treatment. It translates the points the picture is to make into units of thought and/or action by forcing you to

* This is the rate for sound film. Silent film ordinarily is shot at 16 frames per second. Film shot at speeds slower than 16 frames gives the impression of flickering when projected.

visualize how you're going to present your material on film. It "sells" your basic idea/core assertion step by step, instead of just rehashing generalities on a "Gee, this is great!" plane.

This means that, to write a sequence outline, you must learn to think of your subject matter in terms of related groups of shots—more specifically, related groups of shots each group of which makes a point.

Thus, in the fragment of sequence outline at the beginning of this chapter, the point of sequence 7 is that Dr. Smith is doing valuable work which he enjoys. Sequences 8, 9, 10, and 11, in turn, show—that is, prove by visual demonstration—that Dr. Smith (and, by implication, all research scientists) remains an eminently normal human being who enjoys the same kind of things other men do—home, family, sports, music, TV.

Each sequence does this in a related series of shots.

But that's just a beginning. Actually, to build an effective sequence outline, you need to understand not only how shots are related, the types of sequences, but how to outline a sequence, and how to break a treatment into sequences.

1. How shots are related.

✻ In the fact film, shots may be related—that is, tied together—by such unifying elements as

a. Concept, idea, thought.

A sequence has sphericity as its topic. Footage of such divergent items as basketballs, marbles, world globes, and fortune-tellers' crystals is incorporated into it. These dissimilar objects are tied together by narration which calls attention to the fact that all the articles filmed have the state of being spherical in common.

b. Action.

Last round of a prize fight. Champion comes out of his corner fast, hammering Contender into the ropes. Clinching, Contender heaves himself to one side. The maneuver momentarily frees his right arm, just enough for him to explode a short, jarring uppercut to Champion's jaw. Then—

Film coverage of this action may involve two or three cameras; half a dozen or more shots. Cut together in proper order, these shots form a sequence, unified by continuity of action.

(In all likelihood, sequences 7, 8, 9, 10, and 11 in our opening example will each be developed in terms of such continuous action.)

c. Setting.

The scene is a park. It unites shots of strollers, old men on benches, gnarled trees, a fountain, children swarming over playground equipment, riders cantering along a bridle path. The thing they have in common, the element which makes them a sequence, is setting.

↓ d. Character.

A backpacker strides briskly down a grassy slope, clambers up rocky outcroppings, plods through loose shale, drinks at a spring, pauses and wipes his brow as he crests a rise and gazes out across a broad valley. The idea behind the action isn't revealed, the action itself is far from continuous, the settings are divergent. But the focusing of attention on one character (it might equally well be a group) unifies the sequence.

↓ e. Mood.

Slum streets around the world. Shots of sagging buildings, gutter filth, slumped shoulders, ravaged faces combine to create a mood that, simultaneously, ties together a sequence.

Obviously, there may be wide overlapping areas between these or other categories. An idea, a continuing flow of action, a setting, a character, and a mood all may join in one sequence. The proper label is a matter of context and decision, with no two writers or filmmakers necessarily agreeing.

Internal development of sequences may be chronological, spatial, familiar to unfamiliar, cause to effect, or any of the other patterns for building an entire film which we listed in the preceding chapter. Additional useful tools include

Dramatization: The film deals with marriage counseling. Here is a sequence in which a man and a woman, playing husband and wife, lash out at each other in simulated fury.

Analogy: Same film. A sequence features a snarling dog circling a bristling cat. The analogy to the angry couple previously cited is clear.

Example: An actual couple—the wife with a black eye, perhaps—discuss their problem with a counselor, while a hidden camera captures the moment on film.

Comparison: Here alternating sequences show two couples, one happy and one unhappy, or one unhappy in one way, the other in another.

Yes, there are a host of additional ways to develop sequences. Use your imagination.

2. Types of sequences.

Whatever your material, whatever your handling, each sequence you build will fall into one of two categories: *continuity* or *compilation.* An understanding of how these types differ will go a long way towards simplifying the issues involved in creating a solid sequence outline.

↓ a. The continuity sequence.

A unit of *continuing action,* the continuity sequence may include a host of shots, but ends when there is a break in time. Traditionally (but not always, these days, by any means!) its conclusion is marked by an optical effect—a DISSOLVE, a FADE, a WIPE, or such. Casual reference to a given continuity sequence quite possibly may term it "the fight sequence," "the wedding sequence," "the dinner sequence," or such, thus tacitly acknowledging the fact of continuing action; the lack of break in continuity.

b. The compilation sequence.

A unit of *information* or *thought,* and sometimes called a newsreel sequence, the compilation sequence is particularly common in fact films. Often you'll see it in coverage of a flood, a tornado, a travelogue, a tour of a factory, or the like. This is because it enables the filmmaker to use narration to tie together a wide range of divergent individual shots taken with no regard for continuing action. References to such a sequence frequently focus on topic, rather than continuity: "the manufacturing sequence," "the growth sequence," "the hospital sequence," etc. Just as in the case of the continuity sequence, an optical effect frequently marks the conclusion of the compilation sequence. *Unlike* the continuity sequence, however, and because the compilation sequence's scope ordinarily is too broad to be encompassed by continuous, no-break action, opticals may be used within it, to link the divergent times and places involved. It ends when discussion of the topic itself ends.

c. The combining of sequences.

Both types of sequence—continuity and compilation—often are used in the same film. Thus, a picture may begin with a continuity sequence of dramatized action designed to hook audience interest . . . follow it with a compilation sequence which introduces the film's topic and emphasizes its scope . . . go to a second compilation sequence which establishes the broad outlines of a particular locale . . . . move on to a continuity sequence which pinpoints a bit of dramatic action in that locale . . . and so on.

This technique is particularly useful in the fact film, since it makes practical the introduction of a heavy load of information, on the one hand, while permitting the building of viewer interest, on the other.

3. How to outline a sequence.

As in so many areas in film, there's no set format for outlining a sequence. But a good many writers find it useful to follow a three-pronged plan of attack. For each sequence, they make sure to include:

  a. Point to be made.
  b. What's seen.
  c. What's heard.

Items *b* and *c* are clear enough on the face of it. The main thing to bear in mind in their regard is that a sequence outline is, indeed, an *outline*—that is to say, it should be kept as terse and concise as possible.

Item *a*, however, is a frequent source of problems. Why? Because too often, a writer or filmmaker caught up in an intriguing bit of action tries to incorporate it even though it has no particular bearing on the issue at hand. (On one occasion, indeed, I recall an eager-beaver director on a tight budget burning nearly a thousand feet of 16mm film on the cavortings of a couple of stray dogs. Allegedly, they were going to provide "atmosphere." Actually, they only wasted time and money and ended up on the cutting room floor.)

Let us state the issue loud and clear, then: *A sequence should always make a point.* If it has no point to make, it's pure waste motion. If it has a point but doesn't make it, it's a bad sequence.

This should come as no surprise. As previously reiterated so tediously often, your film itself is designed to prove a point, establish the truth of a core assertion. To this end, you build in subassertions, proof points supporting your main point.

That proof must be set forth visually in a sequence. And if the subassertion is so complex as to require development in sub-subassertions, then each of them, in turn, should be presented in a sequence of its own.

So: Step 1 in outlining a given sequence is to decide what point it is to make . . . after which, you go on to the matter of what's seen and what's heard.

Beyond this, some writers and some producers like to have transitions between sequences indicated in the outline. It's a matter of personal preference.

Here's how all this works, where the outline of a *compilation* sequence is concerned:

> Now we show that a Lakewood vacation
> offers fun for every taste. Mixed shots of
> young and old alike (including plenty of
> closeups of happy faces) pinpoint the
> pleasures of fishing, swimming, golfing,
> skeet shooting, indoor games, sunning, girl-
> watching, etc.
>
> Narrator offers appropriate comments
> that emphasize (with sensory words in profusion)
> the pleasures of each activity, plus the release
> from nervous tension that freedom from care
> brings.   DISSOLVE TO:

Do you see the pattern? The very first sentence makes clear the point the sequence is to make: . . . *a Lakewood vacation offers fun for every taste.*

The remainder of the paragraph summarizes what viewers will see when the film's completed. The description of the footage to be included makes it clear that the camera is going to be jumping all over the place, catching a flash of this, a few frames of that, a cut or two or three of the other thing. But all the shots are related, in that they deal with the same topic: a Lakewood vacation; and paragraph 2 sees the narrator pinpoint this in terms of what the audience will hear from the soundtrack.

Finally, the DISSOLVE TO: nails down the transition device designed to move the action from this sequence to the next.

Note also that while the writer covers the ground involved adequately, he keeps his presentation brief.

What happens in a *continuity* sequence?

```
        Back to Bob and Jill.  In the dining room

now, they help their plates at the evening buffet

...eat at a properly appointed table, complete

with snowy linen, shining silver, flowers, and

maybe even candlelight.  Both of them (or

narrator, if it's decided to handle this

sequence voice over) comment ecstatically on

the wonderful variety and gourmet preparation

of the food.

                                DISSOLVE TO:
```

There's no jumping here, please observe. The flow of action is continuous, beginning to end—even though quite possibly the director will cheat a bit by compressing time, via one of the devices we'll explore in the next chapter, when we deal with the shooting script.

The *point?* Here it doesn't appear until the very end, where the characters "comment ecstatically on *the wonderful variety and gourmet preparation of the food."* What's seen and what's heard *proves* it visually— seeing is believing—and we exit to the next sequence via a DISSOLVE TO:

But outlining a sequence isn't all there is to building a sequence outline. Equally important is the matter of

4. How to break a treatment into sequences.

Allegedly, by the time you've finished your treatment, you have your film's action clearly in mind.

Allegedly.

Yet more often than not, when the time comes for you to prepare a sequence outline, problems arise. In spite of all your previous work, you find yourself floundering through gaps, miring down in confusion, wandering off into a maze of false paths and dead ends.

Why? Frequently, because your original concept and line of development just don't work out well in visual terms.

⚡ Solution: Go back over your treatment, and make a list of all the major and minor points to be made.

⚡ Then, devise a way of putting each across on film—that is, visually—via either continuity or compilation sequences.

I hate to tell you how much hard work this is going to take. Or how much additional research. Or—especially—how much creative imagination.

The reason is that it's not going to be enough merely to come up with a disjointed series of fragments. What you're after is a picture that's a unified whole, with each sequence integrated smoothly into the film's overall line of development.

This is why it's greatly to your advantage to have worked out a strong information line and an equally muscular interest line back when you prepared your treatment. Now, out of the research that went into them, you can draw incidents, units of data or thought or action to plug holes, illustrate abstractions, drive home principles, or perform whatever other creative miracles you need.

On the other hand, I'd be kidding you if I pretended that the building of a sequence outline—or any other phase of a film script, for that matter—is entirely neat and logical and by the rules. More frequently, in truth, it's a matter of flying by the seat of your pants, catch-as-catch-can, and then developing these ideas via continuing elaboration. Here's an intriguing bit, there a block of solid information. Then along comes an incident or two; a colorful setting; a brisk exchange. Finally, you gather them all together, and somehow tie them into a package.

I still remember one such instance. The man was a former state politico, a powerful figure of yesteryear. Now his son had attained high office and officials of one governmental subdivision in particular were fearful that reprisals for past affronts might be meted out.

A short film honoring Politico for his place in history might help calm the storm-tossed waters, it was decided. The task of scripting the picture fell on me. All I had to work from was a back-of-envelope list of high points in Politico's career.

Each note, clearly, was basis for an effective sequence. Trouble was, the footage available on Politico was strictly limited, to the point where it seemed impossible to make anything of it.

For days I paced the floor. Still no answer.

Then, one afternoon, someone's private angel led him to thread up a reel of stock footage on the projector.

You couldn't have found anything much more remote to politics. All it offered was a few hundred feet of color film shot from the front bumper of a pickup truck as it bounced and jounced down a narrow woods road. Lord only knows why anyone had taken it.

Yet there it was, the living, breathing answer to our problem: "It was a long, hard road old Sam Smith"—not his name, of course—"traveled on his way to state leadership and a place in history . . ."

Well, after that, the rest was easy. We did it with stock footage of hands, mostly: hands chopping wood, hands laying brick, hands holding law books, hands pounding gavels. Each bit made a point as we traced Politico's career. Where footage of the old man was available, we used it, along with shots of houses, roads, state buildings, and the like that fitted in. Where we had nothing that would fit, we fell back on our bouncy woods road color, with appropriate comment about Old Sam's climb to glory.

The result was hardly a prize picture. But it did solve the immediate problem. And, to my amazement, not long ago I discovered that it's still in circulation.

So what's the lesson to be drawn from this epochal incident?

Would you believe "It's easier to make an acceptable picture when you have points to make but no footage than when you have all sorts of footage but no points"?

Finally, a word of warning: Sometimes a rushed or sloppy producer won't ask you to prepare a sequence outline. Do so anyhow; you'll find it helps you build a solid script far beyond any time or trouble it may take.

Particularly, it's vital when you come to the next stage of your job: preparation of a shooting script.

CHAPTER 5:

The Shooting Script

A shooting script is the detailed plan for a proposed film. Sometimes called a "shot list," it consists of a description of each shot to be incorporated into the picture.

Though largely supplanted by the master scene script (see Chapter 13) where the writing of feature films is concerned, the shooting script remains more or less standard in the fact film field. In effect an instruction sheet for technical people and talent, it tells the actors what to say and do; the crew, what to take pictures of. In major measure, it determines what the audience will see when they view the finished film.

Because these things are so, the shooting script should at all costs avoid (a) pictures which confuse the audience, and (b) instructions which confuse cast and/or crew.

To this end, you need to learn how to break down action, how to describe shots, and how to set up a shooting script in proper format.

1. How to break down action.

The first step in writing a shooting script is to break down each sequence from your sequence outline into its component individual shots.

The trick here is to get in the habit of projecting the finished film in your head as you write it. Visualize each scene in careful detail as it develops. Watch the flow of action in your imagination.

Simultaneously, break down said action into shots: single runs of the camera.

This is a knack, believe me. The simplest way to master it, in my own experience, is to make contact with some amateur or professional worker in the field who will grant you the loan of some reels of edited film, a couple of film winds, and a tabletop rear screen projection device called a viewer. You then wind the film back and forth through the viewer, as slowly as need be, until you're aware of shots as shots, not just a flow of action.

Indeed, there are worse ways to learn to write a shooting script than to maneuver yourself into involvement in the process of film editing, whether as participant or as observer. Watching, watching, watching over some old hand's shoulder as he labors at editing bench or Moviola, asking as many questions as you can get away with as to where and why he's cutting, can prove a major step in your education as a scriptwriter.

Another possible though tedious procedure is to sit through the screening of a feature half a dozen or more times, till you're so totally bored with the story that you can see the cuts—that is, the individual shots.

In any event, and whatever route you take: Do learn to see not-yet-filmed action in your mind's eye.

Simultaneously, keep asking yourself, *"What do I need to have the audience look at next?"*

Your primary guideline in answering this question is of course the point you're trying to make in the particular sequence: the subassertion it's designed to prove. This is why it's so devastatingly important that you write a sequence outline before you start your shooting script, whether anyone demands such of you or not. Without it, you can wander in endless circles, getting nowhere. It's a major reason for films that drag and jerk and ramble.

So: What do you need to have the audience look at next? A tight closeup that will call some crucial detail to their attention? An establishing or reestablishing shot, far enough back to orient them to the broader action? A reaction shot, to help shape their attitudes?

And always, the issue will be the subassertion you're trying to back with visual proof.

Break the question down, if need be. Consider such matters as
—What point am I trying to make *in this shot*?
— How does said shot tie in or relate to the point I'm trying to make in the sequence? In the film as whole?
— What should the action be, in order to make the point most convincingly?
— Am I forgetting anything, leaving something out that needs to be included?
Again, a guideline: The answer, in one word, is always *perti-*

nence . . . logical fitness, applicability, relevance. Every shot should be designed to intensify the effect you seek.

Pertinence is of two types:

Visual pertinence . . . shots that sustain the flow of action or impression.

Emotional pertinence . . . shots which create the audience reaction you seek.

Naturally, in a host of instances—perhaps most—these tend to overlap. But both are elements you create with malice aforethought . . . products of thinking, pre-planning, floor-pacing, organization . . . calculated selection and arrangement of action/footage. And while a large part of the responsibility for the finished product of necessity falls on director and/or editor, the fact remains that the writer plays a major role just by the way he blocks things in. The better he understands film principles, the more likely he is to come up with a script that offers the other people involved ways to put an effective presentation on the screen.

a. Problems of visual pertinence.

Visual pertinence consists of visual flow honed razor-sharp with applicability to the point you're trying to make.

In the continuity sequence, the issue will be to maintain the flow of action. To this end,

(1) *Coverage must be functional.* That is, image size and angle must fit the needs of viewers where the particular situation is concerned. Thus, at certain times, it's essential to orient your audience by establishing the relationship of characters to the background and to each other. At others, the action and/or appearance of characters and/or objects are what's important. Or, the issue may be attention to certain key details.

The writer must anticipate these needs, this functional aspect of visual continuity, and provide for them in the script.

(2) *Coverage must be logical.* Here the issue is less viewer needs than viewer desires, anticipations. If a character gives sudden, intent attention to his watch, Viewer is going to want to see the watch face. If murky shadows stir, Viewer will want to see what's stirring; or, perhaps, Character's reaction to it. If Character races down the street, Viewer will want to see what he's pursuing, what's pursuing him, or what hazards lie ahead.

(3) *Coverage must give the illusion of continuity.* Confusion is a black sin indeed in the continuity sequence. Change of angle, image size, or the like must be motivated, as when the camera jumps from a position aside and behind a running character to aside and ahead, in order to prepare for his sudden veering into an alley. It must also be substantial enough not to appear accidental. Yet on the other hand, it must not take

so great a leap as to leave the audience groping as to where the action is taking place, who's who, or what's going on.

The shots must also be so smoothly joined that no break in the action is apparent.

To this end, continuity sequences are developed in terms of *match cuts* and *cutaways*.

A match cut is one in which the second of two shots of a continuing action includes part of the action in the first shot. The shots are cut together where the action overlaps in a manner to insure smooth transition from shot to shot.

The cutaway, in contrast, does not include any part of the preceding shot.

Thus, we might open with a shot of an office, complete with desks, chairs, filing cabinets, and the like, but devoid of people. A door opens. A man and girl enter.

A second shot gives us a closer view of the pair. Girl moves a few steps further into the room. Shot 3 concentrates on Man as he closes door. Shot 4 sees Man cross to Girl. They embrace. Man unbuttons top button of Girl's blouse. A fifth shot zeroes in on the doorknob, out of frame in shot 4. Knob turns slowly.

Since shot 2 includes part of what was seen in shot 1, it's a match cut. Shot 3 includes part of what was seen in shot 2—again, a match cut. Shot 4? Another match cut.

Shot 5, however, was *not* included in shot 4. In consequence, it's a cutaway.

The value of the cutaway in maintaining the illusion of continuity is beyond measure. Among other things, cutaways can successfully mask spots where the flow of action in two shots doesn't quite mesh together properly. They can introduce parallel lines of action. They can clarify situations. They can break up an otherwise static scene. They can add suspense. They can speed up time passage.

Take our example. The cutaway of the doorknob introduces a parallel line of action, breaks up what might otherwise be a static scene, adds suspense. Perhaps, if we have been wondering what's become of some other character, it clarifies the situation. If, after the cutaway, we cut back to Man and Girl and discover that three of Girl's blouse buttons are now unbuttoned, we've speeded up time passage. And if this new shot reveals that Man is doing the unbuttoning with his left hand, when he was using his right in shot 4, we've also masked a break where two shots don't cut together properly.

Visual pertinence operates a little differently where the compilation sequence is concerned—for in such, unity is provided by *topic* and *narration*.

In consequence, the goal in cutting often is to *avoid* the impression of continuity, continuing flow of action. Shots very well may be chosen for contrast, with emphasis on dissimilar colors, dissimilar sizes, dissimilar objects or action. Extreme closeups may be juxtaposed with extreme long shots, high angles with low, books with bursting bombs, people with machines or monsters.

So much for visual pertinence. In and of itself a fascinating subject, it rates intensive study on the part of every would-be screenwriter. The best place to carry out said study is in the cutting room, under the tutelage of an experienced film editor. Lacking the opportunity for that, much can be learned from the books in Appendix C.

b. Building emotional pertinence.

Emotional pertinence—shots which create the audience reaction you seek—is at least equally vital to visual, in that it has in it the power to make interesting what might otherwise be dull footage. Indeed, when someone tells you that you need to "build" a particular sequence, what he often means is that you need to add shots that will give it greater emotional pertinence.

You give a sequence emotional pertinence through your control of (1) *time*, (2) *emphasis*, and (3) *reaction*.

Take *time*. In a typical factory tour—live, not filmed—90 per cent of the actual, chronological time may be waste motion devoted to chitchat, bad jokes, walking from department to department, and so on. To include it in a film is to reduce effectiveness via boredom. Therefore, in building the tour from sequence outline to shooting script, you eliminate such immaterialities, leaving only essentials to be filmed—a montage that catches the key action in each unit, perhaps.

Emphasis may be the issue where a new widget-stamping machine is concerned. Though each step in its operation occupies only a fraction of a second, one particular meshing of gears or junction of parts is tremendously important. Made aware of this by your research, you break the overall process down, filling the screen with strong, pertinent extreme closeups which *emphasize* the details to which you want to draw attention. The split second involved in the actual stamping thus may end up stretching to a minute or more on the screen.

Or consider a continuity sequence in a home accident film. Our hero, disgruntled after a fight with his wife, goes out to move a heavy trunk from the garage to the basement via an old-fashioned outside stairwell. A broom lies across the threshold. Tossing it into the basement, and more irked than ever, Hero begins backing down the steps, bracing himself against the trunk's weight. Past him, as we watch from above, we can see the broom, now caught crosswise across the stairs close to the bottom.

Cutting back and forth between man and broom, emphasizing each in turn, we can prolong Hero's descent to an endless agony of suspense: Will he trip? Will he fall? Will the trunk crush him? Witness

Alfred Hitchcock's famous *Psycho* scene of Tony Perkins stabbing Janet Leigh in the shower; it built through 78 shots!

Reaction? In a compilation sequence, it quite possibly will be provided by a narrator, who in effect tells the audience what to think, how to interpret the mixed shots on the screen. Or, perhaps a dialogue interchange between actors calls attention to the emotionally pertinent points.

In the same way, a reaction factor can be injected into a continuity sequence on squirrel hunting by appropriate interpretation via narrator. Or, the reaction—and emotional pertinence—may be supplied by the enthusiastic behavior of the hunters themselves.

So much for the principles and procedures by which you build a shooting script. Now, on to mechanics:

2. How to describe a shot.

For clarity's sake, let's work from a sample, checking it against eight points:

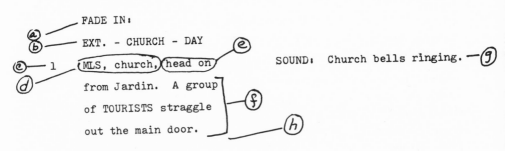

Now, our checklist:

a. How do you get into the shot?

That is, does the shot come onto the screen by means of a FADE (the screen black at first . . . then the picture appearing, brighter and brighter) . . . a DISSOLVE (one picture gradually fading out while another fades in) . . . a WIPE (one picture pushing another off the screen in any one of a wild variety of ways, from straight vertical or horizontal to explosion), or what have you?

(If one shot follows another instantaneously, with no transition device specified, a CUT—the end of one piece of film simply pasted to the next—is taken for granted. Ordinarily, it isn't mentioned in the script, unless perhaps used for shock effect.)

In our example, we FADE IN—all caps, note—because *every* shooting script so begins.

b. What are the conditions of work?

Three items are included here. All go on one line of the script, all are typed all caps, and all always go in the same order. They're omitted if no change in conditions from the previous shot has taken place.

The three items, all essential information for the crew, are:

(1) Interior (INT.) or exterior (EXT.).

(2) Place (MACHINE SHOP, BEDROOM, STREET, RIVER BANK, etc.).

(3) Time (DAY or NIGHT).

c. *What's the numerical designation?*

Shots are numbered in sequence from a film's beginning to its end. In production, before the action of a given shot starts, the shot itself is "slated." That is, its number and other identifying data is chalked on a slate and filmed. This enables the director to avoid confusing the editor when he shoots out of sequence—as he almost certainly will, at one point or another.

d. *What's the image size and subject?*

Both size and subject *must* be included. There's no such thing as a "medium shot," or whatever, in and of itself. But more of that later.

e. *What's the camera position?*

This is the kind of thing you mention only if a particular position is essential to the point to be made—"high angle," "low angle," "shooting from bank window," etc. Fool around with such too much, or try to get fancy, and the director will both hate you and ignore your instructions.

f. *What action is seen?*

What—if anything—happens? Does an actor move? Does a machine function? And remember, the closeup of a knife on a table may be vital and highly dramatic, yet involve no action.

g. *What sound is heard?*

The thing to bear in mind here is that sound includes *effects* (motors roaring, hooves pounding, bells ringing) and *music* (which may or may not be designated according to type—BACKGROUND-PASTORAL, MYSTERIOSO, FANFARE, BACKGROUND-INDUSTRIAL, etc.) as well as *narration* and *dialogue*.

Any sound element you specify should be labeled, ALL CAPS, each time there's a change—as from narrator to actor, actor to actor, sound effects to music, music to narrator/actor, etc.

h. *How do you get out of the shot?*

The issue here is precisely as in item *a*, above. Since no technical effect is mentioned, we assume that the shot closes with a cut.

*   *   *

So much for how you describe a shot. Beyond this, however, in item *d*, above, we made mention of image size. This is such an important—and potentially confusing—subject as to be worth particularly detailed treatment.

IMAGE SIZE DESIGNATION

How large should a given object and/or action appear on the screen at a given time—and how do you label it in your script so it will come out within gunshot of the way you want it?

Your three basic image sizes are *long shot, medium shot,* and *closeup.* More often than not, scripts abbreviate these to LS, MS, and CU . . . or to such variations as ELS (extreme long shot), MLS (medium long shot), MCU (medium closeup), ECU (extreme closeup), and so on.

The key principle to bear in mind in using these various shots is *relativism.* That is, a long shot of a man may very well be a medium shot of the car he's driving—and a closeup of the stoplight in the foreground.

In essence, each type of shot has its special function. You don't use it just as a matter whim, but because you have a particular job that needs doing.

Thus, a *long shot* is an orientation shot, an establishing shot. It relates a particular object and/or action to its surroundings, its background. In consequence, there's no such thing as a "long shot," *per se* . . . only "LS, Susie. Wearily, head down, rain hat pulled about her face, she plods up the walk."

A *medium shot* is a subject shot . . . the object and/or action in and of itself, with a minimum of distracting background. "MS, Susie. She reaches the porch steps," probably will include Susie, head to toe, but very little else save perhaps enough of the steps to make them identifiable.

A *closeup* is an emphasis shot—one which calls attention to the specific detail of the subject which makes the factual or emotional point you seek. Thus, in our imaginary sequence, we might very well follow the two shots above with "CU, Susie's head. She raises it full face to camera. Her right eye is blackened, her cheek scraped and bruised. Tears stream down her face."

And there you have it. No matter what story you seek to tell, what information you want to convey, you forever work with LS-MS-CU and their variations, even though for effect you choose to combine them in all sorts of outlandish orders.

Remember, however, that too great a jump—from ECU to ELS, for example—quite possibly may confuse your viewers; that too many closeups in a row may disorient your audience: frequent reestablishment of characters or whatever in relation to background is a must; and that your inspired dream of a shot that zooms in on Earth from outer space to a closeup of a gnat's eyebrow may of necessity have to be tempered a bit in view of technical limitations.

Remember also that a given director or cameraman may not see a given image size as you do. Your "long shot" of a dining table may, in his eyes, be a "medium long shot"—or even a "medium shot" or "medium closeup." Your only defense is clarity and precision of description every step of the way. If you want someone's eyeball to fill the frame, say so!

And yes, there *are* other terms in use, almost unto infinity. A *full shot* takes in a person, head to toe; a *knee shot* chops him off at the knees; a *waist shot*, at the waist and so on. A *close shot* is a sloppy designation which indicates only that the camera is near the subject. In Britain, you'll run into the BCU (big closeup)—we'd probably call it an ECU. But don't worry about such; you'll pick up the terms you really need as you go along. (I've listed some in Appendix D, the *Terms You'll Use* section.)

3. Shooting script format.

The fact film shooting script ordinarily utilizes a two-column format, as per the sample in the following pages. Shot descriptions are in the left-hand column. Sound (a term which here includes dialogue, narration, music, and effects, remember) is on the right.

Set up with your paper's left edge at zero in your typewriter. Assuming your machine has pica type (and industry practice says it should have), the following horizontal spacing will ordinarily be observed:

> 10—shot numbers
> 15—shot descriptions—40
> 30—transitions
> 45—sound descriptions—70
> 75—page numbers

> Vertical spacing:
> Page number—two spaces below top of page
> First line—four spaces below page number
> Conditions of work, shot descriptions—four spaces below preceding copy
> Transitions—two spaces below preceding copy

Note that while directions, speeches, etc., are *single* spaced in the master scene script (see Chapter 13), the tendency in most fact film shooting scripts is to *double* space both shot descriptions and speeches. This will vary from shop to shop, however, so it's always wise to try to check a sample.

Note also that sometimes the fact film will use master scene format.

Where capitalization is concerned, the following should be typed ALL CAPS:

Character names (often on first appearance only)

Conditions of work

Image size

Camera movement

Transitions

The pages which follow are designed to give you an idea of how a typical two-column fact film shooting script looks. Probably it spells things out more than is necessary. But the director can always adapt to his own taste and style, whereas too sparse a presentation may give him too little to work with.

BOOKS AFIELD

(Shooting Script)

FADE IN:

EXT. - CHURCH - DAY

1	MLS, church, head on from Jardin. A group of TOURISTS straggle out the main door.	SOUND: Church bells ringing.
2	MS, church's main door. Last of the tourist group is ED CRAWFORD (40s, good-natured, non-handsome, tired). He pauses on the threshold.	
3	MCU, Ed. Wearily, he looks this way and that...starts forward.	
4	TAIL-AWAY SHOT, Ed. He plods towards the Jardin.	SOUND: Bells down. Segue to MUSIC: In and up.

EXT. - JARDIN - DAY

5-
10

Mixed shots, Jardin, from
church angle--men and
women of all ages reading
papers or chatting...girls
and boys flirting...kids
playing around bandstand,
etc.

11 MLS, Ed. He enters Jardin.
Camera (in Jardin and
slightly to Mojica side)
PANS to hold him center
frame. He turns in the
direction of Colibri.

12 MS to MCU, Ed. Camera is
in front and slightly to
one side of him now. He
plods towards Colibri.

13 CU, Ed's face. He frowns
slightly and sighs.

14 MCU, Ed. Camera is at
Jardin corner, across
street from Colibri. Still
frowning, Ed pauses...
glances up at Colibri sign.

15 MLS-MS, Colibri sign (Ed's
POV). Camera ZOOMS in to
MCU-CU of sign.

16   CU, Ed. His frown fades,
      replaced by interest. He
      starts forward.

17   MS, Colibri entrance,
      perhaps from angle to
      include Ed or over his
      shoulder.

      INT. - COLIBRI-- DAY

18   MS, store interior, from   MUSIC: Down to BG.
      doorway. LUPE (30s, eager
      to please, Mexican) stands
      back to camera on ladder,
      hanging uppicture frame
      or the like. MARJ (40s,
      volatile, American),
      smoking cigarette, works
      on book display wall.

19   MS, Colibri doorway from
      inside store, to favor Ed
      as he pauses at threshold,
      glancing about.

20   MS, Lupe (Ed's POV).
      She still hasn't noticed
      him.

21   MS, Marj (Ed's POV). She
      doesn't see him either.
                                        MUSIC: Out.

22　MCU, Ed. Looking a bit
　　helpless, he advances a
　　step or two...speaks.　　　　ED: Uh...

23　MS, store interior, to
　　favor Lupe and Ed. She
　　turns...sees him...looks
　　slightly nonplussed.　　　　LUPE (GETTING DOWN FROM HER
　　　　　　　　　　　　　　　　PERCH): Oh...lo siento;
24　MS to MCU, as Ed　　　　　I'm sorry. May I help you?
　　approaches Lupe.

　　　　　　　　　　　　　　　ED (WRY GRIN): I guess I
　　　　　　　　　　　　　　　just can't take any more
　　　　　　　　　　　　　　　churches. What have you
　　　　　　　　　　　　　　　got to read?

　　　　　　　　　　　　　　　LUPE (LAUGH AND SMALL
　　　　　　　　　　　　　　　HELPLESS GESTURE): Well...

　　　　　　　　　　　　　　　MARJ (O.S., INCREDULOUSLY):
　　　　　　　　　　　　　　　What have we got to read--?

25　MS three-shot, to favor
　　Ed. He's obviously
　　startled. Marj now
　　faces him.

26　MCU, Marj (Ed's POV).
　　Smoke curls about her
　　face.　　　　　　　　　　　--Man, are you crazy?
　　　　　　　　　　　　　　　(GESTURING TO SHELVES,
　　　　　　　　　　　　　　　RACKS) I mean, here you
　　　　　　　　　　　　　　　stand in the big fat middle

27   CU-MCU, Ed. He bursts out   of the biggest bookstore
    laughing.   north of Mexico City and
    ask us what have we got
    to read--?

28   MCU, Ed and Lupe. Their
    eyes meet. She laughs with
    him.

29   MS three-shot, to favor
    Marj. Laughing, she
    crosses to join the others.
    Camera ZOOMS back to
    entrance.

DISSOLVE TO:

EXT. - COLIBRI - DAY

30   MLS, Colibri, from Jardin   MUSIC: In and up.
    corner...normal foot and
    vehicular traffic. Shot
    holds as

TITLES COME ON OVER:

The
Book Publishers
International Council
presents

BOOKS AFIELD

(OTHER TITLES AS DESIRED)   MUSIC: Down and out.

FADE OUT

FADE IN:

EXT. - CHURCH - DAY

31   REPEAT OF SHOT 1.   NAR. (CHUCKLING): Yes,
                    DISSOLVE TO: sooner or later we <u>do</u> get
                                        tired of churches--even if
                                        that's what we came abroad
                                        to see...

EXT. - MARKET - DAY

32   MCU, American COUPLE and   We get tired of shopping,
      appropriate foreign   too.
      MERCHANT. They bargain,
      merchant displaying some
      native craft work.
                    DISSOLVE TO:

EXT. - FIESTA - DAY

33-   Mixed shots, fiesta.   Fiestas.
38
                    DISSOLVE TO:

EXT. - DESERT - DAY

39   MS-MCU, spinsterish WOMAN   Even travel itself.
      on camel or burro. Her face
      mirrors comic anguish with
      the animal's every step.

40   CU, woman's anguished face.
                    DISSOLVE TO:

```
       INT. - HOTEL ROOM - NIGHT

41     MS-MCU, fat MAN (nice guy     When that time comes...
       type) in pajamas. Wearily,    well, what better answer
       he gets into bed. A table     is there than a good book?
       with lamp and book stand
       beside him.


42     CU, man. He sighs with
       relief...takes the book
       from the stand.


43     INSERT:  CU (man's POV),
       appropriate book jacket.
```

...and so, onward and upward, through 10 to 20 minutes of script.

But we can't take time right now for all that. It's more urgent that we move on to the next chapter and learn a bit about how to write narration.

CHAPTER 6:

Writing Narration

CYNTHIA

4-1 CU, C rubs bottom | Learning to ride really wears you down...especially in some places!

2 MS, A at C's door, Atascadero | But the setting helps you to recover. I can't imagine a lovelier spot than the Atascadero...~~six thousand~~ *6500* feet...so cool, so comfortable.

4 | Especially with ~~Bill to help~~ *Adrian around to* *show me the town.* ~~me to enjoy it.~~

6 LS, town | ~~The town, too.~~..San Miguel de Allende. ~~It's~~ *A* storybook town, straight out of Colonial

days...a place to see for
yourself what the ~~really~~
truly ~~truly~~ Mexico is like.

9   MS, C&A entering Instituto

The Instituto was another plus
...a center for all the arts,
arts &
from ~~crafts~~ crafts to writing...
~~credit on a master's in your~~
~~free time if that's your thing.~~

17   MS, C&A walking to corral
     MS, colts playing

Is there anything more
beautiful than young colts
playing?

19   MS, tennis serve

Tennis is big with most
~~got a big play from~~ horsemen.
~~a lot of our friends.~~

24   MCU, C watching dive

But
I liked swimming best. ~~though.~~

26   MS, water skiing

Where else can you water-ski
a submerged steeple
past ~~towers of villages~~
~~submerged~~ in a mountain lake?

29a   MS, setting sun

Then, ~~the~~ end ~~of~~ the day. with a
~~the~~ parties. My ~~Your~~ kind of
talk...My ~~your kind of friends.~~

36   CU, C&A drinking

My ~~Your~~ kind of drinks, too--
~~oh,~~ how I loved those
margaritas! ...Or maybe
I should just say, oh, how
I love San Miguel!

JONATHAN

5-1	LS, pan three rings	Play's fine, all right. But
2	MLS, J laffing	that girl's here to learn to
		ride. I'm going to see she
		does it.

8   MLS, students going over cavelette bars

I like to watch the students working out on the cavalett~~e~~. ~~bars. It's~~ Good training. ~~for~~ ~~The~~ horse and ~~the student~~ *rider.* ~~learn together.,~~ The bars *& elevation* give cadence to the horse's action. Elevation, too. As the bars go up, the horse gears himself to accommodate

Shorten

to them... ~~learns to plant his hind feet right, too. If he doesn't, he trips.~~

15   MS, students over a low jump

switch shots

You space the bars to match the gait you want...walk, trot, canter, ~~gallop~~ ...A few days' practice, pretty soon last week's beginners are taking low jumps off a trot from the cavalettes.

Narration is the sound-track commentary that sometimes accompanies a fact film's visual images. Most often it's "voice over"—that is, spoken by one or more off-screen commentators. Thus, the sample from the final narration script polish job of *Riding Holiday in Mexico* on which we opened features two alternating speakers, a girl, Cynthia, and—so help me—Jonathan, a talking ram.

The writing of narration ordinarily goes through two phases. First, while writing the shooting script, you block in tentative lines to go with it, so that client, producers, director, and whoever can follow your think-

Excerpts from *Riding Holiday in Mexico* © 1975 Allende Productions.

ing. Second, you prepare a revised track to go with the film itself, as shot and edited. Polishing on it continues straight through to final recording, as witness the penciled changes on our sample.

Before any of this can take place, however, you have decisions to make. Grouped together, they constitute what has been called

THE PROBLEM OF APPROACH.

Your film has been conceived with a particular slant and mood in mind. Now, it's important to be sure the narration matches that tone.

Sometimes that's easier said than done.

Should the lines, for example, be formal, casual, folksy, or what? With vocabulary reflecting the classroom, the office, the laboratory, or the street? In first person, second, third? Sober or slangy, light or authoritative, cool or warm? Heavy on the information, or letting the pictures tell the story?

The best solution quite possibly may be to try out several styles till you find one that seems to fit. Then, having found it, hang onto it! This is an area where unity's especially important.

Naturally enough, this search for the right narrational approach won't be a separate enterprise, but one you feel your way through as the shooting script takes form. For even if you thought you had the problem solved 'way back when you were writing your treatment, you now may discover that subtle changes in your concept have taken place, forcing you to revise your approach appropriately.

GETTING IT DOWN ON PAPER

The best way to learn to write narration is to write narration. In quantity. In all sorts of styles and on all sorts of subjects. It helps, too, if you study the sound tracks of a host of films for narration devices and techniques, good and bad.

Procedure in writing narration is pretty much a catch-as-catch-can matter, in most cases. Ideas for phrases, lines, modes of attack, frequently begin to take form early, as you develop your core assertion and organize your approach to proving points and sub-points.

The trick is to jot down such bits and pieces, setting them aside for future reference. With luck, by the time you're ready to block in your shooting script, you'll have at least the broad outlines of your narration in mind also.

The two things *not* to do with these preliminary fragments are (a) to ignore and forget them, thus losing them forever, and (b) to try to develop them too rapidly or too completely, ignoring the script's visual aspects.

Assume, now, that you're ready to write your shooting script. What happens where the narration is concerned?

With most of us, I suspect, the rough draft of both picture and sound columns of the script go down on paper pretty much simultaneously—sometimes with the action momentarily leading the narration, sometimes vice versa.

There will also, of course, be those stubborn blank spots where nothing takes form in either area and you have no choice but to grope and fumble your way through. Ordinarily, it's not desirable to let these roadblocks hold you back too long. Better to skip ahead, then return later. Most such problems tend to solve themselves once you've slept on them.

The key fact to remember where your first rough draft is concerned is, let it be rough. From your sequence outline, you know the points you need to make, and how you plan to make them. Beyond that, better to slop down half a page where a line is needed, scraping every last sliver of idea from your brain, rather than limiting yourself to neatly developed, pre-packaged concepts. Only thus can you hope to capture the right words, the right phrases, the alliterations, euphonies, images, rhythms, and twists of language that go to make up truly effective narration copy.

Once that first awful rough is done, it's time to start cutting, chopping out the deadwood.

Herewith, a few points and principles to guide you:

1. Good narration sets the stage.

That means narration should *establish* a number of things as needed—the subject, the setting, the mood, the core assertion; whatever.

Which is *not* to say that narration should try to take over the whole show. If your film starts with breathtaking footage of the Cornish coastline, for heaven's sake let your viewers enjoy it in peace. Narrator can always name the locale later, as a shot zooms in on a crumbling fishing village.

2. Good narration keeps your audience on the right track.

Are there things your viewers need or want to know that can't be communicated visually? Do you need to call attention to something? Set limits? Lead the way through tricky transitions? Recapitulate? Tie up the package when the film ends? The right narration very well may be the answer.

In the same way, nail down the subject and/or setting of each new sequence as soon as possible in said sequence. That means getting in the key word ("cue word") of your commentary early. Don't hold it back till the end of the sequence or other unit—by then, the footage to which it applies may already have gone by.

Also, unless you're using it as a planned transition device, do *not* let the commentary for one sequence "bleed over" into the footage for another.

3. Good narration stays with the subject.

This is another way of saying you shouldn't talk about things not on the screen. On the other hand, neither should you describe things that *are* on the screen and therefore obvious. The solution? Good narration *interprets* the subject. To that end, often the best trick is to generalize when the film shows specifics . . . talk in specifics when the footage is general. Always bearing in mind, however, that specifies *may* require specific comment; general footage, general.

4. Good narration involves the viewer.

Second person and *active voice* are two of your most useful tools in writing fact film narration. "You go right at the crossroads . . . across the moors, all the way to the sea" comes through infinitely stronger and clearer than "A path will be seen to veer right by the observant traveler."

5. Good narration is clear and to the point.

Terse, conversational copy helps. So does a preponderance of simple declarative sentences. Wherever practical, use complete sentences. Don't fall prey to long, bridging pauses in which the audience has to hold the first part of a sentence in mind for six seconds before you let them hear the rest.

A particularly deadly trap is the *list*, in which single words are tied to individual shots. The timing never quite matches the footage, with the result that the whole sequence comes out jerky, disjointed, and awkward.

Specialized terminology is another pitfall. Just because *you* know what a megalith or a macule or a kelp skeg or a lych gate or a roach clip is, don't assume your audience does.

6. Good narration is uncrowded.

A foot of 16mm film can carry about four words of narration. But the fewer feet you ask to do it, the better. Few things wear down an audience more than an overloaded narration track and a narrator who ends up panting. Many writers limit themselves to 100 words per minute (36 feet) of 16mm film, and even that can prove too many.

The remedy for too tight a track? Cut back and space out. Eliminate all the words you can. Then group those that remain into units: one sentence here, three there, two the other place.

Remember, too, that silence, music, and sound effects all have their value. After all, the audience deserves *some* time just to look at the pictures!

7. Good narration is imaginative.

Narration is an area in which to be creative. Don't hesitate to experiment with contrasting narrators, one-man dialogue (rhetorical questions and answers, etc.), sound effects as personalities (remember Alec Guinness in *The Man in the White Suit*?), and the like. It can not only prove effective, but fun—as witness a picture I once scripted with a pseudo-folksong for narration. The junior high audience towards which it was aimed loved it.

Now, four negative points to balance off the positive:

1. Avoid statistics.

True, you can fit in a few figures, if they're essential. But a narrator reading a long list of such onto the sound track is deadly. If figures must be used, try integrating them with filmed charts and graphs.

2. Soft-pedal "commercial copy."

All too often, over-eager clients will want to work in the name of the company or product every other sentence. Result: an alienated audience.

It will help, sometimes, if you point out to such clients that this injection of what amounts to advertising is about the quickest way possible to kill their chances of seeing the film win free public service TV time.

3. Nobody likes a phoney.

Pomposity, grandiloquence, pseudo-intellectualism, forced humor, oversold gimmicks, kettle-drum finales, and the like will win few friends for your client.

4. Don't play it again, Sam.

A cliché is a word or phrase that has worn out its welcome; an expression so trite and hackneyed as to have lost its impact. Most of the time, when you say something's *neat* or *cool* or *sharp as a knife* or *black as night*, you're talking to yourself, not to your audience.

The same principle applies to other forms of repetitiousness. Singing a reprise of your paean of praise to the triple-scragged framistan is more likely to induce snores than conviction. What you need, rather, is a new twist, a fresh angle.

AFTER THE STORM

So far, remember, you're just writing the script.

Finally, it's finished and approved.

Time out while the camera crew gets busy. Eventually, they and the editors will have had their way with your epic. You get a call to come back to do a polish job on the narration.

Know in advance that you're in for a shock. Almost always,

expedience will have taken over, lock, stock, and barrel, changing—it will seem to you—virtually every scene you wrote. In consequence, your original narration no longer fits either time or footage.

This is hardly the best of moments for any writer. But you have little choice but to grin and bear it.

While you're grinning and bearing, you can pass the time by running the picture again. Said picture, at this stage, will be an edited workprint—a special print of the film used for preliminary cutting and juggling in order not to damage the original. It will be much scratched and patched, and minus optical effects and sound track.

Forget the lack of sound and opticals; the scratches, the patches. Just how does the film, as a film, look? Does it make visual sense? Is there a clear-cut, well-balanced beginning, middle, and end? Are the sets and locations well lit, realistic? Do the actors look human, or are they forever falling over each others' feet and staring into the camera? Do the continuity sequences follow the flow of action; the compilation, the developing idea? Is the cutting smooth, shots fitting together with a minimum of jerking and confusion? Are there well-planned cutaways to cover bobbles?

This is a list of questions without an end. Further, the first few films you script, your impulse will be to slash your wrists on the spot. Looking at a workprint and seeing the potentialities for a decent finished product that lie in it is a skill that takes learning. But count on it, given perseverance and a strong nervous system, you'll eventually get there.

The real issue is whether the footage constitutes a good silent picture. If it does, quit worrying and settle down to your polish job.

Narration polish jobs are done in one of two ways: You can write to the footage, by measure, using the four-words-per-foot rule. Or, you can read against the projected picture.

A combination quite possibly will prove your most satisfactory solution. Thus, a long strip of film may best be run through the footage counter to give you an idea of how many words maximum you have room for. Later, you can read your first efforts against the projected picture, for precise timing and smoothing of details.

It will help considerably if you make it a practice to read your copy aloud, unit by unit, as you work it over. Nothing will go further towards unmasking strings of sibilants, difficult words, tongue-twisting phrases, inadvertent double entendres, deadwood sentences, and the like. Even at the recording session, you'll probably have to make last-minute changes to accommodate the verbal patterns and idiosyncrasies of the narrator.

A tedious task? It indeed can be. But though it takes all night upon occasion, there's simply no other way you can trim and hone and insert and rearrange till the finished product is just right.

Finally, the job's done; and with it, in all likelihood, your contribution to the picture. Now there's nothing left for you but to wait out the laboratory till at last the day arrives when you and your fellow workers/craftsmen/artists sit down to view the answer print, the first copy of the picture in release form, complete with sound and opticals.

How does it come off? Like a dream, of course? A rhapsody of pure perfection?

If it does, you're luckier than most. All too often, the print's a bit on the green side, the music track fights the narration, two crucial shots are juxtaposed, your best twist's bombed, and someone's forgotten to include your credit.

Don't panic, though. These are details that can and will be fixed. Besides, a film always looks worse to those who've worked on it than to anyone else.

The big thing is, the picture's finished; your first picture. But don't take too much time out for self-congratulation. You need, instead to be scrambling around for Contract Number Two—another script to write; and this one, you promise yourself, is going to be better.

Or, if your interests lie in that direction, you might move on to consideration of the feature filmscript, which is the topic of Part 2. It begins with Chapter 7, an appraisal of how a film story's put together.

PART TWO

THE FEATURE FILM

∎ ∎ ∎ ∎ ∎ ∎ ∎

CHAPTER 7:

The Film Story

A story is the record of how some imaginary person copes with life.

(No, don't tell me that stories may very well concern actual people. Any person in a story is fabricated. Though I write of Charlemagne or Catherine the Great or my 11-year-old daughter, I am none of these people, for I cannot get inside their skins. No matter how faithfully I record their actions, my interpretation of their dreams and thoughts and motives, their inner worlds, must of necessity remain my own. This being the case, these characters are in truth as imaginary as if I had created them from whole cloth.)

So: A story is the record of how some imaginary person copes with life. It satisfies a need in us by the way it gives a sense of form and order to our chaotic world.

A *film* story is a work of fiction, designed for presentation in motion picture form.

An *effective* film story is one that, when produced and released, pulls audiences into theaters. Often it achieves this feat in the face of competition that headlines bigger stars, a higher budget, greater "production values," and more promotion.

The effective story does this by its use of desire and danger to manipulate tension in viewers. That is to say, it poises them for action, then relaxes them, according to a preplanned pattern. People attend films because they find this ebb and flow of tension stimulating and pleasurable.

How do you learn to manage these so-vital tensions?

A first step is to come to grips with precisely what constitute desire and danger.

Desire is Humankind's yearning for happiness, the one objective we all seek. But different things symbolize happiness to different people. One man dreams of eagerly wanton females. Another aches for the luxury wealth buys. A third pursues the power to make others fawn and grovel. And yes, you find desire at work in a suicide, too, or a misanthrope, or a failure.

Danger, in turn, is something, anything, which threatens our present or future happiness to the point where we're forced to feel an unpleasant emotion: loneliness, loss, anger, inferiority, fear, hatred, or what have you.

Emotion is another name for inner tension; and tension is the driving force that powers all action.

Whatever fails to evoke emotion is worthless in any form of fiction. Anything which *does* involve a character, so deeply and disturbingly he'll fight dragons to change the precipitating situation, will unfailingly involve viewers also. Why? Because the people, the mass audience, pay little heed to anything they view objectively. They *want* to be hooked on tension, drawn taut by feeling. They yearn to see a hero win, a villain lose: a human struggle against odds.

Thus, the drive of desire is the life's blood of every film. And danger is its heartbeat.

"We go to the theatre to worry," observed the late Kenneth Macgowan, outstanding Hollywood producer and long-time chairman of the University of Southern California's Department of Theatre Arts. (p. 36, *A Primer of Playwriting,* by Kenneth Macgowan. New York: Random House, 1951.) "Whether we see a tragedy, a serious drama, or a comedy, we enjoy it fully only if we are made to worry about the outcome of individual scenes and of the play as a whole."

A writer's plan of action for thus manipulating tension, evoking worry, is called a plot.

So, how do you plot a film story?

One of the easiest ways to start is with the old Hollywood springboard, "Who wants to do what, and why can't he?" In other words, you pick someone who aches with desire. (No one else is worth a hoot, remember. Unless Character aches, he won't strive; nor can he be defeated.) Then, threaten that someone's hopes of attaining his objective, via dynamic opposition—a man or a task or a world that fights back.

But we're getting ahead of ourselves, for a film story doesn't spring into being full-blown. Rather, it's developed through a process of continuing elaboration, in a series of five phases: premise, outline, treatment, step outline, and master scene script.

We'll deal with it that way, then. In steps, phase by phase. Building from nothing to something.

Where do you start?

You begin by tracking down a premise.

FINDING THE PREMISE

A premise is the basic idea or concept behind a feature film.

It's not an outline of the story itself, you understand; not even an explicit statement of the situation.

Indeed, it's a most peculiar entity. All sorts of people get confused about it.

Why do they become thus confused? Mostly, because in the motion picture industry premise tends to be lumped with what I like to term a presentation.

Now a presentation *is* a sort of outline—a selling outline, as it were. If you try to include it with the premise, or attempt to pretend it's the same thing, you end up with a mishmash that makes little sense to anybody.

Here, then, let us separate the two, disregarding any screams of outrage that may arise.

Also, let us reiterate the point we first made: A premise is the basic idea behind a film; the bedrock from which your story springs. It is *not* an outline.

Think of it, rather, as a hypothetical question—one that lays the foundation upon which your story situation is to be built.

How does a solid premise come into being?

1. *You find a topic that intrigues you.*
2. *You discover/develop a unique angle from which to view said topic.*
3. *You cast this idea within the framework of a hypothetical question.*

Like the fact film, you see, the feature is undergirded by *topic* and *point of view*. The difference between them lies only in the way they focus.

In the feature, they combine to create a central "What if—?" question: the premise from which the feature's story springs.

Do these events take place in neat 1-2-3 order: topic—angle—premise?

Well, hardly. Indeed, you often may find yourself with little control over how, when, or even if, they take form.

The situation is somewhat like that of a girl walking down the street. She remains just a girl—until someone, looking at her, suddenly sees her as a potential subject of seduction.

Similarly, a bank is just a bank, until someone views it as a potential source of loot, rather than a business institution. Or a wardrobe is just a piece of furniture until mental lightning strikes and, in some mind's eye, it becomes a place to hide a body.

Now obviously this is nothing new. Your point of view is simply your subjective attitude towards a topic: the potentialities you see in it as foundation for a fictional situation. Its basis is your own heredity and conditioning, and no two people see any topic exactly the same.

The "good" topic is the one that stimulates your imagination to come forth with a "good" angle.

The "good" angle? It's one that excites you, preoccupies you, sends your imagination soaring off on flight after flight of story-focused inspiration.

And yes, this *is* important. Tricks, techniques, mechanics, facility with language—all are vital to the scriptwriter. But they can never hope to substitute for the surge and drive born of your own very personal excitement.

But back to premise proper. Consider the picture of a few years ago, *Guess Who's Coming to Dinner.* Undergirding the plot lies one simple yet provocative thought: *What if an upper class white girl fell in love with a black man?*

That question is the story's premise. It sets forth an idea that hooks your interest, needles your imagination. What you do with it, how you develop it, depends on your own taste and talent. You may produce a work of genius, or pure garbage, or copy at any level in between. But without the premise, you have nothing, even at the garbage level. Premise remains the writer's firm foundation. All else is superstructure.

Take the recent Disney hit, *The Apple Dumpling Gang.* Behind it too lies a simple premise: *What if a footloose gambler in the pioneer west suddenly found himself saddled with a brood of children?* Mel Brooks' *The Producers* takes off from *What if two theatrical producers found it financially expedient to mount a flop—only to have said flop turn into a smash hit in spite of them? The Wind and the Lion* explores *What if a Berber sherif kidnaps an American woman to make a political point, only to discover they're kindred spirits?*

Or, suppose we here devise a premise of our very own.

Let's begin with a topic: in this case an object, a Brinks-type armored truck.

Why an armored truck? Because, in the past few days, I've been reviewing a top-notch suspense novel, *The Kidnapping of The President,* by Charles Templeton. The author makes excellent—and unique—use of an armored truck in his story. This has served to focus my own attention on the topic. Now, in spite of myself, I find myself preoccupied with the challenge of finding a different yet intriguing point of view on armored trucks to play with. What shall it be? Robbery? A hiding place? A mobile fort? Some sort of red herring?

Well, robbery's out, of course; too commonplace. And neither the hiding place nor mobile fort bits strike any sparks in my imagination. As for the red herring gimmick . . .

But wait—! Suppose we use robbery, after all, only the robbery's not really a robbery, but a cover-up, a red herring! Maybe, for instance, someone wants to conceal an embezzlement with a fake robbery. Or to distract attention from a bank heist with a noisy, flamboyant attack on an armored truck. Or to launder hot Mafia money by switching it for the truck's load—

Hey, that's it! A switch! But not the Mafia thing; that's old hat and besides, if Mafia types are going to the trouble of knocking off an armored truck, they're going to hang onto *all* the money, not just part.

No, we need something much more human; much less routine. But we'll find that, given a little time. Meanwhile, what's important is that we've found our angle—an angle we can frame neatly in an appropriate, intriguing "What if—?" question: *What if someone robbed an armored truck just in order to switch hot money for that aboard the vehicle?*

The important thing about working from a premise thus is that it forces you to razor-sharp awareness of your story's basic concept.

Every story has such a core idea, you see. The only issue is, is said idea strong or weak? Unless you zero in on it, in its simplest, starkest form, you may discover too late that it holds fatal flaws that point you straight down the track to disaster before you ever set a line on paper.

Given a clear, incisive premise, on the other hand, your story is stripped of many of the ills that might otherwise beset it. In writing, you're able to avoid the extraneous . . . shear away fuzziness and sharpen focus. You present a concise, tightly organized product, geared to maximum impact and effectiveness.

Producers and story editors like that kind of work. They find a place in their hearts and checkbooks for the writer who writes it.

How do you create a solid premise?

1. As already described, you frame the basic idea of your story, the concept on which it rests, in terms of a "What if—?" question.
2. You check this question for
   a. Freshness.
   b. Relevance.
   c. Dramatic implications.
   d. Practicality.
3. You sharpen and strengthen the idea at any point where weakness becomes apparent.

Point 1 is, I trust, already clear. But what about point 2a, and *freshness?*

Your goal, in premise, is to catch attention, arouse interest. The trite or familiar just won't do this. Clichés in speech constitute a reasonably apt parallel: The first time you heard someone speak of something as "smooth as glass" or "cold as ice" or "sharp as a knife," it probably caught your ear . . . created a vivid image in your mind.

Today, as we observed in our chapter on narration, those same phrases no longer touch you. Overuse has worn away the edge of each to where you're hardly aware the words are spoken.

It's the same with stories. *Freshness,* the unique twist, stands all-important. Tell someone your tale concerns boy meets girl and his mind goes off—until you add, "and the girl is a Siamese twin!" A girl having a baby is too routine to hold interest on the screen. But if the father is the devil—well, remember *Rosemary's Baby*?

Relevance? That's simply another way of saying your story must make emotional sense to your viewers. To that end, it needs to catch them up in the kind of feelings they themselves have felt and so understand, all projected in terms pertinent to life today. Thus, the success of *The Andromeda Strain* lay in its brilliant use of technical detail to evoke a fear that lurks in all of us: that human life some day may be wiped out by a plague from across the void. *The Godfather* captures us with disturbing insight into the workings of the Mafia. In *Valley of the Dolls* we see not only sexual titillation, but a way of life that threatens ours and so becomes relevant to us.

For a premise to have *dramatic implications,* in turn, means that it must show the possibility of plunging people into conflict. Preferably, this conflict should be visible and involve other people. For while the story rooted in a monk's inner struggle as he kneels in his cell will fascinate a certain number of viewers, far more will be caught up in clashes that match man against man. (Or against woman—conflict exists wherever will battles will, of course, and this holds as true in a seduction as in a fist-fight.)

Practicality becomes an issue on two levels: First, technical difficulties involved in filming can stop a project cold. A premise of "What if the world came to an end and our hero alone, surviving, had to reassemble Earth from atoms?" involves complications few producers would care to tackle.

Level Two is cost. If you're trying to connect with a shoestring independent who lacks even set rent, it seems unlikely he'll be interested in a script based on the premise, "What if Napoleon, rising from the dead, led France's legions through a new conquest of Europe?"

On to point 3: Is it easy to sharpen and strengthen a premise?

Here the answer is, "Sometimes yes, sometimes no." Despite your best efforts, on occasion, your premise will remain tired and trite. You'll find yourself unable to give it appeal to a sufficiently wide audience. Or you'll recognize intuitively that the public will feel it irrelevant or view the conflicts it offers as too shallow or trivial. Or you'll be forced to acknowledge that practical problems or costs will simply prove too great to warrant producer interest.

When such happens, the answer is to move on to another, stronger project, rather than to waste time and energy beating the dead horse of an idea gone sour.

But more often than not, things will fall into place far better than you anticipated. The secret of success is to use the principles we dipped into in Chapter 1, in discussing how to make the most of your creative powers. Get in there and juggle pieces! Inject new elements! Work till you hit a combination that captures your own imagination! A couple of young fellows traveling cross-country by cycle is mildly intriguing—who hasn't had a yen to do so? But make the pair hippies and you add whole new dimensions of freshness and relevance and conflict. A producer seeking a hit is old hat; one striving to fail comes off as new, different, funny.

So keep analyzing; keep rearranging; keep striving. Even though your first efforts seem incredibly clumsy, totally fruitless, the very effort of trying to set up a clear, sharp premise can't help but whet your own skills at thinking and at writing. And such keen-edged tools are a first step towards success in this scripting business, believe me!

Bear in mind, however, that not every idea, not every premise which you develop, is going to strike sparks in others also. A good many times, you'll discover someone else has already made use of the same concept. In other instances, prior producer/director/actor commitments, technical difficulties, financial involvements, or just plain ineptitude on your own part will shoot you down. You'll find you're lucky indeed if you hit with one "What if—?" out of five or ten.

Further, a gleam of interest in regard to the presentation you build from a given premise is no assurance said interest will continue. Quite possibly you'll be cut off at the next stage, or the next. I still can bleed when I think back . . .

But that's enough on the negative side. Right now, let's assume you've found a truly satisfying premise.

Next question: What do you do with it? Who do you show it to?

If you take my advice, in all likelihood you won't show it to anyone. Why not? Because a premise, in and of itself, is a poor calling card.

Instead of charging off in all directions the moment you come up with a premise, therefore, consider your idea as a seed only—a seed which may or may not sprout. You, because you know it so well, can already envision the lovely plant which—potentially—will spring from it.

It's unlikely, however, that anyone else will be able to appreciate it fully. So it follows that it's wisest not to show your treasure around at this stage. Rather, be patient. Cultivate and nurture your prize in private. Work on it till you have it developed into a fuller form; one more likely to excite others.

This form is one that goes by many names—synopsis, outline, story line, synopsized theme. The term I prefer, the one we'll use here, is the *presentation*.

PREPARING THE PRESENTATION

A presentation is a sort of sales-pitch for a premise. Its purpose is to set forth your basic idea and to sketch in your story's broadest outlines—and to do so in such terms as to hook producer interest.

What persuades a producer to o.k. an idea?

First, a belief that the premise itself has strong audience appeal.

Second, a demonstration of the premise's dramatic potential.

How do you give such a demonstration? Every writer has his own system—and every one of them that works is right.

You, too, eventually will develop private notions on the subject. Meanwhile, however, it may help to have some sort of rule-of-thumb procedure to fall back on while your own ideas are jelling.

Remember what we said about desire and danger, back in our section on the film story? About the necessity of building our attack around a someone who wants something desperately, but whose chances of getting it are somehow jeopardized?

Well, there are worse places than that to start, when you set about laying out your project.

It will also improve the odds, I suspect, if you'll plan your epic work in terms of an old-fashioned, Aristotelian beginning, middle, and end.

Above all, you'll chalk up brownie points if you work from a thing I call a *starting lineup*. For while many will snort, and while it certainly isn't the only approach to building a story, it does offer a simple, practical procedure for the beginner to use as springboard.

The lineup is a sort of checklist designed to focus story elements into a pattern which allows appraisal of their dramatic potential. To that end, it zeroes in on five factors:

1. A character.

The central character in your story, that is.

Actually, a character isn't just a person; he—or she—is a point of view. An individual with a strong attitude towards your topic, he's someone you can involve in the "What if—?" of your premise with full faith that he'll react.

2. A predicament.

A predicament is a premise-related state of affairs somehow sufficiently uncomfortable as to arouse emotion—that is, tension—in Character; and so, hopefully, to arouse emotion and create tension in viewers also. The issue is empathy, as we observed in Chapter 3.

3. An objective.

An objective is a prize for Character to fight for . . . a new and different state of affairs, happier than that revealed in Predicament, which Character hopes to attain.

4. An opponent.

An opponent is someone or something for Character to fight

against. He, like Character, is a point of view—but one in such contrast to that of Character as to insure conflict within the situational framework arising from the premise.

5. A disaster.

A disaster, as I use the word here, is the potential terrible fate with which you confront Character at climax as his penalty should he lose. It also provides the ultimate focal point for audience tension.

So much for the ingredients of our lineup. Obviously, they're designed to provide broad outlines only. But don't worry about holes; we'll plug them later.

Next step: Group the five ingredients into two sentences—the first a statement, the second a question.

> *Sentence 1:* A statement of story situation in terms of character, predicament, objective.
>
> *Sentence 2:* A "will or won't Character succeed?" story question, compounded of Sentence 1 ingredients plus opponent and disaster, and all designed to keep your viewers panting with excitement.

Together, these two sentences will go a long way towards keeping your script soundly structured, on the one hand, yet tautly gripping, on the other. For the pattern they provide does work.

Let's take the sample premise we built earlier . . . develop it as a case in point.

Remember the premise? *"What if someone robbed an armored truck just in order to switch hot money for that aboard the vehicle?"* Where do we begin, in turning this into a starting lineup?

Well, why not start with the "someone"? Arbitrarily, we'll assign him the name of Earl Parrish. Age 30, in order to appeal to a young audience. And since robbing an armored truck may prove on the strenuous side and call for appropriate skill with weapons, we'll make him a Vietnam vet. After all, if any part of this doesn't work, we can always change it later.

Next question: Why has Earl decided to go into the armed robbery business? Is he vengeful, money-hungry, criminal psychopath, or what?

Somehow, none of those angles turn me on. For even though I've barely met Earl, I find myself liking him. I doubt he's just a common thug.

So what would turn a non-thug to robbery? Duty? Blackmail? Altruism?

Duty, in these circumstances, strikes me as a little too James Bond-ish. Blackmail? Well, maybe. Altruism? Hmm . . .

Then, while I brood, the right word comes. It's *loyalty,* a trait admirable in and of itself, yet in whose name all sorts of crimes have been committed.

Shall we try it for size? To whom or what is Earl loyal? A relative? A friend? A sweetheart? A Service buddy?

But no. All such are too routine, too predictable. Let's reach farther out . . . try to find some figure who'll give our plot-to-be a logical yet unanticipated twist.

Like one of Earl's former school teachers, for instance.

And there we have it—we hope: One of Earl's old school teachers is in trouble. Maybe, for an added touch, she doesn't even know it. Innocently enough, she's bumbled into a situation where she's in possession of a suitcase full of demonstrably stolen money. The only way to get her off the hook is to switch the hot cash for cold. One thing leads to another, and the next thing Earl knows, he's committed to making the exchange via an armored truck robbery.

Fine! But that's only the first unit of our lineup, the statement of the story situation. Now, what about the second, the vital, suspense-building story question?

Well, for one thing, we need an *opponent,* an adversary for Earl to battle. Not to mention a *disaster,* a startling—and devastating—twist around which to build our climax.

For now, let's take the easy road where Opponent is concerned: We'll keep his identity a secret from Earl.

As for the disaster, there's an old rule of thumb about such that says make it the most appalling thing that can possibly happen.

What might that be, in Earl's situation?

A possibility: Earl robs the truck, gets the clean cash—and then Villain not only steals it from him, but frames him for the theft!

Here are how these points look, set up within the framework of a starting lineup:

Predicament:	Too loyal to abandon a former teacher,	
Character:	Earl Parrish, 30, footloose Viet vet,	Statement of Situation
Objective:	sets out to rob an armored truck in order to switch hot bills for clean, to save Teacher's funds and reputation.	
Opponent:	But can he succeed, when an unknown adversary	Story Question
Disaster:	heists the clean cash and lays the robbery at his doorstep?	

Please note that the lineup offers basic story elements only. Starkly skeletal, it makes no pretext of revealing the entire picture. Like the premise, it's more a writer's working tool than something to pass on to others. Its greatest value is that it forces you to think in fundamentals. Yet because it lays out a dynamic plan of action, certain elements to look for and decide on, it blasts you off dead center. Do learn to use it!

Clearly, this kind of thing takes practice. Go see three or four or five feature films, entertainment movies. Then, write out a two-sentence starting lineup for each, as outlined above.

Once you begin to get the knack, frame up potential film stories of your own. To acquire facility, work out one each night before you go to bed. You won't believe how much you'll improve in a month. Besides, it's not that much work . . . only two little sentences per night . . . just the kind of preparation you need for your next step, the sketching in of

BEGINNING, MIDDLE, END

Lay out a story based on one of your starting lineups in whatever manner best suits your tastes. Then, break it down into beginning, middle, end. Develop each in a paragraph or two, not more—the idea, remember, is to frame up broad outlines only.

The *beginning* establishes your character within the framework of his predicament, nails down his objective, and carries the story forward to that point where Character commits himself to fight to the bitter end to attain his desire.

The *middle* reveals the various steps of Character's struggle to defeat the danger which threatens him. And if you want your viewers to sit through it, you'd better cram it with fresh ideas, intriguing twists, and intensity of feeling.

The *end* sees Character win or lose his battle. Remember, in this regard, the story doesn't truly end until the struggle between desire and danger is resolved, with some kind of clear-cut triumph of desire over danger, or vice versa.

Applying this breakdown to our money truck caper story, we might end up with something like this:

Beginning: What if someone robbed an armored money truck just in order to switch hot money for that aboard the vehicle? This is the situation we confront in this different caper story.

Our setting is Appalachian Chicago—the decaying Uptown neighborhoods along Kenmore, Wilson, Argyle . . . our central figure, 30-year-old Viet vet Earl Parrish, currently footloose but in all likelihood en route to a mercenary's job training troops in Latin America. Now he learns that the safety deposit box of a dying hillbilly schoolteacher who helped shape his life when he was a boy back in West Virginia contains $60,000 in sequentially numbered bills, hot currency from a bank robbery. If the authorities discover it, it will not only destroy Teacher, but put an end to her dream of a small private program to help disadvantaged hill country kids from her home county.

At present, Teacher knows nothing of all this. It's unthinkable that she could be involved. So the only way out is to switch the stolen money for clean bills. To that end, and despite the fact he's an ex-deputy sheriff, Earl agrees to head up the robbery of an armored truck.

Middle: Gathering together a weird assortment of Teacher's other ex-pupils to help him, Earl plans and carries out the switch . . . halting the truck by spray-painting all windows, forcing crew to open it by pumping tear-gas through the ventilating system, etc. His task is made immeasurably more difficult by the divergent personalities and motives of his aides.

End: The time to put the switched cash into Teacher's safe deposit box arrives. Only now Earl discovers that the money's missing; the only likely suspect, dead. But the very fact of Suspect's death clears all members of the heist group . . . lays guilt in the lap of an ex-hillbilly minor bank official who had access to Teacher's box.

When Earl goes to confront Official, he himself is trapped. Though he kills the bank man and recovers the cash, he now has no way to get it back into Teacher's box. The cops are hot on his trail, too. He has no choice but to run. His girl, a social worker who first discovered the hot money in Teacher's box and then conceived the robbery scheme, asks to go along. Earl refuses; he must take the mercenary job. Her assignment, in turn, is to deliver the suitcase of cash to a small-town West Virginia bank. Banker, Earl's friend, will see that it's used to carry out Teacher's plan.

Earl leaves. Girl watches him go . . . sets off down street with suitcase . . . pauses to greet a pre-planted Mexican or Puerto Rican vendor: *"Buenas noches,* Ramon." And then: "Tell me, *amigo,* how long will it take me to learn Spanish?"

Note, please, that our story is growing as we go along. Just as premise expanded into lineup, so lineup now has been fleshed out into a more coherent story.

This is as it should be. If there is one principle that underlies every form of writing—and, especially, of film scriptwriting—it's this concept of continuing elaboration, building from seed idea through step after step to finished form.

Thus, Earl Parrish is taking on stature almost by the minute . . .

becoming less a name and more a person, complete with past and future as well as present. "Plus" elements—colorful people, striking settings, unusual scenes, unique mood material, and the like—also are beginning to appear: Note the incorporation of the "Appalachian Chicago" background; the assembling of transplanted hillbillies to pull a metropolitan caper; the halting of the armored truck by spray-painting the windows, and so on.

These bits are still in embryonic form, of course; only just beginning to develop. But that's all right. It takes time to build a solid film script.

Finally, there's the matter of a working title. Make it as intriguing as you can, naturally. But even a bad title is better than none at all. It at least gives people some sort of label by which to designate your opus.

What shall we call Earl Parrish's saga? Tentatively—and with apologies to all concerned with that thrill-packed epic, *The Taking of Pelham One Two Three*—let's title it *The Heisting of Money Truck Four Five Six*.

HOW ABOUT FORMAT?

As you'll see from the sample that follows, and those in Chapter 18, there are few rules as to how to set up a presentation. Striking content, plus enthusiastic dramatization, are what count. Just be sure to include—in whatever form or order—premise, starting lineup elements, beginning-middle-end, "plus" factors, and title, and you're not likely to go too far wrong.

```
                    Film Outline


                   The Heisting of
       M O N E Y   T R U C K   4 5 6

                  (Tentative Title)


        Earl Parrish is a man cool and tough enough to rob

an armored money truck, but he has principles.  Indeed, it's

precisely because he has principles--especially a sense of

loyalty--that he agrees to stage the robbery.

        Our setting is Appalachian Chicago--the decaying

neighborhoods along Kenmore and Wilson and Argyle.  Thirty-year-

old Earl, our central character, is the coolly dangerous
```

product of a West Virginia mining county, now jobless and
footloose like thousands of other Vietnam veterans. Chicago
is a last fling for him before he signs on as a mercenary to
train troops in Latin America.

Quite possibly we first meet Earl as he tramps
purposefully along a drab Chicago street. Then an armored money
truck pulls up across the walk and blocks him off. Guards get
out and take posts while money is loaded or unloaded. Earl
scowls at the car. We follow his glance, zoom in to a frame-
filling closeup of its number, 4-5-6, and then cut back as
titles come on over.

Earl has a problem. One of the most important people
in his life has been a hillbilly schoolteacher who helped shape
him when he was a boy back in West Virginia. Now that teacher
lies dying here in Chicago. Her life savings of ⌄60,000, which
she wants to see devoted to helping disadvantaged hill country
kids from her home county, are in a safe deposit box in a
neighborhood bank. The only catch is that a girl social worker
has discovered that said savings have been replaced with
sequentially numbered bills, hot currency from a bank robbery.
If the authorities discover it, Teacher's dream will be shattered,
her heart broken, and her good name besmirched. The only way
out, as Girl sees it, is somehow to switch the stolen money for
clean bills. To that end, she wants Earl to direct the robbery
of an armored money truck.

Loyalty to Teacher overrides good sense, for Earl.
He agrees...recruits a weird assortment of other ex-pupils of
Teacher now in Chicago.

Planning and carrying out the robbery is made immeasurably
more difficult by the divergent personalities and motives of
these aides. But Earl finally succeeds in bringing off the
heist by spray-painting the truck's windows so it has to stop,

then pumping tear-gas through the ventilating system to force
the crew to open the doors.

When the time comes to put the clean cash into Teacher's
safe deposit box arrives, however, Earl finds the armored truck
money is missing; the only likely suspect in the theft dead.
But the very fact of Suspect's death clears all members of the
heist group...lays guilt in the lap of an ex-hillbilly minor
bank official who had access to Teacher's box. Confronting
him, Earl himself is trapped. But though he survives to kill
the bank man and recover the cash, he now has no way to get
it back into Teacher's box. The cops are hot on his trail,
too. He has no choice but to run.

First, though, he takes the money to the social worker.
Unhappily, she reveals that it makes no difference now, for in
the interim, Teacher has died. As for Earl's running, she
wants to go along.

Earl refuses; he's off to take the mercenary job.
Girl's assignment, in turn, is to deliver the suitcase of cash
to a hill-country West Virginia bank. Banker, Earl's friend,
will see that it's used to carry out Teacher's plan.

Earl leaves. Girl watches him go...herself sets off
down the street with the suitcase...pauses to greet a pre-planted
Mexican or Puerto Rican vendor: "Buenas noches, Ramon." And
then: "Tell me, amigo, how long will it take a girl like me
to learn Spanish?"

The End

A final question: What about the validity of the pattern I've
outlined?

Have no illusions. Jean-Luc Godard won't approve, and neither
will Jonas Mekas. But the approach *does* work—most successful feature
films fit in—and it *is* the pattern of life . . . which is to say, the pattern of
People with Problems. You can see this even in your own conversation:

"Mrs. May left for church at 10:15 today" interests no one. "Mrs. May left for church at 10:15 today—and no one's seen her since," captures instant attention.

So it is with your presentation. Its goal is simply to cast whatever raw material you choose to use into some sort of interest-catching form, with a central character set up to move in a particular direction. Then, because the human animal likes life to show at least a semblance of meaning, order, you make sure to include an ending that rounds things out by postulating the victory or defeat of Character in his efforts.

Observe, too, incidentally, how free this approach leaves you. Though I've here developed *Money Truck 456* as straight melodrama, it could equally well be shaped for dramatic comedy on the *Cops and Robbers* order, or *Asphalt Jungle* brand tragedy, or almost anything else you might choose.

*   *   *

So much for the film story. Now, let's take a closer look at its most vital ingredient: the film character.

CHAPTER 8:

The Film Character

Three guests dropped by last night. One was a gaunt, fragile man in his middle 70s, the second a sexy widow approaching 60, the third a proper Englishwoman of 32.

Our visitors' chief topic of the evening was Sexy Widow's impending marriage to an older man several states away. Sexy Widow's approach to the subject was one of wholehearted enthusiasm. As she somewhat tritely phrased it, "A woman needs a man."

"You should know," Male Guest muttered dourly. "At your age, though, you're right. You need to get settled into another marriage."

"No, no!" Proper Englishwoman protested. "She's only buying trouble. An older chap especially—he'll be forever fussing."

"Let me worry about that," Sexy Widow retorted. "I can be quite persuasive in the dark."

Male Guest snorted. "That may not count for as much as you think. Not if this fellow's really ten years older than you are."

"Old or young, what does it matter?" Proper Englishwoman shrugged. "I played nanny to one husband for seven years. I've no desire to take on another." A sidewise glance. "I do wonder, though: How will this chap react if he finds out about your affairs?"

Sexy Widow shivered. "Please, don't talk about it! —Oh, I don't know what I'd do!"

*   *   *

I bring up this episode because it constitutes an excellent lesson in the basics of film characterization.

Thus, the broad externals of character can be reduced to three elements: sex, age, dominant impression: man, middle 70s, gaunt and fragile; sexy widow, approaching 60; proper Englishwoman, 32.

Do you see how simple it is to draw the picture? And how effective? Actors and casting directors alike will love you for it!

Character's inner aspects? Again, they can be approached in terms of three elements: point of view, dominant attitude, interests.

Point of view, you'll recall, is a character's subjective outlook on a given topic. Take Sexy Widow. She viewed marriage enthusiastically, and strongly in terms of the man-woman relationship involved. Male Guest went along with the idea too, but with emphasis on the security angle. Proper Englishwoman, in contrast, disapproved: In a flash, she could see potentialities for disaster.

These reactions to the specific situation were only a reflection of the trio's broader attitudes; their total approach to life.

Thus, Sexy Widow is a woman who views bed as a solution to all problems. With advancing years, Male Guest's preoccupation is with old age and the fear of inadequacy, insecurity. Proper Englishwoman sees close involvements of any kind as fraught with peril.

Interests, in turn, flesh out the picture. This became particularly apparent as the evening wore on. Sexy Widow had trained in interior decorating. Already, she was visualizing the things she'd do with her new home. Proper Englishwoman, who was into sculpture, tended to sniff at that as dreadfully middle-class. Male Guest, a retired oil company accountant, found all such artsy-craftsy stuff wryly amusing in comparison with the man's world of business through which he'd moved.

For my part, as a writer, I found myself involuntarily considering each of my visitors as possible hero/heroine in a film. To that end, I measured by the two standards—goal, and what I term climax potential—which habit leads me to apply.

Where goal was concerned, Sexy Widow came in first by a country mile. She wanted to get married, and she had no intention of letting anything stop her.

Male Guest and Proper Englishwoman, on the other hand, were bystanders, spectators—at least, insofar as the evening's situation went. On the surface, they were interested, but they weren't deeply enough involved to really strive. In consequence, they had drift, rather than direction.

Climax potential, in turn, in my view, centers on a goal-motivated character's capacity for harboring two strong emotions at once.

I say this because I feel the peril at the climax of any story, whether for print or screen, should be emotional as well as physical. It's not enough that hero or heroine should simply kill or otherwise defeat the villain. In addition he/she should also have to win a battle within, in which desire is ranged against duty, honor, integrity, principle, uprightness, spirit, or what have you. If you want a brilliant example of such, think back on that classic, *The Maltese Falcon,* in which honor is enough more important to Humphrey Bogart than is his love of Mary Astor that he sends her off to prison at the climax.

It's this inner clash, coupled with the outer, that gives real depth and interest to a story. And you get it by choosing a central character who has climax potential—that is, a character who, though driven well-nigh compulsively by desire, still can feel the pull of another, contradictory emotion.

How does Sexy Widow meet this test? Pretty well, I think: for even now, before the fact, she shudders and whispers, "Oh, I don't know what I'd do!" Clearly, the right circumstances could set up a strong state of conflict in her. Desire might very well have to battle it out with some other emotion—honor, for example, or pride, or love.

And there you are: characterization basics, alive and breathing, as exemplified in one evening and three visitors.

Have I oversimplified the issues? Of course; and that's as it should be, for it brings us down to the key principle of film character development: *A film character is a simulation and simplification of a person. Though played by a living actor, he is not an actual human being.*

A person, a human being, is a creature of infinite depth and subtlety, infinitely complex; and this whether you label him the product of Deity or evolution.

A person is also infinitely confusing. Philosophers and savants have spent centuries probing for personality's essence. Psychotherapists without number have grown wealthy delving for the source of the troubleds' troubles. Generations of husbands have striven—and failed—to understand their wives; and vice versa.

Film scriptwriters find all this cold comfort. Nor do motion picture audiences show much desire to share in such confusion. They prefer, instead, to be entertained.

That is, they like film characters who *appear* to be living, breathing human beings, but who have been simplifed to the point that they are understandable. Indeed, it may be said with little fear of contradiction that far more film characters fail through being too complex than being too simple.

Which is not to say that a film character cannot come to exist with perhaps even greater reality than a person. Witness Vivien Leigh (*Gone with the Wind*), Charles Laughton (*Mutiny on the Bounty*), Gary Cooper (*High Noon*), Marlon Brando (*On the Waterfront*), Humphrey Bogart (*Casablanca*), July Garland (*A Star Is Born*), Ingrid Bergman (*For Whom the Bell Tolls*), and a hundred—a thousand—others.

It would, in fact, not be too far amiss to title this chapter "An Ode to Actors," on grounds that all we writers give players to work with, on the face of it, are things to do and things to say . . . after which, it is they who translate the dead words from our pages into vibrant, dynamic individuals, on the screen and in the hearts of viewers.

Yet beyond all our debts to actors—directors, too—there are at least two crucial aspects of film character manufacture that rest squarely on the writer's shoulders: the original *conception* of the character; and the *presentation* of said character, as conceptualized, within the framework of the script.

Both these phases of the writer's work are superskilled; inventive to the *n*th degree. And it is here, in carrying out these master services through creative application of a few basic principles, that the writer earns his pay.

(It is also, incidentally, at this point that the whole ridiculous theory of the director as *auteur* collapses. Film characters, film stories, are born in the brains of writers. The director only interprets. If the original conception is his, it is only because, at that moment, he is wearing the writer's hat. Or, as one irate scriptwriter is reputed to have bellowed, throwing a swatch of blank paper at a director, "Here, damn you! Give *this* your famous touch!"

How do you *conceive* a character, then?

The best procedure, always, is first to let your fancy run completely free, in any direction and as far as it will go. Let it catch a flash of today's friend here, a bit from yesterday's foe there, an overheard fragment of conversation after that.

The key principle to bear in mind, at this point, is that it's essential that you cast your script for contrast.

That is, you decide just what characters should be in your story, and—roughly—what kind of people they are.

To this end, you balance necessary characters one against the other.

As a general rule, each character should be different from his fellows. Different physically. Different in point of view. Different in the impression he makes. Different in attitudes. Different in interests. Different in goals. Different in tags. Different in potentialities and background.

Because they're all so different, these characters will have different relationships to each other. Character A will like Character B, love Character C, hate Character D, distrust Character E, think Character F a fool, and so on.

This is important. Failure to contrast characters and to develop meaningful relationships between them is one of the commonest causes of shallow pictures.

Consider the people in our money truck epic. Earl Parrish, the central figure, is a 30-year-old Vietnam veteran, originally a deputy sheriff from a West Virginia mountain county, but now discharged from the service and roving the streets of Chicago.

Selection of these first rough characterizing details for Parrish is a purely arbitrary matter. Young enough to appeal to youthful movie-goers, he also has enough years and experience to come through with a more mature audience. His service as a deputy sheriff and in Vietnam not only gives him a certain color, but provides him with the potentialities called for by his role—a matter we'll take up in more detail later. His years in West Virginia offer sharp contrast to his present presence in Chicago—yet is entirely believable, in view of the heavy influx of Appalachians into midwest metropolitan areas.

Please note, incidentally, that we've given Parrish no physical description. This is with malice aforethought. Beyond the broadest generalities ("burly, bull-necked," "sex symbol," "ribbon clerk," "roughneck," "sickly looking"), most such is a waste of time. Picking people to play roles is the assignment of the casting director. To limit him by picturing a character as "six feet tall, 140 pounds, stoop-shouldered and with crossed eyes" is to make his job unconscionably difficult. Or it would, if he paid any attention to what you say, which in such circumstances he won't. So, hold back on all such, unless physical detail has a definite bearing on the story—as in the case of a plot that makes essential a girl with one hand, a man who stutters, or the like.

How do you distinguish between your characters, then?

You give each *things to do* and *things to say* which are in keeping with *the kind of person he or she is.*

How do you determine the kind of person a character is? We'll get to that shortly.

This probably is also the place to bring up the matter of casting "to type" and "against type."

Casting "to type" actually is casting to *stereotype*—the traditional image of a particular type of person. Thus, "type casting" is the kind that features the "dizzy blonde," the "Italian gangster," the "Irish cop," the "nutty teenager," or what have you.

Casting "against type," in contrast, may have the accountant built like a professional wrestler, the thug wearing horn-rimmed glasses, the heroine overage or overweight.

Each approach has something to be said for it. Casting to type has the virtue of offering audiences familiar people—easily recognized, easily accepted. Casting against type offers realism, freshness, interest. You pays your money and you takes your choice.

Or, you can combine the two: type-casting some of your roles, breaking free in others.

But back to our money truck film, and the key people with whom Earl Parrish will deal in the course of the picture.

Arbitrarily, let's decide that three of these characters will be male

West Virginians from Parrish's home county. Two will be females, also from that background. We'll also include a Chicago girl and a Chicago man.

Bear in mind that in conceptualizing each individual, we'll strive for contrast between them, so that each can be easily recognized on a variety of levels.

Thus, Parrish is a veteran and an ex-deputy sheriff. *In contrast,* we'll make one of his associates Appalachian-born Clyde Felders. Felders is both physically small and a small-time hoodlum, an egotistical career criminal whose pride it is that he has no Social Security number—that is, he's never held a legitimate job.

Next, *for further contrast,* let's toss in a shambling hulk of a man. We'll call him Abel Wood. Another former West Virginian, Abel's a car nut. Amoral though not basically criminal in his orientation, he frequently finds himself involved with thieves because he gets his kicks from dangerous driving, as in getaways.

Now, *again contrasting,* we'll add one Quintus James. Older than the others by 20 years or more, he's greedy and conniving, but wary—a hillbilly shylock with a superficially clean record back in West Virginia. At present he's assistant manager of a Chicago branch bank.

The Appalachian females? Let's start with Florence Tate, retired spinster schoolteacher, an obese lump still hooked on kids. Ceil Robinson, our social worker heroine, is a trim, self-reliant, quietly aggressive woman in her late 20s. Thus, *through contrast,* she offers counterpoint to Florence (pardon me; "Miss Tate," in view of her schoolmarm role), as well as to our Chicago woman, Hilda Dinnick, Clyde Felders' girl-friend, a *Vogue/Cosmopolitan* fan so unbright she even believes what Clyde tells her.

Finally, for even further *contrast,* we'll toss in a male Chicagoan, Zeppo Perrone, a coldly efficient Mafia trouble-shooter who wouldn't carry a gun if you paid him to.

And there you are: eight story people, each summarized in a neat little word-capsule, and each *contrasted* with the others—even the sound and initials of their names are different, as an extra edge against confusion.

For bit parts, in most cases this kind of thing is good enough. For major roles, no; they demand treatment in greater depth. So before you "freeze" your people, you need to consider further factors. Casting these into categories, we have elements which we'll label *external* aspects of character, *internal* aspects, the matter of character *direction,* and character *modifications.*

1. External aspects.

We've already covered the matter of age and sex. Now, let's give a bit more attention to *a. Dominant impression.*

Each of us makes some sort of impact on people we meet—blusterer, bore, braggart, nonentity. A girl may register as mouse or moose or sexpot.

So, what's with the character on whom you're working? How does he come across—his overall impact? Try to nail it down in a word or phrase; no more. Keep it clear and sharp! The more you try to fancy it up, the less likely you are to hammer it home to viewers.

Further, the clearer and simpler you make it, the easier the part will be for an actor to play, and the more believable his performance is likely to be. Complexity only confuses the issue.

Applying this approach to the cast of our money truck film, let's begin by having Earl Parrish give a dominant impression of *competence.*

Clyde Felders, in turn, is *insolent*; Abel Wood, *vacuous*; Quintus James, restrained *friendly/folksy.* Florence Tate seems *exhausted, worn-out.* Ceil Robinson is *coolly self-reliant.* We see Zeppo Perrone as *frozen-faced.* Hilda Dinnick gives the feeling of being *not bright* and *artificial.*

All these impressions are different, note; all to a fair degree in contrast. Each draws an image an actor can present on film.

So much for impression. Which makes it time to turn to

b. Tags.

A tag is a label. It helps to distinguish one character from another. Consequently, each character should have several.

The screenwriter, fortunately, need not worry as much about this as his friends who write for the print media. Detailed description of his characters is not only unnecessary but, as we've pointed out, for the most part undesirable. Actor and director take care of adding color nicely.

However, it's still not a bad idea to stick in a few tags, *providing you give them a direct relationship to the story.* Otherwise, count on it, they'll be ignored.

Tags, for our purposes here, are of three types: tags of appearance, tags of speech, and tags of mannerism. So, as you build each character, ask yourself,

(1) What are his tags of appearance? In general, appearance will be that of the actor himself and that's all there is to say about it.

On the other hand, it certainly did no harm that Mel Brooks tagged the unregenerate Nazi in *The Producers* as wearing a German helmet. Nor would Long John Silver be the same without his peg-leg, Blackbeard sans hirsute adornment, or the Hathaway shirt man minus his eye patch.

Do we need tags of appearance for any of our money truck caper people, beyond what actors and director will develop? Probably not. Yet neither would it hurt to suggest that Abel Wood limps (a neat tie-in with his passion for cars, from the standpoint of Adlerian organ inferiority theory), or that Ceil wears a swirl of hair over her forehead, to conceal a scar that somehow symbolizes her relationship with Earl or Florence or whoever.

b. What are his tags of speech?

This is a subject we'll take up in more detail when we get to our chapter on dialogue. But it's worth pointing out here that each of us speaks differently—in choice of words, in accent, in pacing, in rhythm, in intonation.

Matters of accent, pacing, and the like obviously fall largely within the provinces of actor and director. The writer, however, is the one who sets down the words which will be said, and it will be hard indeed for an alleged hoodlum to rise above a tag of "dear boy" tied to his every other speech; or for Sweet Innocence to sound convincing in her part if her lines drip double entendre.

On the other hand, it would seem appropriate for Florence Tate to tend to address her former pupils as "young man," in school mistress fashion, or to salt aging Quintus James's lines with hill-country expressions. Clyde Felders obviously would tend to Chicago street slang; Earl Parrish, to military references.

c. What are his tags of mannerism?

Remember George Raft flipping his half dollar in old gangster films? Captain Queeg and his ball bearings? Or, more recently, Kojak's sucker? The *Frenzy* villain's habit of picking his teeth with his tiepin?

All these were tags of mannerism. They helped to make a character distinctive, memorable.

Often—as in Queeg's case—such tags are symbolic, as well as bits of business. They help to define and establish character.

Similarly, Quintus James might jingle change in his pocket, or doodle interest figures, or manipulate wire-framed glasses. Hilda Dinnick could have a thing about mirrors—she can't keep away from them. Zeppo Perrone studies the *Wall Street Journal*.

Or, they might not. You need to use careful judgment. Too much of a good thing can leave your cast acting like a bunch of freaks.

So much for character externals. Time now for

2. Internal aspects.

Here we'll consider three elements: point of view, dominant attitude, and interests.

a. Point of view.

This is a subject on which we touched in the preceding chapter. Its core is that Character—*any* character of consequence in your picture— must have an attitude towards your film's topic/premise. How does he see it? Its significance? Its implications? Its potential?

Not that this necessarily comes as a first step in character conception, you understand. It's quite possible for a story person just to pop up on the scene, sans warning, angle, or function. But there he is, and he keeps on hanging around until you feel as if you have no choice but to find something for him to do.

It also may be, too, that a character not only has no specific attitude towards your film's topic, but he isn't even aware that Topic exists—as in the case, say, of the sweet little old lady in *The Ladykillers,* who scurries about amid a gang of desperate criminals but remains happily oblivious to what's going on. All this goes to prove is that oblivion itself can constitute a viewpoint.

In most instances, however, you'll need to devise a more sharply focused point of view for each major character, based pretty much on the role he is to play; the function you have him scheduled to fulfill. Thus, Hero will have a different attitude towards topic than Villain. Heroine will look at things from another angle than Female Menace.

Does this mean we're talking only about melodrama—the standard hero-heroine-heavy?

Not at all. You and your friend both may be fine fellows. But that doesn't prevent you from liking different girls, different jobs, different lifestyles . . . because each of you has a different point of view.

Thus, where *Money Truck 456* is concerned, Earl Parrish views the robbery as a challenge. Why? Because his goal is merely to help Florence Tate. He doesn't care about the cash.

Clyde Felders, in contrast, sees the heist as opportunity incarnate, alive and breathing. All his life a small-timer, he's ever dreamed of making a real score. Now, at last, the chance is with him, for money and for secret glory.

To Abel Wood, the caper is a means to money, sure. But more intriguing, from his angle, is the escape, the driving. All else lies subordinate to those wild moments of excitement in which, quite possibly, he'll match his skill as a wheelsman against the cops.

In Quintus James's eyes, on the other hand, the robbery looms only as an ulcer-aggravating hazard. Give him any choice, he'd have no part in such lunacy. But how can he say no, in the face of pressure from such types as Earl and Clyde?

Florence Tate of course knows nothing of the scheme. Neither does Hilda Dinnick. But we do have some idea of the attitude of each: Florence would reject such a plan out of hand, as contradictory to everything she's ever believed in. Hilda? Well, money's money; and besides, she believes everything Clyde Felders tells her. Too, she knows something's on his mind. She doesn't like that. It takes the stud out of him in bed; makes him hit too hard and without warning.

Zeppo Perrone, our final figure, views the whole business with wary disdain; a professional's chill detachment. He doesn't know quite what's going on, but he's certain something is. Also, it's clear that Something's principals are amateurs. But a syndicate bank, syndicate money, is involved. That makes it personally important to him. A blunder, a miscalculation, could be damaging to his career.

So there we have it: eight points of view, all centering on one central topic/premise: What if somebody pulled a robbery not for gain, but simply to switch one batch of money for another?

It's a good approach from which to start the building of any film. Not to mention a good springboard from which to plunge into consideration of our second internal aspect of character,

b. Dominant attitude.

To a large degree, personality is a matter of attitude.

An attitude, roughly defined, is a habitual mode of response to a particular type of situation. A *dominant* attitude is a person's habitual mode of response to life and life situations in general. It may be optimism, pessimism, belligerence, sweet reasonableness, or what have you. It's an implicit philosophy of life boiled down to a single sentence, and every person has one: "Good looks and sexiness will carry a girl through any dilemma." "If I keep a low profile, don't make waves, maybe no one will give me a hard time." "Don't fool with me, Buster, unless you want a flat nose."

Knowing a character's dominant attitude gives a writer a tremendous edge, for it offers him advance insight into how Character will react in any given circumstance. Thus, faced with trouble, Girl above will turn on the charm; Man 1 will try to stay inconspicuous; Man 2 is likely to come out swinging.

In a word, these characters' attitudes make them *predictable*. So Writer will have little difficulty devising ways to present them believably in dialogue and action.

Earl Parrish? He's a man to count on. In fact, let's focus on that as his dominant attitude: "Loyalty rates for more than anything, when the cards are down."

Checking the other members of our cast, we have:

Clyde Felders: "Don't try to con me, Smart-ass!"

Abel Wood: "I got no time for tomorrow. Today's all I can handle."

Quintus James: "Money makes the world go round—and I know all the prices."

Florence Tate: "I can take whatever life brings, if the children have a better chance."

Ceil Robinson: "You do what's right, no matter what the rules say."

Zeppo Perrone: "It's my mouth, but the Organization's talking."

Hilda Dinnick: "You gotta give the customers what they want."

Clear enough, right? And in case you hadn't noticed, another name for *attitudes* is *values*.

Which brings us to the third of our internals,

c. Interests.

You can tell a lot from a man's—or woman's—interests. The ball fan is a different person from the opera buff. The barfly moves in one circle, the ecology freak in another.

It will add dimension to your characters, therefore, if you give them personal interests, both to individualize them and to give them topics of conversation as required.

Thus, Earl may have a thing where weapons or hunting are concerned. Abel's eyes light up at the sight of a unique car. Hilda seeks good taste in *Vogue*, sexiness in *Cosmo*. Ceil is preoccupied with the world as people. Florence lives through her former pupils; children. Quintus James hates Chicago . . . goes back in retrospect to his West Virginia boyhood. Clyde never tires of talk of criminal cleverness. Zeppo is an enthusiastic seasonal sailor.

This interest element need not be beaten to death, you understand. But it certainly does help to have it handy when you need more than weather talk to flesh out an incident.

So much for character's internal aspects. It's time we moved on to the matter of

3. Character direction.

Direction starts with

a. Goals.

When you say a character has a goal, you mean he keeps trying to move in a particular direction; to accomplish a particular purpose.

Man's goals are of two types: immediate, and long range.

Immediate goals, immediate purposes, are pretty much the product of your story situation. You assign them to your characters, as it were, then devise rationalizations to make such behavior believable.

Goals differ from character to character. Thus, some minor characters may drift with the tide, with no strong immediate goals apparent. The goals of a central character or a villain, on the other hand, ordinarily work out best if they're so strong as to be well-nigh compulsive. Why? Because, as noted in the preceding chapter, the drive of desire is the life's blood of every film.

Take the situation in a recent picture, *Hennessy*. It postulates an Irishman who sets about to blow up Britain's Parliament, despite all efforts of both Scotland Yard and the I.R.A. to stop him.

What would launch a man on such a desperate course? The rationalization offered in the picture has Hennessy's wife and daughter slain in a clash between pro-I.R.A. rioters and British troops. Whereupon, vengeance-driven, grieving Hennessy goes forth to battle.

Closer to home, *Money Truck 456* makes Earl Parrish's immediate goal, his purpose, the switching of bad bills for good via robbery. Rationalization: Earl's sense of loyalty is so strong he's emotionally bound to help save his old teacher.

So much for immediate goals. Long-range are something else again, and a good deal closer to what we usually think of as characterization.

In deciding on a character's long-range goals, we act on the hypothesis that a man's behavior is shaped by his notion of what he considers a desirable future. But our view of what constitutes a goal often is too narrow. We equate such with socially acceptable achievement, when our drives may instead take a negative turn.

Thus, blocking out reality with drugs or gin may just as well prove to be a goal—even if formally unformulated—as getting a raise or marrying the boss's daughter. So may postponing, or pleasure-seeking, or playing with danger. And who among us hasn't known that unhappy man or woman for whom the seeking of a goal to pursue has itself become a goal, even though it stands clear and obvious to everyone but him or her that he never will settle down to actual striving?

In the case of Earl Parrish, he can't imagine a life in which his military skills aren't put to use. Clyde Felders dreams of a really big score. Abel Wood? He doesn't think much about what's to come. But he'll be disappointed if it doesn't include cars to play with.

Quintus James's world is money-bounded. Though he'd be hard-pressed to tell you why, he just wants more and more of it.

Florence Tate, in contrast, hopes only for an easy death . . . while Ceil Robinson, disillusioned with the red tape and basically non-human orientation of social work, yearns for something—anything—that will give her a sense of real self-worth.

Low-profile power is Zeppo Perrone's fantasy . . . a sort of business career within the Mafia, in which its leaders from coast to coast will defer as respectfully to his judgment as they would have in the past to Meyer Lansky's.

Hilda? She'd tell you she wants nothing. But everything she says and does shows that if you'd give her social acceptance, she'd be happy.

So much for character direction. Where the scriptwriter is concerned, however, there's a related factor to consider. Call it, if you will,

b. Rationalization.

It goes without saying, I hope, that you need to know your characters in order to write about them successfully.

Further, you need to know about them infinitely better than does the audience which ultimately views the film in which said characters take part.

On the other hand, it's unlikely you need to know your story people as well as many people who write on writing would have you believe.

Actually, you need to know them only well enough to rationalize their behavior.

To *rationalize* is to make logical, believable.

How do you make behavior logical and believable?

You provide appropriate reasons for it in Character's past conditionings, his past experiences.

Shall we examine this process in detail, beginning with the manner in which a character comes into being?

It all starts, of course, with a script—a story—you want to write.

Sometimes, said story begins with a character. Sometimes, the story situation is genesis.

Actually, which comes first makes little difference. Both must develop—that is, grow—side by side, in either case. Neither can spring to life full blown. Neither can survive separate from the other.

So, a character is born and then develops. But . . . how much do you develop him?

Only as much as you need in order for him to fulfill his function in the story. Why? Because the typical film averages 90 minutes running time. That gives little opportunity for fun and games where either character or story is concerned. The trick is to get the show on the road; build no more and no less than is necessary.

Which doesn't mean you don't need to give your characters their full share of attention. Otherwise they'll reach the screen stillborn, as flat stick figures . . . a sorry fate for the children of any writer's brain.

To avoid this, you provide Character with such past conditionings as are necessary to enable you to rationalize—that is, make logical and believable, remember—Character's present dimensions, present behavior.

A man is a maze of involvements in love, work, society . . . a tangle of tastes, interests, skills, boredoms.

Man develops all these on foundation stones of body and experience. A product of learned behavior, his personality is based on a multitude of procedures he has worked out, consciously and unconsciously, as best suited to coping with his problems, his inadequacies, his world.

Coping means triumphing over heredity and environment alike . . . regardless of good health or poor health or sickness or crippling . . . sharp mind or dull mind or strong mind or warped mind . . . kind parents or cold parents or neurotic parents or absent parents . . . private school or public school or slum school or reform school or no school . . . smart kids or dumb kids or sadistic kids or depraved kids . . . farm town or factory town or suburb or ghetto.

That coping . . . it takes its toll of everyone. Each of us emerges with his share of black eyes and bruises and secret sore spots . . . that sense of uneasiness somewhere deep inside that the shrinks call inadequacy, inferiority, insecurity, frustration.

Still, we have no choice but to battle on, each in his own way. So we bite the bullet and plunge ahead . . . nurse our wounds with laughter, tears, strength, weakness, virtue, vice, cleverness, stupidity, ill health, lust, anger, you name it.

Thus, Earl Parrish stands coolly competent, in command of self and situation, and endowed with a wry sense of humor.

What gave him that competence? A craftsman father? Discipline in Florence Tate's classroom? A body that lacked bull strength, so skill became a substitute?

How about the habit of command? Did it spring from mining camp scuffles? Baseball prowess? Admiration for a hard-nosed old sheriff. Or what?

And the sense of humor. Did he have sisters who sliced him to ribbons with their wit when he tried to take himself too seriously? A grandfather who poked sly fun? Boredom with a dull, drab world, so dreary he could survive it only by seeing its funny side and laughing at it?

You develop all this in notes and scribbles . . . imaginary remembered incidents from Earl's past. Generalities are of little help. What you want are the kind of bits a man might be inclined to tell for a laugh, or a tear, or a brag, or in a moment of bitterness; and frequently a perceptive listener might draw more from what he didn't say than what he did, or focus on elements that seemed at first glance to be side issues—as when you discover the tough cop has three brothers in prison.

Will all this show up on the screen? Of course not; and yes, such probing can easily be overdone. But unless you do at least a modicum of homework on such . . . brood about your hero, get to know and understand him insofar as your story requires, flesh him out to real dimension, devise past history to help you rationalize his present character and behavior . . . count on it, he'll come through on paper and, later, film, as flat and empty.

Now, our final point on character conception: that of

4. Modification.

Not all characters need modification of impression or attitude or goals or what have you. But sometimes you can add immeasurably to a portrayal if you write in incidents which help relieve your character conception's basic starkness.

Take Abel Wood. A shuffling, vacuous nonentity at first glance, he gains dimension if you allow him to display dexterity of a high order. Worn out now, Florence Tate still can show flashes of the peppery disciplinarian she once was. Let Hilda Dinnick reveal uncertainty, Ceil Robinson a warm and sentimental self beneath her cool efficiency. Quintus James can go from fawning servility to cold-eyed greed in a manner that makes clear his folksiness is a cover. Clyde Felders may reveal that he knows when to back down, just when his insolence seems sure to get him into more trouble than he can handle. Still frozen-faced, Zeppo Perrone has been known to rub his sleeve and say, "These threads cost three bills. How much did yours cost?"

As for Earl—well, he's competent and in command, but that can make for a less-than-heartening person. So mightn't it be an idea to let him play with pups, or build up his sense of humor?

Similarly, we may discover he views robbery primarily as a game, albeit a dangerous one. Quite possibly he sees his accomplices in a mellow, nostalgic glow, as if they were still the boys he knew growing up in West Virginia's hills.

How about throwing in a bit of male chauvinism on his part, too? Thus, maybe he considers robbery as men's business . . . objects strenuously to Ceil's involvement. Mightn't it be a good way to throw them into conflict?

Another thing to ask yourself, where modification is concerned, is: Has anyone a secret?

You see, it would be nice if dominant impressions were always right.

It would also be dull.

Fortunately, the human animal fools us ever so often on this score by giving us assorted false impressions.

This is God's gift to the scriptwriter. It enables him to present us with a clear-cut image . . . then slip in a logical yet unanticipated twist that adds depth and dimension.

Like this:

> *A cold-eyed executive type . . . who keeps a bottle in the bottom drawer.*
> *A small, prim girl . . . with a secret taste for black lace lingerie.*
> *A warmly winning elementary school teacher . . . who hates kids.*

Do you see how it works? This kind of secret isn't necessarily a secret in the usual sense of the word. It's just something that doesn't fit the expected picture. By incorporating such a twist, a weakness, an unforeseen aspect as you build a character, you add marked viewer interest. Your audience watches eagerly as each new situation unfolds to see whether Secret will compound Character's problems.

At the same time, you don't want to overdo it. Dominant impression should remain dominant save in those moments when the nature of the situation might logically lead an individual of this particular type to expose his secret.

Note, too, those words, "an individual of this particular type." Nowhere is preparation, planting, more important than when you propose to incorporate a "secret" switch. The ingredients must be there: just not revealed. Otherwise, viewers will feel your character is inconsistent, and be appropriately outraged.

Also, for heaven's sake, don't give *all* your characters "secret" aspects. That grows old in a hurry. Be content to save such Sunday punches for key characters, crucial situations.

Do we need a secret for Earl Parrish? Not necessarily. However, for the sake of example, we'll give him one anyhow: the fact that for all his cool competence and wry good humor, he also rates as deadly dangerous. If the time comes to act and nothing else will do, he won't hesitate to kill.

Is this believable? Understandable? Acceptable? Of course. Probably Earl's demonstrated it repeatedly in Vietnam; maybe in his role of deputy sheriff also.

*   *   *

So. That's enough and too much on character conception. It's time we moved on to another vital matter: How best do you *present* your man or woman?

1. You devise establishing incidents for Character.
2. You maintain Character's character throughout.
3. You stand fast by the principles of character growth.

Each of these points deserves close individual attention. Here we go!

1. You devise establishing incidents for Character.

The only way to capture a character's behavior on the screen is through action and dialogue: the things Character does, and the things he says.

Action and dialogue are most effectively presented in terms of photographable incidents: events which reveal Character's individuality and his relationships.

You the writer devise these events, these incidents, of course. They're born of your script's plot structure. But, in addition, they should be designed in a manner to serve character-revealing functions.

To this end,

a. Establish Character early.

An easy—and hazardous—trap for a writer to fall into is that of failing to establish a given character's character at the earliest possible moment. Instead of "organizing the emotions of the audience" (to borrow playwright Howard Lindsay's phrase) towards Character at the outset, Writer allows Character to meander through a series of bland, non-characterizing scenes, in which Character might as well be part of the furniture.

Need I point out that this is not the brightest possible approach? Not only does it waste valuable screen time, but it very well may—inadvertently—create a false impression.

This being the case, *do* establish early.

b. Establish Character in character.

Failure to establish Character in character—that is, failure to develop him from the start as the kind of person he's to portray in the picture—can prove a real disaster. Why? Because such failure can, as noted above, lead to viewers getting a false impression of Character's character.

Consider, for example, a film I saw the other night. The opening sequence had the hero rough up an unoffending storekeeper who, in accordance with the law, refused to sell Hero a drink on Sunday. Then, as a follow-up, Hero slugged two highway patrolmen who intervened.

What the writer was attempting was clear enough: He wanted to establish Hero as a tough, belligerent type not to be trifled with.

The catch lay in the way he chose to do this. Because where I was concerned, at least, Hero ceased to be a hero, a character to cheer for, the moment he moved in on Storekeeper. He became, instead, a thug and bully, and nothing that happened in the succeeding 80 minutes of the film could change his image for me.

Yet how easily the impression could have been made positive, starting from the self-same situation! This time, instead of casting Hero in hoodlum role, let him sit down with a beer at the same time a couple of biker thugs come in. Let *them* demand the liquor and start pushing on Storekeeper. Whereupon, Hero heroically intervenes. The patrolmen arrive to halt the ensuing brawl and attempt to arrest Hero. But since an arrest is the last thing Hero can afford at the moment there's further conflict, and we end up with the self-same situation—but with a character less distasteful.

Or, to get back to our central point, we've now established Hero *in* instead of *out of* character.

As part of this approach, it's helpful to bear down on four specific yet oft-neglected areas.

(1) Establish dominant impression. If Character is a smoothy, don't have him fall on his face in a mud puddle on first appearance. If Girl is the shy, demure type, it's unlikely she should be introduced screaming like a fishwife at some unoffending nothing.

(2) Establish likability. If a character in a film—particularly the central character—is supposed to be likable, do establish that likability as soon as possible.

How? By having him *do* something likable, for one thing, whether it be helping an old lady across the street, solacing a lost child, or feeding a starving dog. Yes, I agree it's possible to be more subtle about it; but that's a problem for your own imagination.

Or, you can give Character a goal that demonstrates he's on the side of right and justice. Or, you can show him to be an underdog who still clings to his sense of humor. Or, you can reveal him standing up indomitably to disaster. Or voicing views viewers are certain to agree with. Or fighting or sacrificing for others.

But whatever you have him do, do make him likable!

(3) Establish interest. For most of us, interesting people hold an edge over uninteresting. So try to establish Character as an interesting person.

To that end, have him do something interesting. Or put him in an interesting setting. Or a changing setting. Or a dangerous setting. Or contrast him with his circumstances or surroundings: Such social opposites as rich vs. poor, young vs. old, male vs. female, urban vs. rural, landsman vs. seafarer, cops vs. robbers, and the like offer built-in raw materials.

(4) Establish potential. Potential in this sense is of two types: physical and climax.

(a) Physical potential. Character is a mousy little man, scared to death at his own shadow and habitually running from trouble.

Now, at the climax, he whips out a .45 and guns down the villain.

No, I don't believe it. And I doubt that you do either.

Why don't you? Because the writer didn't bother to establish his little man's *potential* for such violence.

Similarly, the frigid girl doesn't turn into a passion flower without warning. The clod doesn't become sensitive. The illiterate doesn't write an epic.

Whatever your character is to do must be prepared for. Show us Little Man staring fascinated at the weapons in Britain's War Museum, or taking instruction on the target range. Let Frigid Girl ponder another character's suggestion that her problem is less lack of sex drive than failure to juxtapose the right man and the right mood. Give Clod sensitivity and feeling where his cat is concerned. And don't even think of casting the illiterate as a writer.

(b) Climax potential. Climax potential, you'll recall, is a goal-motivated character's capacity for harboring two strong emotions at once.

In practical terms, this demands that you show both climax emotions, desire and whatever, convincingly in action at earlier stages. Why? Because a monster can't believably change to a hero *just* at the climax. You have to prepare the audience, make them aware that

Character harbors both emotions, by showing said emotions in action earlier in the picture.

This is the process otherwise known as planting and paying off. You show a gun in a drawer; later, when it's needed—maybe half-a-dozen sequences later—somebody snatches it out and shoots the villain with it. Or, Hero and Heroine find mutual bliss to the tune of a scratchy phonograph record giving out with "Some Enchanted Evening." Then assorted issues separate them. Later—apparently spurned, scorned, and rejected—Hero is about to depart forever. But now the familiar, scratch-shredded strains of "Some Enchanted Evening" echo close at hand. Hero stops short, eyes widening . . . turns, sprints up the steps to Heroine's apartment. Clinch and close.

Similarly, when you seek to build a climax on the basis of a character's decision between desire (for a girl or a job or a million dollars) and duty (to arrest girl's father, or close down the company, or return the million dollars to its rightful owners), you'd better be sure Character demonstrates his moral fiber earlier—like close to the beginning of the picture—by jailing his own mother, or rejecting promotion, or running after the little old lady who's dropped her wallet.

Yes, I grant you that I'm murdering this point via exaggeration. But the fact remains that unless you establish your man's or woman's strength of feeling before the climax comes, said climax is likely to arrive stillborn. And just because I've corned things up to make a point doesn't mean you can't develop your own script with subtlety and taste.

Now, one final detail: No matter what anyone may tell you to the contrary, you need to build plot and character together.

Particularly does this hold true of your central character, your hero.

Indeed, you can do worse than to frame up your climax scene almost before you start, in order to get clear in your mind just what emotions will be in conflict within your hero at that time. Only thus can you block in the earlier action properly.

Which is not to say you can't attack in any other way that suits your fancy, you understand. But it does seem like an awful lot of extra work to go back planting and revising later because, at the start, you never quite thought through your climax.

And that's enough about establishment. It's time now to move on to our second point regarding character presentation:

2. You maintain Character's character throughout.

You don't just establish character once and let it go at that. Dominant impression, dominant attitude, dominant goal, all the rest— they must be brought forward over and over again; hammered home in scene after scene, so that the audience has no opportunity to forget them.

The key issue to remember? Consistency. A character who stays in character from the first frame to the last. Even when his behavior is offbeat, contradictory, it must be so within the framework of personality you've created.

Which is not at all to say that you must be clumsy and obvious about such. On the contrary. Small things, mere hints and touches, can keep viewers reminded that Character A is cowardly, Character B lazy, Character C the kind of girl who remembers the lessons that her mother taught her.

Finally,

3. You stand fast by the principles of character growth.

Character growth is an element critics love to belabor. It means that a character starts out one way, ends up another.

You'll have no trouble with such if you remember one simple fact: *To say a character grows in the course of a film means only that he has learned by experience.*

This being the case, ask yourself how much Character can have learned, and how—that is, through what incidents—he learned it.

The situation is, in brief, much like that we discussed in considering how to establish potential. It's a matter of planning and planting, that's all.

And most of the time, you'll find, you're better off to keep the whole thing straight and simple.

*   *   *

What about the *writing* of character material? Two things.

First, bear in mind that this is an area, like many others, where writing itself is the smallest issue. *Thinking through* your characters is infinitely more important.

Further, said "thinking through" can grow wearing. As one of my old friends, a top scriptwriter, commented not long ago, " 'But would Sam Spade really *do* that?' gets tiresome, finally—especially since Sam is just floating around in your imagination anyhow."

Second, as in all writing, the trick is not to let rules freeze you. Specifically, don't write by rote. Better by far to slop down first thoughts, then check and revise later.

Why? Because, for one thing, your characters will change as you go along. The problems of structuring your script—not to mention satisfying all the people to whose alleged judgment you must genuflect in the course of working through your project—too often will force you to reshape your ideas later.

Even in writing the story treatment, for example, you'll find your concepts developing and modifying, as we'll demonstrate in the next chapter.

CHAPTER 9:

The Story Treatment

A treatment is a semi-dramatized, present-tense, preliminary structuring of a screenplay; an elaboration of the presentation.

What issue is most important in the treatment? The answer, without question, is unity; the solid development of a single story with a strong central spine. Though side issues and subplots may be introduced, ever and always they remain subordinated to the basic scheme.

This is why clear thinking on premise and starting lineup is so vital. If you've done your work on them well, they provide you with a firm foundation on which to build your treatment. In consequence, unless you deviate too wildly, your treatment too is likely to prove sound.

The treatment has three functions: to sharpen the proposed script's focus, to flesh out the story, and to emotionalize the handling.

Fleshing out and sharpening focus go hand in hand. The idea is to block in the story in sufficient detail that its flaws and weaknesses may be uncovered and remedied.

Not that cures are always to be found, you understand. The Hollywood hills are full of stories whose ailments proved so incapacitating that they never got beyond the treatment stage.

The emotionalization angle is a somewhat different matter. Here, the issue is the need for the treatment to create and carry forward an air of excitement such as, hopefully, viewers will experience when they see the finished film. And this, it seems to me, is an aspect oft ignored yet desperately important.

How so? Because, through most of its phases, a script is in essence a blueprint, a set of instructions for cast and crew. Its language and approach are therefore factual. The surge and flow of emotion which are the very heart of the finished film are of necessity left out, save insofar as typed description of action and dialogue reveals them.

The treatment, in contrast, offers an opportunity to write in all such . . . to capture mood, to experiment with emotional effects, to play with feelings.

Further, it's essential that mood, emotion, feeling, be communicated—to two people, in particular.

The first of these people is the *producer*. It's urgent that he become conscious of the spirit of the property—not just the facts—if he's to pass intelligent judgment on it.

Even more vital, the *writer* must acquire that awareness also.

This is not as ridiculous as it sounds. Though the writer may start with a feeling for his material, that doesn't necessarily mean he knows what said feeling is. Only as he works through the script, both in framing and in writing the treatment, does he discover how best to incorporate and handle emotional content.

FRAMING THE TREATMENT

How do you frame up a treatment?

The answer, of course, is: any way that works. But for learning's sake, let's take a logical, five-step approach:

1. You block in the background of the action.
2. You establish story elements.
3. You focus your opening.
4. You plan your peaks.
5. You resolve your issues.

First step coming up!

1. You block in the background of the action.

Every story, every film, is rooted in the past, if only because the people involved in any event have pasts.

Thus, a knife flashes; a man dies. But in a very real sense, that is the end of the event, not the beginning. Knowledge of *why* one particular individual wielded the blade on a particular other is vital to any real understanding of the event.

A woman abandons her husband and her children. But that is only the tip of the iceberg. Data on the states of affairs and states of mind which led up to it are essential to true insight.

A poverty-stricken black couple takes in a crippled white child in the face of neighbors' resentment. Only awareness of what has gone before can bring any degree of comprehension.

It's to your advantage as a writer to recognize this fact. Then, whatever your story, sketch in the background of the action. Lay bare its roots. Track down the events that first brought your characters together. In your own mind, at least, clarify the basis for their relationships . . . the reasons they became involved with your topic/premise.

True, most of this will never reach the screen. But without it, you may never have a script to begin with.

Money Truck 456 offers ever so many examples. The first to come to mind is: How did that $60,000 in hot bills get into Florence Tate's safety deposit box in the first place?

Well, it's a cinch Florence herself didn't put it there, soul of rectitude that she is.

Suppose, however, that Florence shared the box with a trashy nephew, now dead. Blind to his faults, she held her box jointly with him . . . had him run financial errands for her after she became an invalid.

Nephew's just the type who might have been involved in a bank heist. Nor would he have hesitated to switch the loot for Florence's savings.

Just to complicate things, though, let's pretend Nephew isn't guilty. Rather, our villain is old Quintus James, the minor bank official. Maybe Nephew left his box key with Quintus for safekeeping. Later, when Nephew's killed, that gives Quintus access to the box—and a chance to switch Florence Tate's money for that from the robbery.

You can take it from there. Had not Ceil Robinson discovered the switch, she would never have thought of trying to involve Earl Parrish in a robbery. Had not Earl been Miss Tate's pupil back when he was a boy in West Virginia, he wouldn't have considered going along with Ceil's lunatic idea.

All this constitutes *background of the action*: the roots from which the present story springs.

Needless to say, this kind of backtracking can go on endlessly. Also, it can be run into the ground. But without at least a little of it, plot pits will open in your script before you like crevasses in a glacier.

It's a chance you can't afford to take. Not when you almost always can solve your problems so easily with just a little cogitation.

Oh, yes. There's a point that fits in nicely here which you should by all means remember: Frequently, when you start developing the background of a story's action, you'll discover there's simply no substitute for coincidence and happenstance. Life just works out that way sometimes, that's all.

Which is perfectly all right, so long as you bear in mind that audiences will forgive you for breaks that get your hero *into* trouble; never for those that get him out. It's like the old business of always including bad luck in a picture's budget, but never good.

2. You establish story elements.

To establish, cinematically, is to make some element or aspect of the film in some way recognizable and identifiable in the audience's eyes. Thus, you have an establishing or reestablishing *shot*, which relates people or objects to a background or to each other or both.

In the story treatment, the issues are somewhat different. Here, the question is, where and how do you bring in various *story elements*— characters, situations, settings, and so on.

a. Characters.

We've already belabored this subject in the last chapter. We'll say nothing more about it at this point save than to reiterate that you establish not only the characters themselves—their physical beings—but also their *characteristics,* their *relationships and reactions* to each other, and the *impressions* you want them to make on viewers.

b. Situations.

Situations are the states of affairs in which your characters find themselves in relationship to your topic premise. Sometimes these states of affairs constitute *predicaments*—situations which arouse unpleasant emotions in certain characters. On other occasions, they don't. But whatever the situation at a given time or place, it's essential that you establish it—that is, that you let readers know about it—sharply and clearly in your story treatment, so that it will both carry full impact and avoid confusion.

c. Settings.

Obviously enough, every story is acted out against one or more settings. What writers sometimes overlook, however, is that settings have personalities just as much as do characters.

That personality should be pinned down on paper, in your treatment, in appropriate description. Keep it brief, of course; but at the same time try to capture the essence of the milieu, whether it be bar or brownstone, barn or bungalow.

d. Moods.

Moods vary from film to film—not to mention from segment to segment within a given picture. A story treatment that doesn't zero in on this vital element isn't fulfilling its function.

Nor are mere labels enough. It's one thing to say "It's a sad day for Susy;" another to flesh such out with "Everywhere, it seems, she meets with scowls. Wind whips rain down in gusting sheets. Even the cars that pass seem bent on splashing her."

Does this mean all such will be used when it's time to shoot the film? It's unlikely. But in the meanwhile, right now, a picture has been drawn, a feeling created, to help bring your story alive in the minds of those who read your treatment. And that can make the difference between a go-ahead and a cutoff.

3. You focus your opening.

Getting a film off to a good start involves two things: a hook, and a commitment. Both are ever so important.

a. The hook.

You start any film with an attempt to capture viewer interest. You do this by fading in on some incident or action which—you hope—will arouse sufficient curiosity or other feeling in the audience to lure them into involvement with your story as it develops.

This hook—in TV, it's called a teaser—may feature anything from a bomb burst to raindrops running down a windowpane; a car crash to a baby's gurgle. Quite often, it will run before or during the picture's titles. All that really matters is that whatever happens must appear to hold potentially disastrous or otherwise intriguing consequences for someone, on some level or other, so that the audience, anticipating dramatic developments to come, will sit enthralled.

This being the case, it's worth your while to devote a fair number of hours, a good deal of floor-pacing, to devising the most captivating hook you can.

One warning: Don't overkill.

That is, don't build a hook so strong, so hard-hitting, so attention-compelling and emotion-evoking that the rest of your story can't live up to it and so comes as anticlimax. And yes, this can and does happen upon occasion, and you can't afford it. So . . . hook your viewers—but do it with at least a little sense of proportion!

Chances are your best results will come if, while hooking, you also work on

b. The commitment.

As pointed out earlier, the central character in any story should have a *story goal*, a purpose he seeks to accomplish within the framework of the topic/premise. Indeed, on a practical level, story very well may be defined as the record of a quest: a striving and its outcome.

Your story begins—*really* begins, that is—when Character commits himself to attaining his goal, for it is only then that you establish the tale's unifying "story question": Will Character succeed in his efforts to accomplish his purpose, or won't he? Will boy get girl—or won't he? Will woman get job—or won't she? Will convict get freedom—or won't he? Will mother get child—or won't she? Will cop get robber—or won't he? Will alcoholic wife beat booze—or won't she? Will mouse win self-respect—or won't he?

Now though this simplistic approach appears ridiculous at first glance, it works. Skillfully and subtly handled, it needn't prove so artless, either. And other ingredients, without it, add up to little.

In weak scripts, all sorts of preliminaries have been known to precede the moment of commitment. A central character may move through this sequence and that, assorted incidents and events, all with no goal in view, no purpose he's dedicated to achieving.

To try to make bricks without straw has nothing on trying to build a story in which the central character has no clear-cut goal. And the sooner he's committed to that goal, the better.

On the other hand, it's by no means necessary to jump in feet first when considered judgment opts in favor of a smoother entry. Here, as everywhere, horse sense does count!

Indeed, often it's wise to *build* to Character's commitment. Perhaps, for example, you'll want to begin by establishing situation . . . revealing that Character can go in two or more directions. For him to choose to strive and struggle quite possibly will seem insane—even though Audience aches for him to do so. In consequence, when Character decides to plunge ahead despite the odds, audience satisfaction is intense. Your viewers are hooked so firmly it will take truly bad work in the sequences that follow to disenchant them.

Cases in point? They range from *Shane* to *The Odessa File*, *Support Your Local Sheriff* to *One Flew Over the Cuckoo's Nest*. In all, you find carefully built commitment.

Nor does any of this mean Character needs to recognize or babble about his goal or his commitment. Quite possibly all that's needed is an apparently minor action—a flipping away of cigarette, a tossing down of cards, a turning on or off of lights. The issue is merely to let the audience know, somehow, that Character has direction.

It also should be noted that sometimes we fight to retain rather than to attain. A girl may battle for the right to stay single, a man to keep his job past compulsory retirement age, a couple to defend their home against an encroaching freeway. It still adds up to purpose and commitment.

A corollary: Character's goal when the film begins may not be the goal your story deals with. Quite possibly he's "just passing through," in the words of veteran scriptwriter William Bowers, when the story situation brings him up short and plunges him into adventures unrelated to anything he's previously anticipated.

In brief, then, the whole wide world is open to you where openings are concerned. You can play it any way you like—from the silent dope-dealing of *Easy Rider* to the blood-and-thunder of *The Wild Bunch*—so long as you end up with a hook and a commitment.

What about Earl Parrish? Faced with an appeal to join in the money truck robbery, he too must make a decision, a commitment. Until he does, we have no story.

It's also important that

4. You plan your peaks.

Just as a story begins when the central character commits himself to a goal, a purpose, so it ends when he either succeeds or fails in his efforts.

Between beginning and end, in a series of confrontations, Character strives against odds to reach his goal.

The writing of confrontations is an art in itself, spelled out in our next chapter. Here, suffice it to say that a confrontation is a unit of conflict—the entity sometimes known as the dramatic scene—and is the basis on which any story develops and progresses. These units and the transitional episodes that join them, when linked one to another, make up the body of your picture.

Beyond this, in framing your treatment, three things are important to bear in mind.

a. Avoid the predictable.

Your goal in blocking in your picture should be a series of logical yet unanticipated developments, sufficiently exciting to keep your viewers intrigued with your story. Even though experience tells them that the hero will surely win, *how* he wins should come as an exciting, delightful surprise to them.

This same principle applies at every stage. Take it for granted the audience will know *something* is going to happen at a given moment. But gnaw your nails if they know *what* that something is.

How do you avoid the predictable?

In theory, it's no problem. First, you put yourself in the audience's place and figure out what they anticipate will happen. Second, you list possible alternative developments and then choose the one you feel will prove most effective. Third, at the proper points in your script you plant the elements/objects/events necessary to make the twist you've choose come off.

Thus, in one distinctly unmemorable horror script, I had my hero prowling the Mad Scientist's lair. There he discovers a group of The Fiend's zombie-like servitors standing in a trance state in coffin-shaped boxes. Moving on, he enters another room . . . sneaks up on Scientist. But just when it seems as if he's finally triumphed, the doors of two cabinets flanking the entrance swing open. A zombie lunges from each and seizes Hero, and he's right back where he started, only worse—for now he's Scientist's prisoner.

The pattern is, I trust, clear. Audience knew something must surely happen, but not what. Since the zombies already had a known potential from earlier sequences, I simply planted them in the room adjoining Scientist's laboratory, then let Hero proceed. Obviously, in their trance state, they were harmless.

Now Hero enters laboratory . . . creeps towards Scientist. Only then, behind him, the cabinets open, revealing non-cataleptic zombies, their presence logical yet hardly predictable. They lunge, and—well, you get the idea.

Unfortunately, such tricks seldom work out quite that neatly. Hair-tearing, breast-beating, and plain old dogged hanging in there often will be required before you find the right answers.

b. Accentuate the negative.

The example above illustrates this point also. Since audiences come to the theater to worry, it follows that they enjoy themselves more if Hero gets into deeper and deeper trouble as the film progresses. To that end, follow the out-of-the-frying-pan-into-the-fire principle. Each of Hero's efforts to improve his situation should end up making said situation worse: Villain, knocked down, comes up with a knife in either hand. Heroine, saved from dungeon, turns out to have lost her mind. Treasure chest, opened, sets off a blast that sinks the ship.

Too melodramatic? Then how about Hero returning to family after 18 months' service overseas. His wife waits for him at the gate . . . ever so obviously pregnant. Or he reaches down to pick up his two-year-old son . . . and the child bursts into screams of fear. Or he opens the kitchen door . . . and two rats race across the filthy floor.

'Nuff said?

c. Space out your crises.

It's essential that, in planning, you decide which incidents are going to be the big, important, decisive ones. Then, having decided, space them out, so that your viewers have an opportunity to recover from one before you overwhelm them with the next.

Thus, suppose you have six, eight, ten crises: some major, some minor; some mountains, some foothills. Ordinarily, you'll arrange them in a pattern of what's termed *rising action*, ascending intensity, with tension building from beginning to end.

The tension can't *just* build, however. You need valleys between your peaks.

This being the case, you'll need to insert quiet episodes to balance the taut . . . maybe introduce a subplot (a sort of separate-but-related minor story probably centering on minor characters), or comedy relief bits, or material that concentrates on passage of time or space briefly instead of bearing down with such emphasis on story progression.

And yes, the place to work all this out is in your story treatment . . . even though you'll deal with it in more detail later, in step outline and master scene script.

5. You resolve your issues.

Sooner or later, you're going to have to end your story. That means, also, that you're going to have to release the climactic tensions you've built up in 80 or 90 or 100 minutes of manipulation of desire and danger.

How do you release climactic tensions? More specifically, how do you release them in a manner satisfying to your viewers?

Two issues are involved.

a. Releasing topic-engendered tensions.

Topic tensions are those based on largely mechanical issues: How do you get Heroine out of burning building? How do you save Hero from firing squad? How do you decipher the code, find the will, control the dread disease?

This obviously can be a problem. By the time you've built your story to a climax, odds are you've created a state of affairs that's tangled and taut indeed.

Fortunately, you've already mastered the principles of the unraveling process. It's the procedure you used in inventing logical, unanticipated, non-predictable complications and crises back in your film's middle sector.

Now, you use this same approach to resolve instead of complicate: You figure out what the audience expects . . . you devise a different alternative . . . and plant (or expunge) such elements as are necessary to bring it off.

b. Releasing character-engendered tensions.

Your viewers' tensions won't be totally released till they're satisfied with the way things worked out for the characters in your film. Solutions to mechanical problems alone just aren't enough.

Again, however, the answer is relatively simple: You give each character what he's demonstrated he deserves, on a basis of both competence and conduct.

Competence? That means only that you don't have a dub golfer winning the championship over a pro, or a janitor stumping the college physics faculty, or the town hag claiming the cup in the beauty contest. It's the element of *potential* that we discussed in Chapter 8.

Conduct is something else again. For lack of a better word, let's equate it with morality. It means that if a character has behaved the way the audience thinks he should, he wins; if he hasn't, he doesn't.

The problem here—and not just for scriptwriters—is that morality is changing, especially for the young people who make up the overwhelming majority of the film audience. "Situation ethics" increasingly is taking over, with "right" and "wrong" determined on a basis of circumstance, rather than absolutes.

Thus, not too many years ago, the penalties for sexual irregularity, for the girl, included illicit pregnancy, venereal disease, community scorn, and economic disaster.

Today, the pill has given a considerable degree of control over pregnancy. Antibiotics keep disease pretty much in line. Mobility and women's lib have blunted scorn's edge. Girls' movement into better paying jobs has made economic survival feasible.

That this has influenced film attitudes goes without saying. As much or more shattering has been the change in outlook where crime—and, particularly, crime against property—is concerned. Raised on the "human rights are ever and always superior to property rights" theory, the Watergate mentality, and the acceptance of corruption as a way of life, viewers flock to pictures which accept the rationalizations of garment industry chiselers (*Save the Tiger*), agree that it's o.k. to cheat so long as it's crooks who are being cheated (*The Sting*), approve a successful bank robbery (*Charley Varrick*), and happily watch two New York policemen steal a fortune (*Cops and Robbers*). (Obviously it's no accident that the theme song of this last picture is titled "Everybody's on a Caper.")

Not that crimes against people are out. Implicitly, *Death Wish* says violence by villains justifies violence by self-appointed vigilantes. *Clockwork Orange* matches villain's guilt with society's. *Bonnie and Clyde* wade through blood to folk-hero status. *Straw Dogs* demonstrates that the berserk intellectual can prove more deadly than the bruiser.

What it comes down to is that, today, a central character's likability, need, or desire, or the fact that he confronts an evil or faceless opposition, is accepted as excusing all but the most serious violations of yesterday's moral code. If the audience is sufficiently involved emotionally with Character, it will cheer virtually anything he does—or be outraged at anything negative that happens to him. Indeed, it takes no great insight to see that much of *Easy Rider's* impact was product of youthful viewers' empathy with the two dopers who are its central characters, and Viewers' conviction that said characters didn't deserve to die.

There's no particular point to bewailing all this. But it *is* important to understand it. The root of the matter, in all likelihood, is that morality is changing because the world is changing. Shrinking globe and exploding population more and more have shattered Man's sense of individual worth and responsibility. An affluent society has made possible/practical a contemporary equivalent of the "beggars' wage" so beloved of Kropotkin and other anarchist theorists. Dehumanized by mechanization, regimented by government, increasingly lost in the Society of the Whole, large numbers of us have taken refuge in private worlds, segmental societies of our own.

Such being the case, the scriptwriter must stay ever so aware of his audience and its thinking. He dare not deal out penalties or rewards to his characters blindly or by the old standards, lest he lose contact and shatter believability in the process. Indeed, he need not—should not—even forsake his personal standards. For if said standards truly make sense, and Writer truly possesses a modicum of creative imagination, he still can sell them to any audience, providing he approaches them in terms of that audience's point of view.

*   *   *

So much for the *do's* of framing your treatment. Now, how about the *don'ts*?

We'll limit them to five notes of warning:

1. Beware of idiot plots.
2. Beware of static situations.
3. Beware of diffuse opposition.
4. Beware of too many characters.
5. Beware of theme and symbolism.

Here we go!

1. Beware of idiot plots.

An idiot plot is one in which one or more key characters have to behave like idiots in order for the story to come off.

These are the tales that feature heroes who defy killers, heroines who make appointments to meet murderers in isolated castle towers, villains who decide the detective has suddenly switched over to their side.

To avoid such, merely make it a practice to ask yourself, "*Why* does Joe (or Sam, or Suzy, or Griselda) do this? Is there so much pressure on him (or her) that, in the same circumstances, an ordinary, non-retardate man or woman would act this way?"

2. Beware of static situations.

A moving picture should move, should tell its story in action. Otherwise it's not taking proper advantage of the film medium's potential.

Unfortunately, all too often, writers write scripts in which people merely sit around and *talk about* past, present, or future action.

Even worse, they choose topics which offer little opportunity for things to happen: for the story to develop in terms of people doing things.

Now good films can be and have been made in which settings were restricted, action limited. But special problems always are involved, so be sure you're prepared to take on such before you dive into such murky waters.

3. Beware of diffuse opposition.

Simultaneously or in sequence, all sorts of elements may oppose your central character as he moves through your story towards his goal. Not only is the weather against him, the ferryman won't cross the river with the water this high, the Mennonites down the road resent his use of tractors, Banker is determined to foreclose on the old family homestead, Heroine's brother wants to knock his block off, Rival has sworn to have his blood, and Neighbor is loading his shotgun with buck instead of bird.

One of these factors should emerge as dominant in Character's struggle—and the sooner, the better. Why? So that Character will have a specific someone or something to defeat—or be defeated by—at the climax, the culmination of his fight to attain his goal: witness Rick versus Strasser in *Casablanca*, Ringo versus the Plummer brothers in *Stagecoach*, Joe Gillis versus Norma Desmond in *Sunset Boulevard*.

This is tremendously important. *Without* such a dominant opposing element, it will prove difficult if not impossible to bring your climax into effectively sharp focus. There will be no way to demonstrate, through your hero's victory or defeat, that he has won or lost.

A climax which does not pivot on such a demonstration will prove vague and mushy. In consequence, it will fail to give your audience that sudden release of pent-up tension that constitutes ultimate and total satisfaction.

4. Beware of too many characters.

Pay no attention whatever to how many characters you use when you set down the first draft of your treatment.

The second time round, cut out half.

The third, trim to bare-bone minimum.

Thing is, most of us tend at the beginning to bring in story people not as single spies but in battalions. Which is fine, except that (a) actors cost money (how many spectaculars has MGM released lately?) and (b) too large a cast confuses your viewers.

Further, that mass of players is seldom vital. The people you need are those who build your story, advance the conflict, stand for or against your hero in his struggle to attain his goal. Drop all others.

Then, go over the list of those who remain and ask yourself if you can't combine one with another, or perhaps cut bits or incidents to eliminate a few more.

Yes, I grant you all this is tedious and painful. But you'll be glad you did it when, later, producer or director pokes at this role or that and you're already primed and ready to justify the character's retention.

5. Beware of theme and symbolism.

It's impossible to write a script or make a film without a theme—and this includes even the most inept of blue movies.

It's equally beyond anyone's ability to create a picture that doesn't use symbols.

However, the chances are good that the writer will have no idea as to what said theme is till the picture's released and someone tells him. And the things he'll discover about the symbols he's incorporated—well!

The reason these things are so is that a film's theme is merely the message it conveys. Thus, the theme of the blue movie cited above very well may be only that sex is on the sickening side when served up in such a package.

The trouble with themes is that if you bear down too hard on them, your films tend to grow stiff and preachy. You'll fare better, in most cases, if you follow the advice someone passed on to me long years ago. "You want to build in a message? Great! Just don't let any of your characters know what that message is!"

*   *   *

A symbol is something that stands for something else, on a basis of relationship, association, convention, or the like. A noun is a symbol of an object. A flag is a symbol of a country. A cross is a symbol of Christianity. A sickle and hammer is a symbol of Communism. And so on and so forth.

It follows that, in order for symbols to be meaningful, you have to know the ground rules: just what each symbol is supposed to stand for. If you don't, the whole business becomes senseless.

When a writer decides to incorporate specialized symbols into his script, he runs the grave risk that the device that seems so clear and obvious to him may totally miss its mark where his viewers are concerned. Even 75 years of Freudianism haven't yet gotten it across to everyone that they should equate church steeples and snakes with penises, windows and doors with vaginas.

This being the case, it might be wise for the scriptwriter to ignore the whole matter. No matter what he decides, symbols will be present, and he can leave it to the critics to decide what they mean.

Even better, he might make any key symbols he chooses to include clear to all—like bedbugs and cockroaches equal squalor. Then audience, as well as critics, will have a fighting chance to understand!

WRITING THE TREATMENT

How do you write a treatment?

You've already heard enough and too much about my favorite tricks for getting words and ideas down on paper: focused free association, continuing elaboration, and so on. I won't repeat them here.

More important at this point, I think, is a warning not to let facts engulf or overwhelm you. A good film is feeling first of all, remember. Your task in the treatment, in large measure, is to capture same on paper.

How do you manage this? The secret is surprisingly simple. It begins with clear realization that an urge to write anything indicates, in a high proportion of cases, that the topic holds some element you find exciting.

Apply this excitement yardstick to each successive sequence of your treatment. Ignoring plot lines and bridging bits (they're the kind of thing you can stick in later as needed), ask yourself what there is about each person, setting, incident, speech fragment, or what have you that creates—or in the past created—a sense of eagerness or enthusiasm in you.

Get these exciting touches down on paper and, from them, write your treatment. Try to capture the feeling they evoke as you go along, setting your interlinked ideas down as if they were a story told in present tense: not "Joe turned," but "Joe turns." Not "Sue's eyes widened," but "Sue's eyes widen." Strive for words and phrases that will help your readers—and you too—to feel not only the flat facts of what happens, but also mood, color, tension, spirit, tone. Give heed to connotation, denotation. Make maximum use of action verbs, pictorial nouns.

Here, for example, is a passage designed to nail down the feelings that go with an opening—a time, a place, a bit of action:

```
FADE IN:

    Night.  A Lincoln's headlights flash along the

Pacific Coast Highway.  The beam picks up a sign that

says VENICE, with a row of civic club emblems below...

races precariously along darkened streets and over Venice

canal bridges to a jolting halt in front of a sagging,

unlighted, shadow-mottled old house.  A burly male figure

with a flashlight surges from the car, stalks onto the

rickety porch and into the house without bothering to

knock, and sweeps a cluttered room with the light.  The

beam focuses on WARD HOLCOMB, 23 and disheveled, as he

sleeps on a mattress in one corner below an askew

psychedelic poster.  Coming half awake as the light

moves in on him, he peers up blearily.
```

We shift to Ward's POV, the light blazing in his
eyes. He mumbles half-coherent "Huh--?"-type sounds.

An older male voice, quivering with rage, pulses
from the darkness: "Damn you, you bastard! What have
you done with my daughter?"

Here, later, comes a touch of color:

A huge livingroom, epitome of hippie opulence--
parachute silks hung from the ceiling, psychedelic light
projectors blazing kaleidoscopic color, and so on. The
host is EDELBERT KORNITZER, 28, high mogul of the hippie
chemists and a man who prides himself on his devious mind.
With him are two genie-garbed Neanderthal bodyguards, OG
and WOG, and his tester-taster-jester, moronic CYRANO DE
HASSENPFEFFER.

Puzzled, Ward comments on how familiar the guards
look. Whereupon, they lift falls to reveal neatly cropped
cop locks beneath: They're the same two narcs who shook
him down earlier. "Moonlighting," one explains, winking.
"Mr. K. opts for quality, even when it comes to **fuzz**."

Or again:

Ward tries a broken field run for the door...shoves
the mummy case into his assailants' path. A frantic comedy
battle follows, in which he and Judy tangle Og and Wog
in the beaded curtain, conk Cyrano with Judy's crystal,
and otherwise discombobulate the establishment. Someplace
along the line, too, an oil lamp is upset. In seconds,
flames are racing across the floor and up the drapes.

Finally:

```
Ward flees, out of the house and down the street.
Ahead, Judy still stands waiting for a ride.  The sound
of Ward's footsteps reaches her.  She turns into his arms.
Both cry and laugh at once.  No words are spoken.  As
their mutual embrace tightens convulsively, Ward sticks out
his thumb.  A car brakes.  The happy pair scrambles in.
The car roars off.  We follow it in a reversal of the
opening action--up the Pacific Coast Highway, past the
VENICE boundary marker and off into the night as we
                                        FADE OUT
```

And there you are. Your goal in your treatment is persuasion—persuasion of a very special kind: You want to convince the key personnel who read your effort that your story's strong, tight-knit, gripping: the kind of property that will pull viewers, fill theaters.

Nor do you want to leave any doubts as to your epic's cinematic practicality. That means: no holes, no flaws, no problems; no doubts but that the story will take form effectively on film.

Treatment length? Don't worry about it too much. Good treatments have been written in ten pages, and in a hundred. What counts, as more than one old hand has pointed out, is not how many words you write, but how convincingly you sell your idea.

I should also remind you here, in all fairness, that there are all sorts of ways of handling treatments. Writers range from those who like to write extremely "full" to those who prefer to keep their copy "tight" or "lean." Most fall somewhere in between. Again, you pays your money and you takes your choice.

Whichever route you choose, though, one thing is absolutely essential. It's mastery of the art of creating and building and bridging confrontations, and we'll take it up in the next chapter.

CHAPTER 10:

The Art of Confrontation

A story is compounded of desire plus danger. It begins when the central character commits himself to attaining a story goal in the face of opposition. It ends when he either succeeds or fails in his efforts.

This means Character starts a story with one state of affairs and state of mind. He ends with another.

The Great Gatsby begins with Gatsby seeking new contact with his lost love. It ends with him betrayed and dead in his own swimming pool.

Lady Sings the Blues begins with Billie Holiday working as cleaning girl in a whorehouse. It ends with her singing at Carnegie Hall, with newsclip flash-forwards to her continued drug addiction and death at 44. *Chinatown* begins with Jake Gittes agreeing to check on an allegedly unfaithful husband. It ends with both husband and wife dead and Gittes in a state of shock.

How do you move Character from State of Affairs/State of Mind 1 to State of Affairs/State of Mind x?

You impel him forward on twin wheels of *confrontation* and *transition*.

A confrontation is a unit of conflict; a time-unified meeting of opposing forces.

A transition is a change from one condition, one state of development, to another. In the sense I use it here, it's a topic-unified passage from one confrontation to another.

Story-wise, each confrontation and each transition changes the state of affairs and state of mind of each character involved, to some degree. In so doing, it moves the story forward towards its climax and resolution.

Thus, your story opens with your hero faced with a predicament, an emotionally disturbing situation.

In the typical film, you have approximately 90 minutes in which to resolve this predicament . . . replace Hero's disturbing situation and unpleasant emotions with something more satisfactory.

To this end, you link together a chain of confrontations alternating with transitions until, timed out, they add up to 90 minutes of screen time.

Indeed, there are worse questions to ask yourself before you start on any script than "Does my idea offer good opportunities for building confrontations? That is, will my protagonist have to fight to get what he wants, and can I devise incidents to dramatize that fight?"

Next question: How do you build confrontations and transitions?

Confrontation, first. It breaks down into three elements: *goal, conflict,* and *disaster.*

CONFRONTATION DYNAMICS: *GOALS*

Confrontations are the backbone of your script; the big moments in which your story advances.

A confrontation is a meeting of opposing forces; a time-unified clash between them. It's based on a conflict of goal-oriented actions: Someone wants something. Someone else doesn't want him to get it. They struggle.

"Something" = the attaining of a new, different, changed state of affairs.

Or, the retention of an old, same, *un*changed state.

So. A confrontation starts with goals. *Mutually incompatible* goals. Which is to say, if Character A gets his way, Character B can't have his.

A successful confrontation must first of all bring the two—or more—participants together in such a manner that they can join combat. Ordinarily, this means a face-to-face encounter. But variations are possible—witness the wars between lovers waged by telephone. The issue is merely one of imagination; the degree of creativity the scriptwriter brings to bear.

Beyond this, the confrontation should offer conflicting goals which are

a. Specific and concrete.
b. Immediate.
c. Strongly motivated.
d. Established early.

A few examples will clarify the issues.

a. Specific and concrete.

Suppose Character's goal is to win the acceptance—indeed,

friendship—of the woman in the riverfront house next door, despite her tight-lipped antagonism. How can the audience know whether or not he's really succeeded? How can the cameraman film appropriate footage of anything as abstract as acceptance, or friendship?

On the other hand, let's assume the same situation—but this time, Character's goal is to borrow Woman's car. Not only is this a photographable act, instantly comprehensible to viewers, but it also demonstrates the working fact of Woman's acceptance of Character far better than could any abstraction or generality.

In addition, Character's goal should be

b. *Immediate.*

A good goal, for confrontation purposes, is one you can take action to attain *right now*.

In fact, it's even better if you *must* take immediate steps to achieve it. Time pressure adds urgency to any scene.

Take the case above of Character, Woman, and the car. If Character merely thinks it would be nice to be able to borrow Woman's car some day, we haven't got much to work with.

If, on the other hand, Character's infant child has just gulped down some lethal fluid, and getting Child to the hospital fast is a matter of life or death, and Woman's car is the only available transport—well, the confrontation over borrowing the vehicle is going to come on hard and fast.

Which brings up yet another important point: The goals in a confrontation should be

c. *Strongly motivated.*

Frivolous, unmotivated, or weakly motivated goals seldom throw a confrontation into appropriately high gear. Those strongly motivated, in contrast, may speed your story to new peaks of tension.

Back to Character and Woman. Character, with Child's life at stake, obviously is highly motivated. He'll fight to get use of Woman's car.

What about Woman, however? Where does she stand?

Suppose, for example, that refusing to loan her car isn't just a matter of whim with her. Rather, her earlier antagonism is an intentional ploy designed to hold contacts at arm's length. She's rented this waterfront house because the state prison is just across the river and her convict husband's planning an escape. He's slated to make the break this very afternoon. Unless she and the car are here and ready when he scrambles from the water, he's a cinch to be captured and dragged back.

Now: What will be her reaction to Character's demand for loan of the car?

As noted previously, it takes specific, concrete, immediate, strongly motivated goals to build a proper confrontation!

Finally, said goals should be

d. Established early.

The earlier someone involved in a confrontation demonstrates that he has a goal, the earlier said confrontation can get under way.

Next question: How does a character demonstrate he has a goal? By getting up on a soapbox and sounding off about it?

Sometimes, maybe. But not very often.

Far better, let Character create the *impression* that he has a goal by what he does. Let his actions *show* it.

Exhibit A, from our sample episode: The door of Character's house bursts open. He lunges out onto the porch . . . looks frantically this way and that . . . pivots abruptly and, leaping the railing, sprints towards Woman's house.

Not one word has been spoken, note. We don't know that Character has a child, let alone that Child's been poisoned.

But because of the way Character's behaving, we *do* know something's going on, and we have reason to believe it's on the important side.

Naturally, there are other ways this can be handled. Opening on Child's scream, for example, or Child's face, or even the can of drain cleaner. Or earlier, perhaps, with Character watching TV, or setting down a bag of groceries and unloading items which include the can.

Why make such a fuss about establishing goals early and in action? Because once said action's under way and conflict develops, a confrontation may go in any number of directions.

CONFRONTATION DYNAMICS: *CONFLICT*

Mutually incompatible goals bring characters into conflict. Which seems simple enough, save that too often too many writers fail to remember that conflict comes in a variety of shapes and sizes.

Thus, a clash may be brief, or it may be protracted. It may be major, or minor. It may be taut, or almost lackadaisical. You build it to fit the requirements of your developing story.

How do you expand or contract a confrontation, a unit of conflict?

You add intensity, time pressure, twists, complications, or whatever else comes handy, as needed.

In the case of Character, for instance, he might come charging into Woman's house without knocking. "Quick!" he gasps. "Your car keys! Buddy—I gotta get him to the hospital!"

What now? Does Woman refuse, cry out, flee, faint, or what?

And how does Character react?

Let's suppose Woman flatly refuses to loan the car. Character grapples with her. Breaking free, Woman tries to flee. Character pursues. Woman—a desperate type, obviously—hauls out a gun. Character knocks it aside, wrestles Woman for keys.

And that's the way it goes, in confrontation.

Though it should also be noted that this horrendous battle might, under other circumstances, have been brought to an end before it started had Woman said coolly, "Oh, I'm sorry. The battery's down. That's why I haven't been driving this week."

Or, were we dealing with comedy rather than melodrama, an involved scheme on Character's part to get car away from Woman for whatever reason might have ended with the vehicle—Character at the wheel—rolling into the river.

CONFRONTATION DYNAMICS: *DISASTER*

Confrontation starts with goal. Then conflict's added.

It ends, finally, in *disaster*.

Disaster: a new and unanticipated development which worsens Character's situation.

Or, if you prefer, one which offers unforeseen consequences for Character.

Or, one which raises intriguing questions in regard to Character's future.

Consider the potentialities in our car loan episode: Character knocks Woman's gun aside; wrestles her for the keys.

Only then—new and unanticipated development—Woman jerks free for the fraction of a second—and hurls the keys out the window, into the river.

Disaster, right? Character's situation is worsened. Confrontation has ended with him the loser in the conflict, just at the moment he thought he'd won.

Also, happy day, it's given us a strong curtain.

A "strong curtain"—obviously, the term is of the theater—is a striking, unanticipated development that, coming suddenly, in effect acts as a cliff-hanger, a shock device to freeze the audience's attention with an implicit "Ai! What on earth will Character do now?"

Well, what *will* he do? It's a vital question.

Further, it brings us to our second dynamic element, transition.

Transition is a bridge between battles: non-conflict action that carries your characters from one confrontation to another. For all practical purposes, it takes in everything in your film which *isn't* confrontation, conflict. The trivia of living—the chance meetings, the casual chats, the buying of groceries and eating of meals and brushing of teeth—goes into transition.

Yet it isn't all quite as loose as it seems, for transition has it own unifying element.

That element is *preoccupation*: preoccupation with the "What-will-I-do-now?" factor that's the aftermath of the preceding confrontation's disaster.

In other words, Character may drift from here to there; talk of this and that; involve himself in which or wherever. But always, one way or another, whether by implication or oblique reference or side-issue development, you the writer see to it that he's still pondering his future, his next step.

This being the case, transition constitutes a dynamic element in your story just as much as does confrontation. By no means is it mere waste space or empty lines. For through its tacit focus on the future, transition provides the motivation/justification/springboard from which Character plunges into his next confrontation.

Just as confrontation breaks down into goal, conflict, and disaster, so transition subdivides into three elements: *reaction, dilemma,* and *decision.*

TRANSITION DYNAMICS: *REACTION*

Reaction works this way: Overwhelmed by the disaster of Confrontation 1, Character *reacts* to it in characteristic fashion.

Let's take the case of a specific character and situation—a female character, this time, an executive in her mid-30s whose doctor has just told her that what she thought was a touch of stomach trouble actually is liver damage brought on by years of excessive drinking. She can lay off the booze and go on a strict diet plus medication, or she can watch her condition deteriorate to cirrhosis.

Exit Executive. Back out on the street, what is her *reaction*? Shock? Rage? Incredulity? Helplessness? Hopelessness? Panic?

That will depend, of course, on her character, the kind of person she is—a matter which you, the writer, should already have pretty clearly in mind. Whatever the answer, you'll need to devise ways to reduce her response to photographable form: some sort of doings a cameraman can capture on film.

Let's make it simple. What would *you* do, if you were a long-time heavy drinker, reeling under the impact of a sudden, paralyzing shock?

Habit says: Grab a quick drink. Right? So you scuttle into the nearest cocktail lounge, there to gulp down a double vodka (vodka's an old rule with you, to keep you "breathless" on the job, as the ads say), in the same moment calling for another.

By the time Number Three's down the hatch, a greasy-looking type has moved to the stool beside yours, smiling in appropriately unctuous fashion. How's about letting him buy the next one?

You cut him off with a tart, "No, thanks." But his try shakes you. Do you look *that* bad? And whether the answer's yes or no, one thing's certain: You've got to bring yourself under control. You've got to face the salient question: *What do I do now?*

It's a state of affairs we label *dilemma*.

TRANSITION DYNAMICS: *DILEMMA*

On film, dilemma may take the form of anything from deliberation to discussion; from driving down endless roads or walking across endless landscape to praying for divine guidance.

Female Executive has her own pattern. Abandoning the cocktail lounge, she hurries home to her apartment. There, ignoring a convenient vodka bottle, she sets about stirring up a batch of thick, gooey, chocolate pecan fudge. That at least will get her away from the vodka . . . keep her hands busy while she thinks things out.

Only then a wave of guilt overwhelms her. Holding down her weight is an eternal battle for her. She even suspects there's a link between that and her drinking.

Yet here she stands, mixing bowl in hand, stirring in more brown sugar and more chocolate.

Anguish, erupting. With a choked cry, she hurls the fudge-to-be into the trash-pail, bowl and all, bursts into tears, and rushes to the bathroom.

Now, however, she finds, she can't even be satisfactorily sick. All that's left for her is to stand leaning on the washbowl, staring into the mirror at her tortured, tear-streaked face.

The real problem, she knows, is that drinking's not just a pastime for her; it's a defense. Fighting her way up through the ranks to a top executive post in a male-centered world has taken far more nerve than nature or her background gave her. So, she's drawn courage from a bottle. And when tension stretched her too tight, she's relaxed the strain with more of the same.

Now, if the doctor's to be believed, that period's over.

If she wants to live, that is.

Yet how can she quit? Popularity has never been her strong suit; the fights she's fought to get where she is have bred far too much bitterness for that. Particularly, the male chauvinist pig-type rival who covets her job is ever hovering close, alert for any opening, any hint of weakness.

TRANSITION DYNAMICS: *DECISION*

Decision comes, finally. That is, Executive makes up her mind what to do next, what course of action to pursue: She'll quit drinking, cold turkey. Right now, effective tonight, without benefit of Antabuse, A.A., or any other crutches.

Executive's decision, please note, provides her with a new *goal*, something to strive for.

Further, to prove to herself that she really means it, she'll attend a beach-house party tonight as scheduled, despite the fact that it will put her right in the sights of her hated rival.

It's a frightening thought. A drink would do so much to bolster her resolution. . .

Her knuckles go white as she grips the washbowl. Then, with a convulsive twist, she pivots . . . strides to the kitchen, seizes the vodka bottle . . . and pours its contents down the sink.

And there you have the pattern on which is based the art of confrontation: goal-conflict-disaster; reaction-dilemma-decision. It's a sequence which you repeat, time after time, till you reach the end of your film.

Now, one word of warning: In developing this example, note that I've left Executive alone most of the time. This can be dangerous. The screen offers few opportunities for neat asides of explanation. That means the actor must convey his inner world through action . . . must *show* us his thoughts and feelings, drives and conflicts.

A fine actor, well directed, can do this. A poor or mediocre one, ill guided, may fail, or turn us off, or win wild gales of mirth with what he hoped would be a scene of tenderness or anguish.

Be careful of asking too much in this regard, then. Better to write the bit for two, not one, most of the time, or to plan on cutting away to parallel action. The neck you save may be your own!

WHAT ABOUT RIGIDITY?

New writers sometimes make the plaint that the confrontation/ transition pattern is unduly mechanical. Actually, however, the events of your own life fit within it. The only difference is that, because of time/length limitations, film forces a certain compression and neatness of ordering which life foregoes.

Thus, in life, I may spend weeks or months debating whether to quit my job, or move, or marry. On film, quite possibly I'll have only a couple of minutes' running time to do so. But the decision, if presented convincingly, is no less valid.

Take the case of our female executive. Her reaction, dilemma, and decision are perfectly logical. The only issue is how to present them most effectively on the screen. For though, in print, it's easy enough to describe Executive's thoughts and feelings, film demands that we devise ways to dramatize them; to externalize her inner turmoil.

Can such be done? Of course it can—and that as crudely or subtly as your talent will permit. We've already seen how *reaction* translates itself into a cocktail lounge and double vodkas. *Dilemma* becomes fudge and tears and mirror; *decision*, potables poured down the drain.

Now obviously this isn't the only way the situation could be handled. Some writers might have developed it in a bedroom with the greasy type from the bar. Others would have brought in concerned friends, or telephone dialogue, or psychedelic d.t.'s, or ambulances screaming through the night.

Indeed, elimination of any or all parts of a transition is sometimes not only possible, but advantageous. Thus, Doctor might have curtain-lined his session with Executive with a blunt "There it is, Miss Jones: Quit drinking, or quit breathing." She stares at him, face stiff with shock. Whereupon we dissolve to the beach-house party. Someone offers Executive a drink. She shakes her head. "No, thanks. I'm on the wagon." A crisis has been met; a decision has been made. All we see are the results.

The same principle holds true for confrontation. Instead of Character wrestling Woman for the car keys two falls out of three, Woman might simply have let his door-pounding go unanswered, leaving him no choice but to take off in a new direction.

What about the business of cliff-hangers, strong curtains? I acknowledge freely that there are those who object to such. On occasion, they're left out, by some writers and in some pictures. Yet by and large, audiences do favor them—simply because said audiences go to the theater far less for intellectual enlightenment than emotional experience. They buy tickets because they enjoy the ebb and flow of tension; and nothing brings tension into sharper focus than does the build to an unanticipated twist that threatens pure disaster.

Another conclusion easily jumped to is that the use of confrontation and transition to build rising action applies only to certain types of picture—the thriller, the chiller, the action epic.

Nothing could be farther from the truth. The moment purpose becomes apparent, whether that purpose be explicit or implicit, there stands confrontation. Wherever a character struggles to reach a decision, transition is aborning. And this is as true when a child climbs a forbidden tree, then tries to decide whether to tell the truth as to how he tore his shirt, as when a woman seduces her best friend's husband, then strives to make up her mind if she wants to marry him as well.

In a word, the patterns of confrontation and transition are eminently fluid. To assail them as false or mechanical or rigid is pure self-delusion. It indicates only that we ourselves feel so engulfed and overwhelmed by life as to convince ourselves that life itself is formless— an obvious enough misreading of the facts, if you stop to consider that all of us are born, do live, and finally die.

In much the same way, and because death and tragedy do come to each of us, we pretend that life has no strivings, no triumphs, no happy endings. Yet who among us hasn't known happiness, even if only briefly? To demand that film show only aimlessness or defeat is to distort life grossly.

THE MATTER OF SECONDARY FUNCTION

Failure to understand and use the secondary functions of confrontation and transition in your film script is to throw out some of your most helpful tools.

Thus, in addition to moving your story forward, confrontation and transition perform three valuable services:

1. Regulation of excitement and acceptance.
2. Establishment and exposition.
3. Spacing and pacing.

What can we say about each of these categories?

1. Regulation of excitement and acceptance.

Conflict, confrontation, is what creates tension in your viewers. So, to add excitement to a dragging screenplay, you increase the proportion of confrontations to transitions, in terms of number, or running time, or both. For cases in point, consider the well-nigh obligatory car chases, karate combats, and mattress maulings in a host of recent pictures.

If your script lacks logic and believability, on the other hand, the solution often is to build up the transitions. Particularly, emphasize the logic of your hero's actions and the clear good sense—nay, inevitability—of his choice of goals.

The usual word of warning, though: You can always run a good thing into the ground. Let the confrontations crowd too fast and furious on each others' heels, and the film becomes a joke. Stretch out your transitions to too great length, in striving for greater believability, and the audience goes to sleep.

2. Establishment and exposition.

I group these elements together because, by and large, they're two sides of the same coin.

Establishment, as noted in previous chapters is making some aspect or component of your film in some way recognizable and identifiable in your audience's eyes.

Exposition is providing your viewer with information about the past which he needs in order to understand and appreciate the present and future of your story.

In general, it's desirable to limit your use of confrontation for purposes of establishment and/or exposition, *except insofar as said establishment and/or exposition are an integral part of the action*. Or, to put it another way, avoid explanations of anything in confrontation: It breaks the flow of the action.

However, it's hardly desirable to overload your transitions with background either. So, herewith a few hints on how to get maximum mileage with minimum pain:

a. Limit what your audience needs to know.

Remember what we said in Chapter 9 about building yourself a private picture of the background of the action?

Now is the time at which this homework comes in handy. Why? Because now you know all the things *you* need to know about what's gone before . . . so you can, without confusion, choose from that mass those items essential to your viewers also.

Which means you can leave out all the rest, with no fears or worries or qualms of conscience.

Well, at least not too many.

b. Make your viewers want to know the past.

The picture that sticks in my mind in this regard is an old Spencer Tracy vehicle, *Bad Day at Black Rock*. Tracy, as a one-armed World War 2 colonel, drops off a train in a sun-baked desert town in the west. Virtually from the moment he arrives, he's under attack by forces within the tiny community. Yet the town has raised a wall of silence against him. Consequently, both he and the audience are writhing in paroxysms of frustration as to just why all this should be so. And you don't get the answer till you're at least two-thirds through the picture.

c. Make your characters need information and have to fight to get it.

A variation on *b*, above, this concept takes off from the old saw that nothing is duller than information someone forces on you.

Corollary: Few things are more intriguing than information someone's trying to hold out.

Apply this principle to exposition. Instead of having Aunt Susie volunteer information about her impending gall bladder operation, let her make a secret of it. Since she's a key figure in an inheritance squabble around which our story centers, various people—probably including our central character—are going to try to worm the facts from her. Result: What might have been insipid exposition is transformed into taut confrontation. How so? Because that exposition is now an integral part of the film's action and progression.

d. Tie exposition to action.

Back in our section on the fact film, I made mention of the importance of translating information into terms of people doing things.

That same principle applies in features. Instead of telling about or discussing the height of a tower, *show* us the darn' thing. Even better, make someone have to climb it.

If you want to see a master's hand at work in such, drop by your nearest Hitchcock festival and see how he handles the issue in *Vertigo* and in the Mount Rushmore sequence of *North by Northwest*.

3. Spacing and pacing.

There are going to be times in your film when crises crowd too close together.

On other occasions, interest sags because they're too far apart.

Elsewhere, things move too fast or too slow.

In each instance, manipulation of confrontation and transition are virtually sure-fire solutions to your problem.

If the crises are too close together, the answer may be to insert a minor confrontation or two—foothills we have to climb before we reach the mountain, as it were. And each confrontation, in turn, will make necessary a bridging transition, a decision to be reached which provides the goal for the next confrontation. Or, if things really are on the frantic side, you might even consider a little cutting—reducing one of your confrontation peaks to foothill size.

Crises too far apart? Same remedy.

Things moving too fast? Slow 'em down by needling in transitions.

Too slow? Build or add confrontations.

Where do you get the raw material for insertions?

Well, imagination can be a help, of course. But I assume you're already using all you've got of that. Merely to tell you to find more would be a cop-out.

But there *is* a trick that can help, upon occasion. All it calls for is a list of characters to refer to.

Check said list, character by character. Ask yourself: *What's this man—or woman—doing, right this moment of the picture?* Or, if that comes out dull: *What MIGHT he or she be doing, in view of role and background and motivation?* Will it make for an insert or, perhaps, cutting to a parallel line of action?

So much for confrontation and transition. Master them, and you'll have tools that will serve you well in many a crisis.

As a case in point, consider the problems you'll face when you break your story treatment down into a step outline, the script phase we'll examine in the next chapter.

CHAPTER 11:

The Step Outline

A *step* outline is the feature film's (and especially the TV film's) equivalent of the fact film's *sequence* outline. It is, indeed, the sequence outline applied to fiction in a dramatic presentation.

This being the case, life will prove simpler for everyone if, forthwith, you will go back and re-read Chapter 4. The basics are there.

A sequence, as noted in said chapter, is a related series of shots, a filmed unit of thought and/or action.

Where the feature film is concerned, each sequence in effect constitutes a step forward in your story's development. The step outline's function is to help you check out, strengthen, and clarify said story by breaking it down into its component episodes. To this end, it reduces each unit or sub-unit of confrontation and transition to the briefest of descriptive bits—a sentence or two or three, preferably.

The important thing to remember is that these "steps," these segments, should, when strung together, incorporate the picture's entire flow of action. Every sequence—that is, every related series of shots to be photographed—must be included. To leave one out is bound to create problems later.

Here's how a chunk of a reasonably typical step outline looks:

6. The UN General Assembly...a crucial meeting. Country
    X's delegate makes fearful threats. The delegate of
    Country Y reminds him of his nation's solemn treaty
    obligations. Country X's representative responds with

the familiar line that treaties are just "scraps of paper"...and demonstrates his contempt for same by ripping up the documents in question. Whereupon, Villain Kurt, in the gallery with a covey of followers, leaps into the fray with a threat of his own: If Country X persists, not just treaties will be scrapped. He'll destroy **all** paper. Country X's delegate and his backers laugh aloud. Guards converge on Kurt. But before they can reach him, Kurt whips out and smashes a petri dish, thus freeing Papelivimus, the devastating, paper-consuming bacterium John Reynolds has developed. This is hardly spectacular, however, and our emphasis as the sequence ends is on Country X's group as they rise and demonstrate their resolve via clenched- **fist** salutes, pounding on desks with shoes a la Khrushchev, or the like.

7. On an SFX bridge of marching feet, drumbeats, or such, we DISSOLVE to the general headquarters of Country X's army. It's crowded with high-ranking officers. A courier enters, salutes, opens his dispatch case... then gapes as he finds it empty save for a few crumbling scraps of paper. Appropriate hubbub and byplay follow, with maps disappearing, files disintegrating, and the like. While the High Command stares at each other in shock, we DISSOLVE to

8. China. A warehouseman starts to lift a cardboard carton. It crumbles into shreds.

9. The U.S. A woman confronts a supermarket manager and demands to know how she's to shop...drags him to the nearest shelf. Rows of unlabeled canned goods stretch as far as eye can see. Interspersed are heaps of bran flakes sans boxes, sackless flour, empty paperback racks, and the like.

10. Paris. A couturier announces his new fall line of paper dresses--certainly the coming thing this year. Model steps forward, then stops short as her gown disintegrates. Squealing, she tries to cover herself with her hands, while the spectators gape slack-jawed or whoop with mirth.

11. A toilet booth, camera positioned to simulate position of stool's occupant as he reaches for the paper. The roll dissolves beneath his fingers. Occupant gives vent to a v.o. cry of anguish.

12. A newspaper newsroom. Shirt-sleeved managing editor confronts the staff. Two or three girls sit at a coin-heaped table off to one side. "It hits me just as hard as it does you, friends," m.e. tells staff. "But it's still a fact of life you can't have a paper without paper. We're all being paid off." A gesture to the money-stacked table. "In hard money, needless to say." "But this kind of thing--good Lord, we're going back to the dark ages!" someone exclaims. "What's going to happen to the country?" The m.e. shakes his head. "I wish to God I knew."

13. A shabby conference room. A grinning villain Kurt stands before his crew. All order has broken down throughout the world, he says. The room rings with congratulations. Then, a question: What comes next? Retention of control at all costs, Kurt answers. He sees himself as The Man Who Kept the Peace. The simple life--under his dictatorship, of course--is the answer to all problems. Another query: What about John Reynolds? He's upset that Papelivimus has created such chaos. Indeed, there are rumors he's seeking a bacteriophage. Kurt goes rigid. Any attempt to control Papelivimus constitutes high treason, in his view. And that makes John Reynolds an enemy of the state.

What's the simplest way to put a step outline together?

A fistful of 3 × 5 cards and a few square feet of corkboard along a workroom wall can be a major aid. A "step" description goes on each card. Then, you thumbtack cards to corkboard in sequential order. If problems of spacing out climaxes or balancing peaks and valleys arise, all you have to do is insert or remove cards, or reorganize by shifting the cards involved to more satisfactory positions. Similarly, if weak sequences turn up, or changes in plan of attack force revision, it's just a matter of retyping a few cards, not a whole manuscript.

What do you look out for in building a successful step outline? Let's put the issues in checklist form—eleven questions, grouped into three major categories:

1. The overall framework.
    a. Which are my main scenes?
    b. Are they properly spaced and placed?
    c. Do my characters come on at the right times and places?
2. The internal development.
    a. Does this sequence move the story forward?
    b. Is it necessary?
    c. Is it interesting?
    d. Is it logical?
    e. Am I telegraphing my punches?
3. The presentation.
    a. Does each outline unit tell what's seen?
    b. Does it tell what's heard?
    c. Is it clear?

So much for summary. Now, a look at the elements in detail:

1a. Which are my main scenes?

Certainly you should know by the time you get to your script's step outline stage!

A useful trick to make the pattern instantly recognizable is to put a big red check on each main-scene card.

Closely related to this is our second question,

1b. Are said main scenes properly spaced and placed?

The answer, of course, comes through at a glance, once you arrange your cards in order on the corkboard. In general, you probably should have something fairly strong at the start, to hook audience interest, and your strongest scene of all, the climax, close to the end. In between—well, check any TV drama to see how a subclimax/cliffhanger is introduced just before each station break. Do *not* follow quite such a mechanical pattern yourself, however, unless your film is specifically aimed at TV—a movie-of-the-week or such. Rather, try to ride with the natural peaks your material itself develops, insofar as possible.

Helpful in spacing and placing your main scenes are three oft-used but still effective elements: subplots, parallel action, and relief scenes.

A *subplot* is in effect a secondary story, ordinarily involving secondary characters, which takes place simultaneously with the main story. Shakespeare loved these: witness the Jessica-Lorenzo love story that runs alongside the main Portia-Bassanio line in *The Merchant of Venice*. Or, from today's films, recall the Steiner episodes in *La Dolce Vita*, the love affair of the Jewish boy and girl in *Cabaret*, or the development of the various secondary lines in *The Godfather*.

Parallel action refers to two lines of action which take place more or less simultaneously. By juxtaposing—and quite possibly contrasting—sequences from each line, you can both control time and suspense and, often, achieve neatly ironic effects. Thus, in one British picture of a few years ago, the central character is desperately—and dangerously—busy with a burglary. The occupant of the house being burglarized, in turn, is attending a concert. By alternating sequences from burglary and concert, tension is heightened immeasurably, and striking contrast achieved.

Similarly, several viewpoints may be developed within a picture, as in *Frenzy*, where part of the time we live the story with one or more of the various victims, part with the murderer, and part with the police.

Relief scenes or sequences offer a technique for changing mood or time or place, or reducing tension which has risen uncomfortably high, or introducing humor or contrast. At the same time, they have to tie in with the picture's general tenor and story line if they're not to prove disruptive.

Often, this is most simply accomplished through use of a comic character whose appearance signals a relief scene. A good case in point is the introduction of that master of ineptitude, Inspector Clouzot, into *The Pink Panther*.

(Note, however, how easy it is to get too much of a good thing. In *The Pink Panther*, Clouzot was side-splittingly hilarious; in *The Return of the Pink Panther*, something less.)

What about question number three,

1c. Do my characters come on at the right times and places?

Do I need to tell you that all major characters should appear on screen reasonably early? Or that they should reappear often enough to keep your audience reminded of their existence?

The answer is, yes, I do. Over and over again, I've critiqued scripts in which Hero or Heroine or Villain failed to show until the last half of the picture. Or appeared once and then vanished until the climax. Or played a major role in the opening scenes and then disappeared forever.

Any of these ploys can be managed, of course, upon occasion. Consider the way Alfred Hitchcock brought on Janet Leigh as *Psycho*'s apparent heroine, only to kill her in the first third of the film. But this kind of thing takes skill and a sure hand. You're better off to hold back on such until you gain experience.

How to check character presence? List the characters, one to a line, down the left side of a sheet of graph paper. Then, put the sequence numbers across the top, one per column. Finally, enter a check-mark in the appropriate crosshatch square if the character plays in that sequence.

What do you do if characters fail to appear where you want them? The answer, of course, is to juggle, manipulating characters and relationships and action until, at last, all pieces fall into place.

A good case in point that recently came my way was the story of a man whose brother is murdered. Try as he might, the scriptwriter couldn't figure out a way to bring in assorted key characters—including the woman who'd done the killing—until relatively late in the picture.

The ultimate solution proved to be introduction of a funeral scene, at which all the missing characters were present. Further brooding developed sound reasons for them to be there, and the script was off and running.

Do note one point, however—that focused upon in the previous sentence: . . . *sound reasons for them to be there*. One of the great curses of the beginner is a plague known as *author convenience*—which is to say, things happen in a script in an obviously phony and contrived manner, because the writer needs them to happen that way.

This is a cardinal sin, and then some. Yet it can be resolved far more easily than you may imagine.

The first step in this direction is for you to recognize that *everything* in a story is contrived—and contrived for author convenience, at that! So the real issue isn't "Is it contrived?" but "Is it contrived in a believable manner?"

This can prove a murky question. Ordinarily it will come clear, however, if we give proper attention to the five issues involved in the *internal development* of each sequence:

2a. Does this sequence move the story forward?

The issue here is, does this sequence bring the picture closer to its climax? Or, to put it another way, if the state of affairs and state of mind of your key characters are the same at the end of a given sequence as they were at the beginning, then that sequence, that step, constitutes pure waste motion.

A case in point: Ever so much in love, Hero and Heroine visit a fair . . . ride a particularly wild loop-the-loop. The action's so violent Heroine is half sick by the time they get off. Hero is appropriately solicitous. After a moment, however, Heroine recovers completely. They go on their way without further incident, still ever so much in love.

Observe, now, the flaw in this sequence:

Beginning state of mind:
   Hero and heroine are ever so much in love.
Beginning state of affairs:
   They visit fair.
Concluding state of mind:
   They still are ever so much in love.
Concluding state of affairs:
   They continue their ramble through the fair.
   Do you see what's wrong? Time has passed. Action has taken place. *But we can see no evidence of any change in Hero or Heroine's state of affairs or state of mind—at least, no change that we can interpret as having consequences for the future of our characters within the framework of the story.* Result: The sequence has not moved the story forward. Nothing meaningful has happened.
   For a sequence to move its story forward believably, certain events must transpire, certain developments take place. Leave out any of them and the whole structure stands in peril of collapsing.
   The situation is much like that which you face when you climb a flight of stairs. Each step consists of a riser and a tread. Leave out any one of them, and you very well may fall and break your neck.
   The same principle applies where a film is concerned. Leave out crucial steps in the transition of Character from predicament to resolution, beginning to end, and that invisible entity we term suspension of disbelief quite possibly will be shattered. That is, the picture's spell over the audience will be broken; the viewers' enjoyment of the ebb and flow of tension ended. Departing the theater, they'll tell their friends, "Don't go. This one's a dog."
   The essence of moving a story forward most often is the introduction of new (and, most often, unanticipated) developments which change Character's state of affairs and/or state of mind . . . actually or potentially for the worse.
   Could the fair bit cited above be developed in such a manner as to move its story forward? Of course. Instead of recovering promptly, Heroine might have gotten worse. Result: a trip to the hospital, with Heroine's family holding it against Hero that he's so endangered her.
   Or, an attractive carny girl helps Hero with Heroine. Result: Hero finds himself comparing his fragile flower unfavorably with the helper. He wonders if he's made the right choice of fiancees.
   Or, Heroine's bag is stolen in the furore. Result: Heroine blames Hero for carelessness. The unreasonableness of this sets Hero to looking at Heroine with new eyes.
   Or, seeking some medication to aid Heroine, Hero rummages through her bag. Result: He discovers information about her that casts her in a new—and unfavorable—light.

Or—to switch the situation around completely—it's Hero, not Heroine, who gets sick. Far from sympathetic, Heroine mocks him for his weakness. Result: Hero finds his feelings of love replaced by hostility.

Now none of these thoughts rate as gems, by any means. But they do show how relatively small changes in a character's state of affairs and/or state of mind can transform a sequence from static to dynamic . . . keep a story moving forward rather than standing still.

How do you come up with such twists?

One highly effective technique is to bring in a new character (the carny girl, for example) or a character already introduced who's been forgotten (perhaps some hostile member of Heroine's family).

To this end, it's not the worst idea in the world to tack a list of all characters on your corkboard. Then, when you're stuck, you can check them over with minimum waste motion, asking yourself the twist-pregnant question mentioned earlier: "What's Joe doing—or what *might* he be doing—that would jar this sequence off dead center?" Same for Sam, Rose, Eddy, Glenda. By the time you're through, nine times out of ten your problem will be past history.

An even better approach is to root your thinking in thorough and intimate knowledge of your characters and their relationships to each other. The "blamer" heroine who berates Hero for letting her purse be stolen, when his only sin was solicitude for her, is a definite and special kind of human being who shows possibilities for adding extra dimensions to your story as it moves onward. So is the heroine who ridicules Hero because he can't control his stomach. And so would be a heroine who, outraged at her guy's discomfort, proceeded to punch the ride boss in the nose.

One final point: To build a strong sense of forward movement in a sequence, it's best in the majority of cases to end on what might be termed the counterpunch.

This is a concept which perhaps can stand a bit of clarification. Let's begin with reconsideration of those key story elements, confrontation and transition.

The pattern of confrontation is one of goal-conflict-disaster; that of transition, of reaction-dilemma-decision.

The counterpunch focuses on your character's response to a sequence's disaster: his mounting of a new attack via choice of a new goal and/or implementation of that decision in goal-centered action.

Thus, in our fair sequence, when Heroine's wealthy uncle arrives at the hospital and, in a rage, announces withdrawal of vital financial support from Hero's cherished project, Hero might very well conclude the episode with a chill announcement that the hospitalization concerns him and Heroine only; and that as far as the project goes. Uncle can keep his money: Hero will carry on without it.

Instantly, a question is raised in viewers' minds: What will be the consequences of this challenge Hero has thrown in the face of fate? It's a good note to break on.

On the other hand, it certainly is not the only one possible. We might also end on the disaster/cliffhanger (Uncle's announcement that he's cutting off the money), or on the dilemma (Hero's strained effort to figure out what to do in the face of the Uncle-precipitated cataclysm). But centering the sequence's conclusion on Hero's indecision tends to emphasize weakness and stasis rather than the strength and forward movement most audiences seek, while ending with Uncle's cliff-hanger announcement puts the spotlight on Uncle instead of Hero.

Which is not to say that either of these alternatives may not prove desirable in specific instances or for variety's sake. But *in general*, the counterpunch approach is stronger.

2b. Is this sequence necessary?

Now why would I raise such a question as this, after all the attention I've already given the matter of the importance of each sequence moving your story forward?

The answer is that quite possibly you've built two sequences, where one could have done the job as well.

Here, for example, is a sequence in which a friendly elevator operator helps Hero locate Villain's office. Following is one that sees Hero coaxing information from Villain's secretary. A third has him trying to find Villain's car in the building parking garage.

Next question: What is Hero seeking?

Answer: He wants to talk to Villain.

So, why not just let him talk to Villain? Elevator operators, after all, are fast becoming rarities, secretaries who talk too much are hardly unusual, and a tour of a parking garage stands a good chance of lulling your audience to sleep unless someone's taking potshots at Hero.

This business of less-than-vital sequences can be particularly important when you're running long. So don't hesitate to ask yourself, "Can I combine this sequence with another? Is it possible to merge this character/set/action with another?"

2c. Is this sequence interesting?

Again, author convenience rears its seductive head. For it's ever so easy to become so preoccupied with getting in plot lines or essential information that you forget that such can also prove dull, dull, dull, unless you give heed to keeping each sequence entertaining in and of itself.

Thus, Professor Zeitelbaum's lecture on the physics of the fourth dimension may be crucial to understanding your film's climax, or Aunt Agatha's youthful involvement with music the key to the way she reacts to Jean's joining the Hare Krishnas. But that won't help if the audience goes to sleep.

In a static situation, you see, boredom soon takes over. Viewers yawn and squirm; perhaps even leave the theater. A disastrous turn of affairs indeed!

What it all comes down to is that, all statements to the contrary notwithstanding, you don't just hold an audience's attention; you *capture* and *recapture* it.

How do you do this?

First and foremost, you do it by *manipulating tension*.

Because this is so, you'll be well advised to so plan your script that it develops that generally rising state of excitement among viewers upon which we've commented previously. Such a state will be based on the ebb and flow of fear that some immediately dreaded or desired thing will or won't happen; an *anticipation of potentially impending disaster*, as it were.

Secondly, you do it by *translating abstraction into people being human*.

This demands that you be ever conscious of the human animal and his foibles—the way people really react as contrasted with the way they're supposed to; the contradictory things they do, cutting out mashed potatoes to lose weight, even while they eat a box of chocolates; the irrationality that makes them laugh and cry and love and hate and behave the way they did on *Candid Camera*.

Thirdly, you do it by *focusing on the logical yet unanticipated*.

These are the twists of fate, the things that shouldn't happen but do, the wrong people in the wrong places at the wrong times. They're the efforts that fail, the schemes that go awry, the roofs that cave in.

And the diamond-studded cloudbursts too.

One way or another, trickles from one or more of these three streams should seep into *every sequence* of your script. Let sinister forces be gathering outside Professor Zeitelbaum's lecture hall, with cross-cutting to give his words importance as well as build suspense. Bring the abstraction of Aunt Agatha's "involvement with music" to life via an affair with a tramp trap drummer. Or, by way of relief when tension grows too great, break the dreariness of a long afternoon by the river by including a comic character trying to retrieve a jug of moonshine from a sunken scow.

But *do* keep interest pulsing!

2d. Is this sequence believable?

Believability is largely a matter of character behavior. It comes in two parts: things your story people do and things they don't do: the same coin, but different sides.

The things your characters do raise certain crucial questions: Why does Character do this? Would the average person—or, at the very least, a character of Character's character—do it? What other, more logical paths might he take to reach the goal he's seeking?

Thus, why does Character date the ugly sister, not the beauty?

Why does he support his drunken brother? Why does he back down before his boss or mother? Why does he agree to take a job that he detests?

The issue where things your characters *don't* do are concerned is even simpler. It boils down to one question: Why doesn't Character quit?

As, why doesn't he ride out before the gunmen come? Why doesn't he refuse to doctor the books? Why doesn't he refuse to marry the hellion? Why doesn't he put his father in the rest home?

If Character does things viewers see as illogical and unbelievable, their suspension of disbelief in the film is shattered. Consequently, they *must* be made to believe—and the answers the audience wants are visual: living demonstrations of the points you're trying to make. Verbiage is not enough.

2e. Am I telegraphing my punches?

That is, am I being predictable?

What you're after is the unanticipated but logical development. To get it, you need to set up an *anticipated* development . . . then pull a different rabbit out of the hat. But don't cheat, or audiences will hate you.

Let's suppose, for example, that your hero has faced untold perils to get to the room where his girl allegedly is waiting. At last, panting with a combination of fatigue and passion, he knocks at the door.

The door opens—and there stands his girl's mother.

Assuming that you can make the switch logical, it's the kind of twist that will help to keep viewers awake.

Now, what about your presentation?

3a. *Does each sequence, each step outline unit, tell what's seen?*
3b. *Does it tell what's heard?*
3c. *Is it clear?*

For once, in this volume, little need be said. In essence, it's enough that you make it clear that you have something which can be photographed.

*   *   *

So much for the step outline. It's almost time to move on to our final feature film topic, the master scene script.

Almost, but not quite. First, we need to consider a tool essential to writing any effective feature script, that of dialogue.

We'll take it up in the next chapter.

CHAPTER 12:

Dialogue Devices

...Dr. Orbis twists back the dial, turns on the red spots,
switches off the green. The humming SOUND fades away.
The girls stop short in their exhibition of rapture...look
blankly at each other, the audience, and Dr. Orbis.

>   DR. ORBIS
>   So! Ladies, you weren't hurt,
>   were you?

Giggling and whispering, the girls shake their heads.

>   DR. ORBIS
>   Nothing bad happened to you, did
>   it? ...And you <u>did</u> have fun?

Complete affirmation from the girls, perhaps with AD LIBBED
COMMENTS.

>   DR. ORBIS
>   Then back to the fair with you!
>   Have the best of times! And
>   remember, all of you...
>   (arms flung wide,
>   to take in crowd
>   and girls alike)
>   ...Dr. Orbis is the man who
>   rules your mind!

It's been a good show. The crowd's in a good mood as it
starts to leave the tent. But now the roughneck noted
earlier breaks the spell.

154

```
                    ROUGHNECK
                  (bellowing)
        Bull shit!

                    DR. ORBIS
        What was that--?

                    ROUGHNECK
        Bull shit, that's what I said!
        You're a fake!
```

The departing crowd stops...turns. Dr. Orbis peers down
at the man through his thick-lensed glasses.

```
                    DR    ORBIS
                  (dangerously
                  gentle)
        Sir, do I understand you doubt
        my powers?

                    ROUGHNECK
        You bet you do.  I know your kind
        --crooks, liars, frauds--

                    DR. ORBIS
        Of course you know.  What's the
        saying--'It takes one to know
        one'?

                    ROUGHNECK
        Why, you--!

                    DR. ORBIS
        Since you feel so strongly, why
        don't you join  me up here on
        the stage?  Prove to everyone
        just how much of a fake I am?

                    ROUGHNECK
        You think I wouldn't!

                    DR. ORBIS
        Oh, no, sir.  I'm sure you would.
        So, if you'll just step up here
        now...
```

Dr. Orbis's reaction is totally unanticipated by the roughneck.
It dawns on him he's started something he's not sure he wants
to try to finish. He starts to turn away.

```
                    ROUGHNECK
                  (in fake disgust)
        Ah--!

                    DR. ORBIS
        You're not going, sir--?  Not
        before you've exposed me?  ...Or
        could it be you're just a bit
        afraid I'll do the exposing?

                    ROUGHNECK
        Bull shit!
```

He's eager to leave, but now the crowd won't let him.

                         MAN 1
             Go ahead! Get on the stage!

                         MAN 2
             What's the matter? Where you
             going?

                         WOMAN
             He's scared the brujo's going
             to cast a spell on him!

                         DR. ORBIS
             Is that it, sir? Are you
             <u>afraid</u> to come up?

                         ROUGHNECK
             I'll show you who's scared!

He charges up the nearest stairs onto the stage.

                         DR. ORBIS
                    (gesturing to area
                    beneath the green
                    spots)
             Right here, sir.

Simultaneously, he backs to the light board...throws the
mind machine control switch...twists the submission dial.
The raging roughneck stops short, caught in the cone of
green light. (SOUND: humming.)

                         DR. ORBIS
             Now, my friend. Surely we can
             talk this out like reasonable
             men. ...Actually, I'm glad you
             came. I can see you have a
             problem. ...You've always
             wondered: Are you really macho?

The crowd guffaws. The roughneck cowers, wordless.

                         DR. ORBIS
             Oh! That was unkind of me,
             wasn't it? Your kind of man...
             who could doubt you are a
             lover? ...Here!

Stepping to the table, he whips off the rebozo...tosses it
in the direction of the roughneck. It falls at the man's
feet. The roughneck stares stupidly at it.

                         DR. ORBIS
             Yes, indeed, you are a lover.
             And every lover needs someone
             to love. For you...
                    (Turning to
                    coffins, clapping
                    hands)
             Jorge! Join him!

The worst-looking of the "undead" men steps from his box...
crosses to and enters the cone of green light. Dr. Orbis
goes back to the light board.

                    DR. ORBIS
                 (adjusting dials
                 carefully)
        A little lust, now...
                 (to roughneck)
        Isn't Jorge beautiful? Your
        heart pounds, your blood heats
        at his very nearness, doesn't
        it? ...Oh, we all understand
        how it is with a real macho
        like you!

                    ROUGHNECK
                 (hoarse, guttural)
        Aahhh...

                    DR. ORBIS
        Kiss him, lover!

The roughneck clutches Jorge...buries his face in the "undead"'s
neck in an impassioned kiss. The crowd roars.

                    DR. ORBIS
        Muy macho!
                 (stopping short,
                 faking shock)
        Or--could I be wrong? Was there
        somehow something womanly about
        that kiss? ...Sir, the rebozo!

Letting go of Jorge, the roughneck picks up the rebozo.

                    DR. ORBIS
        Wrap it around you, my dear.
        You must be modest, maidenly.
        This is your lover, Jorge, that
        you meet here in secret in the
        campo. How your lips burn for
        his kisses!

The roughneck drapes himself in the rebozo...stands
simpering: head down, eyes averted.

                    DR. ORBIS
        Jorge! It's your sweetheart!
        Kiss her!

Jorge smothers the roughneck with kisses. Again, the crowd
roars.

                    DR. ORBIS
                 (arms spread,
                 mocking)
        Oh, such rapture! Oh, such
        passion!

In a frame-filling REACTION SHOT, the crowd roars with
laughter.

   What we see above is a sample of dialogue: that portion of a script
in which people talk . . . the things they say, word for word.
   The writing of good dialogue is an art in and of itself. For the film
scriptwriter, it's a vital skill.

What issues do we need to consider, where dialogue writing is concerned? They fall into three categories: dialogue functions, dialogue continuity, and dialogue realism.

1. Dialogue functions.

Dialogue has four primary functions; four main jobs to do:
a. To give information.
b. To reveal emotion.
c. To advance the plot.
d. To characterize the speaker and the person to whom spoken.

To a very considerable degree, these functions overlap. A given line may simultaneously perform all four jobs. Yet this is often enough not true to warrant our checking out each category separately. We'll start with

a. To give information.

At first glance this would seem so simple and so obvious as not to call for comment.

The problem is, good dialogue must not only convey information; it must do so without being obtrusive or impeding the story's flow.

Thus, in the script from which our sample above is taken, it was important to demonstrate that Dr. Orbis really does have mysterious powers. To that end, and also to lighten an otherwise heavy horror piece, this incident in which these powers are tested was written in. The situation is such that the key fact to be set forth is contained in Dr. Orbis's own grandiloquent proclamation—"Dr. Orbis is the man who rules your mind!"—yet it is so introduced that it is totally in keeping with the situation and so doesn't at all get in the way of the developing action. Indeed, it precipitates said action, by giving the roughneck an excuse to voice his challenge, thus clearing the track for the demonstration of Dr. Orbis's strange abilities. Each line that follows the initial statement builds upon it, adding new data and insights.

Is the point to be made worth this much screen time? That obviously is a matter subject to debate. My own reaction is that it is.

b. To reveal emotion.

Insofar as practical, each line a speaker delivers should reveal his mood, his feeling. Lines which fail to do so are "dead" and tend not to contribute to the sense of rising action viewers seek.

The place beginners' dialogue falls down often centers on the fact that they, writing, are not aware of the continual flux and change of a speaker's mood. In consequence, the words they put into his mouth fail to reflect his feelings.

Thus, Dr. Orbis's first three speeches in our sample reflect a genial mood, an interval of good feelings. In total command and playing to the crowd, Dr. Orbis coaxes and cajoles and radiates confidence.

The feeling flips with the roughneck's interruption. Dr. Orbis's cordiality falls away, but he stays in control. His words mirror smooth menace, as in the very formality of his line, "Sir, do I understand you doubt my powers?"

The roughneck blusters, riding the impact of his initial break-through. But Dr. Orbis takes the sting from the roughneck's words—and the initiative from the roughneck—by the agreement-plus-switch he voices in his "Of course you know" line. Each line that follows puts him more strongly in command, just as each of the roughneck's lines reflects increasing loss of control.

For the writer, the most important issue is less the words themselves than the changes in attitude, mood, feeling, that each line reflects. The state of affairs and state of mind of each speaker are continually shifting.

In good dialogue, the speaker's words and manner mirror this. In poor, the speeches are wooden, mechanical, and for the author's convenience. In consequence, they embarrass the actors called upon to speak them, as well as leaving the listening audience bored, irritated, and unconvinced.

c. To advance the plot.

Good dialogue should not only advance the plot: It should leave the audience unaware that it is doing so.

Our sample offers a good case in point. On the face of it, it merely acts out the humiliation of a hoodlum, making it more vivid through introduction of appropriate lines. Yet simultaneously it reveals Dr. Orbis's ability to distort reality for his victims: The *macho* roughneck is first deluded into caressing a zombie-like male . . . then warped even further, to the point where he himself takes the female role.

Now all this is entertaining enough in and of itself. But it also constitutes preparation for later sequences in which Dr. Orbis exercises such control in infinitely more sinister fashion. The audience accepts it, however, because this earlier, less crucial demonstration with the roughneck has "proved" to them—"Seeing is believing!"—that Dr. Orbis can indeed rule his victims' minds.

What has dialogue contributed to this "proof"? It has made the demonstration infinitely more vivid, by enabling viewers to follow the subtle ebb and flow of emotional change more closely than they could have through sight alone. In consequence, the scene's impact is much more convincing.

The lesson for the writer is clear: In film, dialogue does not—cannot—exist as an element separate and apart from the picture as a whole. To fulfill its function, it must be integrated into the overall pattern that the writer designs in order to create that ebb and flow of tension which we call entertainment.

d. To characterize the speaker and the person to whom spoken.

Inevitably, dialogue reflects the speaker: his background, his education, his social status; above all, his attitudes and feelings.

On the obvious side, garbage collector and college president hardly are likely to speak the same. Dr. Orbis and Roughneck demonstrate this clearly. "Sir, do I understand you doubt my powers?" is one person—and one *kind* of person—speaking; "You bet you do. I know your kind—crooks, liars, frauds—" another.

But it is on a deeper level, on that of personality itself, that the picture really comes into focus. Thus, Roughneck's speech labels him as a loudmouthed bully—ignorant, inwardly insecure. That of Dr. Orbis, in contrast, reflects quiet menace, coupled with the kind of sadism-laced insight that enables him instantly to pinpoint the chink in his opponent's armor.

It goes without saying, I trust, that insight precedes dialogue where this is concerned. If you don't know the kind of man with whom you're dealing and the traits which reveal his inner self, you can't write proper lines for him.

Part and parcel of this insight picture is the matter of reaction. Where Roughneck responded to Dr. Orbis's exhibition with a yell of "Bull shit!" another man might, without commotion, have asked the authorities to close down the show. A lesser figure than Dr. Orbis, in turn, might have cringed or fled or blustered at Roughneck's bellow.

Once you have your understanding of your people, dialogue becomes one of your most useful tools for bringing insight out into the open . . . putting it in such form that viewers can understand and draw full emotional value from it.

2. Dialogue continuity.

How do you make dialogue hang together?

You make use of a device called the *dialogue hook,* which insures that each speech acknowledges the one preceding it.

We see this technique at work in the very first interchange between Dr. Orbis and the girls at the show:

```
                    DR. ORBIS

        So! Ladies, you weren't hurt,
        were you?

Giggling and whispering, the girls shake their heads.
```

The hook, in this case, is *question/answer.* The girls' giggling, whispering, and head-shaking acknowledges Dr. Orbis's question. Without said question, the "answer" would make little sense.

Note also, incidentally, that though this is a dialogue sequence, the "answer" takes the form of action rather than words. An important point for anyone to remember; too often, learners insist on words, words, words and formal speech, when mime would play better. But more of that later, when we deal with dialogue realism.

The question/answer pattern is only one of a host of hooks, of course. Thus, Roughneck's "Bull shit!" stands as *disagreement* with Dr. Orbis's ". . . Dr. Orbis is the man who rules your mind!" Dr. Orbis's "What was that—?" in turn, represents *reaction*. Roughneck's later "You bet you do" and Dr. Orbis's "Of course you know" are both hooks of *agreement*—by agreeing with the previous speaker's statement, each acknowledges the speech and so establishes the element of continuity which makes good dialogue hang together.

Dr. Orbis's "Of course you know" is also a hook of *interruption*—he has broken in on Roughneck's "cheap crooks, liars, frauds—" diatribe, and the fact of breaking in is in itself an acknowledgment of Roughneck's rantings. Some lines later, when he begins, "Now, my friend," he's using a *transitional word* as a hook. The "now" is an "empty" word, like "Oh?" or "Well!" or "You don't say?" It acknowledges prior speech or behavior without taking a stand. In so doing, it constitutes an excellent pivot for changing the subject. Thus, in our example, the whole opening portion of the Orbis speech is really little more than social noise ("Now, my friend. Surely we can talk this out like reasonable men.") But what follows is a total switch which might have jarred had it not been built up to: ". . . Actually, I'm glad you came. I can see you have a problem. . . . You've always wondered: Are you really *macho*?"

Elsewhere in this script, the same transitional word device is coupled with another favorite, *repetition,* and question/answer to keep an expository passage moving:

<pre>
                    LUIS
        Good God!

                    DR. ORBIS
        Why shudder? Daring is always the
        handmaiden of progress. What does
        it matter what happens to the weak
        and stupid, so long as man's
        knowledge marches forward?

                    LUIS
        So?

                    DR. ORBIS
        So, I developed my master work,
        the retinal serum...
</pre>

Here, Luis uses a transitional word to answer a question with a question . . . Dr. Orbis repeats the word . . . and off we go again!

Again, we have this hook, this acknowledgment via *action,* followed by a reaction speech:

```
                    MARINDA
                 (moving head
                  dazedly)
          I--I can't see...
```

Luis removes her dark glasses. Her face is still averted
and/or in shadow. Taking her by the chin, he gently turns
her face to the window. For the first time, light strikes
her eyes. In CLOSEUP, we see they show only blank white
sclera...no iris, no pupil.

```
                    LUIS
          My God--!
```

And so it goes, with speech or action acknowledging preceding speech or action. All constitute dialogue hooks. The classifications into which I've broken them down—repetition, transitional words, reaction, action, interruption, agreement/disagreement, question/answer, and so on are totally unimportant. What counts is understanding of the basic principle involved: *Each speech should somehow "hook" to the one ahead.* Keep that in mind, and you can't go too far wrong.

3. Dialogue realism.

Where realism is concerned, the big thing to bear in mind in working up dialogue is that there's a world of difference between speech and the written word. Good dialogue strives for the tone of conversation. It attempts to avoid the stiffness and formalism that too often envelopes us when we "take pen in hand."

On the other hand, saints preserve me from the script in which the writer has tried to duplicate actual speech. Better by far that he *simulate* the way we talk. Which is to say, you should aim for the flavor and color of spoken language, but eliminate all but a salting of the banality, repetitiousness, and general meandering in which we all tend to indulge.

To that end, be sure your dialogue keeps your story moving forward in a reasonably straight line. Do *not* permit yourself the dubious luxury of bogging down in endless burblings and weather talk in the name of realism.

Beyond this, the going grows hazy. So much depends on taste and talent! An interchange handled with one man's humor comes out as light and clever. In another's hands, it would prove cloddish. The trick is to assess your own abilities, strong points and weak. Then, stay within your limitations or work with the devil's own fervor to overcome them. There is no other way.

A few observations may help you sharpen your attack, however . . . as witness these 15 far-from-all-inclusive points:

a. Dialogue should be characteristic of the speaker.

I've already given this some attention, so I'll keep my comments here brief.

The key principle is: Know your people, and let their speech help differentiate them. A Texan doesn't talk like a Down Easter, nor a cowhand like a coal miner, nor a child like a man. Each nationality, each generation, each social stratum has it own speech patterns. Only as you listen, listen, listen; pay attention to them, can you hope to capture them in your scripts.

b. *Since good dialogue represents our language as spoken, rather than written, it makes full use of contractions, the second person approach, the active voice, and such.*

When Roughneck in our horror film sample roars, "You're a fake!" he's using that specialized verbal shorthand that we call contraction: It reduces "You are" to "You're." In the process, it adds a touch of realism to Roughneck's speech. Same for Dr. Orbis when he asks, "What's the saying?" or says, "I'm sure you would. So, if you'll just step up here now . . ."

Second person? "When you get to the third corner, you turn right a block," instructs Character. "If you want to cut down the alley, then . . ."

This habit of using second person and active voice—the "you get," "you turn," "you want" element—is ever so common with most of us, especially when we're explaining or instructing. Indeed, the more formal third-person usage ("How does one reach the hotel?" "One proceeds three blocks in the direction you are going.") is in itself a characterizing device, useful in tagging the speaker as on the stiff and prissy side.

c. *Ungrammatical constructions, clichés, and slang are a habit with many of us.*

```
                    ALASTAIR
          Precisely what do you mean, young
          lady?


                    SHARON
          I mean, it do take talent, don't
          it? Like she's a doll.  But
          rhythm counts more than rich
          relations.  You know how the song
          goes--"It don't mean a thing if
          it ain't got that swing."
```

Alastair is a man who speaks correctly. But closer to the hearts—and speech patterns—of the masses is Sharon's approach.

Note too that the contrast between these speakers helps to make for livelier, more interesting dialogue.

d. Some speakers fumble, hesitate, and/or interrupt frequently.

```
                    DR. ORBIS
          But where?  Where were they?

                    ZARA
          I--I don't know.

                    DR. ORBIS
          Was it here?  Here, in the tent,
          my show?

                    ZARA
          No...

                    DR. ORBIS
          Not the tent--?

                    ZARA
          No.  The walls...they were
          different...stone, maybe...like
          an old house...
```

As with almost everything else in the writing business, this can be overdone. But occasional gropings by the right person at the right time certainly does help.

e. Most speeches should be kept brief.

Turn back to the sample with which we began this chapter. You'll find it has 11 one-line speeches, ten two-line speeches, two three-liners, five four-liners, one five-liner, two six-liners, and one seven-liner.

Similarly, checking out a random three-page sample in the script of the much-acclaimed *Winning,* I counted 19 one-liners, six two-liners, and five three-liners; none longer. A three-page chunk from the highly successful *Bob & Carol & Ted & Alice* turned up 25 one-line speeches, four two-line, one three-line, and one four-line.

This obviously is not to say that longer speeches are unknown. A quick thumbing of *B&C&T&A* revealed one 24-line speech, plus a number of ten-, nine-, eight-, and seven-liners. *Winning* came up with one 11-liner, as well as assorted sevens, sixes, and fives.

But the overall picture, in life and in film scriptwriting, favors the short speech.

f. Action—stage business–often substitutes for speech.

```
                    DR. ORBIS
          So!  Ladies, you weren't hurt,
          were you?
```

Giggling and whispering, the girls shake their heads.

Again:

```
              DR. ORBIS
    Now, my friend.  Surely we can
    talk this out like reasonable
    men.  ...Actually, I'm glad you
    came.  I can see you have a
    problem.  ...You've always
    wondered:  Are you really macho?
```

The crowd guffaws. The roughneck cowers, wordless.

The issue in dialogue, remember, is *acknowledgment, reaction.*

Often, actions speak louder than words in this regard. What a man does clarifies his stance far better than what he says.

That being the case, your own best approach is to consider response, rather than mere words. You may end up finding silence golden.

g. *Emotionalism dominates factual content in most speech.*

People are not computers, nor logic machines, nor yet taped answering services. Consequently, as pointed out in the section on dialogue's emotional function, they tend to speak more in terms of feeling than of fact.

Thus, when Roughneck bellows "Bull shit!" he's giving vent to rage, rather than good sense.

Anger, even though controlled and masked, is equally evident in Dr. Orbis's "Sir, do I understand you doubt my powers?" And the sarcasm of his later "Oh! That was unkind of me, wasn't it? Your kind of man . . . who could doubt you are a lover?" clearly reveals a sadistic delight in the twisting of the knife.

Your own characters should be equally enmeshed in feelings; and those feelings should show through their dialogue just as clearly.

h. *Well-nigh every speech should reflect an attempt to influence someone's attitude or behavior.*

In life, much speech is empty. That's a luxury you can't afford in dialogue. Screen time is just too precious.

Avoid dull dialogue of agreement, therefore—"Oh, it's a lovely dress!" "Yes, I think so. And brown's my color." "Yes, it certainly is. Besides, when you wear your hair that way . . ."

As much as possible, your players should be goal-oriented, strivers. Then, you should focus on their confrontations, the moments when they're trying to gain their ends in the face of opposition.

i. Beware of letting any character volunteer information.

>   AUNT AGATHA
>   This girl, George. How much do
>   you really know about her?
>
>   GEORGE
>   Please, Auntie, please! Whatever
>   I know or don't know, it's
>   enough.
>
>   AUNT AGATHA
>   George, even before her teens,
>   she was a problem!
>
>   GEORGE
>   Auntie, whatever it is--
>
>   AUNT AGATHA
>   An affair's one thing. Three in
>   a row's another. And those are
>   just the ones I know about. And
>   then, those poor children--

Beware of making life too easy for your hero—or, for that matter, for any other character. To do so takes the edge off your story.

One way of making Hero's life dangerously easy is to allow other characters to present him with needed information as a gift. Better by far that he should have to fight for it, tooth and nail, wresting it from antagonists in bitter battle. For only thus can you build a proper pattern of rising action.

How to cope with such information, if it insists on coming? One solution is to let Hero look gift horse in the mouth . . . question why he's receiving such largesse . . . and so come up with a new and unsuspected twist. Or follow the old "truth, the whole truth, and nothing but the truth" line, letting Hero receive only part of the truth, or truth mixed with falsehood, or a total lie. Or, let Hero be so eager to escape from his informant that he ignores the data he's receiving.

Whatever your solution, however, be certain of one thing: that you keep your viewers' interest aglow with some unceasing element of tension.

j. Always consider the factor of normal reticence in speech.

Few things in this world are more painful than dialogue in which the scriptwriter puts words into actors' mouths that no normal person would speak.

I'm talking about the lines in which the saintly mother describes her sex experiences in four-letter words, or the miser details the fortune he's accumulated, or the priest reveals secrets of the confessional in the course of casual gossip.

How to get such information in, then? Why not let another character hazard a guess or make an accusation?

Another aspect of all this centers on the fact that not all speech is forthright. Few of us always say exactly what we mean. Lies, evasions, euphemisms, exaggerations, irony, and the like are common.

Good dialogue reflects similar patterns of indirection, when character and occasion demand.

*   *   *

Beyond these hints, how do you learn to write good dialogue?

The first step is to learn to listen; to pay attention not just to what people say, but also to how they say it.

It will also help if, as you write dialogue of your own, you make it a point to read each passage back aloud, to see if it really sounds like people.

You'll have a lot of opportunity to do that when you buckle down to writing the master scene script in all its glory.

It's the subject of our next chapter.

CHAPTER 13:

The Master Scene Script

FADE IN:

1   INTERIOR - OFFICE OF DR. SUAREZ - NIGHT

The room is spookily lighted. Large colored wall diagrams
of the human eye, front and profile, are prominent, with
perhaps an optometrist's examining chair for balance. A
SLOW PAN takes us past an eye chart and any other atmospheric
touches available to a desk on which lies the corpse of
DR. SUAREZ (professional type, 30s). He's flat on his
back, face a mask of shock and horror, head and maybe an
arm hanging limp over the desk's edge. A not-new axe is
buried deep in his chest, handle thrusting up at a sharp
angle. Of course there's plenty of blood...perhaps other
hack-marks.

2   INTERIOR - CLINIC CORRIDOR - NIGHT

From OFF SCREEN we hear the SOUND of a woman's brisk
footsteps. The trim lower legs and feet (nurse-type shoes)
of PILAR CASTENON (pretty, early 20s) enter frame. We
DOLLY with them down the hall to the doorway of Dr. Suarez's
office...HOLD while Pilar (SOUND) unlocks and opens door.

3   INTERIOR - OFFICE OF DR. SUAREZ - NIGHT

Pilar (FULL SHOT now) enters...crosses towards desk. She
wears nurse-type uniform, carries raincoat over arm.

(Probably this is shot from a low angle, close beside the
desk, so we can't see Dr. Suarez's corpse.) Then, as Pilar
nears desk, glimpses corpse, and stops short, we CUT to a
shot that includes both her, as she freezes, and corpse.
CLOSEUP of Dr. Suarez. CLOSEUP of Pilar's shocked,
horrified face. She rallies...crosses to phone...throws

(CONTINUED)

3   CONTINUED
     down coat...snatches up receiver. But even as she starts
     to dial, we--and she--hear the SOUND of a man's sinister,
     echoing, strangely erratic footsteps from the corridor.

4   INTERIOR - CLINIC CORRIDOR - NIGHT

     In a shot similar to 2, above, the feet and lower legs of
     KARL (Frankenstein monster type, 40s) enter frame. Karl's
     gait is tentative and erratic because he has only peripheral
     vision: That is, he sees only around the edge of the eye
     rather than through its center and so is, by and large,
     blind. Details are beyond him, though he can still perceive
     large objects and--especially--motion. We DOLLY with him
     as he moves towards Dr. Suarez's office.

5   INTERIOR - OFFICE OF DR. SUAREZ - NIGHT

     Face mirroring panic, Pilar listens as Karl approaches.

6   INTERIOR - CLINIC CORRIDOR - NIGHT

     Karl's feet reach Dr. Suarez's doorway. We still don't see
     much above his knees.

7   INTERIOR - OFFICE OF DR. SUAREZ - NIGHT

     Pilar still stands phone in hand. Karl pauses momentarily
     in doorway, then lurches forward again. A tall, gaunt,
     sinister figure, he wears raincoat, hat, and dark or mirror
     glasses. A slow step at a time, Pilar backs away from him
     in obvious fear. Closing in, Karl seizes the handle of
     the axe...wrenches the blade from Dr. Suarez's chest...lifts
     it for a blow at Pilar. She tries to dart past him. He
     lurches into her path, letting go of the axe with one hand
     to clutch at her. In silence, they struggle briefly--Pilar
     desperate to break free, Karl maniacally determined to hold
     her. The result is a balancing of strength that plays almost
     in slow motion, with no jumping or flailing. Then, as if
     realizing she can't match Karl's strength for long, Pilar
     sags...claws fast at Karl's face. The blow knocks off his
     dark glasses. In a CLOSEUP from Pilar's point of view, we
     stare into Karl's eyes--shockingly strange eyes, in that
     they're blank white; all sclera, no iris. (This effect is
     obtained by having Karl and those other characters whose
     eyes show blank white wear appropriate contact lenses.) A
     reverse angle CLOSEUP of Pilar, in turn, sees her face
     contort as, for the first time, she loses self-control.
     Her mouth opens.

                              PILAR
                           (screaming)
              Aieee!!!

8   INTERIOR - CLINIC CORRIDOR - NIGHT

     In a shot similar to 2, above, and while Pilar's scream
     continues OFF SCREEN, the feet and lower legs of LUIS GARZA
     (non-pretty hero type, early 20s) enter frame at a dead run.
     Camers PANS to follow action, HOLDING on Luis in TAILAWAY
     as he lunges towards the open doorway to Dr. Suarez's office.

9   INTERIOR - OFFICE OF DR. SUAREZ - NIGHT

     Luis rushes in. Karl lurches to face him, flinging Pilar
     aside. He and Luis struggle for possession of the axe.
                                                     (CONTINUED)

9 CONTINUED

Then, strength superior, Karl shoves Luis away from him so
violently Luis smashes against the wall head first. Stunned,
eyes wide and staring, he crumples to the floor. Karl
starts to close in with the axe. But Pilar snatches up her
raincoat and hurls it over Karl's head like a hood, then
hammers at him with a bookend or such. More than ever
blinded by the coat, staggering under the rain of blows,
Karl makes it to the office door in a series of groping
lunges.

10   INTERIOR - CLINIC CORRIDOR - NIGHT

Fighting free of the coat, Karl flees, lurching off down
the corridor.

11   EXTERIOR - CLINIC ENTRANCE - NIGHT

Karl lurches out the door and to the curb...hangs there,
twisting this way and that as he tries to force his semi-
blind eyes to see. Simultaneously, an old-style black
hearse moves into view at a measured pace, out of the
shadows down the street...pulls up beside Karl. Groping,
he yanks open the door...scrambles into the right front
seat. Still at its stately, funereal pace, the hearse
moves on again.

12   INTERIOR - HEARSE - NIGHT

Camera shoots HEAD-ON, through windshield to include both
Karl and the hearse's driver, DR. ORBIS (Peter Lorre type,
40s)...then CUTS to individual or strongly favoring CLOSEUP
of Dr. Orbis. He wears glasses with lenses so thick as to
distort his eyes and lend him an appropriately weird
appearance. He drives calmly, coolly, smiling slightly as
if at a small private joke. This smile serves as a
characterizing tag for him throughout the film, designed
to sharpen his image as a menace. It constitutes clear
visual evidence of his self-confidence and poise...says
without words that everything is going according to plan
and that he's in control--ever the hunter, never the hunted.
In consequence, by implication, his opponents are doomed
before they start. Here, now, as he drives, the smile
broadens. He chuckles noiselessly. The hearse picks up
speed.

OPENING TITLES OVER

In individual HEAD-ON CLOSEUP, Karl slumps panting, bloody
axe clutched to his chest. Perhaps his fingers caress the
lethal axe-head lovingly, as if it were a woman. His face
is a sinister mask. His blank white eyes stare straight
ahead.

INTERCUT with the above footage are appropriate TRAVEL SHOTS
from the moving hearse.

Individual CLOSEUP, Dr. Orbis. His attention is on the
road ahead now, but a noticeable trace of the smile is still
with him. Camera MOVES IN to frame-filling HEAD-ON EXTREME
CLOSEUP of the thick-glassed eyes.

(CONTINUED)

12 (CONTINUED)

    MAIN TITLE OVER:

                <u>THE EYES OF DOCTOR ORBIS</u>

13   EXTERIOR - HEARSE - NIGHT

    On a long curve, the hearse races into frame towards
    and past camera. Camera PANS to follow action as hearse
    continues on around the curve and disappears into the
    night.

                            FADE OUT

What we have here is a sample of what is known as a *master scene script:* a format which, from the writer's standpoint, frequently is the feature film's equivalent of the fact film's shooting script. A final description of what happens in your film, it spells out what's seen and what's heard, the action and dialogue within the framework of the setting. It's your story cast into such form that the director can direct it as a film, the actors can act it, and the crew members can perform their respective duties.

By and large, however, it does *not* go into technical detail, the breaking down of the action into shots or the like, save insofar as these are necessary in order to make clear a specific effect the writer hopes the director will include.

Thus, our sample probably is written with far more loving attention to such detail than normally would be desirable. Why? Because the writer is striving to create a particular mood of shock and horror while simultaneously establishing situation and key characters.

But more of that later. For now, let's consider nine key issues involved in writing a master scene script: format, visualization, point of attack, sequence development, continuity, characterization, dramatization, believability, and clarity.

1. Format.

Yes, mechanics *are* important, no matter what anyone tells you to the contrary. Why? Because your script is, in its way, your calling card. If it shows a lack of awareness of accepted practice on your part, it labels you as an amateur; and we all have handicaps enough to overcome without *that* albatross tied around our necks!

So. Mechanics.

Ordinarily, the master scene script is set up in a single column format, as per our sample pages. With the left edge of the paper at zero and a machine using pica type, give your copy horizontal spacing thus:

10—sequence (step) numbers
15—directions—75
30—speeches—60
40—parenthetical business—55
45—names of speakers
60—transitions
75—page numbers

Now, let's define and discuss our terms.

A *sequence number* is precisely what you'd think it would be: an identifying number in your script's left margin. The number changes every time conditions of work (INTERIOR/EXTERIOR—SETTING—DAY/NIGHT) change.

If, in the course of revisions, new sequences are added (to sequence 7, for example), they become sequences 7a, 7b, 7c, and so on, so that no changes need be made in the numbers (8, 9, 10, etc.) that follow. Similarly, if sequences (steps, that is) are deleted, the numbers remain in the script, but are marked as omitted, thus:

67
thru   OMITTED
69

or,

67
68   OMITTED
69

Directions are those lines describing the action to be filmed.

Speeches are the words the actors voice.

Parenthetical business is any brief instruction as to some action an actor should perform in the course of a speech, or the manner in which the speech should be delivered. Thus, in the following bit, the parenthetical business is underscored. (It would *not* be, in an actual script.)

```
              DR. ORBIS
            (thoughtfully,
            straightening)
Coffins.  Faces without eyes
coming out of coffins.  The
girl and Garza, trapped and
frightened.
            (continuing, to
            Karl, with
            repressed glee)
So!  That's the final set.
            (significantly)
At the house, you note.  Coffin
Hall!  And for bait...
            (a sudden leer
            of triumph)
...well, what better bait then
our friend Marinda!  'Tonight's
Girl--Songs for Tomorrow!'
...Right, Karl?
```

In the same way, in the following passage, the "*(to crowd)*" line is parenthetical business. But the "*He turns the submission dial,*" "*He twists the fifth dial,*" etc., are set up as directions because of their greater length and complexity.

```
                    DR. ORBIS
                   (to crowd)
        You see?  Dr. Orbis is the man
        who rules the mind!  Before my
        power, the strongest surrender
        ...submit totally.
```

He turns the submission dial as he speaks...makes a pass in the girls' direction. Their heads go down. They hug themselves, cringing and groveling.

```
                    DR. ORBIS
        Fear, hate, submission...ah,
        but these are bitter passions.
        Young ladies as nice as these
        deserve better.  ...Rapture,
        even!
```

He twists the fifth dial. The girls' mood changes before our very eyes. They LAUGH (<u>not</u> giggle), cry out delightedly, fling wide their arms, move in small private dances.

A word of caution: Restrain yourself as much as possible when it comes to telling actors how to act or read their lines. For one thing, they "tend to act the adverb, not the line," as a friend of mine phrased it. For another, often they resent it, unless—and here's the key—the situation is such that it's important to story and character that a particular interpretation be given.

Thus, the "significantly" in our first example is probably belaboring the obvious, in view of the speech that follows. The "to crowd" in Example 2, on the other hand, is entirely legitimate, because the actor playing Dr. Orbis *could* decide he should address his line to Karl or the girls—a bad misinterpretation, in view of the image we're trying to build up for Orbis at this point.

Names of speakers are just that. Note that a speaker's name is repeated if *directions* break a speech (second example above), but not if the break is for *parenthetical business* only.

Transitions are the shifts from sequence to sequence. Ordinarily these will be optical effects—"DISSOLVE TO:," "FADE TO:," "BLUR PAN TO:," or the like. Sometimes you'll find "CUT TO:" also, especially if a cut wouldn't be the anticipated technique, but is desired for shock effect or such. Most of the time, however, a cut is taken for granted rather than spelled out.

Don't worry too much about transitions, though. Odds are no one will pay any great attention to your thoughts on the subject anyhow.

A somewhat different aspect of transition is the fairly common practice of writing "(CONTINUED)" at the end of any page that ends in the middle of a sequence. The next page starts with the sequence number and another "CONTINUED." Then, you drop down a double space and proceed.

Page numbers would appear too obvious to require comment save for one thing: From time to time in the course of producing a script, script conferences, changes of mind, or whatever are going to put you in the position of having to add or delete pages. When that happens, treat each page as if it were a sequence. The extra pages can become 89a, 89b, 89c, and so on. And those deleted are accounted for by making the last page number before the break include those deleted. For example, page 61-2-3-4. Then, page 65.

Vertical Spacing?

Page number—two spaces below top of page

First line—three spaces below page number

Conditions of work, directions, speaker names, transitions— two spaces below preceding copy

Parenthetical business—next space below speaker name

Speeches—next space below speaker name or parenthetical business

All capital letters:

Character names (often on first appearance only), conditions of work, image size, camera movement, transitions

As per Sample Page 1, your first page will begin with an all-caps title . . . proceed to a "FADE IN:" . . . and then get down to business.

The rules on conditions of work are precisely the same as those we noted in our section on the fact film. *Always,* you establish whether a sequence is INTERIOR or EXTERIOR, its SETTING, and whether it's NIGHT or DAY; and you present them in that order.

From there on, you set forth what's seen and what's heard, with as little extraneous matter as possible. Particularly, go light on trying to tell the director how to direct your epic, save insofar as technical details are necessary to make clear an effect you're trying to achieve.

Thus, Director may not see fit to use the "SLOW PAN" in sequence 1. But it does show him the way you visualize the scene, and that can be helpful even if he chooses to go another route.

Sequence 2 makes reference to something "OFF SCREEN"—that is, not shown—and, via the word "SOUND," lets Director know you think the sound effect (often abbreviated to "FX" or "SFX") of Pilar's footsteps would be a nice touch here. Calling for a "DOLLY" shot of her legs as she moves down the hall really is out of your domain, but we can rationalize it on grounds that we're trying for a particular effect: building audience interest via curiosity by showing only Pilar's feet and legs. Same for the "HOLD" while she unlocks the door.

Note, too, that we give each character's name ALL CAPS the first time he/she appears—a flag to warn Director that this is a new member of the cast taking the stage. The thumbnail description of the person is designed to help refresh his memory so he won't momentarily confuse Pilar with the villainess or her aging aunt.

Sequence 3 satisfies our curiosity as to whether or not Pilar has two heads . . . gives her a degree of identity through her "nurse-type uniform." We watch her discovery of Dr. Suarez's corpse . . . experience the impact of it in terms of the CLOSEUP of the corpse and the CLOSEUP of Pilar's reaction.

Some directors might object to the writer's usurping their prerogatives by calling for closeups here. But not many. Why not? Because, you'll recall, the closeup is an emphasis shot—which is to say, its use is based on the assumption that you have something to emphasize . . . with *reason,* because you have a point you want to make.

Here, said point is (Closeup 1) the horror and ugliness that is dead Suarez, and (Closeup 2) Pilar's horrified reaction to the shock of Closeup 1.

The logic of this isn't likely to be lost on Director. Consequently, odds are he won't protest too loudly.

Will he necessarily shoot the scene according to your specifications? No. There are a dozen ways to film any sequence. It's quite possible his ideas on the subject are as good or better than yours. But at least you've given him a notion of the way *you* see it, and the effect *you'd* like to get, and that in itself is worth the effort.

End of closeup. Pilar rallies and crosses to phone—and that in itself tells us something about her; she could equally well have fled or fainted. But either of those reactions would have made a different person of her; moved her out of the role she's destined to play.

Observe, also, that we've written this to give our girl a few bits of business—things to keep her busy and the audience's attention focused.

Take the business of keeping her busy: The Pilars of low-budget filmdom aren't likely to be played by the industry's Bette Davises or Katharine Hepburns. It does no harm to offer them a crutch or two in the way of simple action. They can always ignore it if they don't need it; and if they do, it's there and ready.

Similarly, in sequence 4, we've provided Karl with the physical tag of peripheral vision and explained how it affects him. With that motivation at hand, the actor playing the role can work to the limits of his competence—devising all sorts of business if that's within his ingenuity; plodding with just the fact that his "gait is tentative and erratic," if he can come up with nothing more.

So much for technicalities and format. On to

2. Visualization.

The first step in writing any master scene script is to visualize the action, no matter how clumsily. You can always correct flaws later.

So. The preliminaries are over. You've completed outline, treatment, and sequence outline of your new picture. Now it's time to begin the master scene script. To that end, sit down at your typewriter. Check out the first sentence of your thumbnail synopsis of Sequence 1: "Sam Jones rides into town."

Close your eyes, now. Envision that opening scene, the way your imagination would like to see it on the screen.

Next, write down what your imagination reveals as if there were a screen inside your forehead and you were describing a picture projected onto it from the nether reaches of your brain.

Maybe what you see comes out like this: "The dusty main street of a windswept western town. SAM JONES—tall, tight-lipped, saturnine, unshaven—rides in, horse moving at a tired walk. The rider looks neither to right or left, giving no heed to the loafers' curious glances . . ."

Or, maybe you see it differently: "Mud stands fetlock-deep in Pila Seca's main street. A monster draft horse, saddleless and of the type sometimes termed an Oregon puddin'-foot, plods wearily through it. Its rider, SAM JONES, stands out in marked contrast: small, dudishly dressed even unto a derby hat and pince-nez glasses, a man totally out of context in terms of both horse and setting . . ."

Or: "It's business as usual on Packrat's rutted, 1880-model main street. But then someone spots an incoming rider . . . stares slack-jawed. For the rider, SAM JONES, is mounted backwards on a particularly mean-looking mule. Tied aboard his steed, he wears only the nether half of a pair of long johns and a layer of tar and feathers so thick it's well-nigh impossible to identify the man himself . . ."

No shots have been designated, please note; no camera angles specified. Yet in each instance, a word picture of sorts has been painted, specific enough to spell out clearly just what's wanted, even while leaving plenty of leeway for the director.

How do you develop the knack of writing this kind of thing?

A first step is practice. Look out the nearest window—or from your car, or at a picture, or whatever. Then, closing your eyes, try to recreate the scene mentally and translate it into words on paper.

Or, read a chapter from a book and then, following the same process of visualization, cast it into master scene form.

Count on it, the first few times the result will be less than dazzling. But eventually the pictures you seek to paint with words will take form more and more clearly.

It will help, too, if you bear in mind the tremendous value of *contrast,* unanticipated juxtaposition of elements, as a tool, in creating any picture.

Thus, our first Sam Jones, above—"Tall, tight-lipped, saturnine, unshaven"—is the traditional spaghetti western figure: totally predictable within the story pattern. As such, he tends to be routine and so to offer little stimulus to the imagination.

Sam No. 2, the pince-nezed tenderfoot, is less of a stick figure. Consequently, he spurs us to greater flights of fancy. His contacts and confrontations come through more vividly just because they're fresher; less predictable.

Sam No. 3 is even more colorful, more stimulating. His very dilemma is suggestive of all sorts of incidents and bits of business.

This is not to say that contrast is the answer to all problems. But the injection of one unanticipated, out-of-place element ever so often will set inspirational juices to churning in you—and maybe even give you a sharper, brighter, more intriguing presentation.

3. Point of attack.

Just where do you start your story? Or your sequence?

Just where, that is, in terms of the specific image you seek to have placed on the screen.

These are the questions we deal with when we consider the problem of point of attack.

Where your picture's concerned, the opening shots are something you worked out long, long ago, in treatment and in step outline. But it's one thing to plan, another to write, as Bobby Burns observed in his line about the best-laid schemes of mice and men. Quite possibly, when the cards are down, you'll find it desirable to pick a different note on which to start than you anticipated.

The same principle applies to the beginning of each sequence, each group of related shots.

Whether the issue is story or sequence, the issue is the same. Two principles are involved:

a. Know the note you wish to strike—and strike it.

Are you shooting for impact? Mood? Characterization? Whatever your choice, know what you're after and strive for footage that will convey it.

Thus, in our *Orbis* opening, the object is to inspire horror. The point of attack is designed to achieve that end. Viewers first are given a few moments to absorb a proper mood via a "spookily lighted" room. The fact that nothing happens is intentional, in order to build anticipation of fearful things to come.

Then, the first shock note: the corpse of Dr. Suarez, complete with bloody axe and the implication of jeopardy which that implies.

(Would it have been better to handle the corpse less graphically? Using a shadow image, perhaps, rather than actual gore? Who knows? A good case can be made for either view.)

Pilar's approach and entry follows, built by the fact that our view of her at first is limited to her legs. Simultaneously, the shadow of jeopardy grows also: Where before there was only a corpse, now we have a girl whom, we sense, is potentially a living victim.

Closeups build the scene. Pilar reacts courageously—that is, in character—to the shock.

Enter Karl, personification of menace. The sound of his footsteps—a non-normal sound, please note—comes first, in order to build viewer anticipation of something horrible about to happen. When we see him, his sinister appearance intensifies this feeling. But when he closes in. Pilar, though obviously terrified, still reacts with courage, So . . .

Well, you get the idea.

b. Beware the dragging windup.

Most of us tend to go for the long windup, when beginning either film or sequence.

Quite possibly, jumping into the middle of action or tension would prove more satisfactory.

Thus, is it really necessary to show Character ringing the doorbell and explaining the reason for his visit? Might it not prove more effective to cut from him hanging up the phone, say, to the moment he tells Villain he's under arrest?

More and more, in recent years, both audiences and filmmakers have shown less patience with plodding progression and long-winded explanations. From the stroke of the gavel to the clang of the cell door slamming shut is increasingly the rule.

4. Sequence development.

Developing an effective sequence is a complex business, and one learned largely through experience. But we can at least consider some of the elements involved.

a. Action.

Writers, being word people, tend to rely far too much on dialogue when they start scripting.

This is, to say the least, an error. More crucial by far is the matter of who does what, and what happens, for on the screen, especially, actions speak louder than words.

Our *Orbis* teaser offers a case in point. Not one word is spoken, unless you want to class Pilar's scream as speech. Yet the message and impact are strong and clear.

Which brings to mind an instance in which I was hired to write a science fiction script involving a future society where life centered around games. Although I struggled valiantly with it, I was cut off at the treatment. Why? Because, in large measure, my approach was too verbal, too cerebral.

The next writer fared better. He left out all the dialogue, all the discussions and explanations, in favor of simply having people moved about on a sort of giant chessboard.

Please don't make my mistake in your own writing. Analyze what happens in any given sequence, and then try to let the action tell the story insofar as possible.

b. Dialogue.

In spite of what I've said in *a,* above, dialogue is essential in most pictures. How to handle it? The preceding chapter gives some hints.

In addition, before you write, get the sequence's mood firmly in mind. Impose that mood on any information to be conveyed. Then, write your dialogue to fit.

c. Proportion.

Not every sequence in a film is equally important.

That being the case, you need to decide which loom large and which can be held small.

The important sequences—those in which your central characters are in greatest jeopardy, standing to lose all—should be built big. The "foothill" or transitional units can be passed over relatively lightly.

How do you build a sequence big?

You prepare for it by planting and building up its importance and potentialities of peril in preliminary episodes. Then, when the sequence itself arrives, you write it in terms of subjective time, as it were, stretching it out with detail and hazard and complications to match the dimensions of excitement you wish to create in your viewers.

(Objective time is the kind you measure with a watch. Subjective is based on emotion: your feelings, your degree of tension. It's what makes the two minutes while you climb the steps to your girl's apartment seem like ten, or the half-hour spent waiting to see if your agonized, convulsing, strychnine-poisoned cat will live or die drag on forever.)

Consider, for example, the car-elevated train chase in *The French Connection.* Hero's object in this sequence is to capture one of Villain's henchmen who's escaping via el. To that end, Hero drives recklessly in pursuit under the el tracks. A dozen times he barely misses other cars, el posts, and the like. Once, for nerve-shredding seconds, it seems certain that he's going to hit a woman with a baby carriage. But in the end everyone survives, though Hero's quarry still eludes him.

Now this episode (or the chase in any one of a hundred other recent pictures, for that matter) could very well have been presented as a minor transitional sequence. Instead, writer and/or director chose to build it to a major crisis. To this end, (1) the importance of capturing the pursued hoodlum was clearly established, (2) the hazards involved were brought into sharp focus, and (3) the sequence itself was shot and cut with tremendous attention to detail (especially detail exciting to the audience in its empathy-provoking implications or peril), ignoring clock time in favor of subjective time.

How do you hold a sequence small?

You deal with its content as transitional or of minor importance, rather than building it up as vital or climactic. Perhaps this means bridging endless miles of travel with a few shots of landscape sliding by. Or emphasizing trivia or tedium, as when Hero questions three or four people as to Heroine's whereabouts without avail. Or restraining the emotion in a confrontation, so that Audience remains relatively calm and unexcited, as in the wryly ironic pseudo-suicide sequences in *Harold and Maude.*

Beyond this, and as an overall guiding principle, write each sequence the way you feel it. Then, later, expand or trim as needed.

d. Pacing and placement.

In writing any sequence, consider carefully how it will fit into the picture as a whole. Specifically, bear in mind the sequences it follows, and those which will follow it.

The idea is to build to a pre-planned pattern, with crisis peaks spaced for maximum effectiveness—an individual matter with each picture—and intensification of tension from low points to high.

It helps, too, to try to avoid jerkiness, in favor of a reasonably smooth, rhythmic pace.

5. Continuity.

At last your screenplay is roughed in.

Next question: Do the sequences hang together?

Making sequences hang together is a function of continuity and, by and large, is a problem of the director and the editor. But the writer sets the stage for it, as it were, by his selection and arrangement of his material.

Thus, every event and incident should lead logically to the next. Or, as we phrased it in our discussion of dialogue, each unit should, in effect, acknowledge the existence of the one ahead.

In large measure, this comes down to anticipating your audience's anticipations. Setting up your situation, you arouse viewer interest in certain issues, thus developing the old "What's going to happen now?" angle. Then, tantalizing fragment by tantalizing fragment, you incorporate answers to the question. Simultaneously, you introduce new elements, new questions, to build tension—that is, interest—higher. But never do you lose sight of your line of development or the necessity of linking each new bit to that which preceded it.

6. Characterization.

In developing each sequence,

a. Is each character consistent?

Does your heroine act like a sexpot one moment, an icebox the next? Is your hero swaggering now, cringing then, scholarly the other time?

Consistency and believability are virtually synonymous where character is concerned. Do check for it!

b. Does Character break out of his role?

Pilar, in our *Orbis* sample, is the heroine. In keeping with her role, in the course of the script, she demonstrates courage, warmth, and concern for others.

Karl, the maniacal killer who assails her, also demonstrates characteristics geared to his role: coldness, violence, disregard for human life.

A Pilar who combined courage with coldness, on the other hand, would prove less the heroine; and, more important, would tend to confuse the audience. So would a Karl who murdered ruthlessly even while concerned for others.

This is not to say that characters must—or even should—be all black or all white. After all, Boris Karloff's *Frankenstein* was agonized victim more than fiend. But it is a fact that the subtle grays are more difficult to conceive and write. At first, especially, it's wise not to stretch your luck and skill too far.

c. Does Character have something to do?

Nothing is more deadly than a character who sits around waiting for the feathers to grow. If he has nothing story-vital to do, why include him?

d. Does Character have tags to wave?

Dr. Orbis is tagged by his thick glasses and sinister smile; Karl, by his blank eyes, axe, and erratic gait. Pilar has her nurse's uniform; Luis his reckless courage.

Granted, such billboard labels aren't always essential. But neither do they constitute a cardinal sin, especially where easy identification is desired.

7. Dramatization.

To dramatize is to present or represent in a dramatic manner— that is, in a manner striking in appearance or effect.

The essence of dramatization is the arousal of feeling.

Next question: In each sequence, are you making the most of your story's dramatic potential?

The biggest part of this work has already been done, of course, as you built outline, story treatment, and step outline.

Now, however, as you write your master scene script, the issue is to hunt down details that evoke the feeling you seek to arouse. For if you show only the facts of your saga, you'll end up with emptiness and mediocrity.

To this end, be sure that your key characters have strong attitudes in regard to each developing situation—attitudes so intense as to drive them to action and to conflict.

Reveal these attitudes in appropriate description of the details of your characters' behavior. For to capture feelings on film, the production crew must have something to shoot which will create the feeling sought.

8. Believability.

How do you make a film believable?

a. You provide justification for everything that happens.

That is, you motivate your characters to go in the direction you wish. You provide stimuli which lead them to react.

Equally important, you show your audience these stimuli, these motivations so that, seeing, they will unconsciously say to themselves, "Yes, yes. If I were this character, faced with these circumstances, these pressures, then it's conceivable that I, too, might do as Character is doing."

In other words, understanding *why* your character takes the course he does, your audience believes.

b. You proportion response to stimulus in every detail.

When a girl refuses a man a casual request for a date and he bursts into tears, most of us will feel he's *overreacting*.

When a child, screaming and bloody, comes rushing into a room and his mother fails to interrupt her bridge game, we'll tend to think she's *underreacting*.

Overreaction and underreaction are two major sources of disbelief in film. Viewers simply will not accept the character who behaves in a way they believe to be grossly exaggerated, either up or down, except in comedy.

Controlling such exaggerated actor behavior is, of course, the director's job. But again, as in so many other aspects of film making, the writer can help.

Cases in point are beyond number. But one that I particularly remember is Billy Wilder's answer to a question as to why he began *Some Like It Hot* with the St. Valentine's Day Massacre. The issue, he said, was that a truly powerful motivation was necessary to make it believable that Jack Lemmon and Tony Curtis, the two musicians, would don girls' clothes and take it on the run. Anything less than the threat of death would have made their behavior seem gross overreaction. But with the killings firmly established, their flight in drag appears plain good sense—whereupon, the picture was off to a credible start.

9. Clarity.

Your script, presentation of your visualizations, will be helped markedly by clarity of language. A few points to bear in mind are:

The nouns most useful to you are those classed as *pictorial*: those that flash snapshots in your reader's mind.

The specific noun ordinarily is stronger than the general, the concrete than the abstract, the definite than the vague, the singular than the plural.

Active verbs, verbs that show something happening, are stronger than passive. And for film script purposes, you of course use them in the present tense.

Judiciously used, adjectives help to sharpen a word picture: "tall, tight-lipped, saturnine" says something about both man and mood.

Same for adverbs: "turns angrily" is different from "turns tearfully" or yet "turns slack-jawed."

Short words are a virtue. So are short sentences—especially short simple declarative sentences. "Mud stands fetlock-deep in Pila Seca's main street" sets a stage with minimum waste motion.

Clarity comes first, always, in a script. But vividness is no sin if you can manage it without conflict. When we say that a man "wears only the nether half of a pair of long johns and a layer of tar and feathers," hopefully we've established an image that will inspire Director to something better than routine handling.

*   *   *

So there you have it: nine points to help you build a master scene script.

Remember, though, some things writing a script may be, but mechanical it isn't. In getting any kind of words on paper, the trick is first to learn the ropes. This, I trust, is something this book will help you do.

When you write, however, fly by the seat of your pants, following your impulses and instincts. Afterwards is the time to think of rules, when you go back over your epic, checking and correcting.

*   *   *

What about writing a shooting script for your feature film?

Please don't.

Why not?

Because it will waste your time and energy for nothing.

Thing is, as I've so often said before, but now reiterate, directors feel that breaking down a script into shots is something that's strictly their business. So, even worse than resenting your efforts, they'll ignore them.

That means that, for you, the only time to write a shooting script is when Director, of his own volition, suggests that you and he sit down to work out same together.

What about your second draft screenplay, final draft screenplay, rewrites of screenplays, and the like?

Sorry. First draft is as far as we go in this book.

How so?

Because these later stages are something you have no need—or opportunity—to deal with until you've had a first draft screenplay approved by someone.

When that time comes, revision will be a subject of endless discussion and conferences. Your guidelines then will be the decisions reached by you and your colleagues. Nothing I might say here, beyond the principles already set forth, will help much.

Besides, it's more important now that you get on to an appraisal of various and sundry tricks of the trade of scriptwriting, as set forth in Part 3 of the present volume.

PART THREE

TRICKS OF THE TRADE

■ ■ ■ ■ ■ ■ ■

CHAPTER 14:

Adaptation and Its Problems

How do you adapt a novel, play, fact book, or what have you for film use?

Or, to put it another way, how do you translate a printed work into script form?

The big issue is of course relative complexity. A novel may run 500 pages or more. Most films must be squeezed into 90 minutes running time. Cutting—often, drastic cutting—therefore becomes essential.

Thus, consider a novel we'll call *Monster*. Told in first person, it runs 13 chapters, 255 pages. Each chapter is comprised of one segment of present action, another of flashback background material. More than 20 characters are developed.

How might you approach the adaptation of *Monster* to film form, so far as the script is concerned? There are three major possibilities to consider:

1. You can follow the book.
2. You can work from key scenes.
3. You can construct an original screenplay based on the book.

To a considerable degree, each of these procedures overlaps the others. Yet each in its way is also separate and distinct, with individual strengths and weaknesses, advantages and flaws, to the point that each rates individual attention.

1. You can follow the book.

Wild are the anguished cries of critics outraged by the fact that a given film—which is to say, a given script—doesn't follow the book.

These ladies and gentlemen might not scream quite so loudly, however, were they themselves confronted by the problems of adaptation.

Take *Monster*, for example. Much of its impact is gained from its meshing of present and past. Chapter 1's flashback carries us to a point 263 days before the present action. But the gap narrows, chapter by chapter, until, in Chapter 12, the flashback ends just prior to the present action of Chapter 1. Chapter 13 melds both past and present in a final wrap-up.

Do I need to tell you that any attempt to approximate this pattern on the screen can lead only to total audience confusion?

Further, *Monster* is a taut, suspenseful story—perhaps too much so, for each unit of past and of present builds to a stomach-knotting climax.

How can this be handled, in a film? True, it works well enough on paper, where transitions and the first-person central character's introspections provide sufficient change of pace and release of tension to balance the climaxes' mounting suspense and rising action. But development of 25 separate major crises is impossible in 90 minutes running time. To attempt it is to assure a crowded, jerky, melodramatic botch of a picture—and this without even considering the problem of how to introduce and build 20-odd characters.

The only solution, obviously, is to cut, cut, cut. The question is—cut what?

This is a Gordian knot without a sword. Whatever choice you make will unquestionably be wrong in the eyes of some; and odds are you can't conceivably blue-pencil enough to bring the picture within acceptable length, unless you resort to some version or other of procedures 2 or 3, as described below.

2. You can work from key scenes.

At the opposite extreme from slavishly following the book lies this approach. It has Writer shuffling the book's pages in search of scenes which appeal to him as colorful, dramatic, and at least indicative of the author's concept and story line. These he arranges in some sort of climactic order (not necessarily that followed in the book), then builds bridging passages between them, using either materials which the book provides or which he himself develops.

In the case of *Monster*, Writer might very well decide to build his script in a straight time line, ignoring such of the book's alternating flashbacks as he cannot juggle to fit the straight-line concept. For an opening, he picks a luridly esoteric scene in which a sex-oriented satanist cult is meeting. Male and female leads are both in attendance, with Male lusting after Female. But she refuses him—she won't betray her aging husband.

A scene in which Male Lead swims across a lake at night to murder Husband follows. Then, one in which he discovers that Female Lead, now his wife, has tricked him into committing the murder, simultaneously incriminating him in such a manner that he's doomed to be her slave for all time to come.

Further developments see Female Lead slay a fellow-cultist. Realizing he's next in line, Male Lead sets about to commit a series of fake lust killings, in the course of which he can also murder Female Lead; and so on.

His key scenes chosen, Writer now sets about bridging the gaps between them in such a manner as to give the final product some sense of continuity and logic. Thus, he decides that the incriminating evidence against Male Lead will unknowingly be held by Female Lead's younger sister, a girl as innocent as Female Lead is evil.

This touch particularly pleases Writer, since he recognizes that the characters in the original novel are too distasteful and perverted to serve as hero and heroine in any film of consequence. By playing Sister as heroine, he can in effect make the picture one long chase, with both Male and Female Leads secretly trying to kill her, complete even unto a quick save at the climax.

It's not hard to see why many viewers will find this filmed version of *Monster* unsatisfactory. In effect, they've been given a whole new picture—one with little resemblance to the novel save for the characters and buckets of blood.

Shall we draw a kindly veil and move on to our final approach?

3. You can construct an original screenplay based on the book.

This technique follows the line laid out in Chapter 7. To make a film script of *Monster*, attack the adaptation as if you were putting together an original screenplay. That is, start by nailing down what you consider to be the story's premise. (*"What if a man sets out to fake a series of lust murders to mask his killing of his wife—and then discovers he's actually a real lust murderer at heart?"*)

Next, decide on a point of view. (The novel stays with the murderer himself.) But is that best? Would it be better to use the angle of the wife, for instance? Or a psychiatrist? Or a detective?

Now, lay out a starting lineup. (*"Unable longer to endure the harassment inflicted on him by his evil, sadistically domineering wife, Celeste, Blair Hilliard determines to kill her, masking the slaying with a series of fake lust murders. But can he succeed when his arch-foe, mysterious cult chief Master Satan, refuses to stay dead?"*)

And so it goes, as you move on through your story, step by step . . . determining beginning, middle, end . . . writing a story treatment . . . breaking the treatment down into a step outline . . . building up a first draft master scene script . . .

Will this prove easy? Hardly. For where *Monster* the novel may capture thoughts, develop interior monologues, range through years of flashbacked time and the whole United States, and explore an infinity of bypaths and subplots, you the scriptwriter can't afford such.

Instead, you must reduce the mass to filmable dimensions. Which is to say, you must decide which of the maze of potential story lines you wish to follow . . . which characters should be built up, which jettisoned . . . which relationships offer most potential . . . which scenes hold greatest dramatic strength . . . which incidents must be devised and incorporated to draw the various bits together.

Flashbacks? In essence, they constitute someone remembering in the present something which happened in the past. Unless that remembrance is vital to the story, you very well may skip them entirely.

If, on the other hand, a flashback's content must of necessity be included, you may (a) reduce it to dialogue references—that is, let someone reveal the essential data verbally, or (b) play it out as a dramatized incident, dissolving from present to past and letting the characters involved live through the experience, then dissolving back to the present.

As a general rule, however, it's wise to avoid flashbacks wherever possible, simply because they bring your story's forward movement to a halt. This may either bore or confuse your viewers. In consequence, most of the time, it's better to stick with present action: what's happening now.

Yet the task with which *Monster* confronts you is relatively simple, compared with that which faced the writers of the scripts for such books as *Gone With The Wind, Anthony Adverse, The Man With The Golden Arm, Clockwork Orange,* and a hundred others.

Clearly enough, too, the three plans of attack I've outlined are far from exclusive. At one time or another, on any adaptation, you'll jump from tight adherence to the original here to working from key scenes there, to drawing out a premise and starting lineup from your material elsewhere in order to tie otherwise disparate elements together. And that's fine too. As I've said so many times, the big thing is to get the job done.

Over and beyond broad reformulations such as those discussed so far, the question of what details to cut always arises.

The answer is, cut facts—whole incidents, if need be. Why? Because the heart of any film is *feeling*.

This is diametrically opposite to the tendency of most beginners. Faced with a series of seven incidents centering on a boy's or girl's departure, the new writer invariably will try to crowd all in.

What he should be doing instead is asking himself one vital question: What dominant feeling is the novel's author trying to convey through the incidents? Passion? Poignancy? Relief? Or what?

Thus, suppose it soon becomes apparent that Girl feels poignancy, Boy relief, at their impending separation.

Obviously, seven scenes aren't necessary to convey this. All Writer needs to do is write—or rewrite—one to make clear the characters' divergent feelings, and he can move on again with pages saved.

Of course, this is not to say that cutting is necessarily the writer's only problem. Indeed, the opposite may be the case, as when he finds himself forced to expand a short story to fill 90 minutes. Yet that too can be managed—witness the brilliant work of Dudley Nichols in expanding Ernest Haycox's *Collier's* story into the classic *Stagecoach,* or the Mark Hellinger adaptation of Ernest Hemingway's *The Killers.* The issue is merely one of taking the original story as a springboard, then building a broader work upon it.

Play adaptation? It offers its own headaches. Trapped within the limits of the proscenium arch or arena staging, relying heavily on dialogue for its effects, the play's thrust is far different from that of film. To adapt it for screen use demands a willingness to cut it loose from the stage's confines and conventions . . . open it up to a wider sweep of action and of setting. Too slavish adherence to the playwright's conception can only destroy it.

Adaptation of factual material—a biography, say, or an account of some sort of adventure, discovery, or expedition? Your main problem quite possibly will be avoidance of that overdramatization which embarrasses and infuriates participants, heirs, and assigns. Wives of departed heroes rarely enjoy seeing their husbands portrayed as leering rakes, scientists cringe when colleagues kid them about the simplism or inaccuracy of filmed laboratory techniques, and no tough cop likes it when his buddies in the squad room play their own version of his deeds of derring-do.

I wish I had remedies for all such headaches. Too often, unfortunately, the writer is trapped between producer demands and subject sensitivities. Your biggest assets in such situations are a real determination to give your subject a straight count; honest sympathy for survivors; a willingness to develop your people as warts-and-all human beings, and enough of a sense of humor to incorporate such immortal lines as the one I picked up from a detective describing a blood-curdling shoot-out: "Warning shots, hell! I was just plain missin'!"

*　　　*　　　*

One final thought: Whatever your adaptation assignment, often the result will be a script—and film—which on the surface shows little relationship to the material from which it's taken; and viewers and media alike—and, quite possibly, the original author—will rave at the way you've "corrupted" the work.

Yet if you've done an honest job and played in luck, without too much interference from actors or director or front office or elsewhere, quite possibly you will have created a work which not only holds firm to the spirit of the original, but actually offers better entertainment.

If, on the other hand, you try to cling too tightly to chapter and verse of your source material, you very well may end up with a script which never quite jells: a straggly thing replete with loose ends, abortive scenes, jerky development, and characters who never quicken.

On that thought, we'll move on to another subject: the story conference, the writer and his people.

Read it. It's vital!

CHAPTER 15:

Surviving Story Conferences

It may come as a shock to you, but your success as a film scriptwriter probably depends less on your skill with words than it does on your ability to deal with people.

How so? Because scriptwriting is no ivory tower occupation. Too much money is involved in filmmaking for that—so much it makes people in power nervous. Result: They're forever looking over your shoulder: picking holes in your work, shooting angles.

This is true in both fact and feature fields. The scene of the battle ordinarily is a small meeting known as a story conference, in which your script project is dissected and discussed in an effort to produce the best (or at least the most profitable) product possible. To that end, you sit down with a group of script-wise experts—executive producer, producer, story editor, director, other writers, their aides and assigns, or the like—and analyze what you've done, are doing, and propose to do, with special emphasis on what the Powers That Be consider weaknesses or problems.

Since the people involved are certainly experienced, and quite possibly brilliant, where scripts and films are concerned, the result can be fantastically helpful on occasion. But it can also be frustrating, not to mention destructive of your enthusiasm—the more so, since you'll be expected to work within the framework of the conference's decisions. Nevertheless, it's an accepted way of doing business in all phases of filmmaking, so you might as well get used to it.

Ideally, the man in charge of a story conference should be an individual who (a) thoroughly understands the process and problems of filmmaking; (b) knows what he wants, even though he's not inflexible about it; (c) expresses his views freely, clearly, specifically, and persuasively; and (d) makes all necessary decisions without delay and then stands firmly behind them.

Such men do exist. It's been my pleasure to work with a number of them.

Unfortunately, however, they tend to be rather rare birds. More common are those unhappy specimens who don't know film, who demand the impossible or undesirable, who can't make up their minds, who won't commit themselves, and who refuse to take responsibility. The results, for the scriptwriter, can prove very sad.

Sooner or later, you too will encounter one or more such types.

Next question: How can you best cope with each?

The man in the first category, the one who doesn't know film, isn't a variety you encounter often among feature picture executives these days. Among fact film clients, on the other hand, he's as prevalent as ants at a picnic.

For you as a not-yet-seasoned film writer, this type constitutes a special problem, in that it may take you a while to recognize him for what he is.

Thus, when Mr. Jones suggests that your feature's hero turn out to be a transvestite, or that dancing girls costumed as the components of your client's gear train perform a ballet at your fact film's climax, you may be taken somewhat aback. Yet the solution is reasonably simple.

First, unless you're being questioned directly, keep quiet—someone else among those present may burst out laughing, thus both getting you off the spot and letting you know how Herr Jones' thinking rates.

Second, make it a point to stay properly respectful, no matter how stupid or senseless an idea/suggestion/question seems to be.

Third, explain your own position and reasoning as clearly and convincingly as you can. Because before you're through, count on it, enough will have been said to clue you in as to just where your man stands.

Quite possibly, you'll even find he's also Man No. Two, the one who makes impossible demands.

If this should prove the case, honesty is your best refuge. Tell him the truth about Busby Berkeley chorus lines in $15,000 industrials, or the chances of Charlton Heston in drag hitting the box office jackpot. (And yes, I do remember Jack Lemmon and Tony Curtis in *Some Like It Hot*.) Then, if he still insists, go ahead. As to whether you also ask him whether he brushes off the advice of his doctor and lawyer too—well, how much of a gambler are you?

What about the man who can't make up his mind, or won't commit himself? One way out is to misstate his position purposely—not sarcastically, but soberly; straight-faced: "You mean, you want to play this so Sitting Bull is really Custer's lost half-brother?" "Are you crazy?" "Well, if you don't mean that, what *do* you mean?"

Quite possibly, all this will infuriate your man, but it does force him to take a stand. Indeed, if your twist is sufficiently far out, Man's sense of humor may get the better of him, whereupon the conference tension eases and things start falling into place.

The man who refuses to take responsibility can give you special nightmares. Ordinarily, the game he plays is "pass the buck," with you as the receiver. To that end, scared rabbit that he is, he delegates duties to committees which you are supposed to coordinate, sends you "F.Y.I." critiques from people who have nothing to do with the project, and otherwise lays the ground for hanging any failure around your neck and well wide of his.

A case in point: Walking into an alleged story conference at a major governmental agency, I discovered 20-odd "advisors" assembled. All I was supposed to do was incorporate their off-the-cuff notions into my script, and take the rap in case anyone later disagreed with same.

Instead, I walked out. Which may, in its way, be as good a method of resolving such dilemmas as any.

Not that it will often prove necessary. Most often, impasses break as soon as you explain how eager you are to do the job; it's just that you don't want to infringe or take advantage by making decisions outside your jurisdiction.

But this recital is beginning to sound choleric. Let's move on to something more positive—specifically, an experience-gleaned list of ten ways of approaching problems that may help you through your own first story conferences:

1. Go in loaded.

I still recall a meeting I once had with an agent I wanted to impress. Eagerly, I plunged into a description of the opening of my script. It was a good opening, too, believe me.

Finally I paused for breath.

Agent gestured impatiently. "All right. What happens next?"

I gaped. Because while I certainly did know what happened next, I—well, I didn't know it on quite the same level as I did the opening. Matter of fact, when I thought back on it, I'd somehow assumed that everyone would be so stunned with my magnificent beginning the rest would just sort of develop naturally.

I really did know the rest of the story, though, after a fashion, so I managed to grope my way through it.

To say the agent was unimpressed with my presentation is to put it mildly. Our association began and ended in that one meeting. Which was sad, but it taught me a lesson, cheap at the price.

That lesson was: *Go in loaded!* Know everything there is to know about your story, be it fact or fiction. Be prepared for every objection, every question. Even if you do, indeed, your colleagues still will find enough loopholes in your logic!

2. *Play to your audience.*

In story conferences, a scriptwriter needs to a degree to be an actor, adapting himself to the tone of the group.

Thus, you may be the lone, youthful outsider in a group of aging corporate executives. Or the college graduate confronting self-made men up from the foundry. Or the civilian among military, the layman among doctors, the high school dropout among professors, the kid with three one-acts to his credit up against a hundred years of major studio experience.

Your best beginning stance, in each case, is one of pleasant, relaxed friendliness.

Beyond that, play to your audience, the other men and women present. If they're all deadly serious, don't crack jokes. If they talk football, come in on the chorus with a few reminiscences of your own favorite games. Are hangovers the issue? Be sympathetic. Does someone try to bully, or play big dog, or put you down? Stay courteous anyhow.

Which is not to say that you should fawn or grovel, you understand. Self-respect is never out of style. But this is the other man's turf, not yours, so within limits you'll do best to fit yourself to his pattern.

3. *Be prepared to take the lead.*

Some years ago I signed on to script a series of six films for a national organization. The pay was good, the subject interesting, and the steering committee with which I was to work congenial. Yet the first couple of sessions made it apparent nothing constructive was ever going to happen.

Why? Because, most often, unless a strong man is in charge, a committee tends to go in circles. Or, to put it another way, somebody has to take the lead in any creative effort.

In this particular instance, I was the one who took it, laying out a complete—if unauthorized—plan of attack on the project even unto brief synopses for each of the six pictures.

The committee, delighted, promptly approved the whole package, and we got down to work. But the fact remains that if I hadn't taken the first step, Lord knows when or if we'd have gotten started.

Bear this thought in mind with regard to your own projects. Ever so often, walking in cold, you'll discover that no one knows quite where to begin. When that happens, be sure you have some thoughts of your own in mind—some sort of concept or approach to serve as springboard.

For even if your associates reject it, it at least will serve to jar them off dead center.

On the other hand, don't be *too* quick to jump. The human ego is easily bruised, and your "presumption" can give you headaches that go on well-nigh forever.

4. Be prepared to TELL your story.

So there you are, in the story conference. A neatly duplicated copy of your epic lies on the table in front of each participant. Eagerly, you wait for their reactions.

Only then the man at the head of the table pushes the sheets aside. "Let's dispense with this stuff, Joe," he says. "What we want's the story. Just tell us about it."

Yes, it does happen, and more often than you might imagine. Why? Well, for one thing, it gets pretty dull in a few minutes if everyone sits around the table reading. But more important—and believe me, I'm not kidding when I say this—reading is a problem for a lot of people, and that includes even intelligent, educated, allegedly highly literate types. They simply can't cut it comfortably where a script page is concerned.

Result: "Just tell us about it."

So, just tell them, as clearly and effectively as you know how.

It goes without saying you'll tell them *more* clearly and *more* effectively if you've thought through the possibility of verbal presentation beforehand. A bit of rehearsal might not even hurt.

5. Talk scenes, not story.

"Telling" a script can be a tricky business. Often, before you're through, you find yourself tangled in such a maze of plot details that your audience hangs on the ropes.

Two small stratagems will help you:

First of all, *simplify* your presentation. The closer you can come to stripping it to bare bones, the better. (It's alleged that the line which sold Joe Levine on *Panic in Needle Park* was "Romeo and Juliet on junk.") Work for the "Who wants to do what and why can't he?" approach, the Objective-Obstacle-Outcome synopsis. Not too difficult a task, either, if you've built your script solidly, up step by step from a foundation of premise or core assertion. The mushy, unstructured jobs are the ones that kill you.

Second, insofar as practical, *talk scenes.*

That is to say, talk confrontations, color incidents, conflict units: the big, exciting moments that you can build the way you'd build your account of a bank robbery or marital battle that you witnessed. Tell them vividly, dramatically, so that they come alive in your listeners' minds and capture their imaginations, joining each episode to the next with a minimum of transition.

Is this a legitimate technique? It is indeed. As director Henry Hathaway has pointed out, "People never remember what they hear in a movie. They only recall what they see. The big hits have unforgettable scenes in them, usually action. Pictures that are filled with dialogue do not do as well." You're just capitalizing on that angle. Others will bring up any discrepancies of logic later.

6. Be animated.

If you tell a story as if it were dull, that's the way it's going to seem to your listeners. If, on the other hand, you come on strong, with maximum enthusiasm, your audience will respond in kind.

Obviously, you have to adjust this approach to your own style, your personality. And it doesn't mean pouring on the superlatives or adjectives. But if you can, in your own way, show that this is a story that excites you, you'll have won the biggest part of your battle.

7. Listen.

The reason other people are attending your story conference is to help improve your script. Most of them will be clever, creative, experienced. Often, they can and will give you new twists, improved ideas, sharper concepts.

They can do this, however, only if you do your part—that is, listen.

8. Hang loose.

Close corollary to point seven is that your mood as well as your ears must be receptive. Obviously, you're not going to agree with every idea that's tossed at you, but you should give each and every one honest consideration. A chip on your shoulder will only turn people off, and that you can't afford. Remember, damn it: They're here to *help* you!

9. Don't be afraid to keep it light.

Years ago I knew a used car salesman who always was good for a laugh. It got to where I looked forward to seeing him each morning as I walked past his lot to my office, just for the way he brightened my day with his latest gag.

Later, I learned his secret: His company provided its crew with a fresh, new one-liner daily.

You can do worse than to acquire a store of such yourself. Even the serious business of scriptwriting can stand a smile or two when there's a conference in the offing. No need to be a clown, you understand; but no need to wear a long face either. A cheerful group works better.

10. Stop.

Few things in a meeting are more painful than the man who won't let go. Whether he's ridden by insecurity, lacks judgment, or has a nagging wife who makes him want to stay away from home as long as possible, the fact remains that he makes everyone dread sessions with him.

It's worth your while, therefore, to cultivate a sense of timing; a feel for the moment when all that's pertinent has been said.

When that moment arrives, don't hesitate to beam, straighten up your papers, and say, "Well, that shapes things up, right? At least, so far as I'm concerned . . ." Then, if anyone else sees fit to halt the exodus, that's up to him. At least, you won't have been the one to play albatross.

Which makes this a good stopping-place for this chapter, too. For it's high time we were getting on to that most vital chapter of all in this epic work: How to sell your scripts.

CHAPTER 16:

The Scriptwriter as Businessman

This chapter will devote itself almost entirely to economics, pure even if not so simple. We'll tackle the subject on four levels:

1. How to get assignments.
2. How to handle assignments.
3. How to survive as a scriptwriter.
4. The agents and the Guild.
   Ready? Let's go!

1. How to get assignments.

How do you find work as a scriptwriter?

Let's take it for granted you've already explored—or will explore—all the usual routes: help wanted ads, college employment services, personal contacts, you name it.

If you're on the Coasts, East or West, in New York or Los Angeles, you can shoot assorted other angles. I've known people who took jobs as studio typists, for example, just in hopes that pounding through the pro work would teach them pro skills, or give them contacts, or what have you. Others have signed on as page-boys or gofers (go for coffee, go for cigarettes, go for my lucky piece that I left on the dressing table), cheap labor on non-union productions, and the like.

Sometimes, if you have enough of what our Jewish friends call *chutzpah*, you can scrape acquaintance with some old hand who's tired or has a liquor problem . . . get him to let you do the dog's work on a TV episode in exchange for a shared credit.

Again, reading *Variety* or the *Hollywood Reporter*, occasionally you'll
see ads from producers wanting scripts or writing help. And though the
boys in the know will tell you that all such are frauds and wastes of time,
I've still cashed checks from a few of them.

Writer's Digest periodically offers lists of film companies (fact film,
mostly) in the market for scripts. And magazines dealing with the
industry sometimes carry classified ads soliciting writers.

The American Film Institute's training programs are also worth
investigating, as are the internships announced on rare occasions by
various of the studios. And opportunities sometimes appear on the
bulletin boards or by word of mouth at such film schools as the
University of Southern California and the University of California at Los
Angeles.

Whatever path you choose, however, getting assignments and/or
selling scripts is seldom easy. But on the other hand, it's seldom quite as
impossible as it sometimes seems to the beginner; and the first step is
always the hardest.

The problem is, as you know if you've ever hunted for any kind of
job, that the boss always says he won't hire you because you have no
experience. Yet how are you to get experience if no one will hire you?

Well, in film script writing, fortunately, there *is* an answer. Not a
simple answer, you understand, nor a quick one, nor even a sure one.
But then, who ever promised you a rose garden in this business?

So: Your first step is to get yourself a film to script to prove your
worth.

To this end, you take the same road as does the freelance writer in
any other field. That is, you find yourself a subject and then you write a
script.

No, this isn't easy. But it *is* easier than it sounds. The trick is merely
to think and act *as if* you already were a scriptwriter, and so script a film.

Thus, let's assume you're a beginner, without contacts and stuck in
a town or city far from any major production center. Money is something you're short on, but you do have a certain amount of free time. So,
what do you do?

Take it in four steps:

a. Pick a worthy cause.

The world is full of "public service" causes that can't afford
commercially-produced films. So, pick one—anything from the United
Fund to the Listless League for Lost Leprechauns.

Research this group and its goals a bit. Develop some sort of core
assertion you think might help them on their way.

Then, make contact with the people in charge—informally and
casually, if you can. In the course of things, let it drop that you think a
film might do Group some good, and that you'd like to script such—for

free, of course. Would they, in their role of experts, help you get their position straight?

Count on it, they'll help. Or, if they won't, the officials of some other similar body will prove more farsighted.

At this point, you

b. Write the script.

Do this as your contribution to your career. Do it step by step, just as painstakingly as if you were being paid top dollar.

Approach? The big thing is, keep it simple. Avoid sync sound in favor of voice-over narration, or even live commentary by a speaker. Any angle is acceptable, so long as what you produce serves your group's cause and fills its need.

Once you've got a script, and your associates' agreement that it does the job,

c. Shoot some film.

Here you may go in a variety of directions. Maybe, since you can get by with a sample sequence or two or three, you'll find it easiest simply to buy a few hundred feet of film out of your own pocket, borrow an 8mm camera, and shoot and edit the stuff yourself. Or, there may be a movie bug in the group you're promoting. Or, a college film production class might prove willing to take over. Or, a local TV station conceivably will agree to do the picture as a public service project.

However you work it, hopefully you'll end up with a completed film or, at least, part of one.

Whereupon, take said film to every advertising and public relations agency, film production company, and TV station you can find. Show them film and script, tell them you're the guy who wrote it, and would they kindly consider giving you a whack at any script chores that come up in the days ahead?

You'll be surprised how many brownie points this approach will get you. For one thing, the fact that you come to an agency or producer or station with a can of film in your hand automatically will set you head and shoulders above the competition, if for no other reason than that most people involved with film are constitutionally unable to resist looking at the other fellow's product.

In addition, the fact of having that film says you really *are* a scriptwriter: You've conceptualized an idea in film form and set it down in words that someone, somehow, has translated into moving pictures.

Finally, the fact that you're free-lance and not asking to go on the payroll will give you an extra edge, because it offers the man you're talking to extra talent sans outlay. Given half a chance, he'll try to use you just so you'll stay available.

Beyond all this, there's no law that says you can't show your film and present your ideas to companies or organizations which you think might be in the market for a picture of their own. Talking around and reading trade journals might even see you taking off as a shoestring producer.

Also, it's entirely possible you'll find yourself in a film-related job in spite of yourself. TV stations, especially, often make room for a man or girl handy with ideas and typewriter.

But let's not pipe dream too far ahead. The big thing is, you've done a script—an at least partially produced script—and made some contacts.

Next step: Work at keeping said contacts alive. How? Well, one way is to send some sort of reminder—a note or postcard will do, providing you make it lively and clever—reminding each person on your list that you're still looking for scripts to write. Be sure to feature your name, address, and phone number prominently; and it won't do any harm to brag up any assignments you've won since you last saw Contact.

Another visit? Sure, providing you don't make yourself a nuisance by coming too often or staying too long.

Finally, any spare time you have can very well be devoted to working up yet another script/film, for two *are* better than one, if only to prove your first effort wasn't a flash in the pan.

What if you could care less about industrial/educational/documentary/promotional films? What if nothing save cinematic storytelling will satisfy you?

Well, you can shoot some angles there, too. I've never known a college drama department that didn't like original one-acts, for example. For a good reason: no royalties to pay.

So, write yourself a one-act. Then persuade said drama department—or a little theatre group, or a church school unit, or a union, or a lodge, or a high school—to stage it. Take it from one who's been there, you'll learn by it.

But your target's film, not theater, right? So, the very night your play makes its debut, ride the euphoria of the applause with a suggestion: "Hey! Let's film it!"

You're taking on a job, I warn you. But given a little luck, it will prove worthwhile.

First, of course, comes a script: an adaptation. Then, the recruiting of a crew to shoot it, probably in Super 8.

Again, you'll have a script and a can of film to show. Again, you'll be ready to make contacts.

*   *   *

Now one word of warning: Count on it in advance, the overwhelming majority of those of you who try this are going to fail. But that's the way it is, in the film business. It's rough, and you need every one of those nine attributes I listed in the opening chapter if you're to survive.

On the other hand, if you have backbone, persistence, talent, and whatever, this is at least a chance for you to put them on display. And that's all anyone can ask.

2. How to handle assignments.

You've already learned a high proportion of what you need to know on this subject from Chapter 2, "The Proposal Outline," and Chapter 15, "Surviving Story Conferences." But certain key points still can stand attention, as follows:

a. Do ask to see a sample script.

This book has, I trust, given you some idea of how to put a script together. But well-nigh every outfit has its own idiosyncrasies where style and format are concerned.

It follows, therefore, that it's worth your while to learn about these before you start. And the simple way is to ask the producer to loan you a script whose style he likes.

b. Do nail down deadlines.

Day before yesterday can be a pain—especially when it develops that's when you were to have turned your script in.

You see, in the early stages of a job, clients and producers can be ever so casual about when they expect a finished product. But that attitude may change overnight when it dawns on someone that they just might be able to show their gem at the June convention.

For your part, you can't afford that kind of unanticipated non-sense, nor yet the client's sudden assumption that you can produce rabbits out of hats if you just work 48-hour days like he doesn't. So, nail it down at the start just when you're expected to deliver what.

And then come through.

c. Do be certain who has final authority.

I learned about this the hard way, when I devoted a week's hard work to hammering out a proposal—and then discovered that the people who'd hired me didn't have the power to do so.

The kind of authority you need to be interested in is, who has final authority over acceptance of your script?

Point 2: Does everyone else in the operation agree that this man has the authority?

Both of these are questions I'd surely raise in the very first conference, in the course of explaining how a script is written, and setting up an operating procedure to follow.

d. Do be sure you have a technical advisor.

I've already yakked at length on this point. This time, I bring it up just so you'll remember it.

Equally important, be sure Technical Advisor knows what's required of him. Neither you nor he will be happy otherwise.

e. Do insist on signed approvals.

Unhappy is the writer who, starting on his shooting or master scene script, finds that Client has suddenly changed his mind, so now they're going to start over again with a new concept.

He'll be ever unhappier if his agreement hasn't provided for Client approval signatures of proposal, treatment, sequence outline, and so on, so that Client must pay extra for any approved work which, later, must be changed/done over.

f. Do spell out payment terms.

How much are you paid for scripting a film?

Obviously, that depends in large degree on Client, your skill, your reputation, your availability, and the situation.

There's a marked difference, too, between the rates for fact and feature films. Indeed, the circumstances vary so much we'll take up features in a separate section of this chapter.

Fact film hangs much looser. All kinds of rates and deals are possible. Thus, some producers pay by the reel—ordinarily, that's a 360-foot, 10-minute, 16mm reel. Others pay by the film, regardless of length. Most pay on a one-shot basis, without royalties or residuals. On the other hand, I have a contract now in my file that provides that I get $1,000 for the job, with another thousand if the returns on the film go above $20,000. (I'm not spending it until the check not only arrives, but clears the bank.)

A common target writers shoot for is 10 per cent of the cost of production. In other words, if the film is to cost $10,000, the writer wants $1,000 for the script; if it costs $30,000, he wants $3,000.

Another approach is to try for $1,000 per reel, settling for less if that seems too rich for the client's blood. (If you're tops, on the other hand, you may get more.)

Still a third way of tackling the problem—especially if the film shows signs of being a long, drawn-out project in which everything is certain to go wrong and eat up extra time—is to ask to be put on retainer or on the producer's or client's payroll at so much a month for the duration of the project, with the understanding that you're free to work on other scripts when nothing's doing on Client's picture.

It's also vital that you schedule the payments for your work properly. Personally, I like a four-payment system, set up like this:

25% on signing of letter of agreement.

25% on submission of treatment.

25% on submission of shooting script.

25% on completion of film.

Why the business about "submission" of treatment and shooting script, rather than "acceptance"? Mainly, because you never know what may happen between the time you start writing these items and the time you turn them in. For example, appointment of a new advertising manager may result in the junking of your script's basic concept. Death of an organization's president may put a different philosophy in command. Absence of key personnel may result in months of delay.

None of these things is your fault. Yet if your agreement says you must wait for approval, you very well may spend months cutting financial corners even though you delivered a script that fitted all specifications perfectly.

Above all, you must not under *any* circumstances agree to wait for payment until a film is completed or approved. A personal experience may show you why.

The instance in point saw me writing an introduction-of-the-new-model film for a subsidiary of a major manufacturing company. No producer was involved, because the company wanted to put the job out for bids on the basis of the finished script.

As usual, I stipulated that I was to receive my money in four equal payments, as outlined above.

The parent company's representative bridled at this a little—after all, why shouldn't I be willing to guarantee my product by deferring payment until the film was finished and the client satisfied? I in my turn explained that I had no control over the finished film, or whether it would be approved, any more than a lawyer can guarantee to win a case or a doctor can guarantee that a patient will recover. All I could do was my best, just as Company Rep was doing. Indeed (ha-ha), I'd be willing to defer payment, if he'd be willing to defer his salary for the same period. . .

Anyhow, I finally got my way. Things went along reasonably smoothly thereafter, with no more than the usual number of hassles. (I was interested, though, to discover that this firm's accounting department classed a film script as in the same category as bituminous coal, limestone, and cinder blocks.) Eventually, the script was completed, ready for production. I pocketed my third payment, then went on to other projects while I waited for whoever won the production bidding to finish shooting and editing the picture so that I could do the final polish and draw 25 per cent No. 4.

A year passed without further word. Wondering what had happened, I called the subsidiary firm in whose behalf the film was being made.

To my bewilderment, not one of the men with whom I'd had dealings was still employed there. Those who'd replaced them denied all knowledge of the film project.

Now I wrote to the man who'd been my contact in the parent company. In due course, back came a letter from another name I didn't recognize. Mr. Jones, the first man, was no longer with the firm, this epistle explained. Further, a decision had been made to phase out the product my script was designed to promote, and to retool Subsidiary for work in an entirely different field. Consequently, no film would be needed, and my services were no longer required. Very truly yours.

Well, that was that. I'd been cut out of a quarter of my fee—the quarter I'd counted on as profit—and no one had even thought it important enough to write or call me about it.

But—and here lies the important point—if I'd agreed to accept the original, payment-on-film's-completion offer, in all likelihood I wouldn't have received a cent for my efforts.

Bear that in mind when you check out your own letter of agreement.

g. Do hang loose.

Do I sound as if I thought everyone was out to rob the writer? I don't mean it that way. Many times, I've gone to work on the basis of a telephone call or a handshake, with any letter of agreement an after-the-fact proposition.

Ordinarily, though, this was with small operations, where I knew and trusted the individuals involved. With larger concerns, the letter of agreement is a good idea—not because the people are less trustworthy, but because more of them are involved and things have more opportunity to become confused in the course of moving up or down the chain of command.

About letters of agreement in and of themselves: I'm not a lawyer; whereas my clients in most cases have attorneys on retainer. It therefore makes sense for me to let said attorneys draw up any and all agreements, with me merely checking to make sure Client and I understand each other. What I get is nothing resembling a complete contract, nor do I care about such. You never can hope to plug all the loopholes, if someone's really out to clip you.

More important by far, in my own estimation, is maintenance of a relaxed and friendly atmosphere where all phases of your work are concerned, for it's disconcertingly easy to get a reputation as a paranoid or a prima donna. Take my word for it, you're better off with neither label. To that end, hang loose!

h. Do try for credits.

A writer is judged by the credits he accumulates—credits being those film titles which name you as the man or woman who scripted the picture. Indeed, titles are a matter of sufficient moment that the Writers Guild's summary of its 1973 Minimum Basic Agreement goes so far as to spell out such details as "The Company must include the writing credit in all publicity, handouts, screening invitations, etc., if the names of the individual producer and director are included, even if such credit is in the form of a presentation or production credit." And that's only one of the paragraphs!

In the fact film business, unfortunately, some companies make it a policy to give no production credits whatsoever. That means that your only recourse, if you feel strongly enough on the subject, is to refuse to script for said companies.

More often, the question is negotiable. If you fuss enough about it, you get a credit.

So, do fuss! Some potential customer may see the line on a picture you've done that he likes. The result might be yet another contract.

3. How to survive as a scriptwriter.

Would-be writers, script and otherwise, tend to be (a) gamblers, and (b) optimists. Which is fine, but do calculate the odds before you take cards in the game!

Herewith, four ways to improve your hand:

a. Line up clients.

You need scripts to write before you tackle full-time free-lance work: clients and producers who like your copy and who can be depended on to throw a fair number of assignments your way each year.

This of course implies that you've sold enough scripts already, catch-as-catch-can, to build yourself a reputation.

If you haven't done so, do it now!

b. Put yourself on salary.

In addition to clients, you need a strong financial backlog: money enough to carry you till you get established. How much will that be? Enough, I'd say, so that you can survive at least a year—or, better, two—without too much pain if assignments fail to materialize as quickly as you'd like.

It's important in this regard not to overestimate your potential. Or, to put it another way, a good week doesn't necessarily mean a good year.

Thus—and I have been as guilty of this as anyone else and sometimes more so—it's easy to look at a check that says you've made $3,000 for two weeks' work, and kid yourself that this means you're now a $75,000-a-year man.

Fortunately, there's a simple solution to this problem: Instead of dreaming, put yourself on salary. To this end, divide your total resources ($5,120, let's say) by the number of weeks you want to give yourself to succeed or fail (52, for example).

Breaking this down into roughly even numbers, this gives you a salary of $100 a week. You're free to spend it as you will, with a clean conscience—though it would make good sense to calculate your probable business expenses and put that amount aside each week so you won't run short.

Now, here comes check number one. It's for $1,250, and it arrives less than a month after you make the break.

Congratulations! But do be careful what you do with your bonanza. I'd recommend that you put it in a separate bank account and forget about it. Indeed, until the year ends, you should remain a $100-a-week man. Then, if the record shows you can afford it, and you think you deserve it, maybe you can give yourself a raise.

There's also another, oft-overlooked factor to consider: the matter of you and Uncle Sam and New York (or whatever) State and any other tax-levying bodies that may be lurking in the bushes. So long as your current income is in the bank, you'll have no trouble paying off when Judgment Day arrives. If you spend it, you may find yourself in the unhappy situation of having to go hat in hand to beg a boon of your friendly neighborhood loan shark—he of the cheerful smile, sympathetic mien, and brass knuckles. (Why the loan shark? Because your banker may not consider you, as a writer, the best risk. It's just one more occupational hazard. Only later, when you make it into the Writers Guild, will you have a credit union to give you a hand.)

c. Keep proper records.

I once knew an accountant about to retire from a major film company. Eager for words of wisdom, I asked what kind of a system he planned to use in handling his finances in the days ahead.

Dead-pan, he answered, "Whatever money I get, I'm going to put it in my right pants pocket. Anything I have to spend, I'm going to pay it out of there. At the end of the month, if there's anything left, I'll know I made a profit."

Well, ask a stupid question, you get a gag-line answer.

Where you're concerned, however, I'd strongly recommend that you keep some kind of financial record. The best will itemize every penny you receive, and every cent you spend. With good reason, too. No one can fault you if you have a record of *every* transaction, not just tax deductible expenses. One scriptwriter friend of mine in Hollywood, with $100,000-plus annual earnings, has gone blithely through audit after audit from the IRS on just that basis.

In addition to these income/outgo figures, it's a good idea to keep some sort of time sheet to show how many hours you devoted to each project.

Such a record is valuable for three reasons.

First, it lets you know how much you worked, and this can be a more important point than you realize. Thus, you may have assumed that you've been putting in eight hours or more a day minimum. But when you get the facts down on paper, taking out the coffee breaks and bull sessions, you discover that you actually spent little more than three at actual writing.

Second, it lets you know how much your work paid off per hour. Again, the results may shock you, as when you come to realize that the little narration polish job you took on for a flat $50 paid you $25 an hour . . . or $10 an hour . . . or 73¢ an hour.

Third, it lets you know how much to charge the next time.

This last can be a truly vital point, for too many of us tend to set our fees with a ouija board. This was clearly illustrated to me when an advertising agency asked a number of writers and producers to submit their prices for a small job. Incredulously, I discovered that one producer's bid for the complete film was dollar for dollar the same as my price for the script. Needless to say, it came as no shock to me some months later when said producer went bankrupt.

On the other side of the fence, a public relations outfit once asked me how much I wanted to write narration for a tape cassette. The job sounded fairly simple, so I named a low price—and knew instantly I'd made a mistake when the man to whom I was talking laughed and said, "Well, I guess we can afford *that*."

I learned later that they'd charged the firm for which the job was done precisely ten times my price.

d. Develop good work habits.

How do you develop good work habits?

By working.

Specifically, by not just sitting, staring out the window.

No. What you need to do is turn out copy.

To this end,

(1) *Make preparation a part of your schedule.* One of the most difficult problems in writing is "starting cold"—going at a project without having thought it through beforehand.

A good way to beat this is by setting up a regular schedule for preparation. A program I've found effective is to arrange for a daily quiet time of relaxed thinking—a period when you *don't* have to be grinding out anything or being in a hurry.

Set an hour to do this. Late evening's a good time.

Thus, let's say that your appointment with yourself is for 10 p.m. each night, Sunday through Friday. (Why include Friday, unless you're going to work Saturday? Because you need a bridge from which to start on Sunday night; a springboard from which to leap, as it were.)

When 10 p.m. arrives, take scratchpad in hand and sketch in the work you're going to do tomorrow—detailed notes, a rough draft of shots, or what have you. Let your fancy roam free, so long as it stays on the subject in a sort of focused free association. Don't try to organize too tightly. Bear down more on feelings, emotionally colored thoughts—a state of mind that's alert for what's exciting about the project.

When your hour's up, put away your pad. Go on to bed or your chosen leisure.

Now it's next morning. Get to your desk on schedule. Put a sheet of paper in your typewriter, take up your "preparation" notes, and start typing. Not thinking, you understand; not judging or organizing or weighing phrases, but *typing:* words onto paper from your notes, copying or changing as the spirit moves you. Adding, too? Sure thing; but just the bits that come to you. No straining. No forcing.

By the time you're finished with your notes, I guarantee you'll have your day's work on the road. And I mean *really* on the road. Your interest will have been caught. You'll be rolling, turning out a flow of copy. Not window-staring.

Does 10 p.m. possess some magical property that makes me recommend it? On the contrary. Any consistent routine is acceptable. Thus, suppose you find that the last hour of the normal working day, 4 to 5 p.m., ordinarily is dead time for you, waste motion so far as your regular schedule is concerned. Why not put it aside for preparation?

With that in mind, knock off your customary writing at 3:30 and go for a walk or a Coke or whatever. But promptly at 4 p.m.—and I do mean promptly—report back to your desk and scratchpad and start doodling on tomorrow's work.

Do this from the start of your career. Why? Because when you're young your initial flush of enthusiasm for creating will carry you. But as you grow older at the game, you'll tend to drag your feet more and more . . . spend long hours dawdling. Whole days quite possibly may pass in which you'll get little or nothing done. Soon you'll grow depressive . . . wonder if you've shot your wad or lost your marbles. It's a damaging, nerve-wracking state.

The purpose of preparation time is to keep such from happening . . . to drill the right work habits into you before you're desperate for them.

O.K., end of lecture.

(2) *Line up assignments ahead.* Writers sometimes have a weird way of viewing assignments. They think of them as work orders someone brings to them. Consequently, they sit back and wait for them, the way too many actors in Hollywood sit gnawing their nails by the telephone, yearning for the call that never comes.

Believe me, friends, that's not the way to go about it. For while such miracles sometimes happen—be grateful for them!—they tend to be rare birds indeed. You can starve to death while you wait for them.

What you need to do, rather, is *develop* potential assignments. In other words, keep digging up and expanding upon a steady stream of ideas of your own.

Once you've found a concept that you like, one that strikes you as having possibilities, start pushing it in what seems the most likely direction: to agent, client, producer, director, actor, friend—just about anyone whom you can see as helping you get it into production.

Will it sell? Who knows? But whether you place it or whether you don't, it still will get you into contact with film-oriented people and remind them of your existence.

This is important. To finish a film, then wait for a new assignment to pop up, is a sure road to disaster. You need to be constantly promoting, so that jobs overlap. Otherwise you'll have endless wasted days in those periods between the time you finish a shooting script and come in weeks or months later to do the narration polish job.

Incidentally, this business of working up your own assignments is not to be confused with what the Guild terms "speculative writing," in which a producer says, "Hey, that's a great idea, boy! Why don't you work it up into a treatment and then if I like it I'll buy it." No, indeed. Your ideas should remain just that—ideas, presented in a page or two or three at most. If anyone wants you to work them up further, it's up to him to pay you for it.

e. Beware friends.

No one except free-lance writers really believes a free-lance writer works. Consequently, all feel the writer is fair game for idle moments. The amount of your time they can waste is absolutely incredible. Not to mention disastrous, in view of the fact that all you have to sell is time and talent; a different situation by far than that which exists for the man happily ensconced on someone's payroll.

I know of no solution to this problem save rules—and the rules should be yours, not the other fellow's. Thus, some writers refuse to give out their office addresses, or they have unlisted phone numbers, or they see visitors by appointment only. My own system in recent years has been to hold what amounts to open house—from 5 p.m. on. Before that time, I simply see no one.

What about the friend who takes offense at your thus protecting yourself?

Who says he's your friend, when he won't understand your need for work time? Let him lie where he falls. You can do better.

f. Beware bottles.

Once upon a time there was a fact film producer in Santa Fe, New Mexico, for whom I occasionally did work. I remember him fondly for one particular gimmick he developed for use at client lunches.

Thus, Producer would take us to his favorite place, and the first order of business would be a drink around, with Producer ever beaming and convivial. "The usual for me, Vi." he'd tell the waitress.

So then we'd have a drink or two or three and talk some business, with Producer ever hale and hearty with his "usual"—a screwdriver, we all assumed, since that was certainly what it looked like.

Only after a considerable acquaintance with Producer did I learn the truth: His "usual" was straight orange juice, nothing else.

"Booze is great stuff," he told me, when I finally stumbled on the truth. "I like it fine. But I'm not about to try to talk business with two or three belts of vodka or gin or bourbon in me. Good deals are hard enough to make without that. So, the girls here all know that when I say 'the usual,' I want orange juice."

It's not the worst thought for a writer to bear in mind; for writing, too, is hard enough to handle sans liquor. To work with a bottle on the desk beside you—or even with a couple of beers under your belt—can develop a pattern of conditioning that soon proves a prelude to disaster; and Alcoholics Anonymous has the writer-members to prove it. Drinking is something to do *after* work, not during or before it.

4. The agents, and the Guild.

Writing feature films is a somewhat different kettle of fish than anything we've discussed before. There are two main reasons for this. One is the involvement of agents; the other, the activity of the Writers Guild of America, East and West.

Agents, first.

In that never-never land which Hollywood terms "the industry," writing and selling tend to be two different businesses. The man or woman who does the selling is known as an agent. He markets your scripts and/or services, negotiating prices and contract terms.

For this, he receives 10 per cent of your earnings.

It is, for all practical purposes, essential that you have an agent if you wish to sell feature film scripts. Without one, your chances of breaking in are limited indeed.

The reason this is so is that virtually no producer will consider—or even look at—a script submitted by an "unrepresented" writer—that is, a writer without an agent. Scripts mailed in unsolicited are returned unopened.

There are several explanations for this. One, of course, is that most producers are busy people indeed, and the copy of the typical beginner is so unutterably bad as to constitute a total waste of time. Whereas, when a script comes through an agent, that very fact indicates that the product has passed a preliminary screening and so is at least half-way in line with standard practice, format, level of literacy, and the like, as well as having entertainment value.

Secondly, in the view of producers, reading a script submitted by a person unknown to him is an open invitation to a plagiarism suit. Nor is this an idle fear. There actually are cases on record of would-be screenwriters who have had scripts read and rejected later copying down lengthy passages of dialogue from a picture released by the rejecting producer, incorporating it in a new version of the rejected script—and then suing on grounds that the producer had stolen their lines!

This is perhaps as good a spot as any to observe that plagiarism charges in regard to film are almost always groundless. How so? First, because it's easier—and cheaper in the long run—to buy material than to steal it. Second, because similarities between scripts well-nigh invariably are due to what might be termed the coincidence factor, with two writers coming up with the same idea more or less simultaneously.

Thus, I recall one case when I sent a TV producer a treatment for an episode of his show.

Producer returned it in the next mail, together with a copy of a brand-new script which duplicated the story line I'd developed in almost every detail. "I had to send you this," he wrote, "because if I hadn't, you'd have sworn I'd stolen your idea."

Well, he had a point there, of course, because the similarity between the two jobs was absolutely uncanny. Yet the time element was such that plagiarism became a physical impossibility.

After you've had such happen to you three or four times—in both directions—you get so you hesitate to be too quick on the trigger with accusations.

But back to agents. An agent, in California, where the largest part of theatrical film and TV production is centered, is licensed annually by the state, and bonded. He has to maintain an appropriate office, give character references, and have no criminal record.

Beyond this, naturally, there are both good agents and bad agents—and the one who's superlative for your friend may be awful for you, or vice versa.

Since his income comes from his commissions on works or services sold, no agent can afford to be a total altruist. He therefore is unlikely to help you just for love. Promise, to him, is more important—particularly, that type of promise that indicates you may become a big money-maker.

If he thinks you have such potential, an agent can push and promote you in a host of ways, from upping your price to getting you into shops that otherwise might never look at you.

Of course there's a negative side to this, also. Thus, any agent tends to favor his "hot" properties—perhaps to your detriment. Some are more astute than others, too, as quite possibly may be brought home to you when you discover the deals they've signed you to. And each has his own personality, which may or may not jibe with yours.

How do you acquire an agent? The first step is to get a list of such from the Guild: the Writers Guild of America, East, Inc., 22 West 48th St., New York, N.Y. 10036, or the Writers Guild of America, West, Inc., 8955 Beverly Blvd., Los Angeles, Calif. 90048. (Jurisdiction divides at the Mississippi River.)

The Guild is the scriptwriters' union, with approximately 3,500 members in the WGAW and 1,600 in the WGAE. It holds minimum basic agreements with most producers (including broadcasting networks and stations), covering theatrical and television films, live television, documentary film and news programs.

One of the best things about the Guild, from the newcomer's point of view, is that though it maintains a closed shop, it's an open union. This means that no hurdles are put in your way when it comes to selling your first script. If you can write anything a producer will buy, says the Guild, go to it!

Script No. Two is a different matter. To place it, you have to join the Guild. The initiation fee is $200, the quarterly dues $10 plus 1 per cent of your gross income from "the sale or licensing of literary or dramatic material for, and the engagement of their services in connection with, the production of theatrical motion pictures, radio and television programs, programs produced for 'paid television,' and other programs within the jurisdiction of the Guild." Also you must agree "to abide by the Guild Constitution, By-Laws and all rules and regulations issued or promulgated by the Guild."

Among these rules—and now we get back to the matter of agents—is one (Working Rule No. 23) that says, "No writer shall enter into a representation agreement, whether oral or written, with any agent who has not entered into an agreement with the Guild covering minimum terms and conditions between agents and their writer clients."

This is why you get the Guild's list as a first step towards finding an agent. No agent not on said list is acceptable to the Guild. And since the Guild exercises a marked degree of control over whether you work or not, choosing a non-signatory agent shoots you down in flames before you start.

Once you have the list, your next step is to persuade one of these agents to agree to handle your work. The simplest way to do this is to get some friend who's a client of a given agent, and who also thinks you might have the markings of a scriptwriter, to recommend you.

Lacking the right friend, you can make your play the hard way: phoning an agent about whom you've heard good things, telling him you're a writer who wants to work in film/TV, and asking if he'll consider representing you. If Agent agrees to talk with you, take yourself and a sample script to see him. (It will help if the script is one about which you're particularly enthusiastic.) With luck, he'll accept you. If he doesn't, try another agent.

Is your fight won, once you make this connection? To the contrary.

An agent is a salesman. That means he needs something to sell.

Especially when you're just getting started, you yourself simply haven't enough to offer to ring up any jackpots. You have no name, no established market value, no arm-long list of credits.

That means there's promoting to be done. And you're the one who's going to have to do it.

As a writer, your best stratagem to this end is to write something someone might conceivable want to buy. Indeed, agents have been known to tell beginners that their most direct road to success is to author a best-selling book so that Agent then can peddle screen rights to it.

If your major interest is in the film script form, this offers little encouragement. However, a highly acceptable alternative exists: You can write an original screenplay, in outline, treatment, or master scene form.

This gives your agent the "something to sell" I mentioned . . . brings your name before producers and demonstrates your skill and talent, if any. Even if no one buys your gem (and odds are strongly that no one will), you quite possible will arouse interest and perhaps even get offers in relation to other projects.

Further, this is an entirely legitimate approach. For while the Guild's contract specifically forbids speculative writing, it also states that "this does not limit the submission of original stories. . ." Indeed, I know a few writers who, though Guild members and old hands, have no desire to develop properties on payroll. Admittedly mavericks, they prefer to write what they want to write, then turn it over to their agents for placement.

How does this differ from "speculative writing"? In the Guild's sense of the phrase, as mentioned earlier, speculative writing means writing in which a producer in effect says, "You go ahead and work up this idea you've told me about. Then, if I like it, I'll buy it." This the Guild will not allow. If a producer *asks* you to do work for him, or otherwise gives you a go-ahead, he's considered to have hired you and, in consequence, is expected to pay you the going union rate for your services. That is, you are in effect put on salary for the period it takes you to develop your script—though you can be cut off at various points if the producer decides he doesn't like the way your assignment is going.

The accompanying table will give you some idea of how much such work brings, and perhaps make it clearer to you why most scriptwriters love their union. Other benefits include a pension fund, a health and a welfare plan, a credit union, assorted awards, a newsletter, a directory, a TV market list, and the like.

There is, of course, a negative side to the Guild's approach. It centers, for my money, on the concept known as corporate authorship. Under it, when you sign on to develop a script for a producer, you lose all control over what you write. He can change it in any way he sees fit, abandon the project at will, or whatever. Once you take his money, your work becomes his, to do with as he wishes.

Most Guildspeople don't like this idea any more than I do. But for the time being, at least, they're stuck with it since producers by and large view the granting of "creative control" to writers in about the same light the Vatican would see turning over direction of church affairs to the Communist Party.

One final point: Theatrical film production is concentrated in the Los Angeles area and, to a markedly lesser degree, in New York City. Since the development of any theatrical film script almost always involves extensive discussion and rewriting, it follows that it is well-nigh impossible to break into the field if you do not live (or are not willing to move to) these areas.

*　　　*　　　*

So much for the business end of your work as a scriptwriter. But there still are a lot of miscellaneous items and technical details about the film field which you should know.

We'll strike a few of them a glancing blow in the next chapter.

WGA 1973 THEATRICAL FILM MINIMUMS

EMPLOYMENT, FLAT DEALS	Effective 3/6/73-3/31/76			Effective 4/1/76-3/1/77		
	LOW	MEDIUM	HIGH	LOW	MEDIUM	HIGH
A. SCREENPLAY, INCLUDING TREATMENT	$7,280	$9,100	$16,900	$8,008	$10,010	$18,590
Installments:						
Delivery of Treatment	2,730	3,413	5,200	3,003	3,754	5,720
Delivery of First Draft Screenplay	3,276	4,095	7,800	3,604	4,505	8,580
Delivery of Final Draft Screenplay	1,274	1,592	3,900	1,401	1,752	4,290
B. SCREENPLAY, EXCLUDING TREATMENT	$4,550	$5,688	$11,700	$5,005	$6,257	$12,870
Installments:						
Delivery of First Draft Screenplay	3,276	4,095	7,800	3,604	4,505	8,580
Delivery of Final Draft Screenplay	1,274	1,593	3,900	1,401	1,752	4,290
C. ADDITIONAL COMPENSATION FOR STORY INCLUDED IN SCREENPLAY	$1,300	$1,300	$2,600	$1,430	$1,430	$2,860
D. TREATMENT	$2,730	$3,413	$5,200	$3,003	$3,754	$5,720
E. ORIGINAL TREATMENT	$4,030	$4,713	$7,800	$4,433	$5,184	$8,580
F. FIRST DRAFT SCREENPLAY ONLY	$3,276	$4,095	$7,800	$3,604	$4,505	$8,580
G. STORY	$2,730	$3,413	$5,200	$3,003	$3,754	$5,720
H. REWRITE OF SCREENPLAY	$2,730	$3,413	$5,200	$3,003	$3,754	$5,720

I. **FIRST DRAFT SCREENPLAY, OPTION FOR FINAL DRAFT SCREENPLAY**

FIRST DRAFT SCREENPLAY, payable on delivery	$3,276	$4,095	$7,800	$3,604	$4,505	$8,580
FINAL DRAFT SCREENPLAY, payable on delivery	$2,184	$2,730	$5,200	$2,402	$3,003	$5,720

LOW BUDGET   - Photoplay costing less than $500,000;

MEDIUM BUDGET - Photoplay costing $500,000 or more, but less than $1,000,000;

HIGH BUDGET   - Photoplay costing $1,000,000 or more

Courtesy of:
WRITERS GUILD OF AMERICA, WEST, INC.

CHAPTER 17:

What You Should Know About. . .

Writers have an unfortunate tendency to consider themselves writers only. In the film business—especially in the fact end of it—that's a luxury they can't afford. The more they know about all phases of production, the more likely they are to survive. Indeed, a host of the brethren have carried this to the point of abandoning the exclusively "writer" classification altogether, in favor of the increasingly common tag of "hyphenate"—writer-director, writer-producer, or even writer-producer-director.

There's a sound reason for this switch. In the first place, the hyphenates make more money. But beyond that, screen writers get almighty tired of seeing their scripts butchered. By adding directing and/or producing to their repertoire, they insure themselves greater control over the films they write.

Even if you have no desire to produce or direct, however, it's still worth while to learn all you can about production. Why? Because the more you know, the better you can tailor your script to a producer's needs. Particularly, you can to a marked degree help to hold down the budget, simply by limiting the requirements you set up and simplifying the way you handle your material.

A writer with such skills is ever and always in demand. So here we go, with a first lesson in regard to at least a few of the things you should know about. . .

Actors: As every fact film producer soon learns, amateurs generally can carry out actions satisfactorily—especially if said actions are those the actor performs in life, as when a plumber plays the role of a plumber.

Often, however, these sterling citizens find it almost impossible to deliver lines well. They're also prone to tire of the whole tedious business of filmmaking as soon as the glamor wears off—whereupon, disastrously, they may quit in the middle of a picture.

How to avoid such? Hold amateurs' lip-sync dialogue to a minimum; substitute voice-over narration wherever possible.

Regards action, stick as close as possible to the kind of thing found in Amateur's life experience, so that the necessity of retakes—and consequent irritation—is reduced to a minimum.

Professional actors? They tend to be hams, too often—lazy about learning lines; more interested in building their own parts than in fitting into the needs of the production; difficult to work with.

Especially are these things true if Professional is working with an inexperienced or unsure director, or on a job he considers beneath his dignity. Should you perchance be called in to help remedy the situation, try these ploys: (a) flexibility—stand ready to change lines if need be; (b) flattery—do your best to convince the ham that *your* lines show him off to best advantage; (c) lines that play: You find out about this the hard way, by having your harelipped friends read them into a tape recorder . . . then playing them back to see if they really sound like people talking.

Cutting (also known as editing): Film editors are unsung geniuses of the business. The miracles they can perform with inept writing, directing and acting are absolutely incredible, upon occasion.

You can help your film's editor by providing him (in the script) with plenty of inserts, cutaways, reaction shots, and the like, so he has footage available to cover the errors and ineptitutdes that crop up in any picture.

It's to your advantage, in the course of all this, to learn as much as you can about Editor's problems. How do you learn? You study such volumes as Livingston's *Film and The Director*, Mascelli's *The Five C's of Cinematography*, Gaskill and Englander's *How To Shoot a Movie Story*, Bare's *The Film Director*, Reisz and Millar's *The Technique of Film Editing*, Arijon's *Grammar of the Film Language*, and the like. After which, it doesn't hurt a bit to spend any spare time you can manage hanging around the cutting room, watching the viewer/Moviola as Editor runs his work print back and forth and makes his choices, and listening to any gems of wisdom he may let drop.

Directors: Start with the assumption that the director knows a lot more about the film business than you do. So, learn from him, and don't get your feelings hurt when he hacks up your pet sequence.

On the other hand, if you've worked in a clever handling, Director just may use it. As a matter of fact, your only real headache is to figure out a way to make sure Director actually has *read* the script before he starts changing or shooting it.

As with actors, flattery can be a good gimmick here. Tell the Great Man you want to learn from him (true enough!) and therefore will beat your brow on the floor before him if only he'll go over the script with you, line by line.

Many of the best directors will want you close by their warm side while they prepare for shooting. It will be a time to test how well you've done your homework, believe me. Action that previously existed only in your script now quite possibly will be diagrammed in relation to actual sets or locations. Weak sequences will fall by the way. Strong will be rearranged. Characters will appear and disappear and take on new depth or coloration; and you'll be asked, "But would Seth *do* that?" until you'll swear your skull will split.

Will the final script that results be better than your original? Maybe; maybe not.

But one thing's for sure: *You* will definitely have learned by it.

Lighting: The bigger the area you ask a crew to light, the more men and equipment and power it's going to take. While there are tricks old pros can use to achieve the impossible, you're really sticking your neck out if you ask them to make a factory interior look like an MGM imperial ballroom. Try, instead, to use your head to come up with something just as striking that makes its point via closeups, or a couple of exteriors followed by a quick dissolve to a modest office.

Locations: For greater realism and in order to avoid the problems inherent in set construction, a high proportion of pictures today are shot "on location"—that is, in a "real" environment, away from the sound stage.

But before you specify location shooting, remember that (a) transportation can prove both costly and a headache, (b) bad weather can bomb you out, cataclysmically, (c) extraneous sound can make anything but silent shooting impossible, and (d) an eight-foot ceiling has proved a disaster for many a lighting crew.

Movement: Two key elements move in any picture: the actors, and the camera. Though control of each is fundamentally the problem of the director, you can add greatly to your popularity if you'll (a) learn the nature of the so-called "imaginary (180°) line" which limits camera movement in the interests of maintaining screen direction; (b) master the simple principles of overlapping movement that help to create an effect of continuity from cut to cut; and (c) make it a habit to *act out yourself* anything you intend to ask the actors to do, so you're sure it's physically possible. Believe me, getting people on and off screen, following action, reversing, dealing with obstacles—all are more complex than you might imagine. But you can take them in stride if you'll study the books mentioned in the section on cutting, above. Even better, augment the books by sneaking onto a set whenever you can, in order to observe the principles in action.

Sets: Building a set is a difficult, expensive, time-consuming business. The more you can work with what's readily available, avoiding elaborate construction, the happier everyone will be. Really, it's amazing what you can accomplish with a couple of flats, a curtain, some molding, and a few pieces of second-hand furniture! And the resources of any studio scene dock can enable you to perform virtual miracles, budgetary and esthetic.

Set-ups: In lighting any interior, four basic types of light are involved: the *key light*, the *back light*, the *fill light*, and the *background lights*. Eventually you'll learn the whys and wherefores of each of these.

The important thing right now, however, is that you understand that every change in lighting takes time and thus costs money. It is no accident that so many old-timers state flatly that the secret of staying within the budget lies in cutting the number of set-ups.

Consequently, if you can plan ways to limit set-ups by means of simplified sets, narrowed range of action, reduced number of locations, "cheater cuts," or the like, producers will love you and you'll get more work.

Sound: It's always quicker, easier, and cheaper to shoot silent. The moment sound comes in, you not only have extra personnel and equipment, but the problems that arise from power lines, inept actors, traffic noise, planes passing overhead, air conditioning machinery, and (if you're outdoors) the whisper of the spring breeze in the microphone.

Does this mean abandoning sound forever, than? No. Even filming under the worst possible circumstances, voices can be dubbed in later, or voice-over narration substituted.

But it does stand to reason that the writer who's conscious of the problems involved may do a more satisfactory job than one who isn't.

*   *   *

If you think this covers all the ground of what a writer should know about filmmaking, or even a fraction of the headaches he'll encounter—don't kid yourself! From beginning to end, this business is a torturous if fascinating nightmare—with the scriptwriter getting the blame whenever anything goes wrong.

The solution? Time, study, experience.

Meanwhile, however, you might like to take advantage of veteran scriptwriters' techniques; learn by studying the way they tackle writing problems.

You'll find it all in the next chapter: Lessons from the Pros.

CHAPTER 18:

Lessons from the Pros

There are a lot of ways to do things right.

That's why this chapter includes excerpts from the work of nine different scriptwriters. The idea is to show you not The One True Path, but a variety of styles and techniques and approaches.

I'll comment more specifically as we go along, starting with:

NIGHT WORLD (adaptation), *by Robert Bloch.*

An *aficionado* of suspense and horror fiction from the days when, still in his teens, he began selling to the late lamented *Weird Tales,* Robert Bloch is perhaps most famous as the man who wrote the novel from which *Psycho* was made. His credits in both film and television run into the dozens. Author of literally hundreds of short stories (he still would rather work in that form than any other, but the money in films is better), he adapted the script of *Night World* from his own book of the same title.

Night World is the story of a girl whose husband is one of a group of escaped mental patients suspected of murder. In the segment reproduced here, Bloch demonstrates his skill at exposition: the introduction of plot-vital information.

Exposition is important in every screenplay. The problem is how to incorporate it painlessly, so that it doesn't stand out as a study in author convenience.

Excerpts from *Night World* © 1975 Metro-Goldwyn-Mayer Inc.

In this sequence, Bloch uses conflict—a police interrogation of his heroine—to bring in essential data. Marginal numbers refer to comments which follow the excerpt.

N I G H T   W O R L D

written by

Robert Bloch

———

MOLSON-STANTON ASSOCIATES AGENCY, Inc.
10889 WILSHIRE BOULEVARD - SUITE 929
LOS ANGELES, CALIFORNIA 90024
PHONE: 477-1262

17.

33   CONT'D

                       KAREN
                     (cont'd)
        The other two — who were they?

Willis closes his notebook, pockets it.

                     WILLIS
        You'll have to ask the Lieutenant
        for that information.

                     KAREN
        Who?

                     WILLIS
                    (rising)
        Lieutenant Barringer. I'm
        taking you in.

54 INT. POLICE HDQTRS. — BARRINGER'S OFFICE   NIGHT
ANGLE ON BARRINGER, pacing behind his desk in the
brightly-lit, sparsely-furnished office cubicle.
Barringer is a rumpled bear of a man, a stocky
Homicide veteran. No hardnose, he masks patience
and perceptivity behind a facade of pessimism.

                  BARRINGER
        Sorry, that's all we know.
        One of the victims upstairs
        was an orderly named Thomas
        — Elton Thomas.

As Barringer speaks, the CAMERA PULLS out and we
see Karen seated across from the desk — tense,
nervous, listening intently. Seated in bg., a
black POLICE STENOGRAPHER, male, is poised over
a stenotype resting on a portable metal stand
before his chair.

                  BARRINGER
                  (cont'd)
        The preliminary shows he died
        from a blow on the back of his
        head with some sort of blunt
        instrument. So far they haven't
        turned up the weapon. The other
        victim was apparently a patient —

Karen looks frightened.

                    KAREN
                  (quickly)
        What was his name?

                            CONTINUED

(marginal numbering: 1, 2, 3, 4, 5, 6, 7)

18.

54 CONT'D

Barringer gives her a darting glance.

⑧

BARRINGER
The patient was female.

Karen's relief is immediately evident.

⑨

BARRINGER
(cont'd)
An elderly woman, in her late
sixties. Found lying in the
doorway of her room. Looks as
if she saw Thomas being killed
— then keeled over herself with
a heart attack.
(shrugs)
Of course we'll know more after
an autopsy.

KAREN
(nods)
Of course.

BARRINGER
Judging from the condition of
the rooms upstairs, there were
five other patients in residence
— but that's only a guess.

KAREN
What about their records?

⑩

BARRINGER
(sighs)
Records, identification, file
material — everything went up
in smoke in Griswold's fireplace.
(nods)
The lab's examining the ashes,
but I'm not counting on anything
there. Whoever is responsible
for this did a pretty thorough
job.

KAREN
(closing her
eyes)
Horrible —

BARRINGER
Four people dead. Five mentally-
disturbed patients missing. And
the only one we can identify is
your husband.
(eyeing Karen
closely)
Unless you can help us on the others.

CONTINUED

54 CONT'D

>   KAREN
>   (shakes head)
>   I never saw them. I didn't
>   visit my husband.

⑪

In bg. the Stenographer is quietly stenotyping.

⑫

>   BARRINGER
>   Why not?

⑬

>   KAREN
>   Doctor Griswold thought it
>   might be best —

Realizing she's saying too much, Karen breaks off,
but Barringer isn't buying that.

>   BARRINGER
>   Go on, please.

>   KAREN
>   (hastily)
>   It was just a nervous condition
>   — after he came back from service —

⑭

>   BARRINGER
>   Was he a head?

⑮

>   KAREN
>   No. He never got into drugs.

>   BARRINGER
>   Then what was his problem?

                              CONTINUED

20.

54 CONT'D

Karen is obviously trying to protect her husband,
but she can't cope with Barringer.

>   KAREN
>   (defensively)
> I told you — nerves —

55 REVERSE ANGLE - BARRINGER AND KAREN

Barringer moves up to confront her. His manner is
patient: it's his near proximity that symbolizes a
threat. Her agitation increases as he speaks.

>   BARRINGER
> Can we be a little more specific?
> People don't spend six months in
> a private sanatorium unless there's
> been some kind of diagnosis.
>   (pressing a bit)
> What were the symptoms? What did
> your husband do that made you put
> him away?

⑯

Karen breaks into SOBS, shaking her head helplessly.

56 ANOTHER ANGLE ON KAREN AND BARRINGER

⑰

Barringer takes a handful of cleansing-tissue
from a box on his desk, extends it to Karen.

>   BARRINGER
>   Here.

Karen takes the tissue, nodding. Barringer moves
to seat himself behind his desk. He watches as
Karen dabs her eyes and strives to regain a measure
of composure.

>   BARRINGER
>   (cont'd)
> Sorry, Mrs. Raymond. I know
> how you feel.

>   KAREN
>   (fighting for
>   control)
>   Do you?

CONTINUED

21.

56 CONT'D

BARRINGER
(nods)
You've had a shock, you're
tired, you don't like all
these questions.
(sighs)
I don't blame you. Trouble
is, we've got to come up with
some answers. And right now
you're the only one who can
help us.

(18)

KAREN
(defensively)
I've told you the truth.

BARRINGER
(softly)
All of it?

He's touched a nerve. Karen hesitates -- for a
moment she's trapped -- then inspiration comes.

KAREN
(quickly)
Wait a minute.

(19)

BARRINGER
(alert)
Yes?

Karen gains confidence as she speaks, noting her
diversionary tactic has Barringer's full attention.

KAREN
There was a nurse I used to
call out there for a report.
She was in charge of the day
shift. I'm sure if you talked
to her she could identify the
other patients.

(20)

Barringer picks up a pencil, holds it poised
over a desk-pad. Now he's getting somewhere.

BARRINGER
What's her name?

KAREN
Dorothy. Dorothy Anderson.

BARRINGER
(as he writes)
Any idea where she lives?

CONTINUED

22.

56 CONT'D

> KAREN
> I'm not sure.
> (frowns)
> I think I remember her saying
> something about moving, a
> few months ago.
> (nods)
> That's right. She moved into
> an apartment in Sherman Oaks.

57 INT. DOROTHY ANDERSON'S APT. - BATHROOM　　NIGHT

DOROTHY, a ripely-attractive woman in her early
thirties, stands before the mirror over the
washbowl, wearing a shortie nightgown. As she
finishes creaming her face and smooths the excess
into the skin of her neck, we PAN TO OPEN DOORWAY
giving us a glimpse of a short hall beyond and
— in far bg. — the living room: just enough to
ESTABLISH a television set standing there, and
the flickering IMAGE OF A TV NEWSCASTER on the
tube as we hear:

> NEWSCASTER'S VOICE
> For the third consecutive day
> Los Angeles continued to swelter
> in the grip of an unseasonable
> autumn heat-wave. Moderate
> Santana winds from the desert
> drove today's temperature to a
> high of ninety-one registered
> at Civic Center at two p.m.

Half-listening, Dorothy moves to the bathroom
window and OPENS it. The window-pane is opaque.

> NEWSCASTER'S VOICE
> (cont'd)
> Other highs today — Santa Monica
> eighty-five, San Fernando Valley
> ninety, Los Angeles International
> Airport, eighty-seven.

Dorothy stands before the window for a moment,
grateful for the cooling breeze from the alley-
way beyond. Then she turns. CAMERA GOES WITH
HER to a side doorway leading into her bedroom.

58 INT. DOROTHY ANDERSON'S APT. - BEDROOM　　NIGHT

Dim illumination comes from a lamp on a night-
table next to the telephone. The room is
unimpressive, furnished in Early Sears. Dorothy
ENTERS and crosses to the bed: lying on the
spread is her discarded slip and dress.

CONTINUED

(21)

(22)

23

58 CONT'D

Dorothy picks up the garments, turns. CAMERA GOES
WITH HER ACROSS THE ROOM, past a window with drawn
drapes, as she approaches a closet on the far wall.
Next to the closet is an open doorway leading into
the living-room. The closet door is closed and
Dorothy OPENS it. She hangs her slip on a hook,
puts her dress on a hanger. Meanwhile, she's half-
attentive to:

> NEWSCASTER'S VOICE
> And now, a late bulletin from
> our newsroom. Four victims are
> dead and five patients are
> missing in what appears to be
> an escape attempt by the inmates
> of a private sanatorium located
> in Topanga Canyon.

(23)

Dorothy looks up now, stunned, incredulous.
CAMERA FOLLOWS HER as she moves quickly away
from the open closet toward the living room
doorway.

> NEWSCASTER'S VOICE
> (cont'd)
> The bodies were discovered by a
> late evening visitor to the
> Griswold sanatorium which
> specializes in the treatment of
> mental disorders —

59 INT. DOROTHY ANDERSON'S APT. — LIVING ROOM   NIGHT

As Dorothy ENTERS we see her shocked reaction in
the flickering light from the television screen
which is the only source of illumination in the
otherwise-darkened room. She moves up to the
set, listening intently to:

> NEWSCASTER'S VOICE
> Police have released the names of
> three of the victims. Natalie
> Berger, forty-seven, a resident
> nurse — Elton Thomas, thirty-one,
> a staff orderly — and Doctor
> Lyman Griswold, the director of
> the institution —

At the mention of the first two names, Dorothy
looks stunned — when she hears Griswold's name
she GASPS.

> DOROTHY
> Oh my God!

CONTINUED

The numbered paragraphs that follow refer to the marginal numbers in the script excerpts above.

1. The end of the preceding sequence, complete with an interest hook in the curtain line. Jeopardy is implicit when Willis rises and announces, "I'm taking you in."

2. Note the directness of this transition, a straight cut to Lt. Barringer's office. In effect, we jump from crisis to crisis, with pressure heightening on Karen, Bloch's heroine.

3. Barringer here is characterized in terms of sex (male), age (Homicide veteran), and general impression. His dominant attitude is also clearly established, and we know he's a likable character.

4. Bloch plunges us into the heart of the interview without preliminaries. No time is wasted on introductions, weather talk, or social chitchat.

5. Bloch focuses instantly on Karen's mood, her state of mind as revealed in her behavior. He also offers color details (the police stenographer, etc.) to help establish place and circumstance.

6. Realistic—and frightening—detail, blocking in further facts and helping to build our feeling of impending jeopardy.

7. A small, tension-building reaction—a false assumption on Karen's part . . .

8. . . . building to a small, tension-releasing twist.

9. Further information is introduced—information which won't drag or bore viewers, since the structuring of the situation has already made them eager to learn about it and it's being presented in terms of conflict rather than lecture.

10. Here Bloch has anticipated questions which are likely to arise in viewers' minds, and has answered them before they have a chance to erode suspension of disbelief.

11. A statement that can't help but raise a question in viewers' minds.

12. A tiny, added tension factor: All this is becoming a matter of record.

13. Barringer asks the viewers' question.

14. Again, a spur to viewer curiosity—and a slight heightening of jeopardy.

15. Step by step, Bloch is boxing in Karen . . . cutting off her escape routes, heightening her tension.

16. Karen reacts.

17. Handled incorrectly here, Barringer could very well become an unsympathetic figure. But Bloch now reenforces his image as a likable rather than hardnosed type.

18. Even though likable, Barringer has a job to do—and does it.

19. To get the pressure off, Karen takes a new tack.

20. More information—and a pivot on which to switch to a new sequence, a new series of related shots. Also, to a new and logical development. At the same time, Bloch is quitting while he's ahead. That is, he's introduced the information he needed, the exposition required to establish his plot point. But he's done it within the framework of a situation designed to make it seem natural. And since the situation is one of conflict, thrust and parry, interest—and tension—heightens instead of falling off. But he doesn't stay with it a moment longer than is necessary. Jumping forward from the springboard provided by the "apartment in Sherman Oaks" line, he switches to Dorothy's place, where the already rising action can develop further.

21. Parallel action: Bloch establishes Dorothy and her apartment and introduces the TV newscaster—yet another device to bring in needed information.
22. Bloch starts the newscaster on a low level, the most routine of notes. This gives us a moment of relief from the tension of the preceding scene . . . a chance to absorb the new situation.
23. A switch in subject. The contrast between this latest news and the routine which preceded it makes for shock: a sudden leap in Dorothy's—and the viewers'—tension.

From beginning to end, Bloch has developed this episode in terms of punch and counterpunch, thrust and parry. No one volunteers anything, save as a ploy to lure someone else into further revelations. Yet the story keeps moving forward. The situation at the end of the sequence is different than that at the beginning, in that the state of affairs has changed: Barringer, the detective, now knows that a nurse named Dorothy Anderson may prove a source of further information.

Note too that Bloch has not attempted to push his story ahead too fast. He's content to build rising action, tension, a step at a time, with relatively quiet episodes.

Such scenes are important. While maintaining tension and progression, they also serve as necessary counterpoint for the more violent and/or melodramatic moments of major crisis and climax.

CAPONE (original screenplay), *by Howard Browne.*

A long-time Chicago resident before New York and Hollywood claimed him, Howard Browne's knowledge of the Capone era is encyclopedic, his interest in the subject well-nigh compulsive. A former magazine editor, author of much book and magazine fiction as well as numerous TV and film scripts, he was for a time executive story consultant for Twentieth Century-Fox.

Capone is of course fiction, though within a factual framework. As such, it pays more attention to the hoodlum's character and private life than to the creature of the headlines, even going so far as to develop its subject with a certain flavoring of humor.

The key to Capone's personality (at least, as seen by Browne in this script) is revealed in a single speech on page 22 . . . then demonstrated in detail in various sequences, including the six-page segment included here. It shows clearly how important it is for a writer to make his mind up as to the dominant character note he intends to strike in regard to each story person . . . plus establishing, developing, and paying it off as he builds his script.

22.

59.　CONTINUED:

> TORRIO (cont'd)
> (illustrating)
> to killin the whole deal!
> (mimicking
> savagely)
> "Whatta ya so worried about, Mr.
> Stenson? The Feds're a bunch'a
> dopes, Mr. Stenson."

He breaks off, slamming a hand against the car for
punctuation, then takes a slow, deep breath, lets it
out.

> TORRIO
> I'm going to tell you something,
> Alphonse, and I want it to soak
> in. From here on in, we're doing
> business with a lot of important
> people: lawyers, judges, business
> men, big politicians. To get
> anywhere with them, you've got to
> be like them. Look like them, act
> like them, think like them - and
> more than anything else, talk like
> them. Because the minute you start
> shooting off your face like some
> Union Street punk - the way you did
> with Joe Stenson - they won't come
> inside a mile of you.

①

60.　CLOSE ON CAPONE

②

Impressed, he nods thoughtfully.

61.　EXT. COLOSIMO'S RESTAURANT - DAY (SUMMER)

as a sedan pulls up.

62.　INT. SEDAN - DAY

The driver is FRANK GUSENBERG, 30, heavily built;
beside him is PETER GUSENBERG, 24, slender, tall, hard-
faced. Alone in the back seat is DION O'BANION, 29,
a tall, muscular Irishman with a floridly handsome
face and, normally, a hearty manner. To the driver--

> O'BANION
> You wait in the car, Frank.
> Pete, I want you in there
> with me. Just in case.

As O'Banion and Peter Gusenberg leave the car--

56.

③ 143.   INT. COMBINED LIVING ROOM/OFFICE - CLOSE ON WINE GLASS - DAY

as it is filled from a bottle. CAMERA BACK to disclose
Capone at his desk, napkin under his chin, engorging a
huge plate of pasta along with chunks of bread and gulps
of wine. Frank Nitti is seated at the bar, having a
④   sparse lunch of salad and coffee as befits a man determined to stay in top shape. McGurn is not present.

The room is 20' x 30', richly furnished with deep Oriental
rugs, twin couches flanked by lamp tables, several
upholstered armchairs, a couple of floor lamps. Valanced
drapes and curtains grace the three steel-shuttered
windows, a wet bar complete with bar stools occupies one
corner, the back shelf loaded with bottled whiskey, gin
and wine. Near the corridor wall of the room is a large
ornately carved mahogany desk and a high-back leather
swivel chair. Four phones are on the desk top, plus the
usual accessories. On the wall behind the desk are three
portraits in matching frames: Chicago Mayor William Hale
Thompson, flanked by Abraham Lincoln and George Washington.

Capone continues shoveling in the food for a beat, then
one of his desk phones RINGS. He gestures imperiously
for Nitti to answer.

                    NITTI
                (into phone)
        Yeah?... Who wants to know?

Covering the mouthpiece--

                    NITTI
                (to Capone)
        Some dame named Crawford.
        Says you know her.

Capone, utterly taken aback, stares at him incredulously.
He takes the receiver, a "now-what's-she-want" look on
his face.

                    CAPONE
                (shortly)
        Okay, whatta you want?

149.   CLOSE ON CAPONE

⑤   What he gets back completely floors him.

                    CAPONE
        Do I play...what?

                                    FLIP TO:

57.

⑥ 150. EXT. GOLF COURSE TEE - CLOSE ON GOLF BALL - DAY

as a golf club (1924 brassie) hits it cleanly out of
the FRAME.

151. CAPONE AND IRIS

She's the one who made the shot. She's dressed for the
sport. As for Capone - he wears plaid plus-fours, argyle
golf socks, black-and-white golf shoes, a V-neck pull-
over, white shirt and bow tie. Strange garb for an ex-
Brooklyn thug, but somehow it does not make him look at
all ridiculous. A couple of teen-age CADDIES are present;
one of them now hands Capone a ball and a wood. Iris
gets a pinch of wet sand from the tee-box, takes the ball
from Capone, tees it up and steps back. In the b.g.,
some distance away, Nitti and McGurn, wearing dark pin-
striped suits and fedoras, are trying to appear
inconspicuous.

                    IRIS
                (matter-of-factly)
        Go ahead.

Capone, frowning with concentration, awkwardly addresses
the ball. Iris steps in, alters his grip, AD-LIBS some
brief advice on not moving his left foot, following
through on the shot, etc. Capone listens intently, nods
- and hits the ball with astonishing force and grace.

152. THE BALL

as it splits the center of the fairway, finally settles
to earth and rolls to a stop some 250 yards from the tee.

153. BACK TO SCENE

Trying without too much success to keep from looking smug,
Capone hands the club to the caddy as Iris eyes him
quizzically.

                    IRIS
                  (drily)
        It would seem people aren't the
        only things you can hit.

                    CAPONE
                  (modestly)
        I used to play a lotta stick
        ball back when I was a kid.

⑦
⑧ 154. EXT. SCHOFIELD FLORIST SHOP - CLOSE ON SIGN - DAY

The one reading SCHOFIELD CO. From o.s. we hear the
SOUNDS of light traffic. The CAMERA PANS DOWN past a
lowered awning to the flower-filled display window.

58.

155.   THE SCENE

as a small sedan containing four MEN pulls in at the
curb in front of the cathedral across the street from
the florist shop.

156.   THE SEDAN

⑨

While the driver (Angelo Genna) remains at the wheel, the
others step out. One is Antonio Lombardo, the other two
are JOHN SCALISE, 24, and ALBERT ANSELMI, 38. Both are
Sicilian, swarthy-skinned and smooth-shaven. As,
together, they start across the street toward the shop
entrance--

157.   EXT. GOLF GREEN - ON CAPONE - DAY

⑩

He's lining up a four-foot putt. A beat, then he strokes
it much too hard. The CAMERA PANS with the ball as it
misses the cup by a foot, rolls completely across the
green and into a sand trap twenty feet away.

158.   THE SCENE

Capone, looking disgusted, straightens slowly.

                    IRIS
                 (mildly)
          I guess one doesn't do much
          putting in stick ball.

159.   INT. FLORIST SHOP - FAVORING O'BANION - DAY

⑪

He's using a pair of pruning shears to shape a large
potted plant. The room is crowded with plants and fresh
flowers. A Negro Porter is sweeping clippings into a
dust pan. A beat; then a BELL TINKLES as the o.s. front
door opens.

160.   THE SCENE

Lombardo, Anselmi and Scalise enter as the Porter disappears into the back room. Holding the shears in his
left hand and smiling in welcome, O'Banion walks toward
them, his right hand extended in greeting.

                  O'BANION
                (cordially)
          Mornin, boys. You here for the
          Merlo flowers?

                  LOMBARDO
                (smiling)
          That's right.

59.

161.   THE GROUP

Lombardo, still smiling genially, clasps O'Banion's hand.
Suddenly his grip tightens and he pulls the florist off
balance as Scalise and Anselmi yank snub-nosed .38
revolvers from their underarm holsters.

162.   EXT. SAND TRAP - ON CAPONE - DAY

as he swings wildly at his ball, sending a cloud of
sand directly into the CAMERA. (This is hardly more
than a subliminal shot.)

163.   INT. FLORIST SHOP - THE GROUP - DAY

as Scalise and Anselmi each FIRE three quick bullets
into O'Banion's body. He stumbles back, falls on his
back into a bank of lillies and ferns. Lombardo whips
out a .38, bends and administers the coup de grace: a
single bullet between the eyes. Scalise and Anselmi are
already crossing unhurriedly to the door; Lombardo pockets
his gun and follows. As they exit into the street--

164.   O'BANION

Eyes open and staring in death, he lies among the blood-
stained lilies.

165.   INT. CLUBHOUSE PORCH - CLOSE ON TRAY - DAY

as two highballs are removed, set on a table for two.
CAMERA BACK to reveal Capone and Iris, same wardrobe as
before, seated at the table. Both are smoking Iris'
cigarettes. As the middle-aged black Waiter exits the
SHOT, Iris lifts her glass in salute to her companion.

                    IRIS
                 (smiling)
        To the underworld's most
        promising golfer.

She sips from her glass while Capone extracts his folder
score card from his shirt pocket, smooths it, studies it.

                    CAPONE
        Sixty-eight. Not bad, hunh?

                    IRIS
                  (drily)
        For nine holes? Excellent.

The CAMERA PULLS BACK, PANS around the porch. It's
glassed (or screened) in, has twelve or fifteen round
wooden tables with captain's chairs. At a table near an
exit, Nitti and McGurn are drinking highballs and

                              CONTINUED

60.

165. CONTINUED:

looking ill-at-ease. About half the tables are occupied
- mostly by high-society type females of varying ages -
sipping tea, coffee or highballs. The CAMERA STOPS on
two WOMEN - call them RUTH and EDNA - seated at a table
and sneaking furtive glances at Capone and Iris.

(17)

166. RUTH AND EDNA

Mid-twenties, golf togs, drinking highballs. Upper-crust
establishment types. Junior League, hair unbobbed,
restrained makeup. Ruth shows thin-lipped disapproval;
Edna is titillated.

> RUTH
> Imagine - bringing a common
> bootlegger here of all places!
> Last winter it was that New York
> actor. Now this.

> EDNA
> You think he's actually carrying
> a gun?

(18)

Ruth isn't listening. An idea is taking shape behind her
thoughtfully narrowed eyes.

> RUTH
> (suddenly)
> You know what I've a good mind
> to do?

167. CAPONE AND IRIS

as Ruth and Edna, both smiling cordially, enter to them.

> RUTH
> (gushing)
> Iris! How nice to see you!

Capone scrambles quickly to his feet.

> IRIS
> (casually)
> Mrs. Akins; Miss Detwiler;
> Mr. Capone.

> CAPONE
> (big smile)
> Pleased to meetch'a ladies.

Pretending dawning recognition--

CONTINUED

61.

167.　CONTINUED:

　　　　　　　RUTH
Why of course!　Your picture's
been in all the papers.　You're
the famous...

As she hesitates with becoming delicacy--

　　⑲　　　　　IRIS
　　　　　　(helpfully)
　　　　Gangster?

　　　　　　　RUTH
　　　　　(thin smile)
　　　Well.　Since you said it...

　　⑳　　　　　EDNA
　　　　　(delicious shiver)
I've never met anyone in your
- ah - business before, Mr. Capone.
It must be terribly exciting!
　　　　(ingenuously)
Forgive me, but do you actually
carry a gun?

　　　　　　　RUTH
　　　　　(as to a child)
They call it "packing a rod",
darling.
　　　(to Capone, sweetly)
Isn't that right, Mr. Capone?

It's now obvious to Capone that he's being deliberately
baited by a couple of smart-ass bitches.

　　⑳　　　　CAPONE
　　　　　(straight-faced)
　　　Sure.　I pack a rod.　All the
　　　time.

He takes a quick precautionary glance around the room,
then leans toward them conspiratorially.

　　　　　　　CAPONE
　　　　Here, lemme show ya.

168.　CAPONE

　　㉑　as he rips open his fly, reaches in--

169.　THE THREE WOMEN

Ruth and Edna, eyes riveted on the o.s. point of interest,
gasp and shrink back in shocked embarrassment, Iris
begins to laugh uncontrollably.

1. Here, on page 22 of Browne's script, Johnny Torrio (Capone's predecessor as overlord of Chicago's gang world) rebukes Capone for a particularly stupid and ill-timed display of hoodlum arrogance. His pronouncement— "To get anywhere *with* them, you've got to be *like* them," and so on, becomes the key to Capone's approach to the straight world.
2. A model of compression, this one shot sums up Capone's reaction to Torrio's lecture. It also demonstrates the impact and effectiveness of the closeup in emphasizing a point.

We now move ahead to one of the later script segments, in which Browne shows Capone in action in sequences which reveal the contrast between mask and man: the make-believe gentleman and the hoodlum behind the front.

3. There are a host of ways to open a sequence. Here Browne uses one currently much favored: the use of a close shot of an object as a bridging device.
4. Contrast is the order of the day in this description establishing the grossness of Capone in his adopted habitat. Browne builds it in terms of simple yet effective actor business, with Capone "engorging" pasta, bread, and wine in contrast to Nitti's abstemiousness. The luxury of the room, in turn, is jarred by the contrast of the three portraits—with Big Bill Thompson, mob-backed mayor, assigned the place of honor.
5. Again, the value of succinctness: one close shot, then a flip to . . .
6. . . . the small shock of discovering Capone the golfer. Note too, again, the usefulness of bridging on an object. Also the incorporation of period detail (the brassie, the wet-sand tee, the plus-fours, to help build the illusion of the Twenties.
7. Capone the gentleman follows Torrio's advice, not throwing his weight around. He acknowledges (and thus reminds viewers of) his origins, even though his behavior of the moment belies them.
8. Again, contrast . . . matching Capone's attempt at social pretensions with a sudden switch to the parallel action of impending violence—a violence already anticipated and savored by any viewer drawn to a film about Capone.
9. Description here is limited. Conceivably, the casting director will dig out photos of Genna, Lombardo, Scalise, and Anselmi and make a pass at matching them. But if—more likely—he doesn't, tags cited here will give him acceptable approximations.
10. Back to the golf course. Capone is still role-playing, but with somewhat less success than before. Iris points it up with her reference to stick ball.
11. Back to O'Banion's flower shop and impending violence. Browne is building a pattern now—the rhythm of referential cross-cutting between parallel lines of action, in much the same manner as the flipping back and forth between outlaw and pursuer in the western or between happy home and operating room crisis in the medical picture. Note, too, the incorporation of environmental detail and simple business—the pruning shears, the sweeping of clippings. The tinkling of the bell in 159, preceding the entrance of the three men in 160, prepares viewers for impending disaster and, in the process, heightens tension.

12. The disaster, the jeopardy, comes into sharp, specific focus. But Browne breaks the action, stretching out the viewers' objective as well as subjective time and building the suspense.
13. Contrast, parallel action, heightened tension.
14. The episode's obligatory scene, the culmination of what we've been waiting for and building to. O'Banion dies.
15. O'Banion and blood-stained lilies: a study without words in dramatic irony.
16. The clubhouse porch, and more contrast. The effect is heightened by the presence of Nitti and McGurn, Capone's ever-present bodyguards.
17. Browne begins his build to a comic relief scene of sorts, to give viewers respite from the tension of O'Banion's murder.
18. A plant, preparing us for the bit's punch-line. The women are also "typed" as to character as the sequence builds.
19. Iris recognizes the women's gambit, picks up the gauntlet.
20. This is a situation with which Capone the erstwhile gentleman is unfitted to cope. Result: He reverts to Capone the hoodlum. His action is the ultimate twist, the logical, perfectly planted, yet unanticipated development.
21. The payoff. Capone's harassers are shocked and humiliated, their dignity destroyed. It's low comedy, and it can't help but get a laugh. Also, it reaffirms Capone's character. Though he may try to play the role of the straight, under pressure the veneer will always fall away.

THE REAL TALKING SINGING ACTION MOVIE ABOUT NUTRITION (fact film script), *by Gerald DiPego.*

Scriptwriter of such TV movies as *I Heard the Owl Call My Name, The Stranger Who Looks Like Me,* and *Born Innocent,* Chicago-born Gerald DiPego earlier worked as reporter, teacher, and writer of educational films and books. This background serves him well in *The Real Talking Singing* etc., a recent fact film he wrote for Sunkist Growers, Inc.

The title tells the picture's story. It's presented in the single column, master scene script style ordinarily used in features, with effects desired fully described but no attempt made to break down the action into individual shots. Overall, it constitutes an excellent example of the relating of film tone to target audience.

THE REAL TALKING SINGING ACTION
MOVIE
ABOUT NUTRITION

Original Screenplay
by
Gerald DiPego

Prepared for:
Sunkist Growers, Inc.

July 20, 1972

INDUSTRIAL · EDUCATIONAL FILM DIVISION

CASCADE PICTURES OF CALIFORNIA, INC. · 6601 ROMAINE STREET HOLLYWOOD · CALIFORNIA 90038 (213) 463-2121

FADE IN:

1. ECU - CHAINLINKS OF SCHOOLYARD FENCE - NO PEOPLE - DAY   1.

    (The schoolyard beyond the fence will be used for many
    purposes, several sports.)

    ① ROCK MUSIC comes in as the film opens and ESTABLISHES a
    theme which will play under and support this and several
    other sequences in the film. The MUSIC is rhythmic,
    catchy.

    CAMERA is FOCUSED CLOSE on the links so that at first the
    background is not discernable. Possibly, in sync with the
    beat of the music, the CAMERA MOVES from link to link.
    Finally it holds on one link. FOCUS is quickly racked to
    the schoolyard background. The extreme foreground links
    disappear. A STUDENT FILM CREW (ages 12 to 14) now hurriedly
    enters in front of the CAMERA in funny FAST ACTION and
    prepares to shoot a scene. (Except for a few sequences,
    the kids in the film wear casual clothes, that is, levis,
    t-shirts, sweatshirts, shorts.) As the kids position an
    ACTRESS, reposition her, set up reflectors, hurry about,
    etc....we HEAR the VOICES of the narrators.

    ② Three voices are used in the film - two boys and a girl.
    They are very natural, casual voices. Other than in this
    opening sequence, these kids are not "narrating" the film
    as such. Rather, they are talking among themselves as
    they watch the film, and we "overhear" them. Later in the
    film, they will also address the actors MIKE and DEBBIE,
    but they will always maintain a conversational style --
    kids talking among themselves.

                        GIRL (V.O.)*
                This all started at school. The
                class was talking about what makes
    ③   us feel good - eating, exercise...

                          BOY 1
                ...stuff like that. We learned a
                lot.

                          BOY 2
                Then we got this <u>fantastic</u> idea!

    ④ Under this narration, we see the actress, a pretty girl with
    a perpetual smile, handed a large card. Everyone except
    this girl now begins to leave the SHOT, moving O.S. behind
    the CAMERA.

                                            CONTINUED

    *All narration is "VOICE OVER". Speakers are
    never seen

1.   CONTINUED   1.

⑤
                              GIRL
                We'd make our own film and show
                what we learned...and what it
                means to us.

2.   ZOOM IN TO PRETTY GIRL   2.

      Smiling, she holds up the card. It reads:

                STUDENTS OF ADAMS JUNIOR HIGH SCHOOL
                     (and some other people)
                            PRESENT

                             BOY 1
                So this film is our term project...

      Never taking her eye or her smile off the CAMERA, the girl
      drops the first card and is handed another one from OFF
      SCREEN. This one's upside down but she doesn't notice it.
⑥   It is the title card. A second after she's held it upside
      down, a hand comes IN and turns it right side up. The girl
      smiles to the end. The card reads:

                THE REAL TALKING SWINGING ACTION
                            MOVIE...

                        BOY 1 (CONT'D)
                It's to give you some facts --
                the real facts...

      The smiling girl now flips over the card. The back reads:

                    ...ABOUT NUTRITION

                        BOY 1 (CONT'D)
                    ...about nutrition.

3.   LS - FILM CREW   3.

      The film crew now hurries in front of the CAMERA again (in
      very FAST MOTION) and begins dismantling equipment, gathering
⑦   its gear and preparing to leave the yard. The crew includes
      several girls and is ethnically mixed. The kids expend a lot
      of energy with the equipment, cards, scripts, reflectors,
      dropping things, picking them up, etc. During this sequence,
      we SUPER these CREDITS:

      (A) THE ACTORS AND ACTRESSES - members of the 7th, 8th and
                              9th grades
      (B) THE FILM CREW - members of the 9th grade

                              CONTINUED

-3-

3.　CONTINUED　　　　　　　　　　　　　　　　　　　　3.

(C)　THE VOICES - courtesy of the 8th grade

The CREDITS END, MUSIC remains as one crew member hurries toward CAMERA with a lens cap in his hand. He puts the lens cap on.

　　　　　　　　　　　　　　　　　FADE OUT:

NOTE: What we have established here is a style and a tone that will involve the audience and carry them through our story, allowing them to receive our messages in the comfortable context of humor and identification. The style is light, tongue-in-cheek, even zany to a point, reflecting the kind of youthful exuberance that kids might impart to their own film. We know we're going to see a film about nutrition, but we have also established that this film will be fun to watch. It will make serious points, but won't take itself too seriously. The tone is all important - kids talking to kids. No one talking down. No one preaching. The whole thrust of the film is toward - making your own choices.

FADE IN:

4.　SERIES OF SHOTS - STOCK FOOTAGE - SKIING　　　　　4.

Kids and adults skiing, very striking and contemporary photography to capture an exciting spirit of fun and happy people. The MUSIC remains in BG as our VOICES come in.

　　　　　　　　　　　BOY 1
　　　　　　　Do you like skiing?

　　　　　　　　　　　BOY 2
　　　　　　　Never tried it.

　　　　　　　　　　　GIRL
　　　　　　　I think I'd be scared.

　　　　　　　　　　　BOY 2
　　　　　　　I think I'd be -- well, I'd
　　　　　　　fall a lot.

5.　SERIES OF SHOTS - STOCK - ICE SKATING　　　　　　5.

Beginning with a humorous fall, then other action cuts.

6.　SERIES OF SHOTS - KIDS BACKPACKING IN WOODS (SIX BOYS AND　6.
　　GIRLS)

All of the photography emphasizes energy, the pleasure involved in these activities, a strong youthful spirit.

　　　　　　　　　　　　　　　　　CONTINUED

-27-

91. MED. - BASEBALL CENTER FIELDER - BASEBALL FIELD   91.

    He looks up, catches a fly ball -- It's the apple. He
    takes a bite, looks up, catches another "ball". It's an
    orange. He stares at it, tosses it high in the air over
    his shoulder.

                                        CUT TO:

92. MED. - IN PARK - A BIKER (MIKE)   92.

    Mike is standing still, straddling his bike. He looks up
    and catches an orange, begins to peel it, a pack of bikers
    pass him. (7 boys and girls, including Debbie)

                                        CUT TO:

93. MONTAGE - BIKING IN PARK   93.

    A series of SHOTS emphasizing fun and energy. We use LONG
    and VERY CLOSE SHOTS of the bikers (who include Mike and
    Debbie, both looking their best)...

    ...and we have some fun with the photography:

    (A) The pack of bikers pass the CAMERA, move through the
    SHOT. Then the film is REVERSED, and they peddle backwards
    through the SHOT.

    (B) IN LONG SHOT the bikers move through a park IN FAST
    MOTION, reach an open space and bike in a circle, get off
    their bikes and talk, laugh, peel some oranges, eat them
    -- all in FAST FUNNY ACTION. Then they get on their bikes
    and peddle off.

    (C) We use SLIGHTLY SLOW MOTION, too, for beauty shots
    against the sun and trees.

    All the while the song is playing and we are INTERCUTTING
    THE CREDITS --

    CREDITS: THESE ARE BRIEF SHOTS of that pretty, smiling girl
    holding cards reading:

    (1)   Produced by Adams Junior High School
                    with some help from
                        people like...

    (2)   A Writer...
                    Gerald DiPego

    (3)   And A Director...
                    ─────────────────

                                        CONTINUED

-28-

93. CONTINUED   93.

    (4)   And A Composer...

                  ———————————

    (5)   And A Production House
                  Cascade/California

    (6)   And A Sponsor
                  Sunkist Growers, Inc.

94. THE FINAL SHOT - THE PRETTY GIRL   94.

standing, smiling at us, holding no card. In REVERSE MOTION, the card flips down into her hands from above, and as it reaches her hands, the MUSIC hits its final note. The card reads:

                  "THE END"

                         FADE OUT:

1. Clearly, DiPego recognizes that he's competing with TV interest hooks in this film, so he meets them on their own ground. Thus, he specifies rock music and strong, funny, attention-catching, viewer-oriented, pre-title action. However, he pretty much leaves it to the director how to catch all this on film, making no attempt to break down the action into individual shots.
2. Note use of voice-over narration, rather than lip-sync dialogue. But it's a fresh, unconventional kind of narration, with three speakers and an illusion of "overheard" conversation.
3. Here DiPego makes a definite effort to eliminate any feeling that the actors or sponsor are lecturing or assuming superiority.
4. Remember this girl.
5. An even stronger play for audience empathy/identification.
6. You don't just hold interest/attention in film. You capture and recapture it—even if you have to use gag shots to do it!
7. In this day of women's lib and minority protest, DiPego is taking no chances on casting slips destroying his film.
8. In case anyone has missed the style and tone for which DiPego is striving, he nails it down here.
9. Stock footage saves money—when precisely the right shots are available. Here, DiPego is on safe ground, since the footage needed is general and on a readily available topic.
10. Appropriate lines keep the audience reminded of the film's overall tone and frame situation.

So much for the opening and establishment of situation in *The Real Talking Singing* etc. Now, jumping to the end of the picture . . .

11. Again, the process of holding attention, via fly balls that turn out to be apples and oranges.
12. An orange as transition. Or should we say: *imagination* as transition?
13. Even in this final sequence, a strong effort is made (via "fun with the photography") to hold attention. Note, too, how much initiative is left to the director, in terms of improvising "FAST FUNNY ACTION" and the like.
14. Changes of pace are provided also, in terms both of subject matter and tone.
15. If this had been a shooting script, rather than a master scene script, these intercut credits might quite possibly have been listed as separate shots, between the bicycling shots.
16. The pretty girl again . . . neatly tying the end of the film to the beginning, thus giving the feeling of "full circle" and completion.

WINNER TAKE ALL (treatment), *by Caryl Ledner.*

WINNER TAKE ALL (teleplay drafts 1, 2, and 3), *by Caryl Ledner.*

WINNER TAKE ALL (final draft), *by Caryl Ledner.*

Hard work is the name of the game in the film business, and *Winner Take All* offers an excellent case in point. Caryl Ledner, one of Hollywood's relatively rare woman scriptwriters, had scored well with two books (*Ossie, The Autobiography of a Black Woman,* as told to Caryl Ledner, and *The Bondswoman*) and with *A Great American Tragedy,* a 90-minute movie for TV. NBC promptly gave her a go-ahead on *Winner Take All,* the story of a compulsive woman gambler. But even after an approved treatment, the script for the two-hour picture still went through four drafts before, on film at last, it hit the air as an enthusiastically received drama.

The treatment

①

TIME LOCK (W.nu er Time All)

a treatment

by

Caryl Ledner

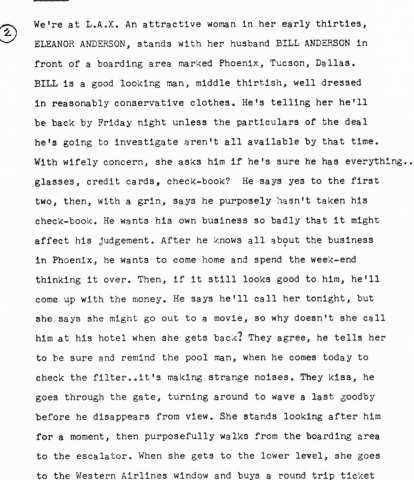

1.

ACT ONE   WEDNESDAY, A.M.

We're at L.A.X. An attractive woman in her early thirties,
ELEANOR ANDERSON, stands with her husband BILL ANDERSON in
front of a boarding area marked Phoenix, Tucson, Dallas.
BILL is a good looking man, middle thirtish, well dressed
in reasonably conservative clothes. He's telling her he'll
be back by Friday night unless the particulars of the deal
he's going to investigate aren't all available by that time.
With wifely concern, she asks him if he's sure he has everything..
glasses, credit cards, check-book? He says yes to the first
two, then, with a grin, says he purposely hasn't taken his
check-book. He wants his own business so badly that it might
affect his judgement. After he knows all about the business
in Phoenix, he wants to come home and spend the week-end
thinking it over. Then, if it still looks good to him, he'll
come up with the money. He says he'll call her tonight, but
she says she might go out to a movie, so why doesn't she call
him at his hotel when she gets back? They agree, he tells her
to be sure and remind the pool man, when he comes today to
check the filter..it's making strange noises. They kiss, he
goes through the gate, turning around to wave a last goodby
before he disappears from view. She stands looking after him
for a moment, then purposefully walks from the boarding area
to the escalator. When she gets to the lower level, she goes
to the Western Airlines window and buys a round trip ticket
to Las Vegas.

2.

We're in the lobby of the Union Plaza Hotel in Vegas. ELEANOR
comes through the main entrance, walks up to the desk and
asks for Mr. Simmons. The desk clerk consults the guest list,
comes back, asks if it's Mr. Edward Simmons she's looking for.
When she says yes, he says Mr. Simmons has checked out..moved
to the Sal Sagev. She can walk there. Just go straight down
Fremont Street.

We pan with her as she walks along the garish street that
constitutes downtown Las Vegas..the sound of the slots, the
men in real and ersatz western clothes, the women in everything
from faded blue jeans with big hoop earrings to shorts,
tight pants, etc. Finally, we're in front of the Sal Sagev,
a run down hotel that looks as though it was built back before
the turn of the century. ELEANOR goes into the depressing
lobby, asks the desk clerk for Mr. Edward Simmons and is
directed to room 424. She gets into the ancient elevator
which creaks alarmingly as it makes its painful ascent to
the fourth floor. She gets out, finds 424, stands in front
of it for a moment, then knocks.

The door is opened by a middle-aged woman who still shows signs
of having been a sensational looking young woman. At the moment.
without make-up and with her hair up in pin-curls, she isn't
the most attractive sight in the world. She looks at ELEANOR
with a complete lack of recognition..ELEANOR uncertainly asks
for Mr. Simmons, the woman opens the door wider and, over her
shoulder tells the other occupant of the room there's a lady

3.

asking for him. In a moment a man appears behind her, a man
in his middle fifties, unshaven, disheveled, with the ruin of
a once handsome face and body. He takes one look at ELEANOR
and seems to shrink. Then, pulling himself together he pulls
her into the room..saying, as he does, that this is no lady,
this is my daughter.

As the scene plays on we learn that ED SIMMONS, a gambler,
was divorced from ELEANOR'S mother when the little girl was
five years old. He was in trouble with everybody, including
the law at the time, and ELEANOR'S mother, a rigid woman, had
secured complete custody of the child. Through the years, ED
had managed to rehabilitate himself..keeping in touch with his
daughter through letters and presents. Then, when ELEANOR, at
eighteen, escaped from her mother's domination by marrying,
she and her father, whom she loved dearly, had re-established
their relationship. ELEANOR and her first husband had had one
child, STACY, born when ELEANOR was nineteen..the marriage was
an unhappy one, for unconsciously the young woman had chosen
a man who was a replica of her mother. In desperation, she
started to gamble..got herself in deep trouble up to and including passing bad checks. It looked as though she was about
to live her father's life all over again, but he wasn't going
to let that happen to her. Somehow, he had scraped up the money
to cover her checks, and after the divorce, he kept on helping
her until she got on her feet. The responsibility of having a
child to raise, and her gratitude to her father, had turned
her life around..she got a good job, worked herself up to being
an executive secretary, managed to keep her daughter in a good
boarding school, and finally, just a year ago, had met and

1. *Winner Take All* began—and continued most of the way—as *Time Lock*. Such title changes are common in the film business. This one was the result of a survey which convinced NBC that most viewers would assume *Time Lock* to be a science fiction picture.
2. The difference between treatment and script is marked. Thus, the treatment's first three pages include action at Los Angeles International Airport and Las Vegas, with protagonist Eleanor Anderson's father, and so on. None of these appear in the final script—again, a not at all unusual state of affairs.

The first three drafts

Each draft, please note, takes a different tack. Any one of them
might have been chosen for production.

ACT ONE   1.

INT. CAR. LATE AFTERNOON.

ELEANOR ANDERSON, attractive, late twentyish
is driving, alone. At first she's listening
to a music station, but after a few moments
her expression changes as if she's forgotten
something. She glances at her watch and quickly
changes the station to a news and sports station,
just in time to hear the broadcaster announce
that they are shifting to HOLLYWOOD PARK for
the sixth race. We HEAR the race and as the
CAMERA moves in very close to her face, we see
the mounting tension, the near sexual excitement
and finally the look of truimph as her horse
wins.

INT. PAWN SHOP (TITLE SEQUENCE)

It is immediately following. ELEANOR enters.
The PAWNBROKER, a youngish man with long hair
and blue jeans is behind the counter, an underground newspaper spread in front of him. He
looks up as the door opens.

                    PAWNBROKER
          Hi. You bringing or taking today?

                              ELEANOR·(reaching into
                                   bag and extracting
                                   pawn ticket)
               Taking.

She holds out ticket, he takes it, pulls book
from under counter, looks up number, exits to
back of shop. In a minute he returns with a
solitaire diamong ring.

                    PAWNBROKER
          I cleaned it for you.

                              ELEANOR (putting ring on
                                   her engagement finger)
               Thank you.

She takes a roll of bills out of her purse and
lays them on the counter. The PAWNBROKER picks
them up, flips through them expertly.

                    PAWNBROKER
          Things going well again, huh?

                    ELEANOR
          I got lucky in a bridge game.

ACT ONE

FADE IN:

1   INT. ESQUIRE BRIDGE CLUB - DAY   1

The club has the look of luxury, done in good taste.
The walls are paneled in dark wood, there is a goodly
amount of space between the tables. There are perhaps
eight bridge games going on. The players, predominently
women, are casually but expensively dressed. We COME
IN CLOSE on one table at which ELEANOR ANDERSON is in
the process of playing out a hand. She is in her late
twenties, attractive, with features that in earlier days
would have been described as patrician. The defending
team are MALE and FEMALE respectively... her partner,
a WOMAN, whose cards are on the table, since Eleanor
is attempting to make the contract they have bid.

All four wear and look of intense concentration. There
is a small burst of conversation at a nearby table, and
Eleanor, about to play a card out of her hand, stops and
looks at the talkers with ill-concealed annoyance. We
FOLLOW her gaze to the table from which the sound is
emanating. The WOMAN at whom she is glaring speaks to
her own PARTNER.

> FIRST WOMAN
> For heaven sake! I wasn't
> shouting, was I?

> SECOND WOMAN
> Of course not. Those four make
> me sick! They ought to play in
> a crypt. That should be quiet
> enough for them.

> THIRD PLAYER (MALE)
> They're not playing. That's a
> blood game. Twenty-five cents
> a point.

CUT TO:

2   ELEANOR   2

her attention rivited on the last two cards in her hand.
She lays one on the table, the other players each play
a card, she gathers in the trick. Then she lays down
the last card in her hand, the player on her left plays,
she takes the last card from the upturned dummy and the
player on her right lays down the card in his hand.

(CONTINUED)

<u>ACT ONE</u>

FADE IN:

1   EXT. ESQUIRE BRIDGE CLUB - DAY   1

    It is a low building, attractive in the Spanish Style,
    with a curved driveway in front of it. Several men and
    women stand in front of it, waiting for the attendant
    to bring their cars. The name of the club is clearly
    visible. One woman, ELEANOR ANDERSON, attractive, late
    twentyish, stands with two WOMEN and a MAN. The man's
    car is brought first.

                     MAN
                (as he goes
                  around to
                  driver's side)
        Don't think you can rest on
        your laurels, Eleanor! Nobody
        sets me five hundred points
        and lives to gloat. I'll get
        <u>you</u> the next time.

    He gets in his car and drives off.

                    WOMAN
                (to Eleanor)
        That'll be the day! He'll
        never be in your class.

                   ELEANOR
        Nothing makes a bridge player
        look smarter than a little
        luck.

2   INT. CAR (TITLE SEQUENCE)   2

    Eleanor's car is brought. She waves goodbye, gets in
    and drives off. At first, she's listening to a MUSIC
    station, but after a few moments, her expression changes
    as if she's remembered something. She glances at her
    watch and quickly changes the station to a news and
    sports station just in time to HEAR the broadcaster
    announce that they are shifting to Hollywood Park for
    the 5th race. We HEAR the race and as the CAMERA MOVES
    IN VERY CLOSE to her face, we see the mounting tension,
    the near sexual excitement and finally the disappoint-
    ment as the race is over and the winner is announced.
    Coldly and suddenly, Eleanor reaches down and shuts off
    the radio.

                               CUT TO:

The final draft

The final draft, it develops, is closest to the first: a frustrating state of affairs, but not at all uncommon.

Rev. 12/10/74

ACT ONE

FADE IN:

1   EXT. CAR - LATE AFTERNOON   1

CAMERA FOLLOWS car as it moves along street in normal
traffic. We hear MUSIC and then a sudden switch of the
dial to a sports station.

2   INT. CAR - RADIO   2

BROADCASTER ANNOUNCES that they are shifting to
Hollywood Park for the Seventh Race. We start to HEAR
the pre-race info and horses are coming to the post,
etc. ELEANOR ANDERSON, attractive, late twentyish,
is driving alone. We HEAR the race as the CAMERA MOVES
IN VERY CLOSE to her face. We see the mounting tension,
the near sexual excitement and finally the look of
triumph as her horse wins.

3   INT. PAWN SHOP - DAY - (TITLE SEQUENCE)   3

It is immediately following. Eleanor enters. The
PAWNBROKER, a youngish man with long hair and blue
jeans is behind the counter, an underground newspaper
spread in front of him. He looks up as the door opens.

PAWNBROKER
Hi. You bringing or taking
today?

ELEANOR
(reaching into
bag and extracting
pawn ticket)
Taking.

She holds out ticket, he takes it, pulls book from under
counter, looks up number, exits to back of shop. In a
minute he returns with a solitaire diamond ring.

PAWNBROKER
I cleaned it for you.

ELEANOR
(putting ring on
her engagement
finger)
Thank you.

(CONTINUED)

Rev. 12/17/74   2.

3   CONTINUED: 3

She takes a roll of bills out of her purse and lays
them on the counter. The Pawnbroker picks them up,
flips through them expertly.

                    PAWNBROKER
          Things going well again, huh?

                    ELEANOR
          I got lucky in a bridge game.

                    PAWNBROKER
                    (grinning)
          I never learned how to play
          bridge.

Eleanor smiles, starts toward the door.

                    PAWNBROKER
                    (continuing)
          See you soon.

                    ELEANOR
                    (half serious,
                     her joke)
          Don't bet on it.   *

She turns and walks out, leaving him with an enigmatic
smile on his face.

                              CUT TO:

4   EXT. ANDERSON HOUSE - NIGHT   4

Eleanor drives into garage, gets out of car. The space
next to hers is empty. She goes around the front door
and we see that the house is a lovely and expensive one.
She is fumbling for her key when the door is opened by
a girl of about eleven. This is STACY ANDERSON, blonde,
chubby, with a pleasant open face which is now wearing
a warm smile.

                    STACY
          I heard you drive in, and I
    ⑥   figured you couldn't find
          your key again. You should
          wear it around your neck.
          That's where I wear my skate
          key.

                              (CONTINUED)

Rev. 12/17/74   3.

4   CONTINUED: 4

⑦
                          ELEANOR
                    (reaching out and
                     rumpling her hair,
                     affectionately)
                Miss Efficiency. Don't give
                up on me, baby. Some day I'll
                be as grownup as you are.

Arms around each other, they move into the entry hall.
As they do, MRS. COLSON, the cleaning lady, emerges
from the kitchen, wearing her coat.

⑧
                          MRS. COLSON
                You're late again, Mrs. Anderson.
                My husband doesn't like his
                supper late. He doesn't take
                kindly to it.

                          ELEANOR
                I'm sorry, Mrs. Colson, really
                I am. It won't happen again.
                    (she reaches into
                     her bag and starts
                     to rummage around
                     for money)
⑨   I've got your money right here.

Finally, in desperation, Eleanor empties her bag out
onto the hall table. There is no money, just the usual
contents of a purse, including a checkbook.

                          ELEANOR
                    (continuing)
⑩   Isn't that just like me? I
                spent it all at the market!

Stacy exits to the car.   *

                          ELEANOR
                    (continuing)
                I said to myself, now be sure
                and bring cash for Mrs. Colson
                and then I forgot all about it.
                The prices -- well, you just
                wouldn't believe the...

                          MRS. COLSON
                I'll take a check this time,
                but no more. I like cash.

                          ELEANOR
                    (starting to
                     write check)
                Shall I make it out to <u>Mrs.</u>
                Colson or...?

                                        (CONTINUED)

Rev. 12/17/74   4.

4   CONTINUED - (2):   4

                        MRS. COLSON
                Cash. Make it out to cash.
                If you make it out to me and
                I don't report it, it ain't
                honest.

        Eleanor extends the check, and taking it, Mrs. Colson
        exits. As Stacy enters out the door after her.   *

5   INT. KITCHEN - IMMEDIATELY FOLLOWING   5

        Eleanor, not stopping to take off her jacket, is busily
        taking things out of the refrigerator, preparatory to *
        making dinner. There is a large pot on the stove, the
        steam coming from it testifying to water boiling in
        it, and a large glass salad bowl with greens already
        cut up in it. Stacy and Eleanor speak, simultaneously. *

                        STACY
                There aren't any groceries
                in the car.

                        ELEANOR
                    (over her line)
                You're an angel, you know that?
                Dinner's got a fighting chance
                of being on time with you at
                home covering for me.

        Eleanor busies herself washing stalks of broccoli.

                        ELEANOR
                    (continuing)
                What happened in your French
                class? Was I right about using
                the subjunctive in that sentence?

                        STACY
                    (nodding)
                Monsieur Goldberg was very
                impressed. Eleanor, what
                happened to the groceries?   *

                        ELEANOR
                What are you, the F.B.I.? Tell   *
                me more about the Frenchman
                from the Bronx.

                        STACY
                    (giggling)
                I told him that's what you
                call him. He says he'd like
                to meet you.

                                    (CONTINUED)

Rev. 12/17/74

5.

5   CONTINUED: 5

                         ELEANOR
       Ooh-La-La.   *

                                            CUT TO:

6   INT. BILL AND ELEANOR'S BEDROOM   6

Stacy at makeup table with eyebrow pencil making herself *
up.

                     ELEANOR'S VOICE   *
       Did your daddy call?

                       STACY
       No. Aunt Connie did, though.
       She says you should call her
       back.

Eleanor emerges from the bathroom dressed more casually, *
just as Stacy begins to try to apply eyebrow pencil.

                     ELEANOR
       Not like that. Make an arch.

                     STACY
       Like this?

                     ELEANOR
                    (going over and
                    studying the
                    problem seriously)
       You have kind of a heart-shaped
       face. Maybe...

(13)

She starts to help Stacy draw new eyebrows. Neither of
them notice that BILL ANDERSON, a handsome man in his
early thirties, is standing in the doorway watching
them.

                     BILL
       Could I make an appointment
       for a haircut, please?

He comes over to them, kisses first Stacy, then Eleanor.

                     ELEANOR
       Mrs. Colson says her husband   *
       doesn't take kindly to having
       a late supper. I'm glad I'm
       not married to <u>him</u>.

                               (CONTINUED)

Rev. 12/17/74   11.

9   CONTINUED: 9

                              PAUL   *
              Odd or even?

                            ELEANOR
                            (musing)
              Odd.

                              PAUL   *
              Okay. Odd for $5?

                            ELEANOR
              Wanna make it $10?

                              PAUL   *
              Okay with me.

                            ELEANOR
              But don't let me catch you
              touching that hose until I
              come out.

                              PAUL   *
                          (innocently)
              Do I ever?

                            ELEANOR
                          (as she walks
                            toward garage
                            area)
              Perish forbid!

PAN with her as she walks into garage and heads for small
room at its rear. She opens the door to reveal a
cluttered desk and a MAN in mechanic's overalls. He is
on the phone.

                            ARNIE
                          (into phone)
              Come on! I only book 'em --
              I don't guarantee 'em. Maybe
              it was the wrong time of the
              month for that filly. You owe
              me five C's.
                          (listens)
              Okay. But no later than noon
              tomorrow, understand? I ain't
              no bank.

He hangs up, turns to Eleanor.

                            ARNIE
                          (continuing)
              Sometimes I think I'm in the
              wrong racket. If I hung up
              a sign, at least I could
              charge interest.

                                        (CONTINUED)

Rev. 12/10/74   12.

9   CONTINUED - (2):   9

                          ELEANOR
              Well, today it's my turn.
              <u>You</u> owe <u>me</u>.

                          ARNIE
              Right, your luck's changing.
                    (starts counting
                    out money,
                    $1,050)
              One, two, three, four.

                          ELEANOR
              It couldn't have gotten much
              worse.

                          ARNIE
              Yeah, six, seven, my customers
              had a good day yesterday.
              Jackpots all over the place.

                          ELEANOR
              We gotta live, too, Arnie.

                          ARNIE
              Ten and fifty.

                          ELEANOR
                    (putting the $50
                    in her purse)
              Anyway, you'll be happy to know
              I'm giving you a chance to get
              it back. I want a thousand
              on Stanley R, in the 8th at
              Arlington to win -- on the
              nose...

                          ARNIE
              He's going off at 20 to 1.
              Are you serious, you'll bust
              me -- A grant on Stanley R.
              What you got, a tip or
              something, I can't cover
              this myself...

                          ELEANOR
                    (smiling)
              You'll find a way. See you.
                    (she exits)

              PAN with Eleanor as she exits TO gas pump area. The
              gas line is still in her tank, the Attendant nowhere
              to be seen. She gets into the car and waits for him.
              Another car, driven by a pretty woman in early middle
              age, drives up to the next pump. This is EDIE GOULD,

                                              (CONTINUED)

Rev. 12/17/74

20.*

12   CONTINUED: 12

(17)
                    ELEANOR
Because you're you and I'm me.
It's as simple as that.
     (beat)
It's hard to have fun with
the Grand Inquisitor.

                  MRS. BARCLAY
Eleanor, all I really want is
your happiness.
     (beat)
How is everything with you?

(18)
                    ELEANOR
If you want to know if I'm
gambling, why don't you just
come right out and ask?

(19)
                  MRS. BARCLAY
     (with deep feeling)
Don't throw away this marriage!
Your first one was a nightmare
-- your life was a nightmare...

                    ELEANOR
Could we talk about something
else, Mother?

                  MRS. BARCLAY
Of course we could, but that
wouldn't fool either of us.
Eleanor, I beg of you...

(20)
                    ELEANOR
I'm not gambling! There! Can't
you believe me?

                  MRS. BARCLAY
I'll try, Eleanor. I'll try.

                                CUT TO:

13   INT. KITCHEN - NIGHT   13

Eleanor chopping celery for dinner. RADIO is on, same
Announcer as opening. Eighth race has just started,
Announcer calling race.

Rev. 12/10/74   21.

14   CLOSEUP - ELEANOR'S FACE (TENSE)   14

(21)   ANNOUNCER'S VOICE
                    And Day Stalker wins with
                    Stanley R second by a nose,
                    with ABC third in the time
                    period.

(22) 15   CLOSEUP - ELEANOR'S FACE (PALE)   15

                                        FADE OUT.

                        <u>END OF ACT ONE</u>

Rev. 12/17/74   22.

ACT TWO

FADE IN:

16   INT. DINING ROOM, ANDERSON HOUSE - EVENING   16

(23)   The table is set with lovely china and crystal, candles,
       flowers at its center. Eleanor is putting the finishing
       touches on it. There is the SOUND of the front door
(24)   slamming, off. Eleanor stiffens, spins around just as
       Bill enters.   *

                        BILL
                  (eyeing table as
                   he kisses her)
(25)   Pretty fancy. Looks like
             Better Homes and Gardens.
             Where's the birthday girl?
             Did you get the puppy?

                        ELEANOR
             Yes, well?

                        BILL
             Well what?

                        ELEANOR
             What happened in Phoenix?

                        BILL
             It looks good.

                        ELEANOR
                  (visible tension)
             Well, tell me about it!

                        BILL
             Later.
                  (at the expres-
                   sion on her face)
(26)   Art didn't come back with me.
             There were things he wanted
             to check on. He'll be calling
             and then we'll know if there's
             really anything to talk about.

       Stacy enters, sees Bill, comes over to kiss him.

                        STACY
(27)   Are we moving?

                                        (CONTINUED)

1. The opening establishes place before moving in on Eleanor.
2. Action establishes character in this sequence. In the treatment, emphasis was much heavier on expository incorporation of detail, with no zeroing in on Eleanor as a gambler. Here, her gambling is nailed down by the very nature of the situation, with no need for author-convenience lines.
3. Though the pawnbroker is a minor character, this brief description sets him up very much as an individual.
4. Note the brevity and natural tone of the lines Ledner gives her characters.
5. Further characterization of the pawnbroker—minor detail, apparently, but of a nature to make him likable and in direct contrast to the traditional Shylock image.
6. Stacy talks as a child—differently, certainly, than either Eleanor or the pawnbroker. And what she says establishes the feeling-tone of her relationship to Eleanor.
7. More feeling-tone, more establishment of relationship—this time, Eleanor's side of the coin.
8. Another character, another speech pattern.
9. More characterization of Eleanor; a tightening of focus—via action, not lecture—on the gambler and money.
10. Eleanor proves herself a liar.
11. A wryly cynical touch—characterization coupled with a chuckle.
12. Eleanor tries to slide past Stacy's discovery. Again, Ledner is characterizing—showing that Eleanor will resort to duplicity, if necessary, in order to hide her secret passion for gambling. It's the kind of thing which could very well make her unsympathetic, had the writer not already established her other side in 6 and 7, above.
13. More characterizing of Eleanor as warm and loving.

A jump ahead, now, to page 11:

14. The compulsiveness of Eleanor's gambling comes through via her inability even to resist betting with a filling station attendant.
15. Quick characterization of a bit player. Note that Arnie's speech pattern matches his mechanic's overalls. Which is not to say *all* mechanics would speak so but, rather, that the speech is not *out* of keeping with the mechanic's label.
16. A long-shot bet—and a new complication. Eleanor's again putting her neck in a noose. Tension automatically tightens. That's the effect a potentially ruinous thousand-dollar bet has on most of us.

Again, a jump ahead—this time, to page 20:

17. Here Eleanor and her mother are clashing. It's the old story of mother being motherly, daughter being rebellious.
18. Exposition via believable conflict: Gambling is an old problem for Eleanor.
19. A serious problem, too. It's cost Eleanor one marriage. Tension can't help but rise.
20. Again, Eleanor demonstrates her inability to refrain from lying; the grip her gambling mania has on her.
21. Payoff to the thousand-dollar bet Eleanor placed in 16, above. It constitutes a devastating complication: a logical yet unanticipated—by Eleanor—new development that puts her far deeper into trouble.
22. Eleanor's reaction shows how bad this is. It also constitutes the screenplay's first-act curtain: a cliff-hanger designed to hold viewers through commercials and station break.

23. Act Two begins with markedly lower tension, to open the way for rising action and, ultimately, a new complication and crisis. To this end, Ledner offers us a time lapse and the routine of homey family life.
24. Eleanor's reaction reflects her state of affairs/state of mind . . . foreshadows trouble yet to come.
25. Bill's non-uptight behavior, in marked contrast to Eleanor's tension, helps through contrast to intensify the moment.
26. Bill becomes aware of Eleanor's tension. His line helps characterize him as a sympathetic and understanding man.
27. A child's reaction—but one which further builds the now rapidly rising tension.

There's much, much more, of course. But throughout, the issue remains the same: a portrayal of the ebb and flow of human emotion, in terms of the things people say and do.

PRETTY BOY, BAD BOY (original screenplay),
by Raymond Friday Locke.

A highly literate man with a taste for history and anthropology, Mississippi-born Raymond Friday Locke was founding editor of *Mankind* magazine. In addition to his scripting of assorted screenplays and teleplays (he recently adapted Ruth Shinsel's *Sign of The Sword* for film), he is author of three books on the American Indian, as well as many national magazine articles and short stories.

It's hard to say how many film versions have been made of the life and death of Pretty Boy Floyd. But that doesn't mean there isn't always room for one more. Locke's script was for Robert Fryer-James Cresson Productions. In it, he shows how imaginative handling can give a fresh, contemporary look to what might otherwise have proved a trite and tedious segment. He also demonstrates another approach to the handling of character in script.

PRETTY BOY, BAD BOY

a screenplay

by Raymond Friday Locke

WGAw
Rep: Ross Hirshorn   Second Draft
     IFA   October 23, 1974
     Los Angeles

Pretty Boy, Bad Boy

a screenplay

by Raymond Friday Locke

Charles Arthur "Pretty Boy" Floyd, called "Chock" by his friends, was born on a farm in north Georgia February 3, 1904. Seven years later his father, Walter F. Floyd, moved his wife and eight children to the hamlet of Akins, Oklahoma, eight miles north of Sallisaw, Sequoyah County. There the Floyd family eked out a living operating a small dirt farm and a country grocery store. The store went broke in 1924, just before our story begins.

Charles Arthur began his crime career at the age of seventeen when he looted the local postoffice of $350 in pennies. The people of eastern Oklahoma had their own method of dealing with such matters; Chock was allowed to give back the pennies and the incident was forgotten. Two years later he married sixteen year old Ruby Hargraves, daughter of a Bixby, Oklahoma, sharecropper.

We pick up Chock Floyd's story in the spring of 1925, less than a year after he married Ruby. While most of what follows is true, this screenplay is not an attempt at film biography or documentation. Biography is the essence of a man's worth in the context of his times and therein lies the truth of this story . . .

1.

Pretty Boy
Locke - 2

Fade in on

1.   The entire screen is white, a white that hurts the eyes.

②   Hold on shot

      Eventually it begins to come clear that the white is
      the afternoon sun in a colorless sky.

Cut to

③   2.   A high shot of a shirtless young man following a plow
           pulled by a tired old mule in a piney woods bordered field.

Pull in

      To the field which is nothing but red dust in which stumpy,
      yellowing stalks of corn are thirsting. The man is
      Charles Arthur "Chock" Floyd, the year is 1925 and the field
      is in the Cookson Hills, Sequoyah County, Oklahoma.

④   Chock is six foot-two, handsome, muscular and his hair is
      black. He has dark blue eyes but most people would
      remember them later as being brown. Right now he is sweat-
      stained and disgusted and would tell you that he's worked
      like a dog on this dirt-poor farm, owned by his father,
      clawing at the dust for crops, dust that increases with
      each passing year through storms and erosion and will
      continue to do so until the entire area will come to be
      known as the Great Dust Bown.

      And he would be damned if he could tell you why he's
      following this plow that slips through the red dust with
      so little ease; no plant will fruit in it. He'd also tell
      you that following this mule's ass is not his ultimate
      ambition.

Cut to

3.   Full shot, field, as Chock wipes the sweat from his face
      and looks off into the distance.

Cut to

4.   Chock and the mule as he unhitches the harness, slaps
      the animal on the back with the reins and follows it
      out of the field, leaving the plow standing in the dust.

Pretty Boy
Locke - 77

Cut to

207. A full shot of Sallisaw, Day, exactly the same as #16.
But this time it is Saturday and the streets are filled
with people doing their weekend shopping. Newt and
Mister Biggers are seated on the same bench. And sitting
directly in front of Old Man Kemp's State Bank of Sallisaw
is Chock's yellow car with George behind the wheel.
As we see Mister Biggers and Newt get up:

NEWT (Off)

He ought to be coming out about now.

Pull in until the bank front fills the screen. Directly
in the center of the screen are the double doors in which
Chock got his machine gun caught the first time.

Suddenly the doors virtually explode open and they stay
open as Chock walks through, his machine gun under his
right arm and carrying the full gray bag in his left
hand.

We pull back as Chock casually walks to the yellow car
and gets in. Newt, Mister Biggers and several others
stand off to the side, watching.

Cut to

208. Chock and George, inside the car.

GEORGE

What now?

CHOCK

Just drive around town real slow like.

GEORGE

Are you crazy?

CHOCK
Smiling.
     Nope.

GEORGE
Catching on, as he eases off.

The hell you're not.

Pretty Boy
Locke - 78

Cut to

209. The street as the car slowly pulls away from the bank.

                        CHOCK
                    G
                     George--

                        GEORGE

           I know. All I have to do is drive. . .

Musical Interlude

⑦

It should begin as Chock and George start driving about
the town. The song can be sung (if so by a male voice)
or it can be an instrumental but it should be very,very
pretty and while there were some very pretty songs popular
in 1930 (But Not For Me, Love For Sale, Sunnyside of the
Street), it should not be an arrangment of one of those.

What we see during the song is a series of shots of
the yellow car being driving about the town, with Chock
throwing all the money he's stolen from Old Man Kemp
to the people in the streets. The people will run and
jump for the bills as they float through the air almost
but not exactly, in slow motion. Chock as George, when
we cut to them, will be having just a high old time as
the streets fill with people of all ages running, jumping
after the money. The feeling should be that of a modern
ballet.

⑧

The song will continue, or at least the music, through
the next three scenes. Chock throws the last of the
money out the window and as the yellow car disappears
down the street we

Lap Dissolve to

⑨

210. Interior of Bank # 1--two bank clerks and they are watching
       Chock and George, dressed diffently than above, busily
       rob the bank.
                    FIRST BANK CLERK

       Whispering to Second Bank Clerk:

           It's Pretty Boy Floyd.

Cut to

⑩

211. Interior of Bank # 2--George and Chock, extremely well dressed,
       are busily robbing it. Now three bank clerks stand in a row,
       their hands in the air.

Pretty Boy
Locke - 79

211. Continued.

FIRST BANK CLERK
Whispering to Second Bank Clerk:

It's Pretty Boy Floyd!

THIRD BANK CLERK
To Second Bank Clerk:

Who'd he say it was?

SECOND BANK CLERK

Pretty Boy Floyd!

FIRST BANK CLERK

And George Cross!

Cut to

212. Interior of Bank # 3--There is a well-dressed banker,
two tellers and an old lady with a hearing horn. They
are, of course, watching Chock and George rob the bank,
and their hands are in the air. One of the tellers, hands
still in the air, tugs at the banker's sleeve. They whisper.

FIRST TELLER

It's Pretty Boy Floyd!

The banker is impressed, almost proud.

SECOND TELLER

Pretty Boy Floyd, you say?

OLD LADY
Almost shouting:

Who'd he say?

BANKER

Shouting into her ear horn:

Pretty Boy Floyd, he said!

Cut to

213. Chock. He smiles and waves as he and George walk out
of the bank with the money. The musical interlude ends.

1. The thing you sell in a biographical or pseudo-biographical script is character. Locke attacks the job straightforwardly in an introductory statement to his screenplay, orienting the script's readers to the time, place, and circumstance of Floyd's world.
2. Time, place, and circumstance again—but this time presented in terms of experiencing and mood, as the film itself will offer them to viewers.
3. One way to create empathy in viewers is to show someone reacting to a simple, universal, easily understood human experience. Here Locke uses heat and fatigue not only to introduce his central character, but to make him human.
4. Scriptwriters vary as to how they feel about this kind of interpolation of background. Some prefer to let the shot descriptions themselves tell the story. Others insist that a fuller, more subjective approach is better.

Jumping ahead deep into the script, we come to page 77 and a different handling of a too-familiar situation:

5. *Déja vu*, the sense of familiarity that makes it seem a thing has been seen before, can have marked value in capturing viewer attention and feeling in a film. Here Locke plays out a sequence against the background of an early Floyd humiliation. His use of leisurely pace rather than slam-bang action is an obviously calculated ploy that reduces tension in preparation for the humor of a unique relief scene. It also strengthens his characterization of Floyd: Only a very special kind of outlaw could have conceived the episode that follows.
6. Relationship: Floyd and George. Repetition of what amounts to a sort of running gag, as well as reiteration of the already-established Floyd/George character relationship and pecking order.
7. Anything goes these days and imagination is at a premium. Taking full advantage of the 1930s nostalgia wave (remember *Bonnie and Clyde*?), Locke draws maximum mileage from and adds charm of a sort to a relatively minor incident, in effect setting it to music and choreographing it.
8. Three bank robberies; or, How to Have Fun and Make People Laugh at Something which Otherwise Might Prove Tedious.
9. Bank robbery no. 1, and the start of a running gag. Note that the music continues through this sequence and the two which follow.
10. A larger bank; more prosperous robbers; a bigger buildup.
11. A still larger bank, more people, and the gimmick of an old lady with a hearing horn for a final sight gag.
12. End of musical episode; end of segment. Verdict: a fresh, shiny handling of what otherwise might have been a tired old routine.

Locke here has given us not only a change of pace, but a demonstration of the use of a musical interlude as a fantasy device to bridge time and space and establish mood.

PRELUDE TO AN EXECUTION (original screenplay),
by William P. McGivern.

Too many writers slack off on their print copy when Hollywood success strikes. One of the outstanding exceptions is William P. McGivern, a giant of a Chicago Irishman who's climbed from the old Ziff-Davis pulps to a continuing output of such best-selling suspense novels as *The Big Heat, Rogue Cop, Caprifoil* and, most recently, *Night of The Juggler.* Ten of his books have been made into pictures.

He also has found time to script a seemingly endless succession of TV shows, as well as theatrical release films ranging from *Gold in the Sky* and *The Wrecking Crew* to *I Saw What You Did.*

Excerpts from *Prelude to an Execution* used with permission of William P. McGivern.

PRELUDE TO AN EXECUTION

An Original Screenplay

by

William P. McGivern

PRELUDE TO AN EXECUTION

FADE IN:

EXT. PARKING LOT - FULL SHOT - NIGHT

From O.S. a flashing neon sign sends criss-cross patterns of
light and shadow across rows of elegant cars. Many imports
gleam in the flickering darkness, suggesting by their numbers,
wealth and influence. We hear nothing except a high wind,
which stirs bits of refuse on the ground. Our impression is
that it is late at night. Some of the parking slots are empty,
no attendants are in sight.

After a beat, we HEAR from O.S. the crisp, lignt SOUND of high
heels on the pavement, distinct and loud in a silence broken
only by rising winds.

ANOTHER ANGLE - TO INCLUDE TRACY CASSIDY

TRACY hurries into the SHOT, looking about with a touch of mild
concern in her manner. In her middle twenties, Tracy wears a
black suede jump suit. She is tall, elegantly slim, with a
suggestion of a dancer's grace in her movements. We will like
what we see of Tracy immediately. There is an engaging warmth
about this girl, something which suggests a swinger with the
heart of a den mother.

Tracy stops, looks off, scanning the rows of cars. We note
now that she has a manila envelope in her hands.

                    TRACY
                  (calls)
              Mr. Arnold?

After a beat:

TRACY'S POV - PARKING LOT

CAMERA PANS SLOWLY across rows of parked cars.

Nothing stirs. The silence is complete.

BACK TO TRACY

She hurries along a row of cars, going deeper into the lot,

2.

continues to glance right and left, obviously looking for
someone. She stops, her manner unafraid, but mildly anxious.

>   TRACY
>   (calls)
>   Mr. Arnold?

CAMERA ZOOMS TO:

DANNY ARNOLD

In his early thirties, DANNY ARNOLD looks the prototype of all
bookkeepers: smooth, closed features, eyes expressionless
behind thick glasses. He stands between rows of cars, looking
off at Tracy O.S. There is something menacing in his silence,
his icy lack of reaction. From O.S. we HEAR:

>   TRACY'S VOICE (O.S.)
>   (calling)
>   Mr. Nelson?

The ANGLE WIDENS to INCLUDE JAKE NELSON. Nelgon stands beside
Arnold, smooth black leather gloves over his big hands. Nelson
is about thirty, taller than Arnold, with the powerful body
and ridged forehead of an ex-fighter. While both men wear
conservative suits, we know at first glance that they are
professional muscle, cold and dangerous. From O.S. we HEAR
Tracy's approaching footsteps. Arnold gives Nelson a brief nod.

MAIN TITLES BEGIN HERE.

SHOT - PAST ARNOLD & NELSON - TO TRACY

She is ten yards away, in profile to us, glancing about the
parking lot. In the B.G. of the SHOT, we see the entrance
to a swank restaurant-nightclub. Uniformed doormen stand
under the ornately canopied entrance.

Above we see a flashing neon sign which reads: THE CARAVANS.

>   ARNOLD
>   Tracy? What is it?

Tracy reacts, turns, walks crisply toward Arnold and Nelson,
a smile of relief brightening her face. In this SHOT, we
will again be conscious of her lovely, graceful body, the
pleasant warmth of her manner.

>   TRACY
>   It's my lucky night.

3.

She stops, extends the manila envelope to Arnold.

                    TRACY (Cont'd)
              Mr. Stone wants you to take
              this to --

⑧ The sentence is chopped off as if by an axe. With brutal and
shocking abruptness, Nelson slams a fist into Tracy's stomach,
doubling her up helplessly. Arnold grabs her slumping body,
Nelson opens the rear door of a black sedan, and the two men
push her into the rear seat. She cannot cry out or scream.
We know from her strangling sobs that she is fighting for
breath.

Nelson leaps in beside her. Arnold jumps behind the wheel,
starts the car. As it roars swiftly AWAY FROM CAMERA,
accelerating under reckless power:

Our title fills the SCREEN:

⑨   PRELUDE TO AN EXECUTION

EXT. A SIX-LANE HIGHWAY - FULL SHOT - NIGHT

In light traffic, we PICK UP Arnold's sedan speeding south
through areas of heavy industry. (Our locale is somewhere on
the north Atlantic seaboard, anywhere from Newark, N.J. down
to Maryland).

In the B.G. of the SHOT, we see blazes of light from the metal
skeletons of petroleum-cracking refineries. They blaze wildly,
erratically against the darkness. White fogs rise from the
frozen salt marshes which stretch out on either side of the
highway.

INT. ARNOLD'S CAR - FULL SHOT - NIGHT

Nelson has a hand clamped over Tracy's mouth while his other
hand locks her wrist behind her back. Tracy, with hysterical
strength, jerks her head free from Nelson's grip.

                       TRACY
                (frantic; pure terror)
              Why? For God's sake, why?

⑩ Nelson clamps his hand back across her mouth, tightens the
grip on her arm, painfully, deliberately.

What's the lesson to be drawn from this script excerpt? It sums up as "How to hook an audience." —or a scriptreader.

1. The visual image here is strong; the setting established with minimal waste motion. Further, it's a setting whose bleakness automatically rouses premonitions of jeopardy in us from the start.
2. The offscreen sound here prepares us for an entrance.
3. Note McGivern's emphasis on feeling, mood, in this description—"We will like what we see of Tracy," "engaging warmth," "a swinger with the heart of a den mother."
4. Again, mood dominates—but a different mood: "smooth, closed features, eyes expressionless," "menacing in his silence," "icy lack of reaction."
5. More mood, not to mention use of characterizing detail—"smooth black leather gloves," "ridged forehead," and so on.
6. Foreshadowing, a signal to the audience that something's coming, even though we don't know what it is. In view of the situation, we're a cinch to assume danger's in the offing.
7. Establishment of characters in relationship to each other and to the broader setting.
8. Here, in a flash, McGivern "organizes the audience's emotions," in Howard Lindsay's phrase, via shock action as Nelson punches Tracy. Empathetic tension is instantaneous, jeopardy established in a rush.
9. The title is a knell-of-doom exclamation point to the teaser's action.
10. Tracy voices the question that's already gripping every viewer. Simultaneously, she establishes her own helplessness and ignorance of the situation.

Prelude to an Execution was written as an original screenplay—and didn't sell. But the ways of Hollywood are devious. The script eventually became the basis for a *Madigan* TV episode, so in the end McGivern's gamble did pay off.

THE GULLIES (fact film proposal), *by Charles A. Palmer.*

THE GULLIES (shooting script, Episode B), *by Charles A. Palmer and Audrey Kaczenski.*

Once upon a time there was a highly successful New England businessman named Charles A. ("Cap") Palmer, Later he became a highly successful film writer. Then, tiring of the major studio routine, he abandoned it in order to set up his own corporation to produce business films for such firms as Kaiser Aluminum, Western Electric, International Harvester, and Hilton Hotels, among others.

Two-hundred-fifty pictures and innumerable awards later, Palmer continues today as executive producer of Parthenon Pictures, the firm he founded.

He also continues to develop and script films, with *The Gullies* an intriguing example of how to promote and package a fact piece.

The proposal

How do you sell a concept? It's a fine art, certainly, and each picture demands its own approach. But this excerpt from Palmer's handling of his *Gullies* proposal is a good example of a highly skilled pro in action.

PARTHENON PICTURES

HOLLYWOOD

2625 TEMPLE STREET, HOLLYWOOD, CALIFORNIA 90026
DUnkirk 5-3911

PROPOSAL

"THE GULLIES"

LAYOUT TREATMENT FOR
A PUBLIC SERVICE FILM SERIES
ON CONSUMER EDUCATION

by
Charles "Cap" Palmer
5/20/74

DOCUMENTARY FILMS FOR BUSINESS

"THE GULLIES"

*A package of 5 5-minute "short
stories" featuring the Gully
family, each concerned with a
consumer "gull."*

The proposed treatment is unique, and the
best way to explain it is via stating the
initial assignment and retracing the analysis which led to "THE GULLIES" solution.

The initial problem is that we are entering into a field where
there is already a great deal of competition. Many pictures
have been made on consumer fraud. Some are really pretty good.
So what we had to do was find some way of handling Consumer
Education -- consumer gulls and cons -- in some new way that
would earn us a general audience by somehow overleaping the
things that are already on the market.

Well, the conventional way of approaching it would be the usual
20-25 minute documentary type movie. That had disadvantages to
it in the beginning, regardless of marketability. Because for
one thing, we'd have to lump too many different things into
the one package and by the time the audience would walk away
from that screening they'd have say 8 or 10 or 15 diffent kinds
of gulls in their minds, and the only residual impression they'd
go away with would be, "There sure are a lot of crooks in the
world -- I'd better not ever buy anything." They couldn't sign
a "resolved that" at the end of it. For another thing, the 20
or 25 minute picture wouldn't reach its adult audience effectively.

THE GULLIES

-2-

PARTHENON PICTURES

You can get almost anything to a school audience -- these kids have to sit there and take it. That is, they have to <u>sit</u> there -- but they don't have to absorb the message. We've got to earn their honest interest. And the adult audience -- which is spending money all the time, and a lot of it wrongly -- is even harder to impress.

More -- even supposing we were to make a perfectly wonderful 28-minute picture and take it to the TV stations to run on their "free time," the TV stations may run it because they've got that public-service log to fill for the FCC -- but unless it's entertaining and interesting, they'll run it at a poor time with little or no audience. Worse, even if we get a good time slot, <u>our message will have only this one shot at the audience</u>, and they won't be looking at it with concentration. So we're not going to get much impact -- at best a melange with little or no lasting <u>effect</u>.

⑤ Our job here is to make the consumer-con message really sink into people's heads. And to do that we've got to have <u>repetition</u>. All good advertising is based on repetition: one ad doesn't get you much of anything -- the second ad helps, the third helps some more. You've got to hit it, hit it, hit it, hit it, hit it.

⑥ So we've got to have some way of doing the same thing. But we cannot give a series of 20-25 minute pictures for TV -- the stations wouldn't run them and there isn't that much money around to produce them.

THE GULLIES   -3-

PARTHENON PICTURES

⑦ So, to get to our proposed solution, we propose a sort of mini-
series of several pictures; but "little pictures" of around
5 minutes; each devoted to <u>one</u> con -- one consumer gull -- and
very interesting and entertaining -- because it's a crime show
in effect, and it's happening to people like <u>us</u>, to our neighbors
down the street -- so we'll identify with it. And since we see
just one fraud, when we've seen that 5-minute picture we go
away realizing the next time we see an ad for a brand-new sewing
machine at $20, we'd better be prepared to resist the switch to
the "better" one at $200. That's all we go away with -- Bait
and Switch. Next week, we get educated on Mail Order. The week
after that, perhaps Home Improvement, then Land Investment; Door
to Door. And each one sinks into us. As a parallel; in school
we teach one lesson at a time, we don't dump the whole semester
course over their heads in one three-hour lecture. It's only
logical that we educate the consumer in the same way. And if
we find a format for this which is interesting enough to people,
we can get them to come back next week and the week after that,
and the week after that.

Our next step is to figure out how to make our shows interesting
enough so that the television stations will accept the series,
and on a scheduled basis, hopefully in "good time."

⑧ Well, what's "interesting"? What catches people and holds them?
One proven answer is family shows, situation comedies -- The
Waltons, All In The Family, The Brady Bunch, and so on. So it

1. Fact films come in all shapes and sizes. Witness that this proposal is concerned with a series of five five-minute pictures.
2. Palmer says he's simply a good explainer, not a salesman. Here he explains why he's giving his explanation.
3. The prevailing situation, briefly outlined.
4. Why Palmer feels the traditional approach isn't the best, in view of said prevailing situation. Observe that this is presented in terms of purpose and audience.
5. Having shot down the traditional approach in flames, Palmer now introduces his first sales—pardon me; explanation—point: the virtue of repetition.
6. Point 2: an attack on the normal-length picture as a solution to the client's problem.
7. Now, the Palmer solution: a series of mini-pictures, each devoted to one technique by which consumers are conned.
8. Next: What approach to take in order to catch and hold an audience.

  . . . and so it goes, point after point. The final product adds up to a pleasant, informal, low-key presentation.

  Is it effective? This time it was, certainly: Palmer got the contract!

The shooting script

A proposal, outline, or treatment can, to a degree, stay general. A shooting script, in contrast, must spell out what happens in such detail that a production crew can capture the desired action effectively on film, as witness these excerpts.

PARTHENON PICTURES

HOLLYWOOD

2625 TEMPLE STREET, HOLLYWOOD, CALIFORNIA 90026
· DUnkirk 5-3911

"THE GULLIES"

by
Charles Palmer
and
Audrey Kaczenski

EPISODE "B"

"BAIT AND SWITCH"
(10-minute Version)

3/31/75
Prod. 211

DOCUMENTARY FILMS FOR BUSINESS

10 MINUTE VERSION

PARTHENON PICTURES

"THE GULLIES"

EPISODE "B"

"BAIT AND SWITCH"

①

②

10-B-1	FAST ZOOM-IN TO HOLD ON CU NAME ON MAILBOX - "THE GULLIES" (SHOOT 15 times @ 5')	⑤ STET MUSIC THEME

	(SERIES OF FLASHES OF GULLY CHARACTERS IN ACTION (LIKE MTM INTR'O) TIMED WITH THE NARRATION: (SHOOT 50')	

NARRATOR

How do you do, I'm Frank Nelson,

bringing you another visit with

that intriguing family, the Gullies.

③ 10-B-2 GUS
    10-B-3 GUS AND GRACIE

Gus, and his wife Gracie ...

④ 10-B-4 GIL
    10-B-5 GIL AND GLORIA

younger brother Gilbert, and his
wife Gloria ...

10-B-6 GRANDMA

feisty Grandma ...

10-B-7 GALSWORTHY

and, the teenager's teenager,

Galsworthy.

10-B-8 SLOW ZOOM IN TO EXT. GULLY
HOME (NIGHT) -- ACROSS MAIL-
BOX ... CAR IN FRONT, MOTOR-
·CYCLE IN DRIVE (CARTOON)

What makes them intriguing is

their devotion to the great

American tendency to fall for

10-B-9 MAIN STORY TITLES SUPER'D
OVER ABOVE SCENE

consumer cons, frauds, pitfalls,

and gulls. In short, utterly

unlike you and I, the Gullies

are -- gullible.

MUSIC THEME CONCLUDES

BAIT & SWITCH (10)   -2-

PARTHENON PICTURES

10-B-10	GULLY LIVING ROOM. GUS, GRACIE, AND GRANDMA LOOKING AT TV ... GALSWORTHY STUDYING AT TABLE IN BG WITH STEREO NEARBY ... ZOOM TO CU GALSWORTHY	⑦ As this episode opens, Galsworthy, as is his nightly habit, is easing the pains of homework with the musical accompaniment of Malice Glooper and his All Electric Aggravators. (WE HEAR IT) Er -- musical?
10-B-10A	3-SHOT AT TV	Not to his father who, after some months of this nightly decibel debauchery is finally going out of his skull.
10-B-10B	CU GUS	⑤ₐ Galsworthy, my son, knock off that expletive-deleted uproar or I will set your hair on fire.
10-B-10C	GALSWORTHY GETS UP, MOVES TO TV AREA AFTER TURNING OFF STEREO	Galsworthy, somewhat surprisingly, obeys. Showing his father a newspaper advertisement, which he has cherished since clipping it from the Sunday paper,
⑥ 10-B-10D	CU ADV - "CRAZY AL'S DISCOUNTS"	
10-B-10E	3-SHOT FAVORING GALSWORTHY	⑤_b he says, stay cool, Father, all will soon be well because I have grown tired of this tasteless music

```
BAIT & SWITCH (10)                                          -3-
                        PARTHENON PICTURES

10-B-10F   GRACIE REACTION           and I will soon purchase an 8-track
           (WHAT'S HE UP GO?)         tape deck on which I can play
                                      selections of

10-B-10G   GALSWORTHY                 my own choosing in the sound-proofed
                                      privacy of my room.

10-B-10H   GUS                        What is holding you back, my son,
                                      asks Gus.

10-B-10J   GALSWORTHY                 Ten bucks, says Galsworthy --

10-B-10K   GRACIE - "NOW I GET IT"    here is the ad, does it not look
                                      wonderful?

10-B-10L   GUS                        All ads look wonderful, his father
                                      replies.  But - a complete tape
                                      deck for $29.95!  Kid, this Crazy
                                      Al is driving without his head-
                                      lights!  Why do you not go to
                                      Michaelson's Music, which we know
                                      to be reliable, and get a set
                                      you can depend on?

10-B-10M   GALSWORTHY                 Because, Father, Michaelson's
                                      cheapest deck is many dollars more
                                      and you will have to listen to this
                                      tasteless music for months before
                                      I can save up the required amount.
```

⑧

```
BAIT & SWITCH (10)                                    -10-
                    PARTHENON PICTURES
```

10-B-19   EXT. MICHAELSON'S   MUSIC BRIDGE
           MUSIC STORE --
           "RESPONSIBLE" LOOK

10-B-20   INT. STORE STEREO DEPT.   Oh, yes, says Mr. Michaelson; Crazy
           (ART). CONSERVATIVE
⑨   LOOKING MAN LOOKING AT   Al's $29.95 come-on, I know it well..
           THE CRAZY AL AD WHICH
           GALSWORTHY HAS HANDED   it is not much good for music, but
           HIM. (MR. MICHAELSON)
                                       it works just great at bringing

                                       victims into his store.

10-B-20A   GALSWORTHY   But sir, says Galsworthy, $29.95 is

                                       all the money I have, and I do so

                                       want a tape deck.

10-B-20B   MR. MICHAELSON WALKS   Well, let's see -- over here is a
           O.S. - GALSWORTHY FOLLOWS.
                                       demonstrator of a really nice set
10-B-21   INT. TAPE DECK DEPT. OF
           MICHAELSON STORE - GALS-   which soon is to be replaced by a
           WORTHY FOLLOWS MR. MICHAEL-
           SON INTO SCENE   newer model, and if you can wait

                                       until the new shipment comes in, I

                                       will let you have this one at the

                                       reduced price of --

10-B-21A   MR. MICHAELSON READS $58.50.
           FROM BACK OF TAG

10-B-21B   FAVOR GALSWORTHY   Galsworthy's eyes light with

                                       happiness for a moment, but then his

                                       face falls as he has to say, but,

                                       sir, I do not have that much money.

                                       Could I purchase it on installments?

BAIT & SWITCH (10)   -11-

PARTHENON PICTURES

10-B-21C FAVOR MR. MICHAELSON	To which Mr. Michaelson replies, do you have a job? Good, then I will take your $29.95 as a down payment, and finance the balance.
10-B-21D CU GALSWORTHY	Galsworthy, now wary, says, one question, sir -- will I get a new-set warranty? And where is your service department? Three thousand miles away?
10-B-21E FAVOR MR. MICHAELSON	My goodness, young man, says Mr. Michaelson, what a strange thing to ask! It's right here in the store.
10-B-21F MR. MICHAELSON STARTS WRITING UP ORDER (SALES CONTRACT)	So now if you wish, we will write up the contract, taking plenty of time to fill in all the blank spaces so we're sure everything is understood.. then you can take it home for your folks to look at, sleep on it, and if you still feel the same way tomorrow, come in and we've got a deal.

⑩   DISSOLVE

10-B-22 GALSWORTHY'S ROOM -- GUS, GRACIE, GRANDMA (SAME SET-UP AS BEFORE)	And here we are, a few weeks later, ready for the grand op -- er, listening. And <u>this</u> time ...

BAIT & SWITCH (10)   -12-

                     PARTHENON PICTURES

10-B-22A   GALSWORTHY HITS THE
           SWITCH
                                        MUSIC STARTS - THE SOUND
                                        IS GREAT, BUT THE SONG IS
                                        THE SAME GROUP GUS HATED
10-B-22B   GUS STARTS TO REACT   IN THE LIVING ROOM SCENE
           TOUGH, BUT GRACIE PUTS
⑪   A HAND ON HIS AND COOLS   And so, as they say, all's well
           HIM DOWN AND HE MANAGES
           TO FOLLOW GRACIE'S LEAD   that ends well ....for the Gullies.
           TO ENSEMBLE APPLAUSE
                                        But you and I can't run our lives

                                        backward when we goof, we've got to

                                        be right the first time around.

                                        So remember --

10-B-23   RECAP MONTAGE OF   since in this world one seldom gets
           PREVIOUS SCENES
                                        something for nothing, if a
⑫   ⑬   proposition seems too good to be

                                        true, it probably is ... and when

                                        people put pressure on you and say

                                        that tomorrow will be too late --

                                        what they mean is, too late for

                                        them.

10-B-24   OVERLAY END CREDITS   So in conclusion, remember --

                                        before you buy -- be wary.

                                              MUSIC UP FOR FINISH

1. Like most fact film producers, Parthenon favors the two-column format—visuals to the left, sound to the right.
2. Shooting instructions are abbreviated to a sort of shorthand. In some instances orders are extremely specific ("SHOOT 15 times @ 5' "), but often they're looser and less rigid than in many shops. Which same is a good example of why it makes sense to ask to see a sample script when you tackle a job for a company with whose format style you're not familiar.
3. This picture and the others in the series are basically brief fact films. But because they're also designed for TV use wherever possible, as per the proposal, they're set up in TV series style, with fast establishment of characters, setting, and general circumstance.
4. Ordinarily the proliferation of "G" names here (the Gus, Gracie, Gil, Gloria, etc., thing) would be a no-no. But *The Gullies'* slant is comedic, so the matching initials add rather than detract from the effect.
5. Voice-over narration cuts costs and simplifies shooting. Note that only one narrator is used, although many passages (5a and 5b, for example) simulate speech by individual actors as they mime their roles. It's one of the many devices by which life and interest can be added to a narrated film.
6. This is the kind of thing that in many scripts would be labeled "INSERT."
7. Frequent use of exaggeration and incongruity help give the narration/dialogue a comedic tone to help build the overall style set for the film.
8. The basic "bait and switch" angle—a low-price come-on, to bring in customers who then will be coaxed and cajoled into buying something more expensive—of the episode is established.

   Now we move ahead to page 10: the episode's climax and payoff.
9. By using an art background—that is, one painted on a flat or the like—instead of dressing and lighting an elaborate set or shooting on location, costs are reduced.
10. A time lapse, and a DISSOLVE to cover it.
11. A final twist, a final laugh: After all the furore, Gus still ends up with the music he loathes.
12. Well-chosen fast cuts (that is, a montage) from what has gone before is a useful device for visually summarizing the points previously made.
13. Meanwhile, our narrator hammers home the message.

ANTONIO AND THE MAYOR (original screenplay),
by Howard Rodman.

One of 1974's most charming films (a television original) was *Antonio and the Mayor,* story of a ten-year-old Mexican child genius sans portfolio. Author of the script and producer of the picture was Howard Rodman, member of the executive board of the Writers Guild of America, West (his resume mentions that he also is "on leave" from the Hod Carriers International), a Brooklyn-born veteran of both print and broadcast media whose credits run to six pages.

Rodman has given his story broad significance by making it symbolic of an underdeveloped nation's leap into the twentieth century. But this pales beside the boy Antonio's conflict with the mayor Acambarros, his village's authority figure.

Even more important, to a writer, is how Rodman successfully developed Acambarros as simultaneously human and (for story purposes) a villain.

ANTONIO AND THE MAYOR
an
original screenplay
by

Howard Rodman

24   CONTINUED 2

Antonio offers Felipe the measuring stick.

                    FELIPE
          Everybody knows a clock can be
          wrong.

                    ANTONIO
          Not this clock!

25   EXT. THE MAYOR'S HOUSE - DAWN - ROOSTER ON THE ROOF

Sleeping first, he wakes abruptly at the TOLLING of the
CHURCHBELL. He flaps his wings and CROWS.

26   INT. WHERE MAYOR AND SENORA ACAMBARROS SLEEP IN THEIR
      HOUSE - DAWN - MAYOR AND SENORA ACAMBARROS

sleeping, side by side, in their bed. The Mayor's gold
watch is under the pillow. Outside the CHURCHBELL TOLLS
and the COCK CROWS and the mayor and his wife are awake,
however unwillingly, with whatever difficulty they leave
their sleep and come to be awake. Automatically, the May-
or reaches for his watch. He squints at it, focuses, reads
the time on the face of the watch, and does not believe
what it tells him. Outside, that terrible sound: A DONKEY
BRAYS. There is no longer any sleep in Tehuaxacatlan this
day.

27   EXT. THE CHURCH - DAWN - ANTONIO AND FELIPE UP ON THE ROOF

where they RING THE CHURCHBELL with terrible insistence,
sending forth such a sense of urgency it is as if the village is being attacked.

28   THE BELL

swings and TOLLS.

29   THE DONKEY

brays.

30   ANTONIO AND FELIPE

ring the churchbell. Pulling the rope hard, silhouetted
against the dawn sky.

Rev. 4/11/74

-9-

31　　AN ANGLE ON THE SQUARE - VILLAGERS

wakened, disoriented, coming to see why the bell is tolling.

32　　ANOTHER ANGLE - VILLAGERS

moving toward the church.

33　　INT. OROPEZA HOUSE - DAWN - MANUEL

holding his shaving mug and brush, goes to the terra cotta
pipe telephone to speak into it.

　　　　　　　　　　　　MANUEL
　　　　　　　Teresa --

34　　INT. CAMARGO HOUSE - DAWN - TERESA

her mouth at her end of the terra cotta pipe telephone.

　　　　　　　　　　　　TERESA
　　　　　　　Good morning, Manuel.

There is a sharp RAPPING, o.s.　Teresa turns sharply to
see?

35　　TERESA AND SENORA CAMARGO

Senora Camargo RAPS sharply against the door frame with a
wooden spoon.　The spoon raps like a woodpecker.

　　　　　　　　　　　SENORA CAMARGO
　　　　　　　Teresa! Are you going to waste the
　　　　　　　whole day?　This house needs some
　　　　　　　water!

36　　EXT. THE PLAZA, ANGLE FAVORS CHURCH - DAWN - MEN, WOMEN,
　　　AND CHILDREN

throng across the plaza, drawn by the TOLLING bell.

37　　EXT. THE CHURCH, ANGLE TO HOLD THE ROOF - DAWN - ANTONIO
　　　AND FELIPE

drop the rope and run into the church to come down.　PEOPLE
throng into the churchyard.

38   ANOTHER ANGLE ON THE CHURCH, TO FEATURE THE DOOR - DAWN
-ANTONIO AND FELIPE

burst out of the church, running. Felipe is a couple of
seconds behind. Antonio shouts as he runs through the
throng of villagers gathered in the church courtyard:

②
                           ANTONIO
                  The bicycle! We have to go to Cam-
                  po Nuevo for the bicycle!

The villagers reverse direction, following after Antonio
and Felipe as they head for the Mayor's house.

39   EXT. THE MAYOR'S HOUSE - DAWN - MAYOR AND SENORA ACAMBAR-
ROS

The Mayor stands in the doorway, his wife behind him, looking out at the world over his shoulder. The Mayor scowls
at the sky, his watch in his hand. He sees the throng running toward his house.

40   ACAMBARROS' POV - ANTONIO LEADING THE VILLAGERS

                           ANTONIO
                        (shouting as he runs)
                Mayor Acambarros! We have to get
                the bicycle today!

41   ACAMBARROS AND ANTONIO FEATURED - FELIPE BEHIND ANTONIO -
BEHIND ANTONIO AND FELIPE THE VILLAGERS

                          FELIPE
                     (corroborating Antonio)
                That's right, Mayor: we have a
                long way to go.
                        ACAMBARROS
           Sh, shh, shhh.

And there is silence. Suddenly, up on the roof of the
mayor's house the COCK CROWS again.

42   ACAMBARROS

turns his head to look toward the cock on his roof.

43   THE ROOSTER ON THE ROOF

crows again.

-11-

44   ACAMBARROS, ANTONIO, FELIPE, THE VILLAGERS

③   The mayor turns, levelling a heavy finger at the bird.

>   ACAMBARROS
>   Get off my roof!

45   THE ROOSTER

obeys.

46   ACAMBARROS, ANTONIO, FELIPE, THE VILLAGERS

Acambarros turns his gaze from where the rooster was to
where Antonio is. The villagers turn their gaze from where
the rooster was to where Antonio is and where the mayor is.

>   ACAMBARROS
>   What is this?

Every eye is on Antonio.

>   ANTONIO
>   Mayor Acambarros, we have to get
>   started. It's very late.

Acambarros looks up at the sky, points for Antonion to look
to.

>   ACAMBARROS
>   The sun is not up yet!

>   ANTONIO
>   My clock says we're going to be
>   late.

Acambarros extends his hand, showing Antonio his watch.

>   ACAMBARROS
>   (of his watch)
④   This. This is what tells us what
>   time it is in Tehuaxacatlan!

He goes back into his house, past his wife in the doorway.
She shuts the door after her husband and herself. People
disperse. Antonio stands a moment, shaking his head in disapproval of the mayor's watch more than of the mayor, himself.
Across the plaza Senora Camargo raps her door with her wood-
pecker-busy spoon.

>   SENORA CAMARGO
>   Antonio! This house needs more
>   wood for the fire!

Antonio and Felipe head for home.

Rev. 4/10/74   -12-

46A   INT. BEDROOM IN THE ACAMBARROS HOUSE - DAY - ACAMBARROS

⑤   stands diconsolately in front of the mirror; wearing his
        trousers, but not yet his shirt. He holds his watch close
        to his ear, listening to it tick. SENORA ACAMBARROS brings
        him a clean shirt. She is struck by something disconsolate
        about him: the slump of his shoulders, perhaps, the sadness
        in his eyes.

                         SENORA ACAMBARROS
                What's the matter?

        He sighs and shrugs. Still holding his watch he makes his
        arms stiff, holding them out so his wife can put his shirt
        on him.

                         ACAMBARROS
                Everything changes. When my father
                was the mayor small boys didn't tell
                him what time it was. My father
                KNEW what time it was. He believed
                in his watch and his watch told him
                the truth!

                         SENORA ACAMBARROS
                Do you think Antonio Camargo is al-
                ways right when he tells you what
                time it is? Do you think his water-
                clock always tells him the truth?

                         ACAMBARROS
                How do I know what that boy knows?
                I can tell you what I know: Who am
                I? - that's what I know; I don't
                know who I am. This is what I know:
                when my father was ASLEEP he was a
                mayor!

                         SENORA ACAMBARROS
                How do you know what your father was
                dreaming?

                         ACAMBARROS
                He was a different man; I'm just
                like everybody else. I have to
                make myself a different man. When
                I go out of my house I make myself
                look like this --
                        (he makes a stern face)
                But I like to smile.
                        (his shoulders slump)
                I have to tell people what to do,
                but I want someone to tell me. Is
                that an honest man? What kind of
                a mayor is that?

                                        CONTINUED

-13-

46A   CONTINUED

                        SENORA ACAMBARROS
                You're the best man I know.

He sighs a profound sigh. She walks out. Acambarros sits,
the weight of the world too heavy for him.

                        ACAMBARROS
                If I could make the world all over
                again -- I would make everything
                exactly the same way. But I would
                put Antonio Camargo in someone else's
                village.

47   EXT. A NARROW DUSTY ROAD - DAY - LS, TO ESTABLISH

        a great cloud of dust moving toward us.

48   THE MEN AND BOYS OF TEHUAXACATLAN

        going to the railroad station at Campo Nuevo to get the
        bicycle. They walk easily and swiftly, too, accustomed
        to walking great distances.

49   ANGLE TO FEATURE ACAMBARROS

        leading them. Setting a brisk pace.

50   ANGLE TO FEATURE FELIPE AND ANTONIO - AMONG OTHERS, INCLUD-
        ING JAIME (FELIPE'S LITTLE BROTHER)

        They are toward the rear of the group. Jaime has fallen be-
        hind somewhat. He stops and calls out.

                        JAIME
                Felipe! Wait!

        Antonio and Felipe run back for him.

51   ANGLE TO FEATURE ACAMBARROS

        as he comes on toward us, leading the OTHERS. The haze of
        dust stirred up by their passage becomes thicker and thicker.

52   EXT. WATERING HOLE ON THE WAY TO CAMPO NUEVO - DAY - THE
        MEN AND BOYS OF TEHUAXACATLAN

                                        CONTINUED

-91-

238
thru
238C VARIOUS ANGLES - TO COVER -- ACAMBARROS

is the first to turn away, certain now that no one can reverse his will. He goes into the house. His wife follows.
Manuel and Felipe and Senora Camargo release Antonio. He no
longer struggles. He has accepted that the bicycle is gone.
He stands quietly, looking at the fire with a strange, intense expression we cannot decipher.

                    TERESA
          Come on, Antonio. Come back to our
          house; don't stay here?

Antonio looks into the fire.

                    ANTONIO
          Why did he do it?

The fire burns on. Antonio sits on the ground near the
fire, looking into it, looking for his bicycle and seeing
only its ashes. Already the fire is dwindling. One by one
and by twos and threes the others go away, leaving the boy
to his lonely sorrow.

239 EXT. THE PLAZA OF TEHUXACATLAN - NIGHT - ANTONIO

alone is there. The fire is dark except for a dull red ember here and there. The bicycle has been consumed. Finally, Antonio gets to his feet. He walks to stand in front
of the Acambarros house, facing it, making no sound, just
staring at the house.

240 INT. ACAMBARROS' HOUSE - NIGHT - ACAMBARROS

⑦

hiding himself so that he cannot be seen from outside, Acambarros locks out the window, watching the silent boy, o.s.,
outside.

241 ACAMBARROS' POV - ANTONIO STANDING OUTSIDE THE HOUSE

staring, as if he may be able to see Acambarros, though in
fact he cannot.

                    ACAMBARROS (O.S.)
                    (quietly)
              Sabinosa. Sabinosa.

242 ACAMBARROS AND SENORA ACAMBARROS

She sits, braiding her hair as her husband looks out the

                              CONTINUED

242   CONTINUED

window.

⑧

>ACAMBARROS
>Go tell him I said I don't want him
>out there.

She ignores him.

>ACAMBARROS
>Go out there and tell him!

>SENORA ACAMBARROS
>Don't shame yourself, my husband!
>Don't send me. Go yourself.

Acambarros moves his hand in a small gesture which doesn't
deny his wife's accusation. He pleads.

⑨

>ACAMBARROS
>Talk to him for me, please. Please.

She goes, finally. He returns to the window.

243   EXT. THE ACAMBARROS HOUSE - NIGHT - SENORA ACAMBARROS

opens the door and is framed in the doorway, facing ANTON-
IO. She speaks gently.

⑩

>SENORA ACAMBARROS
>Antonio, go home now.

Antonio doesn't move.

>SENORA ACAMBARROS
>Antonio, nothing can come of stand-
>ing there.

244   INT. THE ACAMBARROS HOUSE - NIGHT - ACAMBARROS

stands at the window, watching.

245   EXT. THE ACAMBARROS HOUSE - NIGHT - CLOSE SHOT - ANTONIO

his face expressionless and yet implacable. He simply
stares at the house.

246   SENORA ACAMBARROS

her face sad, somehow.

310 ■

TRICKS OF THE TRADE

247   WIDER - SEÑORA ACAMBARROS AND ANTONIO

and ACAMBARROS comes from within the house to the doorway,
putting his wife aside very gently, so that at last he can
confront Antonio himself.

                    ACAMBARROS
                (without much conviction)
          Go home, Antonio.

248   ANTONIO

extends his arm, his fist tightly clenched about the two
silver pieces his father put into his hand. He turns the
fist upward and opens it so that the two silver pieces are
revealed on his palm.

                    ANTONIO
          This is what I got for my bicycle.
          That I made with my hands and my
          mind and my heart. Here is the
          coin for my hands, mayor: I still
          have my hands.

He throws one coin to the ground at the Mayor's feet. He
still has the second coin.

                    ANTONIO
          I still have my mind, Mayor; you
          don't have to pay me for that.

He throws the second coin at the mayor's feet and reveals
his hands are empty now.

                    ANTONIO
          But, Mayor Acambarros, now I have
          no heart left.

He holds out his empty hands.

249   ACAMBARROS AND SEÑORA ACAMBARROS

                    ACAMBARROS
                    (gently)
          I asked you to go home, Antonio.

249A ANTONIO

                    ANTONIO
          I wanted my bicycle to go to school
          in Azara.

-94-

250　ACAMBARROS AND SEÑORA ACAMBARROS IN THEIR DOORWAY

Señora Acambarros turns and goes into the house. But still Acambarros stands there. Like stone. Because he is so moved he is like stone. Because he doesn't know what to do so he just stands there. Then, finally, he simply turns and goes back into the house. He shuts his door quietly.

251　ANTONIO

stands there a moment more. He turns and looks at the ashes of his bicycle in the dead fire. Somewhere in the fire a last ember cools and SNAPS. Antonio leaves the fire and crosses to the water clock between the two houses.

252　EXT. THE PLACE BETWEEN THE CAMARGO HOUSE AND THE OROPEZA HOUSE, WHERE THE WATER CLOCK STANDS - NIGHT - ANTONIO

looks at his clock a moment.

　　　　　　　　　　　ANTONIO
　　　　　Nobody cares about water clocks.

He pushes the water clock over.

253　WIDER - ANTONIO

goes to his house. Just as he reaches the door it is opened by his mother, waiting for him. He goes in and she closes the door.

254　THE ENTIRE PLAZA

empty. Silent. There is no longer even a red ember in the fire which burned the wooden bicycle. It is all done.

　　　　　　　　　　　　　　　　　　FADE OUT

FADE IN

255　EXT. THE PLAZA OF TEHUXACATLAN - NIGHT

Nothing moves. But the CHURCH BELL begins to TOLL.

255A　INT. THE CAMARGO HOUSE, WHERE CAMARGO AND SEÑORA CAMARGO SLEEP - NIGHT - CAMARGO AND SEÑORA CAMARGO

wake from sleep, startled by the BELL TOLLING. Perhaps even frightened, so strange a sound is this in the middle of their night.

255B   INT. WHERE MANUEL, FELIPE, JAIME, AND THE OTHER OROPEZA
        CHILDREN SLEEP IN THE OROPEZA HOUSE - NIGHT - ALL

        wake at the TOLLING OF THE CHURCHBELL, with various indi-
        vidual reactions.

255C   INT. WHERE ANTONIO AND TERESA SLEEP IN THE CAMARGO HOUSE
        - NIGHT - TERESA

        wakes. She gets out of bed and as she rises the CAMERA
        FRAMES UP TO HOLD HER and thus we are able to see the up-
        per bunk now, where ANTONIO sleeps. But he lies with his
        back to us, facing the wall, curled into himself not car-
        ing.

255D   EXT. THE PLAZA OF TEHUXACATLAN - NIGHT - THE PEOPLE OF THE
        VILLAGE

        come to their doors and come out into the plaza, all fac-
        ing the church from whence the sound of the CHURCHBELL
        goes on and on.

255E   EXT. THE ROOF OF THE CHURCH, WHERE THE CHURCHBELL IS --
        NIGHT - SENORA ACAMBARROS

        tolls the bell with a strange , incessant clamor.

256   EXT. THE PLAZA OF TEHUAXACATLAN - NIGHT - THE PEOPLE

        move toward the church, but when they come to the road
        which runs along the front of the church to come into the
        plaza they stop, looking at something we cannot yet see.

257   EXT. THE ROAD WHICH RUNS ALONG THE FRONT OF THE CHURCH
        - NIGHT - POV FROM THE PLAZA - A TORCH

        appears first. And with the appearance of the torch the
        BELL STOPS curtly. Silence. The torch is moving, coming
        closer. Now we see it is held by a man, and now we see
        the man is ACAMBARROS, and beside him, moving in a strange
        way, is the BICYCLE SENT FROM MEXICO CITY. And we see
        that it bobs up and down in this strange way because the
        wheel is crumpled from the fall into the canyon. And now
        Acambarros reaches the gate of the church courtyard and
        SENORA ACAMBARROS emerges from there and walks just behind
        her husband as he turns into the plaza.

258   EXT. THE PLAZA OF TEHUAXACATLAN - NIGHT - ACAMBARROS

first, wheeling the bicycle; then SENORA ACAMBARROS just
behind him. Now MEN, WOMEN, and CHILDREN of the village,
some bearing torches. They cross the plaza to come to
THE CAMARGO HOUSE.

259   TERESA

in the doorway. Just behind her CAMARGO and SENORA CAM-
ARGO watching the procession coming toward them. Teresa
is the first to understand what is happening. She pushes
back into the house, excitedly, to get Antonio.

260   ACAMBARROS

brings the bicycle to the house.

261   CAMARGO AND SENORA CAMARGO
thru
261E   come out of their house. THE OROPEZAS, one and all, come.
ANTONIO comes out of the Camargo house, against his will,
actually. Pushed by his sister, TERESA, behind him. She
makes him face Acambarros.

For a moment the mayor and the boy face each other in silence. Then the mayor pushes the bicycle forward, presenting to to Antonio.

                    ACAMBARROS
            Now this is yours. I did not mean
            to hurt your heart.

He thrusts the bicycle into Antonio's hands. Then, his
wife by his side, Acambarros walks away back across the
plaza to his own house.

Antonio takes the bicycle. He looks at it, feeling how
it is hurt and moving in his mind to understand how to
heal the machine. He lays it down on the ground and opens the tool kit which hangs from its frame. He takes
out the tools and begins the work of repair. Someone
holds a torch closer. FELIPE goes into the OROPEZA HOUSE
and gets a lantern, and brings it back. TERESA gets a
lantern from the Camargo house. And now, from everywhere in the village of Tehuaxacatlan the people bring
light for Antonio to work by: a torch, a lantern, a lamp,
and a candle; light of every kind. So that darkness will
not keep Antonio from what he needs to do.

262   EXT. THE PLAZA AT TEHUAXACATLAN - SUNRISE - THE ROOSTER
ON ACAMBARROS' ROOF

wakes with the sun and greets the new day with his voice:
CROWING. The CAMERA PANS AND FRAMES DOWN to traverse the
plaza and bring us to THE CAMARGO HOUSE where Antonio has
just finished healing the bicycle and Felipe is pumping
new air into the tires. Antonio mounts the bicycle, his
father holds him, then pushes the bicycle until it gains
momentum and Antonio pedals off across the plaza. They
all watch him: CAMARGO, SENORA CAMARGO, TERESA, MANUEL,
OROPEZA, SENORA OROPEZA, JAIME, and the others.

263   ANTONIO ON THE BICYCLE

he pedals and makes the bicycle circle. He is getting
control of it. He makes a complete circle. He waves at
his family and friends as he passes them. Now he heads
for the far end of the plaza.

264   THE ACAMBARROS HOUSE - DAY - ACAMBARROS AND SENORA ACAM-
BARROS

and ANTONIO pedals by them. He waves as he passes.

265   ACAMBARROS POV - ANTONIO ON THE BICYCLE

reaches the end of the plaza, but he doesn't stop. He
turns onto the road which will eventually take him to
Azara.

266   ACAMBARROS

nods. He has thought and thought and he thinks that Antonio having the bicycle is a good solution to everyone's
problems. He turns to his wife and nods his reaffirma-
tion of his own conclusion to her. She smiles.

267   EXT. WHERE THE ROAD PASSES PABLO RODRIGUEZ' HOUSE - DAY -
ANTONIO ON THE BICYCLE

passes the house. PABLO RODRIGUEZ is in the doorway. He
waves as Antonio waves as he pedals past.

268   (A MONTAGE)
thru   EXT. VARIOUS PLACES ALONG THE WAY BETWEEN TEHUXACATLAN AND
268E   AZARA - DAY - ANTONIO ON THE BICYCLE

CONTINUED

1. Rodman introduces us to his villain. And since time is to be a major issue in *Antonio and the Mayor,* he brings him on in a setting and circumstance that focus on time: the churchbell tolling, the rooster crowing, the donkey braying, the mayor awakening and groping for his watch. The situation is both human and emotionally neutral, however. It doesn't commit viewers to being either for or against Mayor Acambarros.
2. A bicycle is the bone of contention in the picture. Antonio, in his eagerness, is already committed to a course of action: He wants to get the bicycle at once. Acambarros, the mayor, still is presented on a neutral plane.
3. Acambarros vs. rooster. Acambarros wins. It's good for a laugh, but it also says something about Acambarros and his ego.
4. Conflict between Antonio and Acambarros begins. The mayor's sense of his own dignity and self-importance demands that he rule even on this matter of what time it is . . . a minor point, but one that foreshadows the attitude to be expected of him in the sequences to come.
5. Aftermath of and reaction to the preceding argument, this sequence establishes Acambarros' character, his humanness: the uncertainty that lurks beneath the stern facade; the desire to be loved that clashes with his self-image of himself as the voice of authority.
6. A summing up of Acambarros' frustration: He has nothing against Antonio, but he just doesn't know how to cope with him.

The pages between 13 and 91 cast Acambarros more and more in the villain's role, a victim of his own false pride. With no malice on either part, he and Antonio are continually at odds. Forever trying to preserve his cherished dignity from the wounds Antonio unintentionally inflicts, the mayor first throws the bicycle the train has brought into a canyon . . . later buys and burns a wooden bicycle Antonio has made.

Then:

7. The face Acambarros turns to the world is that of villain—a man using his strength and power to crush a child's dream. Here, however, hidden from view, stands the human being, wavering and uncertain.
8. Rodman puts Acambarros' self-doubt into words . . . sharpens it with Senora Acambarros' reply.
9. Acambarros still can't master his distress. He pleads with his wife—and, in so doing, builds the sequence.
10. Senora Acambarros fails to move Antonio. The fact of her inability to budge the boy is more impressive than any effort of the mayor's might have been, since it would have been only natural for Antonio to resist any plea from the man who has caused him so much grief. Also, again, it represents a new attack and so builds the sequence.
11. Acambarros at last comes forward himself, for the ultimate confrontation: hero and villain, meeting face to face.
12. Antonio attacks—and in an unanticipated way. His weapon is his portion of the money Acambarros paid the father for the wooden bicycle.
13. On the face of it, this line would appear to be pure hyperbole. Instead, it's preparation for the payoff, a super-plant.
14. Getting a bicycle wasn't just a child's whim. It held great import for this boy's whole future and (by implication, within the film's context) for Mexico.

15. Acambarros just stands. Since this is subject to a variety of interpretations, suspense holds; perhaps even builds a bit higher.
16. Antonio's defeat is total. The audience anguishes with him and for him.
17. The segment ends. But because there has been no real resolution to the "Will he or won't he?" of the story question, viewer tension still holds.
18. The FADE OUT/FADE IN denotes not only a passage of time but a chapter break, in the grammar of the film.
19. The tolling church bell, repetition of a pattern established at the film's beginning, also brings a familiar response: The villagers assemble. Observe, too, that Rodman is content to let these scenes play without words. Viewer anticipations can say more at such a point than any dialogue.
20. Now, at last, speech. But only one, and that brief and so touching it makes you want to cry—in considerable measure, because it so beautifully pays off the plant from 13, above. Also, it's logical even if unanticipated that Acambarros should have this change of heart. For inside, despite his authoritarian self-image and false pride, he's a good man and human. Rodman established that clearly back in 5, above.
21. Nor is it just Acambarros who reveals himself. The whole village now joins hands to help heal Antonio's heart.
22. Finally, visual proof that all's well. Not only is the bicycle successfully mended, but Antonio can ride it.
23. At last, our resolution, the answer to our story question: Antonio *can* win over (or maybe "with") Acambarros. But it's in no sense a bitter victory, for everybody's happy. Even Acambarros stands as a bigger, more insightful man.

Rodman's script goes on for a few pages more, paying off those elements of broad significance mentioned (and planted) earlier. But that's merely the last touches of the denouement. The story is already over, with the conclusion of Antonio's struggle with the mayor.

Also, in case you hadn't noticed, Rodman not only has shown how to develop a very human villain. In addition, he's demonstrated how to build a climax to a truly striking peak.

Lessons from the Pros   ■ 317

TERROR ON THE FORTIETH FLOOR (outline), *by Jack Turley.*

TERROR ON THE FORTIETH FLOOR (sequence cards), *by Jack Turley.*

TERROR ON THE FORTIETH FLOOR (treatment/step outline) *by Jack Turley.*

TERROR ON THE FORTIETH FLOOR (elaborating notes), *by Jack Turley.*

TERROR ON THE FORTIETH FLOOR (teleplay), *by Jack Turley.*

Jack Turley prepared for a scriptwriting career with TV production experience in such places as Oklahoma City and Albuquerque, then moved to Los Angeles and enrolled in TV writing courses at UCLA. His first sale was to *Route 66*—a collaboration with his instructor, Milton Gelmer. Now, with 20 years' experience behind him, he is turning more and more to the movie-of-the-week type of thing. *Pray for the Wildcats, Hurricane,* and *The Day the Earth Moved* are among his recent credits.

Terror on the Fortieth Floor, airing as a two-hour, seven-act show, kicked off NBC's 1974 season. It also has been released in Europe as a theatrical film, as well as rerun in the U.S.

Turley's handling of *Terror* offers excellent insights into the entire process of script development. Here we see how it was built step by step from a story by Turley and Ed Montagne.

Excerpts from *Terror on the Fortieth Floor* used with permission of Jack Turley.

The outline

⑴

Jack Turley

" THE ONLY WAY IS DOWN "

This is not meant to be a storyline. It is a preliminary
sorting of possibilities...a springboard.

②
③

THE PHYSICAL ELEMENTS

④

Christmas Eve. An office party on the top floor of a
modern skyscraper. The building is empty except for those
at the party--and even these people are finishing their
drinks so they can hurry home to families for the long
holiday week-end.

An exodus to the elevator. No one is aware that a small,
die-hard group of revelers has slipped away to continue
the party in the plush inner sanctum of the boss' private
office. There is, however, one witness to the secret--
the OFFICE MESSENGER BOY. But one of the party participants,
an Executive, swears the Office Boy to secrecy, half by
implied threat, half by allusion to promotion.

⑤

The mass of departing office workers get off the elevator
at the main floor, unaware that they have left a few
revelers behind. The people say goodnight to the WATCHMAN,
tell him that they are the final remnants of the office
party. No one else left upstairs. The Office Boy,
protecting his Executive conspirator, says nothing as
he leaves with the others.

2

The remaining seven or so people still on the top floor
in the boss' private office have effectively isolated
themselves from discovery, stealing a little more time
to enjoy themselves. No one knows they are there, except
the Office Boy--and the Executive assures his friends
that their secret is safe

THE DISASTER

Because it is a holiday week-end and the building will
be totally unoccupied during that time, the Maintenance
Supervisor has left orders for some minor repair work to
be done on the building's heating system. The Maintenance
ENGINEER comes on duty this Christmas Eve begrudging his
lot for having to work at all. He is assuaging his
discontent with a bottle of cheer he has brought with
him.

The Engineer begins his repairs, getting drunker as he
works. There is a gas leak, then a spark caused by a
careless mistake. A massive EXPLOSION knocks out all
the support systems in the building--lights, phones,
heating, elevators, etc.--enveloping the basement in a
blazing fire.

The Engineer is killed and the watchman, making his rounds
and pausing to pass the time with the Engineer, is critically
injured.

Firemen answer the electronic alarm and a frantic effort

3

⑥ begins to get the fire under control before it guts the
skyscraper. The Watchman is conscious enough to inform
the firemen, erroneously, that the building is deserted.
The Fire Commander utters a fervent "thank God." If the
explosion had occurred two hours earlier, hundreds of
people could've been killed.

THE PEOPLE

and their separate stories will begin to unfold now against
the ominous threat of the raging fire far below, which
appears to be climbing toward the top, floor by floor.
The people are trapped, aware of the danger below them
but unable to make their presence known to the firefighters
below. Communication systems are gone...no lights...stair-
wells are choked with heavy, deadly smoke...windows designed
for gale force cannot be broken.

Let us consider these trapped victims, identifying them,
for the moment, by the simplest of names:

⑦
               MISTER PLAYBOY

               MISTER SENIOR EXECUTIVE

               MISTER DESPERATE

               MISS NAIVE

               MISS LONELY

               MISS OPPORTUNIST

               MISS PREGNANT

Contrary to the names, these people should not be
interpreted as caricatures. They are, and must be,

4

real, very real, people...flawed in instantly recognizable
ways. These people could be found at any office party
anywhere. They must contain the essence of familiarity
for anyone who has ever worked in an office.

Let's look at each character a little closer:

⑧ MISTER PLAYBOY is a young, good-looking stud, four button,
wing-tipped, attache-cased make-out artist. He lives the
virile Hefner image--ski trips, sports cars, flashy
acrylic bachelor pad. Mister Playboy has one primary goal
in life--to make one more conquest, to get one more woman
in bed. It might be interesting to find out that, even
with all his macho and super charm, Mister Playboy doesn't
have anyplace to go on Christmas Eve...or anyone to go to
that he really wants to go to.

MISTER SENIOR EXECUTIVE is a tired memorial to all the
tough years he's spent beating his way to a comfortable
existence. All the right appurtenances are finally his.
The fashionable suburban home...private school for the kids...
the country club membership...an attractive wife perfectly
trained to the executive role. But something is missing.
A spark...a reason for Mister Senior Executive to want to
go home. He's staying at the private party because it
gives him a little longer reprieve, a chance to flex a
rapidly-diminishing male ego before those he mistakenly
thinks actually care.

11

She knows she's starving herself, that her neighbor has
been, innocently enough, what a man should be for her.

THE OVER-ALL STORY APPROACH

(9) The crisis in the skyscraper, the fire and the threat
that it will climb upward through every floor to the people
trapped on top, will encompass most of Christmas Eve
and into the early morning hours of Christmas Day. During
this time, we will interstice--against the ongoing drama
(10) of the trapped victims--individual cameos of the "connecting
people" and how their own lives are being affected by
the crisis.

(11) For a period of time within the dramatic story, the firefighters below would be unaware that the trapped people
are even in the building. It seems deserted by all outward
appearances and, also, there was the reassuring statement
from the unknowing watchman that all the people were gone.
But the Office Boy, the only one who knows about the
secret party in the boss' office, is the ultimate key to
alerting firefighters to the new complication.

Now it becomes not a matter of saving the building, but
(12) of saving people who are trapped on the top floor.
Helicopters seem to be a logical and dramatic answer.
Portable lights are dropped onto the building's roof.
Rescuers acetylene their way through the locked steel door
leading to a stairwell from the roof. They work their

12

(13) way down through the smoke-filled passage to find the trapped people. In these few minutes, personal drama is suspended in favor of pure action. The victims are led back to the roof and carried away by the helicopter in a rope-slung litter.

(14) At a nearby city park, in a hastily-organized rescue area, the victims are reunited with their individual "connecting people"--to resolve, however we choose, their lives from that point forward.

(15) This final scene, or rather scenes, should not, I think, be handled with quick one-liners and then fade out. The resolution of each prime character should, by this point, be more essential than all the drama and action preceding it. We should then savor it, play it out full; not simply treat it as a wrap-up finish to an action adventure story...

1. As observed in connection with Caryl Ledner's script, titles do tend to change. *The Only Way Is Down,* Turley's choice, stayed with his script most of the way.
2. Turley's presentation of his materials is an interesting variation on the traditional outline. His use of subheaded groupings of data ("THE PHYSICAL ELEMENTS," "THE DISASTER," "THE PEOPLE," "THE OVERALL STORY APPROACH") breaks a complex mass down into easily grasped components.
3. "THE PHYSICAL ELEMENTS" is really a statement of the background of the action, the circumstances under which the story takes place.
4. In choosing Christmas as the time for the action, Turley establishes a strong joy/tragedy contrast. Similarly, the disaster stands out starkly against the background of office party revelry.
5. Here Turley establishes the plausibility and logic of his situation, anticipating and answering possible viewer questions even before they arise.
6. More holes are plugged, the sense of jeopardy intensified.
7. It's easy to lose readers—even experienced script-readers—in a mass of details. By simplifying his people to the label level, Turley makes them instantly understandable stick figures.
8. The image of each person established via label, Turley now elaborates them into believable human beings, giving them attributes and backgrounds as required.

   Skipping ahead to page 11 . . .

9. "THE OVER-ALL STORY APPROACH" reveals the broad outlines of Turley's plan of attack in thumbnail form.
10. No one exists in a vacuum. Here characters are revealed in greater depth by showing their interrelationships with others beyond the scene of the fire.
11. Plot angles, tension factors, are developed.
12. The mechanics of resolution. No producer wants to take chances on a writer writing himself into a corner. ·
13. Character's great, but viewers like excitement too.
14. Tension released; physical problems and peril resolved. But a good character has a future as well as a past, and an effective denouement must at least foreshadow it.
15. Tone and residual impression are important. Turley sets forth his own views on the subject.

The sequence cards

A few of Turley's sequence cards: a writer's notes to himself on
how to develop his play. These all are from Act 1.

TOP FLOOR ① a
OFFICE PARTY WRAPPING
UP — XMAS EVE.
A SPLINTER GROUP
SNEAKS OFF TO BOSS'
OFFICE — UNSEEN by others
at PARTY.

BASEMENT ① e

STOSH MAKING REPAIRS,
NIPPING bottle,
getting DRUNKER.

LOBBY ① f Watchman
LAST of MAIN PARTY
leaves, tells WATCHMAN
NObody else UPSTAIRS.
OFFICE BOY silent.
(mention that cleaning
personnel won't be in
UNTIL MON.)

TOP FLOOR   ① g

PARTY get's cozy.
PLAYBOY hitting on Ginger
OVERLAND hitting on Marlene
JERRY FOSTER making drinks
to Lee and Betty.
discuss what's happening.
Lee turns inward, to
her own thoughts.

FLASHBACK   ① h

Lee AND Jim PEARSON
AND his two young
daughters on outing.
Lee tells him she's
pregnant. Pearson
stunned, withdraws

BASEMENT   ① i

Mister Janos drops in to
visit Stosh, making
Rounds. Stosh makes
drunken mistake.
EXPLOSION—FIRE
END ACT 1

The treatment/step outline

Turley prepares neither a treatment nor a step outline as such, preferring instead this combination form that includes elements of each.

<u>"THE ONLY WAY IS DOWN"</u>

                                        Jack Turley
                                        May 23, 1974

<u>ACT ONE</u>

<u>TOP FLOOR - MODERN SKYSCRAPER - AT DUSK</u>

Christmas Eve. An Office Party in progress...drinking...
laughter...presents exchanged. The building has already
emptied out except for this last celebration. Now, even
these celebrants are finishing their last round so they
can hurry home to families for the long holiday week-end.

<u>TOP FLOOR - BOSS' OFFICE</u>

A plush private office. We watch a separate contingent
of die-hard celebrants slip away <u>unnoticed</u> from the main
party to continue their own party privately in the boss'
office.

<u>TOP FLOOR - CORRIDOR</u>

STOSH, the night watchman, gets off the elevator, locks
it open. He pauses to watch the office celebration a
moment, then turns down the corridor to lock the steel
security door at the stairwell. As he turns around, some
of the celebrants exit from the party to jokingly inquire
if Stosh is locking them in for the night. Stosh grins.
No such luck. He's locking the floor because of a recent
office theft. Orders from Mister Overland.

Stosh waits as the mass exodus begins, the celebrants grabbing
their coats and their presents in a noisy, festive crush
to get to the elevator.

-2-

TOP FLOOR - BOSS' OFFICE

The three men and four women who have slipped away unnoticed
from the main party are now silently waiting until the others
leave. They listen behind the closed door, smuggling amused
glances at each other, offering a silent toast to themselves
on their success. We take this moment to meet each one:

④ DANIEL OVERLAND - a tired memorial to all the tough years
it's taken him to beat his way to near the top. Overland
is greying, mature, and long-suffering from a marriage on
the rocks. Like countless other executives who go to office
Christmas parties, Overland is stealing some extra time
to bolster a fading ego, to gain reprieve from the chore of
just going home.

KELLY FREEMAN - the office stud, a young, good-looking
macho chaser who worships at the Hugh Hefner shrine.. Kelly
has a single goal in life--to get one more woman into bed.
There are some suitable prospects here at the party. As
Kelly sees it, it's only a matter for his choosing.

HOWARD FOSTER - a hustler, a fast-talking loser who is
caught somewhere in the no-man's middle of the corporate
ladder. Howard Foster has already peaked in his career
and knows it. He has trapped himself in a wasted lifetime
of playing the angles, of working deals that never work.

1. Presentation is, in effect, by sequences. Each is labeled as to location and, if necessary, by DAY/NIGHT or the like.
2. Handling in this sequence ranges from impressionism to "telling" summary.
3. Key plot factors are included, even though not yet fully developed.
4. Characters also are introduced, within the same general framework in which they'll come on in the final script. Now, too, the characters have names as well as traits and backgrounds.

The elaborating notes

An actual screenplay or teleplay requires infinitely more detail than the summarized versions that go before. Turley works these out on yellow legal pads.

Parker answers: Negative.
~~Er checked to~~ We've
~~just~~ brought out ~~one~~ fatality
and one injured.
Building ~~as shown~~
watchman has reported
no one else in
building.

Voice from stand: "Ten
~~Four,~~ ~~Battalion~~ one.
~~thanks~~ We're dispatching
engines three, eight,
two oh eight, fourteen,
72, and trucks 8,
82 and 43. And
Utilities nine, 13 and
Five.

I'm setting up command
Post on first floor
lobby by elevators.
The incoming Captains
report to command
Post for assignments
We can
use elevators, not
involved. I've
committed 1st alarm
assignment
on the 11th floor. We're
going to try to hold
it on 12.
Batt. one,
Voice from RADIO: "Do
you have a rescue
problem?

The teleplay

"THE ONLY WAY IS DOWN"

Teleplay

by

Jack Turley

Story

by

Ed Montagne

and

Jack Turley

FIRST DRAFT
June 21, 1974

ACT ONE

FADE IN:

EXT. DOWNTOWN STREET - LOS ANGELES - DUSK

Traffic...pedestrians...the thinning residuum of rush hour.
It is <u>Christmas Eve</u>, on the edge of early evening. We're at
an intersection, CLOSE on a volunteer SANTA CLAUS who stands
a lonely vigil beside his coin kettle. Santa is shaking his
tiny bell at passersby, but there are few interested
contributors. People are hurrying homeward to their holiday
weekend, presents and packages tucked under their arms.

CREDITS BEGIN as Santa wearily gives up the bell-ringing, paws
under his uniform to fish out a pocket watch. He consults it,
decides it's quitting time. Santa folds up his portable
kettle rig, slings it over his shoulder, trudges off across
the street. As he passes by in front of an office building,
CAMERA HOLDS, watching him disappear into the distance.

Now, CREDITS CONCLUDE as CAMERA SWEEPS UPWARD on the tall
office building, taking us for a dizzy ride toward the top
floor. OVER THIS, the SOUNDS of an office party in progress...
voices...laughter...

INT. OFFICE BUILDING - TOP FLOOR - THE PARTY

A suite of offices, obviously part of a large corporate
operation. Desks have been pushed aside, a temporary bar set
up on a filing cabinet, a decorated Christmas tree, a few
decorations hung from the ceiling. The voices and laughter
continue to fill the scene as we gently nudge our way through
the crowd of celebrants -- Executives, secretaries, various
office personnel. This is the wind-up of what has obviously
been a wet and festive afternoon.

Perhaps as we circulate our way through the crush, we hear
bits of conversation, familiar bits that might be heard at any
office party:

                    AD LIBS
              "We should have a party like this
              at least once a month--"

              "If I don't get a raise by the first,
              I'm quitting. I mean it--"

              "Look, this is the first time we've
              had a chance to talk...really talk.
              Why don't we get out of here and
              go someplace for a drink?"

2.

One of the celebrants, a slightly tipsy office-manager type,
SAM LEWIS, is making a speech...or trying to. We move in
CLOSER.

>   SAM
>   Now I know this is not what you
>   would call a 'serious occasion'
>   but--

Snickers, some good-natured jeers.

>   SAM (CONT'D)
>   But I still think something should
>   be said...I mean...the real spirit
>   of Christmas...all of us, you know...
>   good friends sharing a little fun
>   with the hard work...

The celebrants don't want to hear this crap. People turn to
search for coats, to gather up packages.

>   VOICE
>   We know, Sam. That's what you said
>   last year!

Laughter. Sam can't help but give his audience a bleary grin,
shaking off his attempt at sentimentality.

>   SAM
>   Yeah and I'll probably say it next
>   year!

More laughter as somebody shoves a drink at Sam.

ADJACENT OFFICE

an open doorway connects it to the main party area. BETTY
CARSON, a plain, slightly-overweight secretary in her middle
20's, is talking on the phone, cupping her hand over her ear
to block out the din:

>   BETTY
>   When I get there, that's all!

Betty is angry. She glances over at her friend waiting for
her in the doorway, GINGER MACKLIN, another secretary. Betty
gives Ginger a long suffering grimace as:

>   BETTY (CONT'D)
>   Mom, quit talking to me like a
>   child!!

Ginger is younger than Betty, prettier, and a new initiate to
the office force. Eager to get back to the party, Ginger
gives Betty an impatient gesture. Betty nods, still suffering
her martyrdom.

41.

④
                    KELLY
          Yeah...and we've both come a long
          way. You're Regional Sales
          Manager, I'm Executive Assistant
          to the Senior Vice President. He
          listens to me, he respects what I
          have to say. Would you say that's
          'paying the freight' now, Howie...?

HOLD a beat, Kelly's smile turning more brittle as he gazes at
the older man, watching him crumble.

INT. FIRE FLOOR (SPECIAL SET) - ACTION CUTS

⑤ The battle continues against the raging flames. Firemen are
moving down a passageway, spraying tons of water into the
crackling holocaust. SMOKE...INTENSE WILTING HEAT...A ROARING,
bellowing monster out of control, lashing in all directions.

EXT. ANGLE IN STREET

⑥ A REMOTE TV TRUCK wheels to a stop. DAVE HARPER jumps out,
gestures his crew to hold a minute. Harper is a local TV news
personality, a professional. He quickly scans the situation,
moves in to intercept a familiar face.

                    HARPER
          Captain Thomas!

ANGLE - INCLUDING CAPTAIN THOMAS

caught in mid-stride. He stops, frowns impatiently. The
Captain's face is smoke-blackened, his coat stained and water-
streaked. Harper beelines to him. No wasted talk. They know
each other.

                    HARPER
          What've we got?

                    CAPTAIN THOMAS
          A bad one. Fire started on
          twelve, it's up to fifteen. If
          you're setting up cameras, give
          us room, Harper. We've got more
          equipment coming in.

                    HARPER
          Right. Radio report said you've
          taken out two victims, one dead.
          Anymore trapped in there?

42.

CAPTAIN THOMAS
Far as we can determine, there's
no life hazard on the upper
floors. Building was deserted
for the holidays.

HARPER
That's a break.

CAPTAIN THOMAS
It's the only one.

Captain Thomas pivots away. HOLD on Harper a beat, his gaze
scanning upward, toward the top of the building.

INT. OFFICE SUITE - THE PARTY ROOM - TOP FLOOR

Lights off. Ginger, weaving slightly, crosses to pick up her
coat, hastily puts it on, gathers up some Christmas packages.
She moves to a doorway and out into the corridor.

CORRIDOR

Ginger pauses, looks off toward Overland's office. The door
is ajar, the SOUNDS of conversation -- Lee and Overland and
Darlene talking. Ginger ruefully considers saying goodnight,
but discards the idea. A quick departure might be more
prudent. She silently hurries on.

ANGLE - THROUGH GLASS DOOR

leading from the elevator lobby into the reception area of
the offices. We see Ginger come around a corner, struggling
to get her packages securely tucked under her arm. As she
reaches the glass door, she looks up to push it open...but
stops, frozen where she stands, her hand still suspended on
the door's handle.

POV - REVERSE ANGLE - THROUGH THE GLASS

and Ginger's horrified expression mirrored on it. Beyond the
door, in the elevator lobby itself, deadly ominous wisps of
smoke are spewing through the slits of the closed elevator
doors, roiling lazily upward to gather on the ceiling. HOLD
as MUSIC STINGS and we--

FADE OUT:

END ACT TWO

43.

ACT THREE

FADE IN:

EXT. OFFICE BUILDING - NIGHT

(11) The floodlights...Firemen hurrying into the building...
emergency vehicles...the Crowd...all ESTABLISHING the
continuing fire fight. SMOKE seeps from the narrow band of
windows at the 12th floor, getting heavier. We can also see
a flickering red glow through the windows two floors above
the 12th. The fire is climbing toward the top.

INT. OFFICE SUITE - RECEPTION AREA - TOP FLOOR

(12) Ginger has sounded alarm to the others. Overland, Darlene,
Lee, Howard, Betty and Kelly converge into the reception
area from every direction. They gather at the glass door
with Ginger, grimly looking out into the elevator lobby. The
smoke, although thin and wispy, is still visibly seeping from
the closed elevator doors, accumulating against the ceiling.
It doesn't take Overland but a second to make a command
decision:

                    OVERLAND
                 (coolly, quietly)
          I think we better get out of
          here--

                    GINGER
          What is it, Mister Overland?
          What's wrong--??

                    OVERLAND
          Probably an equipment fire or
          something in the basement.
          Nothing to worry about, Ginger.

                    DARLENE
          My new coat!! I've got to get
          my new coat!!

She darts off before anybody can stop her.

INT. STAIRWELL - BELOW FIRE FLOOR

(13) A tangle of water hoses snake up the criss-cross stairs,
making the already-narrow passage that much tougher for the
Firemen hand-carrying equipment upward. Other Firemen are
also coming down the stairs, the two streams of traffic
bucking each other in a constantly-congested flow.

102.

POV SHOT - THELMA AND OVERLAND

from across the parking lot. They're locked in each other's
arms, oblivious to everything around them.

REVERSE - DARLENE

⑭ watching them with a brittle detachment. Her gaze shifts.

HER POV - BETTY

Arm in arm with her <u>Mother</u>, crying on her shoulder as they
walk away.

BACK TO DARLENE

She considers it, a bit wistfully, then glances up.

HER POV - A CHRISTMAS DECORATION

⑮ hanging from a nearby street lamp. The light dims OFF,
shutting down as morning approaches.

BACK TO DARLENE

She sighs, brushes at her tattered fake fur coat, turns, looks
off. Somebody else is sharing her loneliness -- <u>Kelly</u>. He's
⑯ hunched down on the bumper of a Paramedic unit, head drooped
in despaired brooding. Darlene crosses to him, reaches out to
touch his shoulder, keeping it light. She doesn't want any
heavy dialogue right now.

                    DARLENE
          Hey, we're alive. That's worth
          something, isn't it?

Kelly looks up, tears in his eyes.

                    KELLY
          I was scared. I didn't want him
⑰   to get killed.

                    DARLENE
          Look, I've got an idea. Why don't
          a couple of losers get together
          for Christmas day? We can talk
          about everything if it'll help.

                    KELLY
          Nothing helps...

103.

Kelly's head droops down again, resigned to his misery.
Darlene reaches to offer her hand, a gesture of sympathy.

>   DARLENE
>   Come on, Kelly baby. We might
>   even find something to like about
>   each other...

Kelly looks up at her, hesitates, then takes her hand and rises,
walks off with her.

>   KELLY
>   You understand, don't you...about
>   Howie?

>   DARLENE
>   Sure...I understand.

WIDE ANGLE - FROM HELICOPTER

Taking in the full street scene, this aftermath of disaster.
We're lifting into an <u>early</u> <u>morning sky</u>. OVER THIS:

>   HARPER'S VOICE
>   Although the fire is still burning
>   through parts of the lower floors,
>   Chief Packer says they now have it
>   under control and he expects to
>   have it completely stopped within
>   several hours...

The Helicopter is rising <u>close</u> alongside the building, floor
after floor after floor. We get brief glimpses through some
of the windows, the fire damage, the smoking debris. Over
this, continuing:

>   HARPER'S VOICE (CONT'D)
>   It's been a long and grim night for
>   a lot of dedicated Firemen...and
>   for the six people who somehow
>   managed to survive this disaster.
>   If there's one thing we can be sure
>   of, we'd be willing to bet those
>   four women and two men just got the
>   best present they'll ever open...on
>   this or any other Christmas morning.

CAMERA RISES UP over the edge of the building, past the
lingering smoke, STILL RISING to take in the vast sweep of
Los Angeles spreading far to the horizon. A clear bright day
has come.

>   FADE OUT:

<u>END</u>

1. Credits are important to every scriptwriter. Here, Turley gets a joint story credit, plus solo teleplay credit. (And though the script terms this a teleplay, remember that the finished picture was released as a feature film in Europe—a clear indication of how much the two media tend to overlap today.)

2. Check the first sequence of Turley's treatment/step outline, above, against these three paragraphs. Time and place now are established in terms of specific images. Thus, the Santa Claus in effect says Christmas; the bit with the watch and kettle sets the time. The camera's upward sweep tells us where the party's taking place.

3. Mood and general situation are established swiftly. Turley begins to zero in on his story people.

   A jump ahead to page 41 now:

4. Action here is at the party.

5. Now, a cut to parallel action: strong contrast, extreme jeopardy.

6. A different scene; more parallel action. Turley brings in necessary exposition via the dialogue between the TV newsman and Captain Thomas.

7. An important plot line here. Captain Thomas's assumption that the top floors are deserted can't help but heighten viewer suspense as jeopardy to the trapped party leaps higher.

8. Back to the party again, but centering on Ginger, one individual, with a consequent concentration of attention.

9. Suspense is heightened and attention focused even more sharply by shooting Ginger's panic reaction before revealing its cause . . . an excellent technique, but dangerous unless motivation not only follows immediately, but is instantly understandable to viewers.

10. Now, the payoff to Ginger's reaction—not to mention the jeopardy pinpointed in 5, above, and Captain Thomas's assumption (in 7) that the building's upper floors are deserted. A tremendous visual cliffhanger for an Act 2 curtain, it's intensified even more by the music "sting"—a sudden, jarring musical note struck for emphasis, like an exclamation point at the end of a sentence.

11. The pickup after the act break: swift, wordless reestablishment of peril.

12. Back to the fortieth floor. Our characters react characteristically to the crisis—Overland coolly, Ginger naively, Darlene in terms that, in effect, make possessions worth more than life itself. All of which is, of course, highly important storywise—for our story concerns not just a fire, but the reactions of people with whom viewers are emotionally involved to the character-testing jeopardy the fire represents.

13. A suspense-heightening return to parallel action.

   Again we jump forward . . . this time to the final scenes of the picture's resolution.

14. The fate of one character after another is resolved. And since we see this through Darlene's eyes, she becomes increasingly the focal point of viewer interest.

15. Christmas morning has arrived. The night of terror is over.

16. There's still no happiness for Darlene, or for Kelly. But Darlene has strength. She's still in there fighting. It's the kind of thing that makes a character admirable to viewers.

17. Kelly, too, gains sympathy, as we discover he has a conscience. And since Darlene understands, at least there's hope for them, even if not instant happiness. Which is fine, for a quick save would have come through as both corny and unbelievable.
18. There's a larger world beyond the problems of Turley's story people, however. Now, it takes over, with Harper clarifying the situation where the fire is concerned.
19. Harper voices a feeling which most viewers will share.
20. A new day . . . peace, and a return to reality for viewers, in contrast to the night's fear and tension.

*　　　*　　　*

So, at last, we end these lessons from the pros; this glimpse at the way the old hands solve script problems.

But there's still the question of where you fit into the world of film. It's the topic of our final chapter.

CHAPTER 19:

You and Film

So there you have it: how to write film scripts, complete in 3½ easy lessons.

Or, who's kidding who? Nothing in this world worth having comes that simply.

One edge is yours, however. In writing, above all fields, you stand as master of your own destiny. Your genes and chromosomes and conditionings shape your tastes and talents. Beyond that, you call the shots. Which way you go is your own decision.

The only way to learn to write is to write, it has been said.

It's also the only way to find out if writing is your thing.

Hopefully, this book has helped you acquire a degree of professional technique. But the fact that you have training and talent is not enough. You also need desire and drive—a continuing desire and drive, specifically; one that functions day in and day out, week in and week out, assignment after assignment, year upon year.

That kind of focus isn't easy to come by, for building any script is hard work. Often the day arrives when you just don't have the push to want to go on. Nor does such a faltering come only to the losers or the fringe types. Even top performers have been known to succumb to it.

Exhibit A: A friend, retired now. Things reach the point where scripting even one more film was just too painful.

Exhibit B: Friend 2. Too bored to write another line, he said, he became a gentleman farmer.

Exhibit C: Yet another friend. "There comes a time when you want to be judged for your own incompetences, not someone else's," was the way he put it.

All these were good writers, believe me. Still, they quit.

Theirs aren't unique plaints. You'll hear them over and over again, from men and women who've reached the peak of their profession. Victims of the old "I hate to write but love to have written" syndrome—it strikes each and every one of us sometimes—they come to the moment where all they want to do is back away.

And yet . . . And yet . . . can you really quit, once you've tasted the excitement that comes with architecting films? I wonder.

Take "A," above. I'd have sworn he was out of the business forever—only then, the chance to script a picture came along, and once again he was off and running.

"B" continues in his role of gentleman farmer. But I notice he seems to find other things to do upon occasion—things involving the scripting of further films, regardless of whatever he may say of boredom.

"C" still hates the way producers and directors and actors blame writers for their own weaknesses and errors. But periodically, he too still involves himself in doctoring scripts in trouble.

You see, there's a sort of fever that goes with film work, no matter whether you're doing loops or feature pictures. Some succumb to it more completely than do others—to the point, sometimes, that they not only catch fire, but continue to burn in spite of themselves.

Such burning is hardly an unmitigated blessing. Frustration comes with it, too often, and so does emotional involvement on a level that amounts to paranoia, and a well-nigh obsessive-compulsive preoccupation with work.

On the other hand, it has its good side also: the excitement that surges up as you face the challenge of each new project; the sense of commitment that grows as the work progresses; the feeling of fulfillment you get when words—*your* words—at last take form as pictures on the screen. . .

Or, as I remarked back at the beginning of this epic work, one of the nicest things about film script writing is that it offers not just a living, but a way of life which allows you to make full use of your potential.

That can prove a satisfying thing, believe me; one worth finding.

Again, good luck!

APPENDIX A:

The Storyboard

A useful tool in scripting either fact or feature films is the device known in the trade as a storyboard. It consists of a series of small sketches of proposed film action, thumbtacked to a corkboard or other background in sequence so that the picture's line of development is presented in visual terms. Ordinarily descriptive comment, narration, or dialogue accompanies each sketch. The finished product is much like a comic strip, with individual panels presenting the film's highlights in such fashion that any and all concerned may understand.

Why bother with working up a storyboard? There are three good reasons.

Reason One is the difficulty fact-film clients and feature-film producers sometimes have in visualizing action from words. A storyboard lays this to rest by letting said client or producer *see* the story as it develops.

Reason Two is the way the storyboard enables a writer to nail down precisely the effect he wants, making his point with pictures instead of struggling vainly to translate complex images into verbiage.

Reason Three is that even the most talented of inexperienced writers—indeed, writers far from inexperienced, upon occasion—sometimes have difficulty knowing whether or not a given sequence will translate well from script to screen. The storyboard offers an excellent way to find out, by forcing Writer to show rather than talk about precisely what he means. Or, to put it in other terms, it's a first-class method to train yourself to think pictorially.

346

Storyboard art ranges from the roughest of rough stick figures to semi-polished work. The most elaborate example I ever encountered was developed as an ambitious executive's gimmick to sell his firm's top management on making a film. Far from constituting a preliminary step in or aid to writing, it came into being only after I'd turned in the shooting script for the proposed picture.

At that point, an artist was engaged to do color sketches of the action, shot by shot. Thirty-five millimeter color slides then were made of the sketches and set up in sequence in an automatic projector, the film's tentative narration timed and taped to play with it, and the whole package presented to the firm's board of directors.

Unfortunately, the board didn't buy the idea. Since the presentation was, to say the least, an expensive venture, I still wonder how Executive hid the costs in his branch's budget.

This incident also illustrates that storyboard art may take a wide variety of forms. Though most boards feature sketches, I've seen some that utilized snapshots, clips of pictures from magazines, and assorted other approaches. So don't let the fact that you're not an artist stop you. Indeed, learning to sketch well enough for storyboard purposes needn't prove too traumatic. Thumbing through a few books on cartooning self-taught and the like at your local library will give you all the information you need. Or, for a whole chapter on sketching for storyboard purposes, get hold of Leo Salkin's *Story-Telling Home Movies* (McGraw-Hill, 1958). It's excellent.

Does this mean you should always storyboard your scripts? On the contrary. While a storyboard can be an exceedingly helpful aid upon occasion, it also represents an extra—and extremely time-consuming—step in the scripting process. Employ it, therefore, only when a client demands it, or when you see definite benefits as accruing from it—as, for example, in working up or getting across some bothersome point.

APPENDIX B:

Judging Screen Time

Few topics generate more debate among beginners than the question of the ratio of script time to screen time. That is, how many pages of script does it take for how many minutes of film?

Of course this is ridiculous. It's obvious that the whole issue can be resolved with a simple formula or two.

Or is it?

Let's try to figure it out, starting with the simple formulas mentioned above:

1. It's ordinarily considered that two pages of a fact film's two-column shooting script averages out a minute of screen time.
2. Similarly, a page of a feature film's master scene script allegedly is equal to a minute of screen time.

Is this true? Well, now, that all depends.

Suppose, for example, that the two pages of fact-film shooting script is made up of descriptions of 15 shots of mechanical components. Each shot is scheduled to run not more than two seconds. In consequence, it doesn't take a mathematical genius to figure out that 15 shots times two seconds comes out at 30 seconds—one-half minute.

Or, suppose a page of your feature film script includes that immortal line, "Five hundred Indians ride over the hill." How much running time does that take?

The issue, you see, is that each page of script is different.

But—and here we get the other side of the coin—they're not all different, and they're not often *wildly* different. Put together, one after the other, the *average* fact film script will run about 30 seconds per page; the *average* feature, about a minute.

Which is not to say that it still doesn't pay to use your head at least a little. Thus, if you have a whole series of pages that strike you as running extremely slow or fast, make allowance for it.

Ordinarily, that allowance should take the form of including a few too many pages, rather than a few too few. Why? Because your script is going to pass through many hands, and be filmed under circumstances you can't control. In consequence, you need to take it for granted that a few lines or shots or scenes just may be blue-penciled somewhere along the line. Also, that when the crew gets out on location, they'll discover that it takes Harold Hero only 17 seconds to climb the cliff, or that the dog flatly refuses to frolic for more than seven, no matter how his trainer curses.

And then, when the boys view the dailies, they discover that two-thirds of the footage in the shot of Hilda Heartlorn swimming across the creek is light-struck, to the point it can't be used.

That kind of thing explains why the old hands would rather write a little fat than thin, as in the case of two TV scripts now beside me. Each is designed for a one-hour show—which is to say, 60 minutes minus commercials, for an actual on-screen time of 42 minutes. Both scripts were done by old pros with years of experience behind them. One runs 72 pages, the other 75.

'Nuff said?

Beyond such generalities, here are ten factors to bear in mind when judging timing:

1. Number of locales.

Every time you change to a new setting, you have to establish it in your viewers' eyes. Establishing takes footage. Footage takes time. So, the more changes of setting, the more screen time will drain away. And if these changes are of a type that take only a line in the script (INT. - SPACESHIP - DAY), the normal balance between pages and minutes can get seriously out of kilter.

2. Subject.

A shot must be held on the screen long enough to convey the essential information about it to the audience visually. Obviously, less footage will be needed if the subject is a simple monument than if it's a complex piece of machinery.

3. Action of the subject.

I've already mentioned the classic gag about the Indians riding over the hill. In general, simple action will be more easily understood— and will take less screen time—than complex.

4. Distance.

A long shot takes more time to grasp than does a closeup. Why? Because Viewer may have to search the long shot for seconds before he can decide the point being made ("What the Sam Hill gives with all that desert? Oh, I get it! There's a rider over there in the corner"), whereas a screen-filling closeup of Chief Running Sore makes its impact instantly.

5. Composition.

The shorter the shot, the simpler the composition is going to have to be. Long S-curves in the D. W. Griffith tradition, patterns within patterns, and the like, take time to comprehend.

6. Color.

Footage in color takes longer to understand than footage in black and white. I learned this the hard way via a shot of a herd of Black Angus cattle grazing on lush green pasture land. Given enough distance to show the herd *as* a herd (see point 4, above), black cattle and green grass so blended that we had to throw out the footage. In black-and-white workprint, in contrast, you had no trouble at all separating them.

7. Size of screen.

A "normal" film frame has an aspect ratio (ratio of width to height) of four to three. The various "wide screen" gambits change this ratio—Cinemascope, for example, offers a ratio of five to two.

The normal screen allows for faster cutting, simply because the audience doesn't have to scan so large a span in search of each shot's point, the thing it's emphasizing. Result: A film designed for wide screen will actually include fewer shots than one shot for normal.

(Incidentally, *do* bear in mind that many theaters project *all* films wide screen, whether they were shot for it or not. Which explains why so many actors' heads are cut off just above the eyebrows, and why audiences leave theaters frustrated and baffled when the final, crucial action happens to take place a bit too low. Television is even worse, of course, in the way it not only trims edges but, because of small screen size, virtually eliminates anything meaningful where shots at any distance are concerned.

8. Depth.

It's easier and quicker for viewers to grasp what's going on if action takes place on a virtually two-dimensional plane. The greater the effect of depth—that is, three dimensions—in a shot, the slower the cuts must be.

9. Camera movement.

Pans, tilts, zooms, dolly shots, and the like tend to control—and to slow—cutting. Consider, for example, the shot in which Our Hero makes a crucial announcement. Camera pans to Heroine so we can see her reaction. Fine, but less time and footage would be involved if we merely *cut* to her shocked face.

Which is not to say camera movement should never be used, of course; merely that it *does* have negative aspects which should be weighed against possible advantages.

10. Context.

Closely related to point 1, above, is the fact that if your audience has already seen given settings, people, equipment, or what have you, they'll catch it faster in succeeding scenes.

Bearing this in mind, you as writer can use such familiar material to speed up the cutting and thus reduce footage and screen time.

On the other hand, you don't dare forget that, overdone, too much of the familiar creates a devastating—and deadly—sense of monotony.

APPENDIX C:

For Further Reading

I know scholarly screen writers, and I know others—equally successful—who have never read Word One on the subject. Nevertheless, most writers of my acquaintance show a tendency to learn by reading; and I myself owe a monumental debt of gratitude to the printed word.

Here, then, is a selection of works I've found interesting, informative, and in some way useful to me as a scripter. Perhaps you, too, will enjoy thumbing through a few.

Obviously, this is anything but a systematic or definitive bibliography. Nor do all the volumes included deal with scriptwriting as such, for much of what you'll need to know comes from other fields. Thus, my own *Techniques of The Selling Writer* is basically an analysis of fiction dynamics. But, hopefully, a little thought will enable you to apply its principles to motion pictures as well as the short story and novel.

Similarly, Stuart Palmer's *Understanding Other People* offers psychology simplified to a level where it's actually useful in creating characters. Aesop Glim's books on advertising include much that's of value to the fact film writer. Marian Gallaway's *Constructing a Play* and *The Director in The Theatre* are stage-oriented, but full of ideas and approaches equally valuable for film. The various technical books on film production contain information that will help orient you to the practices and problems of the medium.

One final point: Don't let the age (dates) of publications necessarily turn you off. Pudovkin and Nilsen still have much to offer that's applicable today, and so do Frances Marion, Arthur Krows, and *The Film Book.*

The editions listed are those that happen to be on my own shelves. Good reading!

A.N.A. Film Steering Committee. *Criteria for Business-Sponsored Educational Films.* New York: Association of National Advertisers, Inc., 1955.

A.N.A. Film Steering Committee. *The Dollars and Sense of Business Films.* New York: Association of National Advertisers, Inc., 1954.

Arijon, Daniel. *Grammar of the Film Language.* New York: Hastings House, 1976.

Baddeley, Hugh. *The Technique of Documentary Film Production, Third Edition.* New York: Hastings House, 1973.

Bare, Richard L. *The Film Director.* New York: Collier Books, 1971.

Barsam, Richard M. *Nonfiction Film.* New York: E. P. Dutton & Co., Inc., 1973.

Barzun, Jacques, and Graff, Henry F. *The Modern Researcher.* New York: Harcourt, Brace & World, 1957.

Blakeston, Oswell. *How to Script.* London: Focal Press, 1949.

Bluem, A. William, and Squire, Jason E. (eds.). *The Movie Business: American Film Industry Practice.* New York: Hastings House, 1972.

Brown, William O. *Low Budget Features.* Hollywood: William O. Brown, 1971.

Buchanan, Andrew. *Film Making from Script to Screen.* London: Faber & Faber Limited, 1937.

Burder, John. *The Work of the Industrial Film Maker.* New York: Hastings House, 1973.

Butler, Ivan. *The Making of Feature Films.* Baltimore: Penquin Books Inc., 1971.

Carrick, Edward. *Designing for Films.* London: The Studio Publications, 1949.

Corliss, Richard. *Talking Pictures: Screenwriters in the American Cinema.* New York: Penquin Books 1975.

———. *The Hollywood Screenwriters.* New York: Avon Books, 1972.

DeWitt, Jack. *Producing Industrial Films.* New York: A. S. Barnes & Co., 1968.

Eastman Kodak Co. *Basic Production Techniques for Motion Pictures.* Rochester, New York: Eastman Kodak Co., 1971.

———. *Basic Titling and Animation for Motion Pictures.* Rochester, New York: Eastman Kodak Co., 1970.

Egri, Lajos. *The Art of Creative Writing.* New York: The Citadel Press, 1965.

Fadiman, William. *Hollywood Now.* New York: Liveright, 1972.

Feldman, Joseph, and Feldman, Harry. *Dynamics of the Film.* New York: Hermitage House, 1952.

Fielding, Raymond. *The Technique of Special Effects Cinematography, Third Edition.* New York: Hastings House, 1972.

Froug, William. *The Screenwriter Looks at the Screenwriter.* New York, Dell Publishing Co., Inc., 1972.

Fulton, A. R. *Motion Pictures.* Norman: Univ. of Oklahoma Press, 1960.

Gallaway, Marian. *Constructing a Play.* New York: Prentice-Hall, Inc., 1950.

———. *The Director in the Theatre.* New York: The Macmillan Co., 1963.

Gaskill, Arthur L., and Englander, David A. *How to Shoot a Movie Story.* New York: Morgan & Morgan, 1959.

Geduld, Harry M. *An Illustrated Glossary of Film Terms.* Holt, Rinehart & Winston, 1973.

Gerrold, David. *The Trouble with Tribbles.* New York: Ballantine Books, 1973.

Glim, Aesop. *Copy—the Core of Advertising*. New York: Dover Publications, Inc., 1963.

———. *How Advertising Is Written—and Why*. New York: Dover Publications, Inc., 1961.

Halas, John (ed.). *Visual Scripting*. New York: Hastings House, 1976.

Herman, Lewis. *Practical Manual of Screen Playwriting*. New York: World Publishing Co., 1952.

———. *Educational Films: Writing, Directing, and Producing*. New York: Crown Publishers, Inc., 1965.

Higham, Charles, and Greenberg, Joel. *The Celluloid Muse*. New York: New American Library, 1969.

Kirsch, Maurice. *How to Write Commentaries for Films*. London: Focal Press, 1956.

Krows, Arthur Edwin. *Playwriting for Profit*. New York: Longmans, Green & Co., 1928.

Lawson, John Howard. *Theory and Technique of Playwriting and Screenwriting*. New York: G. P. Putnam's Sons, 1949.

Lewin, Frank. *The Soundtrack in Nontheatrical Motion Pictures*. Hollywood: Society of Motion Picture and Television Engineers, 1959.

Leyda, Jay. *Films Beget Films*. London: George Allen & Unwin Ltd., 1964.

Livingston, Don. *Film and the Director*. New York: The Macmillan Co., 1953.

MacCann, Richard Dyer. *Film: A Montage of Theories*. New York: E. P. Dutton & Co., 1966.

Macgowan, Kenneth. *A Primer of Playwriting*. New York: Random House, 1951.

———. *Behind the Screen*. New York: Dell Publishing Co., Inc., 1967.

Madsen, Roy. *Animated Film*. New York: Interland Publishing Inc., 1969.

Marion, Frances. *How to Write and Sell Film Stories*. New York: Covici-Friede, 1937.

Marner, Terence St. John. *Directing Motion Pictures*. New York: A. S. Barnes & Co., 1972.

Mascelli, Joseph V. *The Five C's of Cinematography*. Hollywood: Cine/Graphic Publications, 1965.

May, Mark A., and Lumadaine, Arthur A. *Learning from Films*. New Haven: Yale University Press, 1958.

Mayer, Michael F. *The Film Industries: Practical Business/Legal Problems*. New York: Hastings House, 1973.

McGraw, Charles J. *Acting Is Believing*. New York: Holt, Rinehart & Winston, 1955.

Mercer, John. *Introduction to Cinematography*. Champaign, Illinois: Stipes Publishing Co., 1971.

Miller, Tony, and Miller, Patricia George. *"Cut! Print!" The Language and Structure of Filmmaking*. Los Angeles: Ohara Publications, 1972.

Nilsen, Vladimir. *The Cinema as a Graphic Art*. New York: Hill & Wang, 1959.

Osborn, Alex. *Your Creative Power*. New York: Charles Scribner's Sons, 1948.

Palmer, Stuart. *Understanding Other People*. New York: Thomas Y. Crowell Co., 1955.

Parker, Norton S. *Audiovisual Script Writing*. New Brunswick, N.J.: Rutgers University Press, 1968.

Pudovkin, V. I. *Film Technique and Film Acting*. New York: Grove Press, Inc., 1960.

Reisz, Karel, and Millar, Gavin. *The Technique of Film Editing, Second Enlarged Edition*. New York: Hastings House, 1968.

Reynertson, A. J. *The Work of the Film Director*. New York: Hastings House, 1970.

Rilla, Wolf. *The Writer and the Screen*. London: W. H. Allen, 1973.

Rose, Tony. *How to Direct*. London: Focal Press, 1949.

——, and Benson, Martin. *How to Act*. London: Focal Press, 1951.

Salkin, Leo. *Story-Telling Home Movies*. New York: McGraw-Hill Book Co., Inc., 1958.

Shavelson, Melville. *How to Make a Jewish Movie*. Englewood Cliffs, N.J.: Prentice-Hall, Inc., 1971.

Smith, Richard W. *Technical Writing*. New York: Barnes & Noble, 1963.

Snyder, Robert L. *Pare Lorentz and the Documentary Film*. Norman: University of Oklahoma Press, 1968.

Spottiswoode, Raymond. *Film and Its Techniques*. Berkeley: University of California Press, 1951.

Stephenson, Ralph, and Debrix, J. R. *The Cinema as Art*. Baltimore: Penquin Books, 1965.

Stork, Leopold. *Industrial and Business Films*. London: Phoenix House, 1962.

Strasser, Alex. *The Work of the Science Film Maker*. New York: Hastings House, 1972.

Swain, Dwight V. *Techniques of the Selling Writer*. Norman: University of Oklahoma Press, 1974.

Toeplitz, Jerzy. *Hollywood and After*. Chicago: Henry Regnery Co., 1975.

Trapnell, Coles. *Teleplay*. San Francisco: Chandler Publishing Co., 1966.

Truffaut, Francois. *Hitchcock*. London: Panther Books, 1969.

Vale, Eugene. *The Technique of Screenplay Writing*. New York Grosset & Dunlap, 1972.

Wilson, William H., and Haas, Dr. Kenneth B. *The Film Book for Education, Business and Industry*. New York: Prentice-Hall, Inc., 1950.

Yoakem, Lola (ed.). *TV and Screen Writing*. Berkeley: University of California Press, 1958.

APPENDIX D:

Terms You'll Use

Every field develops its own specialized in-group jargon, and the film industry is no exception.

A number of lexicons of this terminology have been compiled—Harry M. Geduld's *An Illustrated Glossary of Film Terms,* Tony and Patricia Miller's *"Cut! Print!,"* and the University Film Association *Journal*'s "Terms Used in Production of 16mm Non-Theatrical Motion Pictures," for example. Indeed, there's even a handy pocket volume (*Film Vocabulary,* published by the Netherlands Government Information Service, Film Division, 43 Noordeinde, The Hague, Netherlands) which gives the equivalents for 1,024 film terms in French, English, Dutch, Italian, German, Spanish, and Danish.

The glossary I offer here is indebted to these others, but obviously makes no pretense to being anywhere near as comprehensive as they are. However, it does place special emphasis on terms the beginning scriptwriter is likely to encounter and hence may save him at least a few moments of bafflement.

action. Movement of the subject within the camera's field of view.

adaptation. A script in which fact or fiction is translated into a presentation suitable for filming.

angle shot. A shot continuing the action of a preceding shot, but from a different camera angle.

animation. The cinematic creation of an impression of movement by inanimate objects or drawings.

356

answer print. The first combined picture and sound print, in release form, of a finished film.

antagonist. The person, element, or force which opposes the central character of a film in his efforts to attain a goal.

anticlimax. An inadvertent drop in tension following the climax of a film because of the scriptwriter's attempt to top the climax with additional material dealing with some secondary issue. The cause ordinarily is the writer's failure to recognize the key element of danger which threatens his central character's desire. Once this threat is resolved, the film is over, save for the tying up of loose threads in the denouement.

art director. The person who designs and supervises construction of a film's sets.

audio. Sound, including dialogue, voice-over narration, music, and effects. The "audio side" (that is, the right side) of a two-column script is the side which tells what sound elements are to be included.

back light. A light thrown on foreground actors or objects from farther back in the set, separating them from the background and giving an impression of depth to the picture.

back lot. That portion of a studio's property equipped with streets, false-front buildings, and the like for use in simulated location shooting.

background. Action, objects, or setting farthest from the camera in a given shot or shots.

background light. A light used to illuminate a shot's background.

beat. A momentary, predesignated pause in an actor's action or delivery of a speech.

big closeup. British term for extreme closeup.

business. Action introduced in order to build up or reinforce characterization, a sequence, a plot point, or the like.

busy. A shot or sequence in which inclusion of too much unnecessary action or setting detail distracts from the impression desired.

camera angle. The point of view from which the camera surveys a subject. Thus, "high angle" means that the camera is looking down on the subject; "low angle," that it is looking up, and so on. "Another angle" means simply that the camera continues to film a given action, but from a different position.

caper film. An adventure film centering on a major theft; generally presented from the thieves' point of view.

cast list. List (and, frequently, brief description) of the roles in a film.

character. A person in a film.

characterization. Any and all details of appearance and behavior devised by a scriptwriter to define a given story person as an individual.

chase. Use of pursuit of one character by another to build suspense in a film.

cheat. To shoot or edit film in a manner that simulates reality by falsifying the relationship between people and/or objects.

climax. The point in a screenplay at which the conflict between desire and danger reaches its ultimate peak.

close shot. A loose term that says only that the camera is close to the subject. Read it as somewhere in the neighborhood of a closeup or medium closeup.

closeup (CU). An emphasis shot that calls attention to some aspect of the subject—a facial expression, a fist-clenching, an inscription on an object.

commentary. Narration for a film, spoken by an off-screen voice in voice-over situations.

complication. A new and unanticipated story development that throws the central character/protagonist for a loss where the attaining of his ultimate objective is concerned. In effect, a confrontation, complete with goal, conflict, and disaster.

composition. The framing of a picture area to achieve a desired distribution and balancing of light, mass, shadow, color, and movement.

conflict. The interplay between forces seeking to attain mutually incompatible goals.

confrontation. A unit of conflict and the main structural component of plot. A time-unified clash between opposing forces in which one person or group attempts to attain an immediate goal and another person/group attempts to prevent attainment of said goal, its basic pattern is one of goal-conflict-disaster, with disaster representing an outcome which has consequences further endangering first person/group's desire.

continuity. 1. A detailed shooting script. 2. British term for story line.

continuity cutting. Editing film to present action in a smooth, logical flow that preserves the illusion of reality for the audience.

contrast. Comparison of one element (situation, object, person, emotion) with another markedly different.

contrived. A pejorative label which implies that some script phase, element, or device is unbelievable, artificial, and for author convenience. Since everything in a script actually is contrived, the label is meaningless and indicates only that someone doesn't like something about the story or presentation. The issue, for the writer, then becomes one of contriving more satisfactorily.

credit. Title acknowledging work done by some specialist (producer, director, writer, actor, technical staff member) on a film.

crisis. A peak in a screenplay's development, brought on by a major threat to the protagonist's chances of attaining his story goal.

cut. Instantaneous change from one shot to another by splicing the two pieces of film together.

cutaway. In continuity cutting, a shot which does not include any part of the preceding shot, as when a character glances out a window and the shot that follows shows what he sees.

cutback. The shot which follows a cutaway if it returns to the preceding action, as when a cutaway shot of what a character sees out a window is followed by a shot that includes the character as he turns away from the window and resumes the action in which he was previously engaged.

cut-in. A medium shot, closeup, or the like, filmed for cutting into a master scene.

cutter, cutting. Editor, editing. More narrowly, the person who actually cuts and splices the film, as differentiated from the editor, who selects the footage to be used and decides where it is to be cut/spliced.

day for night. Daylight exterior shots simulating night by means of filters.

denouement. The tying up of a film's loose ends following the climax and during or following the resolution. Here questions are answered, lingering tensions released, an ending given an emotionally satisfying twist, and so on.

Deus ex machina. When God or the scriptwriter intercedes to save a film from its logical conclusion.

director. The individual who interprets a script and supervises its filming.

dissolve (lap dissolve). An optical effect in which a fade in is superimposed over a fade out so that one shot replaces the other. Its most common use is as a transition through time and/or space between sequences.

documentary. A word with as many interpretations as there are people talking. In general, it refers to a film that avoids artifice and dramatization in favor of extreme realism, shooting in actual settings with non-professional actors who live the parts of the play.

dolly. A small, wheeled platform used to move a camera smoothly while it shoots.

dolly shot. A shot filmed from a moving dolly.

double system. A sound film system in which picture and sound are recorded on separate but precisely synchronized reels of film, thus enhancing sound quality and simplifying editing.

down. Reduce volume of music or sound effects, as in such script instructions as "MUSIC: DOWN TO BG" or "MUSIC: DOWN & OUT."

dramatic scene. A confrontation.

dub. 1. Mix; re-record various sound tracks onto one composite track. 2. To record dialogue or other sound to match action in shots already filmed.

edit (editing, editor). To select, arrange, trim, and splice together film shots for optimum effectiveness.

effects (FX, SFX) track. Sound track on which a film's sound effects are recorded. These may range from footsteps to gunshots to the racing of a car's motor.

empathy. The tendency of viewers to share the experiences of filmed characters, as when they tense at some threat jeopardizing a person in a picture.

episodic. Script or film structure giving strong emphasis to incidents; less to continuity and the building of a sense of rising action. *Barry Lyndon* is an episodic film.

establish. To make clear any element important to understanding and appreciation of a sequence or film, and that element's relationship to the sequence or film's other elements.

exploitation film. A low-budget picture for a specialized audience—horror fans, bikers, or the like.

exposition. Introduction of information from the past necessary for understanding of a film story.

exterior (EXT.). Shots made out-of-doors.

extreme closeup (ECU). A strong emphasis shot, as when a shot of an eyeball fills the frame.

extreme long shot (ELS). A shot that reduces the size of the subject in relation to its background markedly more than a long shot.

fade. An optical effect used as a transitional device, in which the picture on the screen gradually goes to black (fade out) or takes form from black (fade in). Every film opens with FADE IN: and closes with FADE OUT. Between, fades may act as punctuation, separating major segments of a film. As punctuation, a fade is much stronger than—and not to be confused with—a dissolve.

fill light. A light used to fill in shadows cast by the key light and thus balance the picture.

flashback. The introduction into a film of a shot or sequence revealing something from the past, as when a character recalls a past event.

flat. A wooden framework supporting stretched and painted cloth used as a background for action.

follow action (follow shot). The camera moves horizontally or vertically on its tripod or on a dolly in such a manner as to keep attention centered on key action.

foreground. Action, objects, or setting closest to the camera in a given shot or shots.

frame. 1. One single picture on a piece of motion picture film. 2. To compose a shot to include, exclude, or emphasize certain things, as in "This shot is so framed that the narrowing distance between the two riders is immediately apparent."

freeze-frame. Repetition (via optical printing) of a single frame of a film so that its image is held on the screen for whatever time is desired.

French scene. A dramatic unit under a system of designation which decrees a new scene to begin with each non-incidental entrance or exit.

full shot. A shot that takes in all of a subject, be it an individual, a group, a car, or a house.

gimmick. A clever plot device, especially one that helps to resolve the film's problem.

head-on shot. Movement straight into the camera, as in the case of someone striding down a hall.

heavy. A villain-type character.

high-key lighting. Lighting in which light, highly illuminated areas predominate, as in most comedies.

hook. 1. A striking incident, unique action, or the like, used to capture audience attention at the beginning of a picture. 2. A linking device (question-answer, repetition, agreement-disagreement, etc.) used to render dialogue cohesive by tying each speech to the one ahead of it.

identification. The tendency of a screenplay's audience to take sides, in effect cheering the hero and booing the villain.

insert. A shot, frequently an extreme closeup, of some object or detail (a letter, a picture, a hand, a tattoo) which can be filmed in such a manner as to eliminate setting. Thus, it may easily be shot out of sequence and cut into the picture during editing.

interior (INT.). A shot filmed indoors.

jeopardy. Anything which endangers a character's chances of attaining his story goal and fulfilling his desire.

jump cut. Splicing together two shots taken from the same angle, especially if some element of the action is omitted. The effect is one of jerkiness and discontinuity.

key light. A shot's primary light source.

lead. The central character or main acting part in a film.

lighting set-up. The placing of lights to illuminate a given shot or shots. Since this task ordinarily takes at least an hour, it constitutes a major expense. Anything the writer can do in his script to limit the number of set-ups will count as a star in his crown.

limbo shot. In effect, a shot staged in space, with props but without a normal set. Often the action takes place in front of a large, blank fabric backdrop called a cyclorama.

lip sync. Dialogue recorded in precise synchronization with the filming, so that speech and lip movements match.

location. A natural setting for action, as differentiated from a sound stage.

long shot (LS). A shot that relates the subject to the background. Frequently, it constitutes an orientation or establishing shot.

loop. A strip of film with its ends spliced together so that it can be projected continuously as a guide for actors in dubbing lines to match lip movements or other action.

low-key lighting. Lighting in which dark, shadowy areas predominate, as in most horror pictures.

MacGuffin. The bone of contention in a film; the thing everyone is trying to save or steal.

mask. To block out a portion of a camera's field as it shoots, as in masking to simulate the view through binoculars or a keyhole.

master scene. An orientation shot (frequently a long shot) taking in all or a considerable part of the action in an entire sequence. Closer shots (cut-ins) of repetitions of the action then are filmed to build the sequence via emphasis on appropriate details.

master scene script. A script which details the action and dialogue of a film, but by and large does not include shooting instructions or camera angles or break down the action shot by shot.

medium closeup (MCU). A shot whose image size on the frame is between a medium shot and a closeup.

medium long shot (MLS). A shot whose image size on the frame is between a medium shot and a long shot.

medium shot (MS). A shot of the subject in and of itself, with only incidental background.

miniature. Small-scale model of an object or set, used to cut the cost of filming floods, train wrecks, airplane crashes, and the like.

mise-en-scene. A film's environment. The sum total of its setting.

mix (mixing, mixer). The combining of sound elements (voices, music, effects) from various tracks in desired proportions on a single rerecorded track.

montage. A combination of brief shots and optical effects, used as transition or to create emotional effects. It may condense months of searching into seconds or minutes, for example, or reveal the distortions of a character's thinking in insanity or a drug experience.

MOS. "Mit out sound." A gag-line reference to shots or sequences to be filmed silent.

motivation. The logical basis for a character's action.

moving shot (travel shot). A shot made from a moving vehicle.

Moviola. A sound/picture viewing device used in film editing.

music track. Sound track on which a film's music is recorded.

narration script. Commentary prepared for use of a film narrator in a voice-over recording situation.

narrator. A commentator (most often unseen) who voices appropriate interpretive remarks for a film's sound track.

nontheatrical film. Ordinarily, a film shown in schools, churches, clubs, and the like, and used to inform, influence, and inspire, rather than to entertain.

oater. Western film.

obligatory scene. A film's climactic confrontation, the elements for which have been planted. Unless these plants are paid off in an appropriate clash, the audience will be frustrated and disappointed.

one-shot (two-shot, three-shot, etc.). A shot that includes one or whatever people.

optical effects (opticals). Systematic progressive alteration of a motion picture shot by means of an optical printer, generally for transitional purposes. Common optical effects include fades, dissolves, wipes, superimpositions, and the like.

pan. To turn a camera from right to left or vice versa on its tripod while taking a shot. The vertical version of a pan is called a tilt.

parallel action. Footage in which action in different locations at the same time is shown as a series of successive sequences by cutting back and forth from one setting to the other.

pay off. To make significant use of something previously planted, as when at the climax of a film the protagonist faces down the villain with a previously planted pistol.

persistence of vision. The retention of an image of a viewed subject on the retina of the viewer for the fraction of a second after the subject has been removed. This phenomenon makes possible the motion picture, in which the audience sees a succession of still photos as a continuing flow of motion.

picaresque. A film—frequently episodic costume drama—which recounts the adventures of a rogue. Example: *Tom Jones.*

plant. Apparently offhand establishment of an idea, character, or property to be used more significantly later in the film. The fact that a gun is seen in a drawer when said drawer is opened to get a pad or pencil is an example.

plant, false. An apparent plant which is never paid off, as when Hero discovers a Yugoslav dinar in the change on Mysterious Stranger's nightstand—but no reference is ever made to it again. The audience has a right to irritation in such circumstances.

plot. A writer's dramatized plan of action for manipulating audience emotions.

plot line. 1. A line of dialogue essential to development/understanding of the plot. 2. A film's story line.

point of view (POV). 1. A shot in which the camera's position approximates that of a particular character and the audience sees what said character would have seen. 2. Attitude.

predicament. a situation so emotionally disturbing to the central character in a screenplay that he is impelled (that is, motivated) to take action directed at changing said situation.

premise. A hypothetical "What if—?" question that provides the basic idea for and springboard to a film story.

process shot. A shot in which foreground action is staged against a translucent screen on which a filmed background is projected.

producer. The individual who plans, coordinates, and supervises production of a film.

progression. Forward movement of a screenplay towards its climax through incorporation of new information and developments.

proportioning. The matching of emphasis to importance in a film script, building some segments large while holding others down.

proposal outline. A brief statement of purpose, target audience, concept, and specifications for a proposed fact film.

protagonist. A film's main character; the character in whose fate the audience is most interested.

quick save. Resolution of a film's problem in less time than seems believable, generally under circumstances that smack of author convenience.

rear projection. Projection of film onto a translucent screen from behind in order to provide background for live foreground action.

relief. A sequence or sequences designed to reduce audience tension (often through humor) after a period of high excitement.

resolution. The defeat of desire by danger or vice versa in consequence of the protagonist's behavior in the ultimate conflict that is the climax; the payoff for the hero's trauma; the method of solving the screenplay's main problem.

running gag. The building up of the humor of some incident or fragment of behavior by repetition as a film progresses.

rushes (dailies). Film processed overnight (or as soon as possible) for immediate viewing to check quality of photography and performances.

scenario. A largely obsolete term for a script form giving a general description of the action of a proposed film.

scene. A term today so loosely used as to be largely meaningless. Thus, it may refer to (1) a setting, (2) a shot, (3) a sequence, or (4) a confrontation.

script. A set of written specifications for the production of a motion picture.

seat-slammers. Throw-away lines at the beginning of a picture when, it is assumed, viewers will be more preoccupied with getting settled in their seats than with the film.

segue. Smooth transition from one sound (particularly, one musical number) to another.

sequence. 1. A related series of shots, unified by some element they hold in common—setting, concept, action, character, mood, or what have you. 2. A major segment of a film, on the order of a chapter in a novel.

sequence outline. A list and brief description of the sequences to be included in a film.

set (setting). An artificially constructed scene in which action to be photographed takes place.

set list. A list of all settings to be used in a film. If included (it isn't always), it ordinarily will follow the cast list and precede the script's text.

setting. The physical surroundings in which a given segment of a film's action is supposed to transpire—bedroom, ballroom, dairy, dock, or whatever.

sexploitation film. Film (probably X-rated) whose appeal is primarily based on explicit sexual activity.

shooting script. A detailed script which describes a film's action shot by shot and serves as a blueprint for production.

shot. The series of still pictures taken by a motion picture camera between the moment it starts and the moment it stops in a single run.

shot list. A shooting script.

situation. The fictional circumstances prevailing as a film opens.

skin flick. A sex film.

sound effects (SFX, FX). Any sound from any source other than voice over narration, lip-sync dialogue, or music.

sound stage. A building or portion of a building designed for the shooting of sound film.

space opera. A science fiction film.

special effects. Techniques for achieving unusual photographic effects unattainable by ordinary procedures.

speculation. Writing on a contingency fee basis; the writer doesn't get paid unless the producer or other person in charge likes the product. Forbidden under Writers Guild rules.

spine. A script's skeletal backbone; its basic plot.

splice. The joining of two pieces of film by any of various techniques.

split screen. Film so manipulated that different shots appear simultaneously in different sections of the screen when projected.

step outline. A sequence outline for a feature or TV film, specifying the action to take place in each sequence as the story develops.

sting. A striking sound (music, shout, etc.) which is used as emphasis or punctuation in a film.

stock shot. Footage of locales, action, or the like, drawn from film libraries to eliminate the need for shooting the sequences involved.

story. 1. In fiction films, the record of how somebody deals with danger. 2. Loosely, the plan of presentation of any film's contents.

story analyst. A studio story department employee who appraises and synopsizes potential screenplay material.

storyboard. A series of sketches, generally with comment, of proposed film action. It is designed to present the picture's line of development in visual terms.

story line. A screenplay's main line of development. Read the term as *story outline* and you won't go too far wrong.

story treatment. A semi-dramatized, present-tense, preliminary structuring of a screenplay or, more broadly, any script.

structure (structuring). A script's framework, its pattern of organization. The combining of story elements into such a pattern.

subjective camera. A technique sometimes used in instructional films in which the camera approximates the learner's point of view. It's also occasionally seen elsewhere, even in feature films; the outstanding example probably is *Lady in the Lake* (1946), in which the viewpoint character virtually never appears on screen.

subplot. A story-within-a-story, generally involving subordinate characters and developed in terms of action parallel to that of the main plot. A subplot's purpose ordinarily is to provide relief from main-plot tension.

superimposure. One or more shots in which one photographic image is printed on top of another, as in ghost effects, titles, etc.

suspense. Uncertainty of outcome; the fear something will or won't happen.

swish pan (blur pan, whip pan). A transitional device in which a pan so rapid that the images blur is used to change from one setting to another.

synchronization. Exact matching of a film's sound and action, as of speech to lip movements.

synopsis. A brief outline of a proposed film's content.

tag line (curtain line, punch line). The final speech in a confrontation, episode, or sequence; generally, one that tops those lines which have gone before.

tail-away shot. Movement directly away from the camera, as when a shot is of the back of a man departing.

take. One filming of a shot.

target audience. The group to which a film is designed to appeal.

teaser. Intriguing pre-title action used to capture audience attention, especially in a TV picture.

technical advisor. A person with detailed knowledge of a film's subject matter, assigned to assist the scriptwriter in preparation of his script.

tempo. The impression of pace in a film.

theme. A screenplay's implicit message.

tilt. Vertical movement of a camera on its tripod head while making a shot.

time-lapse photography. A technique by which filmed action is speeded up by allowing a greater length of time than usual to elapse between photography of successive frames. By this process, a plant may be made to appear to bloom in minutes, or the seasons to change before an audience's eyes.

titles. A film's listings of who did what in its production.

transition. 1. The bridge from one confrontation to another. 2. Anything that links together sequential units or elements in a film.

treatment outline. A third-person, present-tense summary of a proposed fact film script or, more broadly, any film.

trucking shot. Dolly shot. Shot from a moving vehicle, ordinarily a wheeled platform which in most cases moves with the subject at an approximation of set distance.

up. Increase volume of music or sound effects, as in such script instructions as "MUSIC: IN AND UP."

video. The side of a two-column script describing the action to be filmed. The visual (left) side.

viewer. A mechanical/optical enlarging unit used by editors to examine film.

voice-over. A narrator's commentary recorded for incorporation on a film's sound track.

weenie. An objectification of the hero's desire in simplistic films—and some not so simplistic. The thing sought: the jewels, the formula, the stolen money.

wild. Film shot or sound recorded with no synchronous relationship to each other.

wipe. A transitional optical effect in which one image appears to push another off the screen in any one of dozens of patterns.

workprint. A copy of film footage used in editing so that the original will not be damaged.

zoom. Simulation of camera movement toward or away from the subject, by means of a lens with variable focal length.

Index